Save our Stags

Save our Stags

The Long Struggle Against Britain's Most Controversial Blood Sport

Ian Pedler

BLACK DAPS PRESS

First published in 2008 by Black Daps Press
P O Box 1447, Paulton, Bristol BS39 7WT
www.saveourstags.co.uk

Distributed by Gardners Books
1 Whittle Drive, Eastbourne, East Sussex, BN23 6QH
Tel: +44(0)1323 521555 | Fax: +44(0)1323 521666

British Library Cataloguing in Publication Data
A catalogue record for this book is available from the British Library.

ISBN 978-0-9554786-0-4

Typeset by Amolibros, Milverton, Somerset
www.amolibros.co.uk
This book production has been managed by Amolibros

Printed and bound by T J International Ltd, Padstow, Cornwall, UK

About the Author

BORN IN 1946, IAN Pedler has been opposed to blood sports since first joining the League Against Cruel Sports as a ten-year-old. He was active with the Hunt Saboteurs Association from its inception in 1963, then as founder of the Save Our Stags Campaign, while also serving as an Executive Committee member of the League until resigning as an active animal rights campaigner in the late 1980s. His professional life has been spent in the field of community mental health social work, at which he is still employed part-time. When not harassing animal killers he pursues his other interests of world travel and early American history.

He lives in the West Country with his wife Josie.

Dedication

This book is dedicated to the memory of Sue Smith, who "rookied" many a wood to rouse the harboured stag.

Contents

Abbreviations used in text xv

List of Illustrations xi

Preface xvii

Chapter One

"...one bite, and the deer is dead" 1

Chapter Two

"...the Queen has been strongly opposed to stag hunting for many years past" 33

Chapter Three

"Attila, or St Francis?" 56

Chapter Four

"This wild stag was not a captive animal. It was only temporarily unable to get away" 63

Chapter Five

"The HSA! Vot's the cap and vere's the country?" 87

Chapter Six

"a bunch of yobs and unwashed squatter types" 105

Chapter Seven

"deer must be made a protected species..." 122

Chapter Eight

"a giant game of chess" 133

Chapter Nine

"I did not find her a reliable witness…" 150

Chapter Ten

"…go out as apostles into the world and support this war" 173

Chapter Eleven

"Let him walk" 193

Chapter Twelve

"This has always been treated by the Labour Party as a private members' measure" 219

Chapter Thirteen

"I read these messages; I don't understand them" 243

Chapter Fourteen

"What part of 'no' does the hunting fraternity not understand?" 266

Chapter Fifteen

"It is now lame duck legislation…" 289

Conclusion 321

Appendices 331

Bibliography 395

Index 405

List of Illustrations

Facing page 72

1 Henry Salt (Photo: LACS)

2 Joseph Sharp (Photo: LACS)

3 Edward Hemingway (Photo: LACS)

4 GONE TO SEA! A stag boldly swimming across Porlock Bay. C1920. (Photo: Alfred Vowles)

5 Spectator sport 1926 style. (Photo: Alfred Vowles)

6 STAG IN THE WIRE. c1950s. One of the most dramatic photographs ever taken of stag hunting. Blood sport supporters have long claimed it was taken in France, but the truth is no one knows its origin.

7 WHAT ARE THEY LAUGHING ABOUT? *Daily Mirror* 20th March 1957. The author's first experience of stag hunting. (Note the schoolboy peering from between the two characters on right of picture.) (Photo: Reg Lewis/Mirrorpix)

8 Guard of honour for a dead stag. Devon and Somerset Staghounds. 19th March 1957. (Photo:Reg Lewis/Mirrorpix)

9 Protestor Cicely Norman at a meet of the DSSH. 19th March 1957. (Photo: Reg Lewis/Mirrorpix)

10 1958 leaflet produced in support of Sir Frederick Messer's *Protection of Deer (Hunting Abolition) Bill*

Facing page 136

11-13 Three stills from the 1958 Russell W Fuller footage, with one showing the deer being dragged down by hounds from the Quantock Staghounds. (Photos: LACS)

14 Gwen Barter at the Norwich Staghounds. 15th March 1962 (Photo: *East Anglian Daily Times)*

15 Raymond Rowley with hunt master Col Brian Gooch at the Norwich Staghounds. 15th March 1962 (Photo: *East Anglian Daily Times)*

16 A lassoed stag is dragged up the bank of a frozen stream. A leaflet produced by Gwen Barter as part of her campaign against the Norwich Staghounds. (Photo: *Daily Herald)*

17 A stag held by DSSH hunt supporters in the River Yeo prior to being shot. One of a number of such pictures taken by Raymond Rowley over the years. This one gaining front-page national coverage on 21st October 1966. (Photo: LACS)

18 Twenty years of service to the deer. The woman with her sleeves rolled up in this 1950s photograph is Mrs Nora Cox, master of the DSSH. (Photo: LACS)

19 The woman in hunting gear to the right of this picture taken in 1979 is Mrs Nora Harding, master of the DSSH. Same woman. Different name. Over twenty years apart. Note the huntsman holding the deer's heart. (Photo: Douglas Doig)

20 Young supporters accept their souvenir of the kill. DSSH October 1979. (Photo: Douglas Doig)

Facing page 232

21 Save Our Stags Class of 1980. Off to a demo in the big city. (Photo: Mandy Dawes)

22 John Hicks (Photo: LACS)

23 Lashings of fun on the Quantocks. Saboteur on the run 1st January 1981. (Photo: Francis Stothard)

24 Close to the end. DSSH 22nd August 1981. (Photo: Mike Huskisson/LACS)

25-26 Two stills from a 8mm cine film that was shot by Mike Huskisson at the DSSH on 22nd October 1981. The second one shows hounds attacking the beaten stag. (Photos: Mike Huskisson/LACS)

27 The Doniford hind standing at the water's edge after escaping from the Quantock Staghounds. (Photo: Save Our Stags)

28 Bill Cavanagh's famous 10th October 1987 "stag on a roof" photograph. (Photo: Bill Cavanagh)

29 "LET HIM WALK" Autumn 1992. Having already been shot, this stag was made to walk up a steep slope, where he would be shot again. (Photo: Kevin Hill)

30 L to R: IFAW monitors Kevin Hill and Peter White (Photo: IFAW)

31 Nowhere left to run. (Photo: Save Our Stags)

Abbreviations used in text

ACPO:	Association of Chief Police Officers
ALF:	Animal Liberation Front
BDS:	British Deer Society
BFSS:	British Field Sports Society
CAA:	Cinema Advertising Association
CA:	Countryside Alliance
CPHA:	Campaign for the Protection of Hunted Animals
CPS:	Criminal Prosecution Service
DEFRA:	Department for Environment, Food and Rural Affairs
DSRADP:	Devon & Somerset Residents' Association For Deer Protection
DSSH:	Devon & Somerset Staghounds
FC:	Forestry Commission
FONT:	Friends of the National Trust
GECCAP:	General Election Co-ordinating Committee for Animal Protection
HSA:	Hunt Saboteurs Association
IAR:	International Animal Rescue
ICABS:	Irish Council Against Blood Sports
IFAW:	International Fund for Animal Welfare
LACS:	League Against Cruel Sports
MDHA:	Masters of Deerhounds Association
NAHC:	National Anti Hunt Campaign
NARA:	National Animal Rescue Association
NCADH:	National Committee for the Abolition of Deer Hunting
NFAPG:	New Forest Animal Protection Group
NFB:	New Forest Buckhounds

NFDAA:	New Forest Deerhunt Abolition Alliance
NSACS:	National Society for the Abolition of Cruel Sports
NT:	National Trust
POWA:	Protect Our Wild Animals
QSH:	Quantock Staghounds
RSPCA:	Royal Society for the Prevention of Cruelty to Animals
SOS:	Save Our Stags
SCC:	Somerset County Council
STNC:	Somerset Trust for Nature Conservation
SWDP:	South West Deer Protection
TSH:	Tiverton Staghounds

Preface

ON THE CHILLY MORNING of 19th February 2005 I stood beside the faded splendour of Bagborough House, on the slopes of the Quantock Hills, to witness what I hoped would be the last act of a drama that had been over one hundred years in the making. For while the huntsmen of the Quantock Staghounds still dressed in red, the hounds continued to mill around expectantly as they had done for generations past, and the supporters proffered their undying love for the red deer, today there was a difference. Thanks to the *Hunting Act 2004*, which had come into law the previous day, blood sports were now "illegal". For the first time in my life it was a criminal offence to chase and kill Britain's largest wild mammal for sport, and I had played a small part in helping to bring this day to fruition.

For me the journey to this meet of hounds had begun a long time before on Wednesday, 20th March 1957. For that was the day when the *Daily Mirror* published a two-page centre spread photograph headlined "What are they laughing about", which showed jubilant supporters of the Devon and Somerset Staghounds dragging away the body of a stag at the end of a hunt.

Not in itself an auspicious event, but coupled with the impressionable mind of a ten-year-old pupil of Downend County Primary School, under pressure to produce an interesting newspaper picture for the following Monday morning "current affairs" class (conducted by the formidable Miss Brain) it was obviously auspicious enough. In an age when the expected presentation would be a picture of some royal event, the up and coming Elvis Presley strutting his stuff in *Jailhouse Rock*, or in my case Fess Parker touring the country as *Davy Crockett, King of the Wild Frontier* resplendent with dead racoon headgear, the image of my slaughtered stag with his throat slit was a little hard to take.

Her reaction to my picture of a dead Hungarian freedom fighter of the previous November had raised serious questions regarding my view of the world. Now I was pushing the boundaries dangerously close to the "time to call the parents and have that concerned about Ian chat". I was told in no uncertain terms that such subjects were not for my tender eyes and that if I was to develop a penchant for deer-related issues then Walt Disney's *Bambi* should be my preferred option. Protests that the photograph in question contained a young man suspiciously close in age to myself, peeping out from the merry crowd, only solicited the reddening of the neck. Confirmation, if such were needed, that another word from me would result in spending the remainder of the morning standing in the corner with my back to the class. I had already crossed the line into "controversy".

As ever, it would be my dear old grandfather who would explain the meaning of the *Daily Mirror* picture. What surprised me was the passion with which he denounced the actions of Exmoor's finest. For it transpired that every alternate year during the 1920s, with Tenby the other favourite, the Pedler family would decamp to Illfracombe for the week. It was on one of these holidays, during a "charabanc" trip across the moors, that they had witnessed the killing of a stag. As he told the story to me the "charabanc" was forced to stop by hunt supporters, while the stag was dragged into the middle of the road and held down while the huntsman cut its throat. All this in full view of the passengers, many of whom became quite distressed, including my father, who would still vividly remember the incident eighty years later.

From this inauspicious introduction to blood sports would come junior membership of the League Against Cruel Sports, leading to participation in the obligatory annual Boxing Day poster demonstration. In early 1964 I would attempt to disrupt my first stag hunt courtesy of the fledgling Hunt Saboteurs Association. By late 1973, having formed the Save Our Stags Campaign, I was waging a not-so-private war against the West Country stag hunters.

By the time I quit active campaigning in 1987 I had lost count of the number of non-abolitionist friends and work colleagues who had asked me the question: why was I so obsessed with stag hunting? The funny thing was I didn't know for sure. It had to do in part with a socialist upbringing that encouraged compassion for less fortunate sentient beings, be they human or animal. There were also, of course, the animals which surrounded me throughout my life, who through close association brought me to the conclusion that they exist in their own right and not as objects to be tolerated merely for their perceived usefulness to human kind. The obvious cruelty to such a noble creature was also a serious factor in the equation, as was the undoubted pleasure derived from disrupting the stag hunts. This, coupled with the undoubted belief (no doubt born from the arrogance of youth) that here was a local atrocity against which I *could* make a positive contribution, had always seemed justification enough.

Then late one Friday night, as a guest on one of those dreadful late night chat shows so beloved of '80s TV audiences, I found myself confronted by the quintessential red-faced, ranting, blood sport fanatic demanding to know why I had spent so many years trying to destroy his way of life. The answer, I replied without thinking, was easy: "I simply don't like bullies."

That said, it would be wrong to assume I have not sometimes questioned the morality of attempting to destroy a way of life that at first glance would appear to offer a counter-balance too much of the pointless technical mumbo-jumbo that seems to dominate our lives today. Riding across the countryside in all weathers at one with nature has always seemed preferable to the consumer-obsessed culture that controls every aspect of modern society. Unfortunately blood sport adherents are not at one with nature, more like "at war with nature". Take a look through any of the numerous magazines available, such as *Shooting Times* and *The Countryman's Weekly*, and it's not a love affair with the natural world on display, rather the love of killing nature. The love affair is between the hunter and his hound, gun, crossbow, snare, trap, or whatever other means of destruction comes to hand.

To my old-world frontier mentality the image of the huntsman pitting his wits against nature in the raw is at odds with the reality of mobile phones, four-by-fours, quad bikes and all the other paraphernalia of twenty-first century technology that are employed to pursue the hunted animal. The image of the huntsman as part of the natural cycle is as much a myth of yesterday as the oft-recited "need for control" argument.

Therefore it is the inherent falseness of the premise that modern hunting is anything approaching "natural", coupled with the refusal to accept that killing for sport can ever be morally justified, which enables me to placate my conscience.

So as you read this book always keep in mind the simple fact that every demonstration the blood sports lobby has marched on, every speech about civil liberties, every stunt they have pulled (and what direct action advocate didn't give a wry smile at the "invasion" of Parliament by Otis Ferry and friends), every violation of parliamentary procedure, in fact every conscious action they have ever undertaken over the past one hundred years has had but one single aim: the protection and continuation of the right to chase and kill sentient creatures for amusement and sport. Nothing epitomised this sentiment more than an article appearing many years ago in the *Shooting Times* by a well known writer and self-professed "deer lover" which opened with the lines: "We all know the thrill of killing something. And killing something big."

As a long-time opponent of blood sports there was little in the oft-repeated rhetoric of these people that had much effect upon me, it being a constant reiteration of their own sense of moral superiority and rural guardianship. There was one allusion though, made at the start of the campaign against the *Hunting Act*, which made me see red: the sanctimonious reference to themselves as "rural freedom fighters". For in the 1950s I had made friends with a number of fellow children at my school who were refugees from the failed Hungarian Uprising. What I learned from them would cloud forever not only my view of Communism as a political philosophy, but also my concept of what a freedom fighter should be. For me they would always remain the brave men, women and children who fought out their unequal struggle on the streets of Budapest against the Soviet T54 tanks during the closing days of 1956. To see the term "freedom fighter" sullied by an inflated ego in a red coat chasing after a lone deer, or a little bundle of russet fur, simply to sate some unfathomable need to kill for pleasure, was one insult too far.

Also remember something else: the people who fought against stag hunting did not do so for any of the reasons trotted out during the

Countryside Alliance campaign to kill the *Hunting Act 2004* such as prejudice, bigotry, or some half-baked concept of class warfare, but simply because blood sports are cruel. If you still need to mix the concept of "class" into the hunting debate, then try looking at the issue another way. Try the equation of how an overwhelming majority of democratically elected Members of Parliament had to force the government into invoking the little used Parliament Act to secure the passage of the *Hunting Act 2004* past the opposition of a collection of noble Lords who had been elected by no one. Then add three (no expense spared) challenges by the Countryside Alliance to the Acts validity via the High Court, Appeal Court and Law Lords, all of which upheld the validity of the Act.

This to be followed by almost total subservience to the hunters' interests by government ministers, police and legal institutions combined, which has led to an almost total disregard of the law, that has allowed hunting to continue more or less unimpeded, give or take the odd minor inconvenience, which in turn will be rectified by "a very small one-clause Bill" when the Tories are returned to power. So maybe it is this unquestioned ability to circumnavigate the law of the land by these rural grandees that *could* lead some people to think that a certain class of people are above the law, while at the same time convincing this same class of person that in fact they *are* above the law.

Or put another way the following somewhat apocryphal story related to the American journalist P J O'Rourke by Mike Hobday of the LACS, even if not true, succinctly attests to the hunting sets high opinion of themselves. At a fox hunting protest, during the run-up to abolition, one of the demonstrators had approached a hunter and told him, "We are going to make what you do illegal." The hunter looked down from his horse and replied, "People like you obey the law. People like us make the law."

It was accepting an invitation to give a talk at the HSA's 2002 AGM, on "Sabbing Stag Hunting in the Good Old Days", that brought me back into the fold. For while I had not actively participated in the field for many years (save for the odd foray against DEFRA's irrational badger culling policy) I had certainly never lost my interest in blood sports or sympathy for those who campaign on behalf of animal rights. It was at this AGM that I learnt of the serious illness of someone with whom I had been extremely close for many years. The stupidity of internal animal rights ideological differences had forced us apart. A state of affairs, I was to learn later at her funeral, that we had both bitterly regretted. In many ways it was the death of my friend that brought me back to be there at what we thought was the end of stag hunting.

Since writing this book, a new set of friends and colleagues have asked if all the years in animal rights was worth the effort. The short answer is *yes*. During all that time I was involved with some of the kindest, bravest, most humane and honourable people that anyone finding themselves trapped on this sad little planet for the duration of their natural could wish to meet. Being a part of the animal rights movement is akin to sharing in a large, extended family, with all the diverse emotions that entails. It is true that often we only meet at demos, court appearances and funerals, but it's in the knowing that "out there" are many kindred spirits who will look at the latest atrocity against our fellow creatures, not to mention the impending destruction of Mother Earth herself, and feel exactly the same as you. That you are privileged to share your life with many for whom the sight of nature's incredible diversity does not instantly engender thoughts of how can I hunt it, shoot it, eat it, or turn it into some form of profit-related enterprise. It is all about not being alone.

The issue of not being alone is especially true when attempting to research and write a book of this nature. There are so many people without whose help, advice and input, direct or indirect, the story would remain untold that I would like to offer my special thanks to the following:

Mike Hobday and Jess Barker, along with all the staff at the League Against Cruel Sports in the Union Street office, who allowed me free rein in their archives, along with the chance to lay a few twenty-year-old ghosts of my own. Doreen Cronin who revived my flagging spirits with her kind comments on reading the first draft, coupled with much appreciated suggestions and corrections to subsequent editions. Likewise Kevin Hill, whose positive response to early drafts was more of a boost than he realised. A special thanks to Dave Wetton, who read and corrected the early drafts with "a fine tooth comb", thus vastly improving the finished product. The LACS executive director, Douglas Batchelor, for his help and advice. Mandy Dawes, erstwhile driver of the SOS battle-bus, who brought the memories flooding back, after an absence of twenty years, of the time she was always there to watch my back during the "Quantock war". Graham Floyd, whose views on the need for a realistic deer control policy so mirror my own, for his permission to quote at length from his excellent book *All His Rights.* LACS sanctuary manager Paul Tillsley for his kindness during the trips "to see the deer". The staff at Taunton County Library, whose patience at my inability to master the newspaper archive-copier was an inspiration. Anne Keirby of Ashgate Publishing Limited, who kindly sent me a photocopy of a much-needed reference book when I was unable to find an original. Staff at the *Western Daily Press* and *West Somerset Free Press,* who not only answered innumerable queries regarding long-forgotten news items, but offered much-needed help in tracking down illusive photographs. Likewise to Douglas Doig, Mike Huskisson, Mel Knight of Mirrorpix and Francis Stothard for permission to use their photographs. An extra special thanks must also go to Jane Tatam of Amolibros for her brilliant work of turning a jumbled mass of A4 sheets into this finished book. Also all the former hunt saboteurs and animal rights activists that gave of their time to revive half-forgotten memories of long ago who are too numerous to mention here, or wish to remain anonymous. Thanks, guys.

In conclusion a final thanks must go to the two women who offered endless encouragement during the long hours of writing this book. The spirit of one, my late friend Sue Smith, who stood looking over my shoulder the whole time refusing to let me give up on the project. While last, but far from least, my wife Josie, who may not have been there during the "glory days", but who has shown endless patience with the fall-out, while accompanying me on numerous field trips back to the past. Without you this book would not have happened.

NOTE: During the writing of this book I did consider including a list of source notes at the end of each chapter. Though as this book is intended for the general reader, or animal rights activist, this appeared somewhat superfluous as many direct references are given in the text. Therefore should the origin of any unaccredited quote be required, they are, along with all quoted references, a matter of public record and verifiable source material can be found in the public domain.

Equally, all efforts were made to obtain permission regarding the use of actual, or perceived, copyright materials. Failure to have done so, on notification to the author, will be rectified in future editions of this book.

Furthermore, it must be stressed that nothing in this book is intended to encourage the use of violent, criminal, or unlawful acts in the furtherance of animal rights campaigning. Non-violent direct action must always remain the order of the day.

Chapter One

"...one bite, and the deer is dead"

THE WEST OF ENGLAND commands the dubious privilege of retaining the last stronghold of what is arguably the most controversial, whilst certainly the most brutal, of all blood sports. For here, in an area that extends approximately fifty miles West to East, from Barnstaple to Bridgwater and thirty miles North to South, from the Bristol Channel to Tiverton, are to be found the last three packs of hounds to hunt the wild red deer. From early August until mid-April the Quantock, Tiverton and Devon and Somerset Staghounds hunt down an estimated combined total of between 150 and 200 deer.

Stag hunting has always been the most reviled blood sport on the anti "hit list", sustaining constant attack for over one hundred years. Singled out for special attention far more than any other form of hunting, it has spawned a whole collection of organisations specifically dedicated to its abolition. National committees have been formed to pressure Parliament, hundreds of thousands of pounds spent purchasing land to frustrate its activities, hunt saboteur groups have attempted to destroy it through direct action tactics, while its interests have been ruthlessly attacked via such national bodies as the Royal Society for the Prevention of Cruelty to Animals (RSPCA) and National Trust (NT). Not surprisingly, the support for stag hunting amongst other members of the hunting fraternity has been lukewarm at best, their activities tending to be seen as drawing unwanted attention towards hunting in general. Even the pro-hunt Wildlife Network, close ally of the parliamentary Middle Way pressure group so prominent during the run-up to blood sport abolition in 2004, recommended its abolition by Act of Parliament.

All this has tended to create an entrenched attitude of mind in the small area of the West Country where stag hunting retains a foothold. They have learnt to fight their corner so successfully that they now command an importance far beyond their size. Over the years, they have come to dominate every local structure that may directly, or indirectly, have some bearing on their sport in particular, or the red deer herd in general. They have a company to buy land, or hunting rights, to protect the hunt in perpetuity. When threatened by Parliament in 1930 it was the stag hunt interests who created the British Field Sports Society, the organisation we know today as the Countryside Alliance. Then, if all else fails, there is always the trump card. They will threaten that if stag hunting is abolished then the red deer will be exterminated from Exmoor and the Quantock Hills. Nothing illustrates better this inherent threat than Dick Lloyd's statement in the 1989 *Vive La Chasse* that: "If the evil day should dawn when hunting is prevented for any reason, the deer will start a rapid, bloody slide to extinction from which all the statutes in the House of Commons will not save them. Those who cause that state of affairs will have to answer to future generations for the disappearance of the last remaining large herd of red deer in England and the Exmoor National Park will have to find a new symbol, for the stag's head will become a sad and hollow mockery."

To further justify this argument Dick Lloyd will quote, in the same book, another "leading naturalist and authority on deer" Richard Prior. In his 1965 *Living with Deer* Prior writes:

> "Forget about the ethics of hunting, but make up your mind as to whether or not it would be a calamity if red deer were no longer to be seen in this corner of England... . If I appear to condone hunting, it is not that the idea of chasing any animal for the pleasure of riding after it has the slightest appeal for me, but that no workable plan to ensure survival for the deer has been suggested by those who would like to see the end of staghunting. Hunting does involve cruelty, so does farming for

> that matter, but is it not better for lack of any alternative but final extinction, that one beast should suffer so that the rest may live in safety? I feel that the animal lovers who are now so anxious to protect the deer from hunting would be the first to bewail the loss of this stately creature which has become a symbol of the wild beauties of Exmoor."

There was more than a touch of irony here in that having damned the West Country red deer to annihilation at the hands of well-meaning but ignorant animal welfare groups, rather than the actions of embittered stag hunters who would carry out the threatened slaughter, Dick Lloyd should then invoke the opinion of "expert" Richard Prior to back his statement. For this is the same Richard Prior who in 1985, when appearing as a "deer expert" on behalf of the Devon and Somerset Staghounds (DSSH) during a twelve-day trial at Bristol High Court, admitted under questioning from Louis Blom-Cooper QC that he knew nothing about deer hunting.

A far more candid, or should we say honest, deer expert was Kenneth Whitehead, who had the truth of it about right in his 1980 *Hunting and Stalking Deer in Britain through the Ages.* He thought:

> "The claim, often put forward, that stag hunting with hounds is the *only* satisfactory way of controlling the deer population in this part England, is not borne out in practice, because occasional deer drives still have to be held to kill surplus stock, particularly hinds. Anti-hunting supporters can argue that since some deer have to be shot, complete control should be effected by shooting. Such a thing is of course possible, but whether the farmers, deprived of their favourite sport of hunting would tolerate *any* deer at all on their land is extremely doubtful."

Due to the stranglehold maintained on deer-related issues in the area, the effectiveness of stag hunting as a viable means of deer control, weighed against other forms of control practised by such bodies as the National Trust, Forestry Commission, and independent stalking operations, is an argument that cannot be resolved. The issue is not that such alternatives exist, but rather that if stag hunting is not accepted without question as the central plank of any proposed deer management scheme, then the hunters simply refuse to accept its implementation. There have been many attempts over the years to arrive at a solution, with countless reports attesting to the fact that hunting is not the most effective, nor humane, form of deer control, with all of them either ignored or supplanted with new reports commissioned by the hunters themselves that then supply the required verdict.

Another bone of contention between the pro and anti factions has been to determine the actual number of deer residing in hunting areas. The hunts have always deliberately underestimated the number so as to bolster their claim that deer hunting is the most effective method to keep the herds at an acceptable level. As, for many years, they were the only people with ready access to the deer, it was not difficult to hide the true figures, taking up the slack with secret deer drives to shotguns. Only since the 1980s, with deer counts undertaken by bodies relatively independent of hunting interests, have the true numbers of deer across Exmoor and the Quantocks become known, proving to be twice, or three times, higher than previously thought. The stag hunts now maintain that they never claimed that hunting was the only method of control, merely that it is the most intrinsic element of a wider "management control plan". ***Note 1***

What is not in question is that the activities of stag hunters have commanded the attention of both local and national press, culminating in what must surely run into thousands of column inches. While some has been informed, more well meaning, much has been sensationalist and inaccurate. The numerous attempts to debate the subject in Parliament have, in the main, been little more than slanging matches, consistent only by their lack of reasoned argument. The entire issue has become one of claim and counter claim mired in vitriolic rhetoric emanating from two diametrically entrenched viewpoints with the only common denominator being a lack of common ground.

To appreciate the issue fully, one must, strange as it may seem, study the writing of the hunters themselves, not the self -justifying pamphlets of the British Field Sports Society or Countryside Alliance, but the classics of stag hunting literature. For only here, tucked away between reams of wordy rhetoric extolling the virtues of traditions unchanged, will be found descriptions of animal abuse worthy of the most fertile abolitionist's mind. An entire mind-set will be revealed which, while constantly endowing the hunted animal with human characteristics, singularly fails to offer the slightest compassion for a terrified sentient creature. These books resound with people whose sole motivation is a deep love and respect for the hunted stag, while denying his right to exist except as a quarry for the hounds. Surprisingly, considering that this was once classed "as the sport of kings", few modern books have been written about the hunting of red deer, with the true classics penned from the middle of the nineteenth to the early twentieth century.

While authors such as Richard Jefferies, Philip Evered, Archibald Hamilton and Alfred Vowles offer a wealth of detailed insight into the true face of deer hunting, the book still regarded in many quarters as the "Bible" of stag hunting is Dr Charles Palk Collyns' *Notes on the Chase of the Wild Red Deer.* Although published as long ago as 1862, describing hunting during the period 1780-1860, both the 1902 and 1907 reprints carried statements in the preface that "as to the value of the statements made by the author, it can scarcely be asserted that in the interval of forty years any serious flaws, physiological or technical, have been brought to light. The system of hunting observed in the field is practically the same today." This assertion remains true one hundred years later for, while the technology of the hunt supporter has changed beyond all recognition with his mobile phone, four by four and quad bike, the role of the master, huntsman and whipper-in remain much the same as in the days of Palk Collyns. Equally, as the methodology of the hunt has remained static over the years, so apparently have the cruelties inherent within it. As any hunt saboteur or hunt monitor will know from experience, the incidents described in these books are as prolific today as they undoubtedly were back then. In fact so commonplace were they that not only Dr Collyns, but virtually every writer putting pen to paper on the subject of deer hunting before the 1950s, records such stories as a matter of course.

For instance, Dr Collyns tells us how "the rustics (the equivalent of today's followers) dislodge the stag from its stronghold by shouts and stones" and how, at the end of the chase "the faltering stride, and lowered head proclaim his strength is failing" and that "the spent deer has not the force to leap the hedge or ditch and is ready to fall". He continues "[the deer] runs feebly and painfully along the beaten paths" then "he gives one wild and hurried look of fear and dares the desperate leap. He has jumped from a height of at least thirty feet on to the shore and in the next moment is floating in the salt sea waves." Then "...a man in a boat puts a rope around the horns of the deer and the victim is dragged in triumph to the beach, the knife is at his throat and, amid the baying of the pack and the loud whoo-whoops of the crowd, the noble and gallant animal yields up his life."

The Rev Edward Smith of Enmore, in his 1939 *Quantock Life & Rambles,* will record how they chase a deer for over two hours across the Quantock Hills and then force him to swim a mile and a half into the River Parrett. Once a boat has been found they will row out to him, tie a rope to his antlers and drag him ashore to be killed. The author Richard Jefferies, in his 1884 *Red Deer,* explained that the boatmen "throw a rope round the stag's antlers and draw him on board, and immediately tie his legs. A stag seems an awkward animal to get into a boat, but they manage it without much difficulty and bring him ashore to be killed. The huntsman...always kills, that he may be sure it is a warrantable deer of proper age; if it proves not to be mature, the stag is let go..."

While the "boatmen receive a guinea for bringing in a stag and a half guinea for a hind" the hounds sometimes got a free ride. Such as Credulous who "swam after a stag, seized him by the ear, and partly mounted on the stag's back, was drawn along a considerable way, sometimes pressing the stag's head under water." In a similar incident recorded by Dr Collyns it was more of a group outing after a stag "swam through the waves with six couple of hounds in close pursuit, which they continued until a boat sent out captured him and five of the hounds were towed to land on his back. It was a grand sight to see the stag with the hounds swimming after him for at least half a mile."

At Porlock Weir it was common practice for many years to keep a boat in readiness during the hunting season in the event that a deer took to the sea. The march of progress brought refinements to this process, for according to Kenneth Whitehead: "During the inter-war period the motor boat replaced the rowing boat, and this considerably speeded up the taking of a deer that had taken to the sea. With the motor boat it was no longer necessary to take the deer on board, and during the early thirties the general procedure was to slip a rope over the stag's antlers, or round the hind's neck, and then drive the boat at full speed for a few minutes, with the result that the deer's nostrils were pulled under the water and the animal drowned." In later years a humane killer would be supplied to the Porlock Weir boatmen by the Devon and Somerset Staghounds so that the deer could be killed at sea.

On Exmoor they will hunt a hind for over three hours, then check the ordnance map to confirm that the distance "from the middle of Blagdon Wood to North Common is fully seven and a quarter miles, but, as hounds ran, of course, the distance was made infinitely greater". As the kill was at 2:15 p.m., with daylight left to find another quarry, the hunt will continue afresh until "finally the hind took to the sea at the mouth of Horner Water, where the breakers were coming in with such force that she had to be left". Unable to capture this stirring scene for posterity, the noted Exmoor chronicler Alfred Vowles will later publish in his 1920 *Stag hunting on Exmoor* the photograph "GONE TO SEA! A stag boldly swimming across Porlock Bay", pursued by five hounds. Whether this one drowned or not he omits to record. This same author, not content to confine such stirring scenes between the covers of a book, was also noted for his extensive range of postcards, many showing similar incidents, which were widely available to day trippers and holiday makers.

Hunted deer taking to the sea must have been a common occurrence. Philip Evered writing in 1902 (*Staghunting with the Devon and Somerset)* tells us:

> "The swimming powers of deer are very great indeed, but they have their limits, and deer are more often drowned at sea than is supposed. The chill of the water is sufficient at times to drown a beaten deer, and it has occasionally happened that a stag has

been seen to drown in comparatively still water, when they might have returned with ease to the beach."

In the same book he adds the comment that "steamers, in passing up or down channel, have occasionally sighted the floating carcase of a deer that has been lost at sea in this way".

This author remembers a harrowing incident in early 1965 when two stags were hunted along the cliffs at County Gate, near Lynton, for over two hours before being driven into the sea. The DSSH had a boat waiting offshore to kill them, for as Master Bob Nancekivell pointed out later, "If we had let them go on they would have drowned, because they were exhausted."

Such incidents are not uncommon today as the former stag hunt supporter, now turned LACS activist, Graham Floyd recounted in his book *All His Rights.* The victim this time was a semi-tame stag know to many locals as Percy the Pet that having been pursued by the DSSH was last "seen to be swimming across Porlock Bay towards Hurlstone Point" prior to the hounds being called off.

The end was predictable:

"On reaching the pebble ridge beach I paused to scan out to sea. To my amazement I immediately caught sight of a pair of antlers like a ship's mast rising and falling in the waves some half a mile out. Unfortunately the beach was not deserted. Over by the Point there were some fishermen quite oblivious to everything. I wish there had been time to warn them for by now Percy was obviously making a desperate bid to reach the shore before he was taken around the point by the incoming tide. Keeping out of sight, all I could do was watch the outcome. Closer and closer he came, surely they would see him in a minute. To be expected, when one of them caught sight of him, their reaction was ecstatic excitement. Their shouts and commotion turned Percy back out to sea again. He had no choice but to struggle against the force of the tide and attempt to round Hurlstone Point. As he disappeared out of sight he was clearly being swept closer and closer to the rocks where he would stand no chance."

Later, after reaching the rocks below Hurlstone Point, Floyd discovered the fate of the deer.

"I scanned despairingly with my binoculars. I knew I could not afford to stay long; the tide was rising rapidly and threatening to cut off the rock I was sitting on. Soaked from the spray of the breaking waves, I took a last long hard look. Then something floating in the sea took my notice. It was either a large piece of driftwood or it was the drowned body of Percy. I studied it hard as it was being washed ashore. Eventually I could see that it had hair upon it and my worst fears were realised – it was Percy. I felt shocked and saddened and somewhat amazed at the incredible chance in a million that the body was being carried to the exact rocky area that I was standing on. The last few vital feet then I grasped an antler. Having taken his antlers I eventually had to leave Percy to his watery grave in this inaccessible place. It was somewhat ironic that Hurlstone Point, where Percy met his sad end, was in clear view from his favourite lying bed in the paddock next to my cottage. He might have planned it all."

Though it must be left to Richard Jefferies to explain fully just what "good sport" could be had when a hind went to sea.

"Upon one occasion a hunted hind took to the sea and swam out so far that she was but just visible. The huntsman and one gentleman who had followed close and was with him, tied their horses in cover and watched her from the beach. She swam till their straining eyes lost sight of her; the hounds, wearied and exhausted, returned to the beach. While they still stood trying to catch sight again of the game, a steamer came past, and at this moment the huntsman saw a dark spot on the water which he imagined must be the hind.

"As the steamer approached the dark spot it began to move, and he was then certain it was the deer. He shouted and waved his cap, but the men on the steamer did not see the deer in the water – they were looking at him on the beach and at the hounds. At last, however, they understood the shouting and pointing, and saw the hind floating in the sea. Then began the strangest chase – a steamer after a deer. The men on deck shouted and holloa'd, and the whistle was blown. The vessel easily overtook the hind, but when they tried to take her with a rope, she doubled; this was repeated several times, and each time the hind, though after a long run, avoided them by doubling.

"Presently she turned and swam ashore, but here the hounds met her on the beach, and forced her back again. She swam straight out till the steamer, which had been brought in nearer to land, began to chase her, when she returned to the beach a second time. The hounds drove her to sea for a third time – this time the steamer could not approach near enough to chase her without grounding, but a hound named 'Trouncer' headed her. This hound swam faster than the rest of the pack, and showed greater intelligence. Instead of following the deer in her windings, he endeavoured to keep outside her, so as to turn her and head her for shore. For the third time she returned to the land, fell, and was taken."

Dr Collyns says that the hunting of stags should not continue beyond 8th October because they should not be disturbed during the rut (breeding season) when they "become exhausted and fatigued". He refers to them at the end of the rut as "Sorry looking animals…their bodies lean and drawn up and their gait and movements indicating the state of debility to which they have been brought." Yet, our modern hunters ignore this advice and continue throughout the rut until the end of October. The break that was formerly from 8th October for two to three weeks to allow the rut is now described, in *Vive La Chasse*, "as a break of about a fortnight in early November to rest hounds, horses and hunt staff".

Much the same indifference is shown towards the hunting of pregnant hinds. The hinds are fertile at three years old and bear their first calf the following year. The gestation period is eight months, so the calves are usually born around the end of May to early June, though John Fortescue (1887 *Records of Staghunting on Exmoor)* reported the killing of two heavily pregnant hinds, despite efforts being made to save them, during August and September. The calves are suckled for eight to ten months and remain with their mothers until the second autumn. So instances of pregnant hinds hunted to exhaustion, or calves left abandoned when their mothers are killed, are far from rare.

Again it is the good Doctor Collyns who tells of a hunt in September 1853 when, having tufted a stag unsuccessfully for a long time, a hind broke cover "and the field impatient for a gallop, urged the master to lay on the hounds". After "a fast burst to Oare, Badgworthy, Brendon Common, Farleigh and Watersmeet, near Lynmouth, the hind was killed, and was found to have a fine male calf in her." On another occasion he refers to an enormous leap taken by a hind in a failed attempt to escape the pack. The hunters were amazed because what made it "more extraordinary" was "that on being paunched, a calf was taken from her almost able to stand".

Sometimes the hinds are hunted with their calves, such as the one on 18th August 1819 from Porlock. "In Berry Castle they found a hind and calf, and as the hounds wanted blood, the pack was laid on under Buckethole." The hind ended up taking to the sea and before the hunt could arrange a boat "a sloop going up the Channel saw her, and put out a boat, caught her, and carried her away". What happened to the calf is unrecorded. Fast forward to 16th December 1929 when the *Evening Standard,* under the headline "Exhausted Hind Lassoed" tells us:

> "The Tiverton Staghounds had hunted a hind from Haddon. When the hunt began the hind had a calf running beside it, but it left the calf sheltered in undergrowth. Closely pursued, the hind was hunted in and out of the River Exe several times, and when exhausted it entered the River Barle, near Marsh Bridge. Because of the flooded state of the river the hounds and hunters could not reach it. The hind was eventually caught by a hunter, who threw a rope over its head. The rope was drawn tight and the animal was pulled out of the water and killed."

Again there is no mention as to the fate of the calf.

Nothing much had changed by 31st December 1957, when a "retired police detective inspector" employed by the National Committee for the Abolition of Deer Hunting "to attend and report fully on what took place at stag hunts" wrote the following after attending a meet from Wheddon Cross.

> "Shortly before 3.30pm the hind came down into the water near the pathway to Horner Water. Hounds were on to it, very close. Ran up and down the water followed by hounds, shouting horsemen, riders and foot-followers. For some minutes the whole scene seemed to be in utter confusion. Hind was seen clearly only 20 feet away on the bank of Horner Water. Tried to run away from hounds, up the side of water but was turned back by riders and hunters on other side; it turned again but was unable to get on to the road due to car followers and horsemen blocking the way… . Hind was terrified, its main fear being hounds. (I regret I am unable to explain the actual look in its eyes, but it appeared to express the utmost fear, realising its hopeless situation.) Within minutes about a dozen hounds were around it and trying to pull it down. It was holding its head high. (*It was observed to be a very small hind, and young.)* A man then fired a shot (one shot from shotgun) and it fell amidst the hounds, who were all over it. It took some minutes for the Huntsman, Sidney Bazely, to get hounds off it… . *On close inspection it was observed to be a very, very small young hind.*"

Maybe this time it was the mother's fate that went unrecorded.

Come the twenty-first century and the whole sorry spectacle of calves separated from their mothers because they were unable to negotiate banks and fences, or if they have stayed together hunters riding between them in an attempt to separate the pair, have all been captured on film courtesy of South West Deer Protection. One such film, taken on 25th November 2000, clearly shows a desperate calf clinging to its mother's side, prior to the hind's death at the hands of the DSSH.

While today we are assured that the hounds never touch a hunted deer, merely hold it at bay until the huntsman can humanely dispatch it, this did not seem to be the case during Richard Jefferies' day. He tells us that

"No more able to run, the hunted stag stands at bay in the river, choosing a place so deep that the hounds must swim to reach him, while he is firm on his feet. Though they swarm about him, if the water is deep enough he can keep them at bay with his antlers for a time; but they are too numerous. His strength decreases as their eagerness increases, for they attack him for his flesh; they hunt not only for the joy of the chase, but the savage flavour of blood. After delivering a blow with his antlers, the stag holds his head high up, his large eyes straining down on the hounds, and his mouth shut. They swarm upon him, and weary him out, pulling him down at last by his legs, and he falls with his legs under him as a bullock lies. The hounds are whipped off, or they would tear him to pieces – their teeth marks are generally left in the skin..."

According to the same source it gets even worse for the hinds.

"The huntsman is always anxious to be on the spot when the hounds run in upon a hind, because, as she has no horns, she cannot resist them a moment, and they pull her down at once. Once when the river the hind entered was in full flood...he crossed over swimming his horse, and was obliged to dismount and wade in flooded meadows for some distance beside the stream, encouraging and directing the pack. Presently the hounds found her, but, as it happened, on the other side; he hastened back to his horse, and saw them pull her down as he ran. He swam his horse across again, but when he got to the spot – though it was but a few minutes – the deer was not only eaten, but the bones were picked clean; so eager are the hounds for the flesh of the deer."

It would appear that eighty-six years later a super-hound has been created, for the writer and broadcaster J H B Peel in his 1970 *Portrait of Exmoor* will tell us that, by comparison to shooting, "hunting seems merciful". For apparently "many people do not know, or have chosen to forget that hounds kill swiftly: one bite, and the deer is dead." Whereas E R Lloyd, Chairman of Masters of Deerhounds Association, disagrees with both the previous statements when explaining that "one of the commonest misconceptions is that deer are torn to pieces by the pack: this is not the case. At the end of a hunt the deer is either lost or stands at bay, in which case hounds instinctively stand off and bay until the arrival of one of the hunt staff, with an approved firearm, who approaches the deer and shoots it at point blank range."

While it may be true that such incidents as recorded here are the exception and the comments of naturalist E W Hendy valid when he states that "a great deal of the invective against stag-hunting comes from casual visitors to Exmoor who have seen the kill…", he is honest enough to admit that: "Of course occasionally there are unfortunate incidents: deer sometimes come at bay in positions where it is difficult to kill them quickly." The added assertion that "such incidents are collected and published by the opponents of stag-hunting, often with inaccurate and misleading embellishments" rings hollow when weighed against the evidence of the hunters themselves. Much the same dismissive attitude was levelled against any photograph produced by the anti camp to show the cruelty of stag hunting, with the usual claim that it had been taken in France, as was the reaction to one used in this book. Now it is not so easy to hide the truth for the last twenty years have seen the employment of hunt monitors and "undercover operatives", employed by such organisations as the League Against Cruel Sports (LACS) and International Fund for Animal Welfare (IFAW), whose sole function is to patrol the hunting fields looking for evidence. The accumulated video footage taken by such people as Mike Huskisson and Kevin Hill certainly need no embellishing from head office.

Stag hunters will be the first to tell you that they derive no pleasure from the death of such a noble animal, but view it merely as the regretful by-product of a very necessary culling programme. A few will echo the sentiments of J H B Peel when he says that hunting "does more good than harm to those who relish it. It allows them to exercise certain ineradicable impulses that might otherwise be deflected onto human beings." Most though would agree with Dick Lloyd that "followers of staghounds go hunting for a variety of reasons, such as for the ride (often with the family), watching hounds working, the excitement in horse and rider by galloping with others, a day on the hills, physical exercise away from 'the office', regular out-door activity for large numbers of pensioners, and – for some – what the French call 'La Chasse' (the chase), an inbred human instinct from the earliest days of the human race...". Perhaps Alfred Vowles was more honest when writing in a less politically correct age: "It is the ambition of all good staghunters to be near the finish, and if they are it proves their enthusiasm, keenness and knowledge of the country.... Absence means defeat!"

West Country red deer hunting today is a tiny remnant of what was once the predominant blood sport in Britain. From the 1750s until relatively recently, most counties in England have boasted one or more packs of deerhounds, with Kenneth Whitehead listing the total number of registered hunts throughout the years at 126. Though it is true to say that the majority of these were not hunting wild deer, but semi-tame or carted deer, which had been transported from a park or enclosure to the meet, released from a cart, then chased until exhausted. They were then, barring fatal accidents, recaptured and returned to the park until needed again. The last two carted deer hunts on the mainland, Mid-Kent Staghounds and Norwich Staghounds, lasted until the early 1960s, when they were both disbanded following public pressure, although two packs remained in Ireland. In Northern Ireland the County Down Staghounds lasted until 1998, when it too was forced to disband through public opposition, while the Ward Union continues to hunt in the Republic.

Fallow deer were also a favourite quarry, with the last pack, the New Forest Buckhounds, continuing until 1997. The much smaller roe deer were extensively hunted for many years, but the practice died out around the time of the First World War. Regrettably it has been revived recently in the West Country, with two packs, the Cheldon

Buckhounds and Mr Lawrence Clark's Buckhounds, formed in 1990, with a third, the Isle Valley Buckhounds, in 1992. Following an incident on Exmoor in 1993, all three packs of buckhounds were expelled from the deer hunters governing body, the Masters of Deerhounds Association (MDHA), following a ruling from the British Field Sports Society (BFSS) that roe deer hunting was not a legitimate field sport. They subsequently formed their own body, the Masters of Buckhounds Association, but remain isolated from mainstream hunting. Consequently they are very secretive, fail to advertise their meets, and prove extremely hard to locate.

No such problems existed with the three packs of staghounds whose meets were regularly advertised in both the *Horse & Hound* and the local Exmoor newspaper *West Somerset Free Press* until 2007. The *Free Press* is a wonderful old-fashioned publication that devoted (pre the 2005 ban) half a page to detailed reports of the previous weeks hunting activities, though still manage to retain a neutral stand on the issue.

The Devon and Somerset hunt on a Tuesday, Thursday and Saturday, the Tiverton on Wednesday and Saturday, with the Quantock out Monday and Thursday or Friday. While the deer hunting year is divided into three distinct seasons. From early August until late October is autumn stag hunting, when male red deer of five years or over (warrantable stags) are hunted. There is then a short break, partially to accommodate the rutting season, until the early part of November when the hind hunting begins, which will continue until the end of February. Then from March until the end of April, spring stag hunting takes over, which is the hunting of young male red deer between the age of three to five years.

The oldest and largest of the three hunts is the Devon and Somerset Staghounds (DSSH) which can trace a direct lineage back to 1775, although there has been deer hunting on Exmoor for a considerable time prior to that. The earliest reference, according to Patrick Chalmers, *The History of Hunting,* would appear to be in 878 when we find Alfred the Great "hunting with certain officers and vassals in the forests of Somersetshire". But all we know of that woodland jaunt is that the hunted stag escaped the hounds for a truly original reason: "The Sun becoming totally in eclipse between nones and vespers...the deer disproved the dogs." While Cecil Aldin, writing in *Exmoor, The Riding Playground Of England,* tells us that stag hunting specifically over Exmoor is one of our oldest hunting institutions and that "the first recorded Master of Staghounds was a gentleman by the name of D'Auberville, who lived in the time of William the Conqueror".

According to E T Macdermot in *The Devon and Somerset Staghounds, 1907-1936* "regular hunting on Exmoor dates from 1508, when King Henry VII granted to Sir Edmund Carew of Mohun's Ottery, Devon, a lease of the forest for his life with licence for him and all other lieges by his authority freely to hunt and course the deer with hounds, greyhounds, bows and arrows." By the time of Queen Elizabeth I, Exmoor was hunted as a Royal Forest, with the earliest record found by Charles Palk Collyns for a pack of staghounds here being 1598.

There followed years of ad-hoc hunting packs operating across the area and it was not until 1775 that the first serious attempt to formalise Exmoor deer hunting was undertaken by Colonel Basset of Watermouth. This pack, known as the North Devon Staghounds, operated under various masters more or less continuously until 1824 when it was sold to a German who removed it to Europe. Not until 1827 was hunting resumed when Sir Arthur Chichester raised a scratch pack made up of foxhounds, which he hunted for the next six years. When he quit in 1833 hunting again ceased on the moors.

It restarted in 1837 when Dr C P Collyns raised a pack which for the first time became unofficially known as the Devon and Somerset Staghounds, although this folded in 1842 due to lack of money. After Collyns came the Hon Newton Fellows, who ran hounds for the next six years, after which Sir Arthur Chichester one again resumed the mastership, but for the 1848 season only. That same year the hunt was again disbanded, after which the only deer hunting on Exmoor was conducted by visiting packs of harriers and foxhounds.

It was not until 1855 that Mr M Fenwick Bisset, a gentleman farmer from Berkshire, came to live as a tenant of Lord Carnarvon at Pixton Park, near Dulverton, that Exmoor was again regularly hunted. From that date onwards the Devon and Somerset Staghounds, as they would now be officially known, have hunted continuously to the present day.

It boasts forty-five couple of hounds. In hunting terms the hounds are never referred to in the singular: i.e. ten couple indicating twenty hounds etc., and the hounds are never called dogs. To say such a thing is a sure-fire give-away that you are "an ignorant anti", with the kennels at Exford, Somerset.

The DSSH, apart from being the most powerful of the three hunts, also happens to be one of the largest single landowners on Exmoor. As long ago as 1926 they began acquiring many acres of moorland to protect their sport, registering them in the ownership of the Badgworthy Land Company Ltd for use as a perpetual hunting ground. This company is a subsidiary of the DSSH, owns the kennels, reports its affairs to the annual meeting of the stag hunt, and pays any surplus money it has to the hunt funds. Today the Badgworthy Land Company owns in excess of 7,000 acres outright, with an additional estimated 50,000 acres of "sporting rights", which includes most of the land now owned by the Somerset County Council. These "sporting rights" have been obtained, either purchased or bequeathed, from existing landowners to ensure the hunting of deer "in perpetuity", and legally to pre-empt any future owner from banning the hunt.

Similar measures to protect the future of the sport were undertaken by the more affluent members of the hunt. In 1932, Dunkery Beacon (the highest point on Exmoor) and 4,000 acres of surrounding moorland were purchased jointly by Lt Col W Wiggin, the then Master of the DSSH, and Mrs Allen Hughes, and given by them to the National Trust, on condition that stag hunting should always continue there. In 1935 stag hunt subscribers bought the extensive Anstey Common, near Dulverton, as a hunting ground, in memory of one of their number, Mr Froude Hancock. While a few years before the Second World War the National Trust were given the Winsford and Holnicote estates by Sir Richard Acland, who also laid down the condition that stag hunting should be allowed to continue so long as it remained legal.

The Tiverton Staghounds (TSH) was formed in 1896 as an offshoot of the DSSH in order to hunt the deer which were increasing in number south of the Barnstaple to Taunton railway line. At first it was known as Sir John Amory's Staghounds after the man who created it (Sir John Heathcoat-Amory) and operated until disbanded in 1915. For the remaining years of the First World War the area was hunted by a scratch pack mastered by Mr Charles Slader of South Molton who, upon retirement in 1919, handed over to Mr J Yandle. He not only assumed the mastership, but completely reorganised the hunt, including changing the name to the one we know today. The pack consists of fifteen couple and is kennelled at Mouseberry Farm, near Tiverton.

Until 1901 the Quantock Hills were occasionally hunted by both Sir John Amory's and the DSSH, but this ceased when a local pack was established here. Mr E A V Stanley of Quantock Lodge decided that the red deer introduced onto the hills by Fenwick Bisset, former master of the DSSH (1855-1881) in the 1860s, with the intention of expanding the DSSH's territory, were now becoming a serious problem. This pack, which became known as the Quantock Staghounds (QSH) hunted regularly until 1907, when it was disbanded. There was no deer hunting on the Quantocks until Colonel (later Sir) Denis Boles, master of the West Somerset Foxhounds and Tory MP for West Somerset decided to reform the hunt in 1917.

This followed a request from the Controller of Food in the Liberal war time cabinet under Lloyd George to restart the QSH "so that the farmers could have their hunting and at the same time make sure that the deer herd was allowed to flourish". The Liberal government paid for four horses, ten couples of hounds, the wages of two men for a season, along with horse and hound upkeep. Colonel Boles brought seven stags from Warnham Park in Sussex, one of the finest herds in the country, by train from Horsham to Williton. They were released into St Audries Deer Park and after six months allowed out onto the Quantock Hills, where they soon bred with the few remaining indigenous hinds. There was limited hunting on the hills from now on, but not of the seven stags, with the first of these not killed until 1923, and only then after one was hit by a car. Colonel Boles continued running the pack at his own expense until 1931, when the mastership was taken over by Mrs E M Wimbush who carried through until 1954. Today the QSH is the least prosperous of the three packs, with twenty-five couple of hounds and maintain kennels at Bagborough, a small village on the Quantock Hills.

The most important part of a stag hunt takes place the evening before, and early morning of, the meet. For it is at dusk and dawn that the "harbourer" (a deer at rest in the woods is said *to harbour),* the member of the hunt whose job it is to find a suitable (warrantable) stag to be hunted, will be at work.

The determining factors as to what makes for a warrantable deer are described by E R Lloyd as:

> "In the autumn the oldest stags are selected by the 'harbourer' for hunting; some of these carry very good antlers but this does not preclude them from being suitable for culling; for instance, a powerful stag in his prime in company with the same herd of hinds for the third year, has to be culled if he is to be prevented from serving his own daughters. Antler growth is not the only parameter by which a deer is judged; his physical condition is even more important.
>
> "When hunting spring stags (sub-standard 3 and 4 year olds) and hinds, harbourer and hunt staff make every effort to locate and cull the poorest animals. In the case of hinds, this is assisted by the process of hunting; even an expert may not spot that one hind is over-burdened with lungworm or liver fluke, but the hounds will expose the weakness quickly; consequently, the practice is initially to pursue a herd and then concentrate on one that breaks away, as this is usually due to some hidden debility making it difficult for it to retain its place..."

The day before will find the harbourer in the area of the advertised meet asking local farmers, forest workers, etc. for any sightings or knowledge of deer movements. Any information, for it must be remembered that many locals specifically keep an eye peeled for signs of deer so as to assist the hunt, will be followed up. He will visit a number of locations alleged to be holding deer, then carefully track the animals by their slots (hoof prints). From these, for this man is an undoubted expert concerning deer, he will be able to determine whether the animal is old or young, male or female, has any injuries and, so it is said of certain harbourers, tell the size of the antlers. Once he has decided upon a possible quarry by slotting, the next step is to try and view the animal. This can be accomplished either by following the slots to where the deer is feeding, or to position himself where he has been told or deduced that the stag will harbour for the night. He knows that once a deer has chosen a resting place he will remain there until daybreak.

At first light the following morning the harbourer will return to the same area to make sure the stag has remained at harbour throughout the night. By tracking the slots around the edge of the wood (under no circumstances will the wood be entered for fear of disturbing the animal) he can determine the deer's point of entry, whether it is still there, or has already left the wood to feed. If signs indicate it has left, then the slots will be followed to the grazing site where a sighting will be made.

There are, of course, many variations on the "what will the stag do in the morning" theme. Apart from remaining in the wood or grazing locally, there is moving off with hinds, wandering off to a completely different location or bedding down for the day. If the animal has elected to lay-up, for during autumn months red deer stags will conceal themselves amongst the fern, bracken and heather of the moor with antlers laid along their backs remaining virtually undetectable to all but the most observant, the slots must be patiently tracked to the new location. In fact, the importance of the harbourer to the success of "a good day's hunting" cannot be over-emphasised, for without his information the expectant field waiting at the meet will be totally blind.

Once he has assessed the situation the harbourer will report back to the Master, then subsequently return with the huntsman and four or five couple of hounds to rouse the stag from its resting place. The accompanying hounds are known as "tufters", specially selected because of their experience and reliability. The remainder of the pack will be held in the hound van, or corralled in a convenient barn near to the meet. If the entire pack were used to flush the warrantable stag from the wood it is possible that other deer would be roused as well, causing the hounds to chase off (riot) in all directions. Therefore only the tufters, who can be relied upon to concentrate on a single scent, obey the huntsman's commands instinctively and ignore all other distraction, are used.

While huntsman, harbourer and tufters enter the wood, a number of experienced members of the hunt, including the whipper-in, will be stationed outside to watch for the deer as it emerges. There will also be supporters mounted on motorbikes, not to mention many armed with mobile phones, who will keep the hunted animal under constant surveillance. Once the stag is out in the open and running, the harbourer's job is finished and the rest of the pack will be laid on with all speed. The deer is not given a head start, or "given law" as it is called, for the time between rousing the stag and informing the Master is considered long enough for the animal to collect its wits and make good an escape.

It would appear far more difficult to select a huntable hind than a warrantable stag. For according to Fred Goss, generally accepted in hunting lore as the most famous of all harbourers:

> "Hinds are usually found in herds, and the initial difficulty in hunting them is to separate one of them from the rest. As in hunting stags a start is made with tufters, but on account of the difficulty often encountered in getting a hind away from the herd, as many as six or eight couples of hounds are generally used for this purpose. Once a hind has been driven out of the wood it is necessary to keep her on the move or she will quickly rejoin the herd, and once she is mixed up with them the procedure has to begin all over again."

As a general rule hinds tend to give a faster run than stags as they appear to have more stamina. Though the drawback with hind hunting is that they are more reluctant to leave home ground, whereas a stag will often make a straight run, hinds are apt to take a more circular route, quite often ending back where they started. This is particularly so during the early part of the season when there is a calf afoot, during which time she will attempt to confuse the hounds by constantly mixing with other hinds, in the hope of losing them and returning to her calf.

Once the chase proper is underway what happens next varies greatly depending on the natural abilities of the deer, terrain over which the hunt is taking place, weather conditions, and luck. Some stags will run through a field of cattle, or a herd of hinds, in an attempt to confuse the hounds. Others will follow the course of a stream (beat the water) for many miles, thereby leaving no scent for the pack to follow. It has been known for some stags to "beat the water" upstream, leave the water, cross over to the next stream, then reverse direction back downstream.

Submerging in moorland pools with just the muzzle exposed, taking a "wallow" (mud bath) to mask the scent, or flattening himself against the ground, much as a hare will, hoping that the hounds will race past without noticing, are all ruses that have been witnessed and recorded over the years.

The actual length of the chase also varies enormously, with Kenneth Whitehead reporting runs during the 1959-60 season of twenty-two and thirty miles, while Alfred Vowles devotes four pages of his *Stag-hunting on Exmoor* to what is described as "THE GREATEST RUN OF THE WAR." For:

> "On the 22nd September, 1915, there occurred the greatest hunt of the twentieth century and one which proved a striking illustration of the uncertainty of stag-hunting and how sometimes after a morning's tedious and vexing tufting, a deer will suddenly crash from the thicket and bound away never to hesitate or falter until he has galloped before hounds for hours on end and led them for twenty or thirty miles far into the confines of another shire."

On "this great and memorable day...the stag was a light five-year old..." who would apparently run a considerable distance because from:

> "Hele Wood near by (where the stag was found) to Furzehill Farm (where he was killed at 5:30 p.m.) is exactly seventeen miles straight across country. Following the course he adopted and allowing for the preliminary skirmishing before the lay-on

and the zig-zags en route to the West Lyn, the distance covered must have been quite twenty-two miles, and perfectly open going, over the cream of the moors and at a cracking pace all the way. Sixty miles is the estimated distance covered by hounds-the tufters in fact-from kennel to kennel on this hot September day!"

An even longer jaunt was recorded during the mastership of the legendary Morland Greig (DSSH 1911-1914) during October 1913. When, after laying on the pack at 12.20 near Dulverton, they would eventually take the deer at Denes Court, between Bishops Lydeard and Taunton at 5.30 p.m. We are then told that "after welcome refreshments at Wats House, the home of Col. Boles MP, Major Greig, his daughter and the hunt staff did not arrive home until 11.15 p.m. after having ridden nearly seventy miles."

Even allowing for the undoubted exaggeration of some old time chroniclers regarding these long chase tales so beloved of hunting mythology, there are reports enough to verify that runs of two to three hours, over a distance of seven to ten miles, are common enough. Nostalgia for the "Golden Years" of the long hunt was all too evident in the 2005 book *Staghunter,* which devoted twenty-three pages of detailed reports, with maps, of some great runs of the 1920s and '30s. While the very last legal hunt of the DSSH, following the 2004 ban, was reported by their correspondent Pricket as "one of the great hunts of recent times, including a point of nine miles…".

Maybe that doyen of hunting literature, Henry Williamson, should be given the last word on the issue. In his *The Old Stag and Other Hunting Stories,* does not the hero, Stumberleap, run for some six and a half hours, over a distance of fifty miles to be last seen in the Severn Sea "swimming in the rolling waves…and after him, fifteen and a half couples of staghounds"? The hunting fraternity will no doubt say that Williamson wrote fiction. But they would say that, wouldn't they?

When the hunted animal has been run to exhaustion, or "elects to stand at bay" to use the hunting parlance, the kill is usually carried out using a humane killer or shotgun, although the knife is still used under exceptional circumstances. Prior to 1929, when the "hunt gun", a folding 12 bore with a special cartridge, was introduced, the standard method of killing was to slit the deer's throat, or stab it through the heart. Though according to H P Hewett, this gun "is no more instantaneous than the humane killer or the traditional knife in the heart, which arouses such horror among the ignorant, many of whom are not even aware that the deer must...be bled if the venison is to be fit for human consumption." Occasionally the deer will take the most extraordinary measures to escape from its pursuers, such as swimming out to sea, jumping into disused quarry workings or over cliffs, hiding in the flower-beds of a Quantock conference centre or running through the middle of large urban areas such as Barnstable, Tiverton or Bridgwater. The reason for such behaviour was obvious to Charles Polk Collyns who wrote:

> "It is more than probable that, at times when the deer have sprung from the cliffs, they have done so under the delusion as to the depth of the fall, caused by partial blindness, the effect of severe exertion. In most cases, however, the animal has, no doubt, taken the fatal leap while under the influence of uncontrollable fear."

One such incident, just before the outbreak of the First World War, also involved the "absolute fearless sportsman" who "always rode forward in every hunt" Morland Greig. Having taken "a stag to the steep cliffs at Hurlstone Point, above Porlock Bay and with the pack on the very edge of the precipice, urgent action was needed. Morland Greig was first up and sizing up the operation, could see if the stag was not quickly killed, it would fall over the edge to be dashed to death on rocks below with the bulk of the pack. By crawling down to the edge of the cliff he managed to kill the deer, whilst a coastguard was holding its legs, and hounds were put out of danger."

The opposite would happen on 5th October 1934, "when the Culbone Stag plunged a hundred feet over the cliffs and on to the beach at Glenthorne, followed by half the pack". Eight hounds would be killed outright, with many injured, of which two more would subsequently die. A few days later tragedy struck again for huntsman

Ernest Bawden "whose love for his hounds was a byword" when, following a meet from Larkbarrow, "the stag at bay fought heroically, killing two and wounding several more."

While Collyns will tell of

> "one occasion a stag met his end by leaping from a height on to the rocks, under circumstances which almost justify the belief that he deliberately committed suicide. A stag had been 'roused' in the open, and after a magnificent burst, ran towards the sea. Mr Frederick Knight, having viewed the deer at a great distance, standing on the summit of a rock overhanging the Channel, stopped the hounds, and the deer was observed, for some considerable time, walking restlessly to and fro on the cliff, as if seeking for a path by which he could reach the sea. Suddenly, however, he was missed, and as he did not reappear, some of the field went forward to the spot where he was last seen, and leaving their horses on the high ground, repaired to the beach by a rocky path at some little distance. On reaching the shore beneath the cliff, the stag was found a disfigured object, mashed to a jelly, the horns broken to flinders and scattered on the rocks. It would appear that the animal, though not driven or pursued at the moment, had deliberately leapt from the cliff almost perpendicular on to the rocks that lay some hundreds of feet beneath." ***Note 2***

The hunters will make every effort to try and avoid such incidents, as the result is invariably public outrage and condemnation. When a hunted stag managed to crawl under a furniture van in the Exmoor village of Timberscombe on 30th August 1962 there ensued a lengthy legal case brought by the League Against Cruel Sports, while photographs of a terrified stag on the roof of a Porlock cottage in 1987 were published across the front pages of most national newspapers, followed by angry editorials demanding "end this savagery".

The ideal "bay" from a hunt's point of view takes place in a secluded wooded area, far from the prying eyes of unsympathetic observers, where the animal can make a stand in a shallow river, with its back protected by a bank, while surrounded by the baying hounds. Of such scenes are the stirring legends of stag hunting made, so vividly described by Alfred Vowles:

> "The stag rudely pushed from the precincts of Porlock has made a last desperate bid and has succeeded in reaching his homeland, where he will use all his wits to put up fresh deer, hide away in some secluded and impenetrable thicket or otherwise cunningly defeat his pursuers. And should the worst come to the worst he will elect to die in the friendly and merciful waters of his beloved Horner.
>
> "Although by this time he must be a very tired and weary beast, he remains determined and clever, able to twist, double and mystify with amazing tactics, and unless his enemies keep him in close touch he will, despite his size and conspicuousness, live to be hunted another day.
>
> "But it is not long before many persistent 'View Holloas' are heard in the valley upstream, to be quickly followed by a vigorous doubling of the horn and sounds of baying hounds.
>
> "The stag is standing at bay in the river with his back to a large bush, and baying him are five couples of the foremost hounds. One hound, Darter, more eager than the rest, makes a vicious leap at the stag, but with amazing quickness the latter wields his formidable antlers and the savage brute is mercilessly swept aside.
>
> "A similar fate overtakes another of the best and pluckiest hounds, who goes crashing into the water. Without warning, he breaks bay and with a tremendous and over-whelming charge at the hounds, he bursts through the terrible cordon and with a mighty leap gains the bank and escapes up the valley.
>
> "But the deer is done! This last great spurt is his last and the

beginning of the end. He again plunges into the water, runs a little way and turns to face his enemies.

"With his back to the bank, he stands with his head held high, proud and glorious, defying all comers.

"One fearless hound – with more valour than discretion – leaps at the stag's throat, but the deer is master of the situation. It is a great scene and climax in the life of a deer.

"With antlers and feet he is able to keep off all comers and when set up for his final fight is formidable, resourceful and brave. Amidst the pandemonium of baying hounds and the general uproar of the occasion, the huntsman springs from his horse and administers the *coup de grace* by the approved and most humane method. Assistance in this adventure is given to the huntsman by local men who are always 'in at the kill' and today Fred Sedgbeer and 'Pudding' Floyd – two staggy stalwarts of Porlock – pluckily went in to help handle the fighting stag."

The remainder of the hunt is now purely academic, although strangely enough it is usually photographs of this aspect which, when published in the newspapers, tend to cause the greatest public outrage.

The carcass of the deer will now be bled and disembowelled, the former to make the venison palatable for human consumption, the latter as a reward for the hounds. The heart will be given to the owner of the land upon which the animal has been killed. The liver and kidneys to helpers who assisted the huntsman with the kill, priority is given to anyone who received a soaking while pulling the body from the river. The carcass will be distributed in the area where the deer was originally found, as a reward to the farmers who "fed" the animal and suffered crop damage as a result. It is also during this phase of a hunt that the "rite of passage" ceremony of "blooding" will take place. This is a tradition whereby children, or adults at their first kill, will have their faces smeared with warm blood from the freshly killed deer, or fox, hare and mink, as this ritual applies to all blood sports. The blood must not be washed off, but allowed to wear off naturally over the following weeks. While officially blooding is no longer condoned, it is still widely practised among the more fanatical elements of the hunting world, although these days it tends to be kept well away from public view.

The head (antlers) is always returned to the kennels and, if considered suitable, will be mounted on a wooden plaque with small inscription to present as gifts to favoured hunt supporters or valued locals. The heads of hinds killed are not considered of any importance and are disposed of alongside any other unwanted remains.

The slots (hooves) are given to keen hunt members, or honoured guests, who were in at the kill. The tusks (two canine teeth) are similarly awarded, many of which will later be made into scarf pins or cuff links. ***Note 3. See APPENDIX 1 (description of composition for average hunt).***

★

Such then is the history, heritage, tradition and practice of deer hunting. Admittedly, some of the more barbaric aspects are no longer undertaken, much less boasted of in public. Though it is probably true to say that this reticence is more to do with the changing public attitude towards their sport, than with any newfound enlightenment or heightened sense of morality.

In reality it is only since the late 1950s, with the ever-growing availability of private transport, that such places as Exmoor and the Quantocks have become readily accessible to the general public. Stag hunting to my parents' generation was a few column inches in the daily paper, but is now a common personal experience to my generation of mobile hunt saboteurs. What could be printed for local consumption in books and newspapers has now become the property of the general public within hours of its happening thanks to television. What was once a very private West Country affair is now a very public national property. While it is perfectly logical to accept that succeeding generations of Exmoor folk should wish to keep alive what are essentially eighteenth-century activities and traditions, it becomes illogical when they fail to notice that most of us find difficulty in assimilating the inherent brutalities of their sport with twenty-first-century society values.

Though to be fair, the British Field Sports Society did see the writing on the wall back in the late 1950s, when they employed the public relations firm Benson's (the same company which carried out PR work for the washing powder Omo) to act as their image-makers. The results bore fruit in 1961 with the publication of their pamphlet *You And The Press.* Pre-empting the concept of "political correctness" by some forty years they advised on a range of issues starting from the premise that: "There is always rich entertainment value in being able to present in an undignified light somebody who occupies a position of authority, and it is this, much more than the fate of the quarry, which makes hunting an attractive target for the newspapers." It suggested that editors might be prevailed upon to tone down coverage of anti-hunt activities with the aid of two tickets to the local hunt ball. Hunt officials were cautioned, when talking to the press, never to refer to the physical condition of the hunted animal at the end of a chase, or of hounds deserving a taste of blood. It concluded with the sound advice that an animal is never killed at the end of a hunt, but is always "accounted for". It was from this time on that the BFSS moved away from its image of an exclusive club to promote "field sports", slowly transforming itself into a pseudo conservation movement dedicated to protecting and preserving wild life through the promotion of blood sports.

In the late 1990s it would undergo yet another image makeover, this time into the Countryside Alliance – now allegedly taking on board a range of rural issues, but its main priority remaining the promotion of hunting. Even this agenda would be heavily weighed towards a defence of fox hunting, with little attention given to stag hunting or hare coursing, no doubt on the simple expedient that both were hard to justify. Whereas it was relatively easy to remove any concept of "cruelty" from the fox-hunting debate, turning it instead into an academic argument about "minority rights", "freedom of the individual", or class warfare. Rather than any collective effort by the Alliance to defend stag hunting, the issue would be left to fanatical devotees such as Baroness Anne Mallalieu and Lord Mancroft.

The issue of what would become of the West Country deer following the 2004 hunting ban has remained somewhat contentious. It would appear naïve to trust their well-being to interests solely concerned with the accommodation of hunting – especially when it is these very people who have systematically opposed every attempt to promote the interests of deer through legislation, or implement serious management structures that do not revolve around hunting. It may well be true that in the past the cessation of hunting was directly related to the demise, or elimination of the deer, but to quote situations dating back to the 1600s (Cromwell's Commonwealth period when hunting was banned) or the eighteenth and nineteenth centuries to prove your point is rather disingenuous. The world was a very different place back then when people were forced to kill for food, when society was brutal, with little respect for human rights leave alone "animal rights". We are now in the first decade of the twenty-first century when most reasonable people are willing to accept that wild animals have a right to exist in our countryside other than as mere objects to be harried and killed for sport. The argument that "if we can't hunt the deer then we will wipe them out" is the rationale of the bully-boy and the thug, not an argument for the continuation of stag hunting, but rather a condemnation of the hunters themselves.

There is now such an overwhelming abundance of evidence to prove not only that deer hunting is not the only form of effective control, but that in fact it is not much of a method at all. The argument that shooting cannot be used because of the danger to the local community from stray bullets is a nonsense when you consider that the National Trust, Forestry Commission, and League Against Cruel Sports have all used this method at various times, not to mention that organised deer stalking has been in operation around the Dulverton area for some years past. Also the oft repeated myth that without deer hunting the economy of the Exmoor area would collapse has long since been laid to rest by all but the most blinkered hunt supporter. The truth of which depends on whether you believe the various independent surveys which say that the loss of revenue would be negligible, or hunt sponsored reports that put possible revenue loss in excess of nine million pounds. Maybe if the self-styled "protectors" of the deer were to put more effort into encouraging visitors to the moors to watch and photograph the animals, as already undertaken by two small Exmoor safaris which operate at present, instead of the steady flow of "sportsmen" who come to kill, the financial outlook might not appear so bleak.

So mired has the issue of deer control become in the West Country, mainly because every time evidence is presented to prove a certain point, the stag hunters merely move the goal posts. Until such time as the interference from this small group of self motivated individuals is removed from the equation, allowing a clean slate for such bodies as the National Trust, Exmoor National Park, or better still a government-regulated body to oversee the management and conservation of the deer, the issue will remain unresolved.

Note 1. For instance the composition of the Quantock Deer Management and Conservation Group (QDM&CG) for 2006 was made up of individual Quantock landholders, as well as representatives of organisations including English Nature, Friends of Quantocks, Forestry Commission, National Trust, DEFRA, British Deer Society, The Quantock Staghounds, The Deer Initiative, The British Association for Shooting & Conservation (BASC), and the Quantock AONB Service.

Note 2. Polk Collyns follows this story with another curious incident. "The day upon which this event occurred, in many other respects, was a most disastrous one. The first intelligence at the meet was that one of the best hounds in the pack had been killed and *eaten* in the kennel, nothing having been left of poor 'Gambler' save his head."

Note 3. As already stated this part of the hunt is academic as the deer is already dead, though as a ritualistic spectacle, with hearts, livers and heaps of intestines all over the place, it can appear somewhat nauseating to the uninitiated. Some idea of what it looks like can be see in footage included in the classic documentary *The Animals Film.*

Chapter Two

"...the Queen has been strongly opposed to stag hunting for many years past"

1901 APPEARED TO BE a good year for the opponents of deer hunting. For after years of agitation and criticism it looked as if public pressure had finally forced the Royal Buckhounds, which had been in existence in one form or another since 1362, to disband. ***Note 1***

The campaign had its roots back in 1891, when the Fabian socialist Henry Salt, in company with publisher Ernest Bell, founded the Humanitarian League. While undoubtedly concerned with such issues as prison reform, the abolition of capital punishment and sweatshop labour, it soon became apparent that the league's major preoccupation was "humanity to animals".

Within months of its formation Henry Salt had decided that the focus of attention would be the twenty-odd carted deer hunts that existed at that time. In order not to spread too thinly the League's resources Salt further decided that to represent the deer hunts generally they would attack one specifically. The Royal Buckhounds were chosen, the rationale being, that if this pack could be closed down, regardless of its royal patronage, the rest were sure to follow.

To front the campaign to discredit the hunt Henry Salt enlisted the aid of the Rev J Stratton, Chaplain of Lucas' Hospital, Wokingham, Surrey, who was a reformed foxhunter. His job was made easier by the fact that the buckhounds already attracted a considerable amount of public derision, not only because they chased tame deer in and out of barns and railway waiting rooms, but also because comments by Lord Randolph Churchill that its ranks consisted of "the counter-jumpers of London" – that class of person who were dominated by the generic term "'Arry", had earned them the East End name of 'Arry's 'Ounds.

The Reverend began his campaign in the best reformist tradition, with a letter-writing campaign to the newspapers, followed by the pamphlet *Cruel Sport – Some Facts Concerning the Queen's Buck Hounds.* Writing of the campaign later Henry Salt would say

> "every possible difficulty was put in our way by officials, whether of the Court, the Government, or the Hunt, who in this case, as in all, desired nothing more than to save themselves trouble by letting things go on as before. Red tape cared little whether carted stags continued to be disembowelled on iron palings and worried by hounds. For example, when, in 1898, we wished to lay before Queen Victoria the case *against* the Royal Hunt, in answer to Lord Ribbledale's book, *The Queen's Hounds,* her private secretary, Sir A Bigge, refused to bring the League's publication to her notice; the Home Secretary also declined to do so, as did the Prime Minister, each and all cordially advising us to apply elsewhere."

Blocked at every turn Henry Salt then hit upon the expedient of "petitioning" the Queen to allow the counter-case to be sent to her, and in this way the Home Office was finally forced to do what it had declared to be "contrary to practice". This petition solicited a reply from Sir H F Ponsonby stating that: "I do not wish to enter into a discussion upon a subject with which I have nothing to do. But I may observe, though probably you are already aware of the fact, that the Queen has been strongly opposed to stag-hunting for many years past."

During the course of his investigations Stratton would walk over twenty miles a day following the hounds, in the hope of uncovering atrocities, mostly he found that on being released from the carts a deer would flee in panic, taking refuge in the first shed or barn that came to hand. What he did find was a wall of silence from frightened locals, mounting aggression from hunt supporters, a good many abusive letters, followed by shots fired into his home. After this the Rev Stratton bought a revolver. A rowdy public meeting was organised in Wokingham, which had once been a favourite venue for bull baiting, by the hunts supporters and in 1894 the first organisation to defend blood sports was formed. The Sporting League championed "the protection, support and improvement of all legitimate sports, pastimes and recreation".

The mounting publicity generated by this campaign did keep the subject of carted deer hunting firmly in the public eye, while accelerating the disgust felt in some quarters over such incidents as when an often hunted stag named Guy Fawkes, hard-pressed by the buckhounds, disembowelled itself on a fence it had not the strength to clear, and was finished off by one of the huntsmen.

Undeterred by the threats and intimidation, Stratton continued to organise petitions, memorials, resolutions and deputations, all of which were aimed at forcing Parliament into taking action on the issue. Throughout these activities he made constant use of quotations that he had found in an article appearing in the 3rd September 1892 issue of the hunting magazine *Field.* The writer had equated the hunting of carted deer with the horrors of bull baiting, saying that "nothing but the prescription and aegis of royal patronage have saved it from being consigned to limbo". The author went on to argue

> "that if anyone were to capture badgers, aniseed them, and turn them out in the open with five minutes start of a scratch pack of terriers there would be an outcry; and yet the badger was better able to defend itself than the dishorned buck of modern stag hunting that 'soils' in a river or shelters in a cowshed..."

In 1896 when John Colam, secretary of the RSPCA, quoted this passage in a letter to Lord Salisbury the *Field* decided it was time to distance itself from any perceived support for the abolition of carted deer hunting. In the 28th November issue it announced:

> "Perhaps the time has arrived when we ought no longer to refrain from explaining that the article in question...does not represent

> the views of this paper. The article should have been declined and returned to the writer, the sentiments being quite opposed to the line the *Field* has always taken, but by an oversight the article was inserted during the absence of the departmental editor."

This statement obviously came as no surprise to the Rev Stratton, who had been under attack from the *Field* for some time over his campaign against blood sports, but the accompanying admission must have made him smile. In the same edition he read: "We repeat that we do not seek and never have sought to exalt the hunting of the carted deer to the position of the highest form of sport, but because it falls short of the ideal it does not follow that it is attended with all the barbarities alleged against it by Mr Stratton."

In tandem with the campaign against the Royal Buckhounds was a move within Parliament to ban not only carted deer hunting, but also the coursing of bagged rabbits, and the shooting of birds released from traps. The "Spurious Sports Bill", drafted by the Humanitarian League, was introduced at various times into the House of Commons by Mr A C Morton, Mr H F Lettrell, Sir William Byles, Sir George Greenwood, and in the House of Lords by the Bishop of Hereford (Lord Percival). The Bill made little headway due to vigorous opposition, including one occasion (1893) when it was "talked out" by Sir Frederick Banbury, who was renowned in the Commons as a vigorous anti-vivisectionist and friend of animals!

The House of Lords confronted the issue in 1898, when a Bill presented by Lord Herschell, following a recent decision in the courts had emphasised that cruelty to animals could be punished only if the animals were domesticated, attempted to expand the definition to include wild animals in captivity. While Herschell was thinking of such animals as performing bears, lions in cages and other circus animals the Prime Minister, the Marquis of Salisbury, warned that as it stood the Bill would protect "deer-buck kept for the sport of the buckhounds...". In the event, the Bill was read a first time, then forgotten. Two years later a similar measure, the *Wild Animals in Captivity Protection Act 1900,* was passed into law, but only after strong pressure from deer-hunting supporters ensured that amendments were agreed at Committee Stage which were designed to remove any doubts that the Bill would inadvertently affect legitimate sports such as hunting and coursing.

The death of Queen Victoria would now accomplish what the Humanitarian League had worked so hard to achieve. For following the accession of Edward VII a Parliamentary Select Committee was appointed to recommend economies in the Royal budget. One of their suggestions was the saving of £6,000 a year by disbanding the buckhounds, to which, as Edward had no interest in them, he agreed. So, not on any moral or humanitarian grounds, but simply as an act of economy, an institution which had survived from Plantagenet times was brought to an end. Though it proved something of a Pyrrhic victory, for within months the Berkshire and Buckinghamshire Farmers' Harriers converted to staghounds, inheriting most of the country formally hunted by the Royal Buckhounds.

Henry Salt and the Rev Stratton may well have considered it a victory, but in reality little had changed. They were soon disillusioned to find that the disbandment of the Royal Buckhounds had made no impression on carted deer hunting generally. The next controversy concerning this "sport" occurred in 1910, when the RSPCA instigated a court case against the Master of the Cambridge University's so-called drag hunt. The incident occurred during the chase when a carted hind was first impaled on barbed wire, then took refuge in the yard of a railway gate keeper, where it was beaten and mishandled in an attempt to make it run further, causing it to die of shock. Later in court the magistrates "decided that as the chase was in progress at the time the prosecution must fail". Presumably if the animal had been abused before or after the chase they would have considered a conviction for cruelty.

The Humanitarian League had by now given up on carted deer hunting, but continued to campaign against other blood sports without success. Its most notable contribution to the subject was a volume of essays published in 1914 under the title *Killing For Sport,* with an introduction by George Bernard Shaw. Their militant pacifism during the First World War turned many of their most ardent supporters against them, while their adherence to vegetarianism branded them as cranks, with the consequence that in 1919 the Humanitarian League folded.

The only organisation now fighting for the welfare of animals was the RSPCA, though its primary concern was for domestic animals. The reason for this was quite simple; ever since its formation in 1824 the control of the RSPCA had been firmly under the control of hunting practitioners. The founder of the society, Richard Martin, hunted on his Irish estate, while the Royal patronage had not exactly been conducive for pressuring Parliament to legislate in favour of wild animals. While the RSPCA pressed ahead with legislation, the judiciary was happy to prosecute so long as the law didn't consider acts of cruelty on the hunting field illegal. To this day many magistrates are hunters who routinely convict for cruelty against animals. Nothing epitomised the ambiguity of the law more clearly than this author's "old friend" Bob Nancekivell, Master of the DSSH during the 1960s and early '70s, who on a Monday, Wednesday and Friday could, in his role of JP, convict for cruelty against any domestic animal, while, on Tuesday, Thursday and Saturday, quite legally chase red deer across Exmoor.

It is interesting to note that the first attempt in Parliament to introduce legislation on behalf of animals was Sir William Pulteney's Bill to abolish bull-baiting in 1800, which failed on its Third Reading by forty-three votes to forty-one. The next animal-related Bill in 1809, which aimed to protect farm animals, also failed. In 1821 Richard Martin tried to pass a similar measure, but failed on the First Reading. It did become law the following year, being the first Act of Parliament to offer any kind of legal protection to any animal anywhere. The main beneficiaries were the larger farm animals: horses, cattle and sheep.

In 1835 Joseph Pease's *Protection of Animals Act* was passed, which widened the scope of Martin's 1822 Act to include all farm and domestic animals. This Act also prohibited anyone from "keeping or using any house, room, pit, ground or other place for running, baiting or fighting any bull, bear, badger, dog or other animal (whether domestic or wild) or for the keeping of pits for the purpose of cock fighting".

The *Prevention of Cruelty to Animals Act* passed in 1849 was merely an extension of the 1835 Act in that it tightened still further the baiting of all animals: domestic and wild, along with the complete abolition of cock fighting, rather than just the pits. The next animal-related legislation was 1854, which banned the use of dog-carts, followed in 1869 with the first Act giving protection to some sea birds. Then the 1876 *Cruelty to Animals Act* came into force which made it compulsory to give anaesthetics to animals prior to vivisection experiments.

The first move to attack deer hunting, although inadvertently, came in 1883 with G Anderson's *Cruelty to Animals Acts Amendment Bill* which was meant to extend protection to wild animals in confinement, as well as pigeons kept for shooting. The second clause was designed to protect animals in menageries such as dancing bears, but soon came under attack because pro-hunters felt that the ambiguous wording of the clause "would stop stag hunting and the hunting of bagged foxes and of trapped hares and rabbits".

The main opponent of this Bill was Sir Herbert Maxwell who felt that "if they consented to any Bill that abolished the chase of such animals, the day was not far distant when all field sports would be put to an end, in obedience to the intolerant spirit to which they were unhappily becoming accustomed." Whereas Lord Randolph Churchill supported the measure on the grounds that it would prohibit stag hunting which he opposed and leave fox hunting which he supported.

Colonel Kingscote claimed that hunting wild deer was far more cruel than hunting tame stags which "were trained and kept in perfect condition". In the event, the Bill failed to make headway that year. The following year, having been re-drafted to exclude any possible indirect reference to carted deer hunting, the Bill failed to reach a Second Reading.

In 1898 Lord Herschell presented a Bill in the House of Lords to make provisions similar to Anderson's Bill that wild animals in captivity should be afforded legal protection. In opposition the Prime Minister (the Marquis of Salisbury) pointed out that the proposer of the Bill was on dangerous ground, for as it stood the Bill would protect "bagged foxes and deer-buck kept for the sports of the buck-hounds...".

July 1900 saw the Second Reading in the House of Lords of the *Cruelty to Wild Animals in Captivity Bill* which had passed unopposed through the Commons. Lord James of Hereford assured the House that this Bill was "not intended to deal with the cruelty alleged to arise in sport, such as stag hunting...". At the Committee Stage (12th July) and Third Reading (26th July) amendments were agreed which were designed to remove any doubts that the Bill would – though not intended to do so – affect legitimate sport such as carted deer hunting and coursing. The Bill finally passed into law as the *Wild Animals in Captivity Protection Act 1906.*

On 6th May 1909 the Bishop of Hereford attempted to introduce in the Lords a Bill to "prohibit three highly objectionable forms of sport: the hunting, coursing and shooting of animals which have been kept in confinement". In opposition Lord Newton defended the hunting of carted deer as "a meritorious and laudable amusement...". Lord Ribblesdale and Lord Willoughby de Broke also attacked the Bill claiming that deer hunting was no more cruel than any other type of field sport, adding that "all relations of man to animal when he is pursuing it, must necessarily partake of the nature of cruelty". This Bill also failed to get beyond the Second Reading.

Though it was impossible to make any headway regarding the hunting of carted deer, thanks to the tireless pressure of the RSPCA and Humanitarian League, a legal milestone was reached in 1911. After months of debate Sir George Greenwood was able to successfully pilot through Parliament the *Protection of Animals Act* that would consolidate under this one Act all other existing animal welfare legislation. Though it tightened various ambiguities inherent within previous Acts intense pressure from the blood sport lobby made certain that this legislation was restricted to "captive and domestic animals". To make doubly certain that there was no future misunderstanding a clause was added which specifically excluded the "coursing or hunting of any captive animal unless such animal is liberated in an injured, mutilated or exhausted condition". Therefore wild animals kept in confinement for sport, once released, would immediately revert back to wild animals again, removing from huntsmen any form of legal restriction regarding their treatment. Ten years later, in 1921, following much adverse criticism towards some of the more objectionable practices of the carted deer and bagged fox hunters, a clause was added to the 1911 Act which demanded that once released the animal should be given a "reasonable chance of escape...".

The Royal Assent to the *Protection of Animals Act 1911* brought to an end all further need for additional parliamentary action concerning the well being of domestic and agricultural animals, laying as it did the foundation for what remains to this day the major piece of legislation governing animal welfare. It also succeeded in cementing the ideological differences of two diametrically opposed groups: one who believed it was illogical to protect domestic animals while allowing the ill treatment of wild animals, with the other demanding the legal immunity to perpetrate any cruelty against wild animals so long as it was conducted in the name of "sport". The lines were now drawn for a moral and ethical battle that would rage unabated into the present day.

The issue that brought stag hunting, along with all other forms of wild animal abuse, into sharp public focus had its roots in the attitude of the RSPCA towards hunting. From its very beginning the RSPCA was dominated by an affluent pro-hunt leadership who, while offering the social and financial support necessary to allow for parliamentary progress on behalf of domestic animals, worked equally tirelessly to make sure that hunting remained untouched. The situation was best summed up in 1891 when the Rev J Stratton, about to embark on the campaign against the Royal Buckhounds, wrote: "What has become of the Society for the Prevention of Cruelty to Animals that it seems never to have made a persistent stand against barbarity in high places?" This frustration was highlighted by an incident concerning the Mid Kent Staghounds, which the RSPCA declined to become involved with.

On 17th February 1924 this hunt chased a carted hind from the meet at Tenterden (Kent) to the coast at Rye in Sussex. Hard pressed by the hounds "she plunged into the sea and started to swim away from the shore". Unable to secure a boat to pursue the deer, members of the hunt signalled to a passing fishing boat in the hope the crew would turn the deer back, "but to everyone's surprise the crew pulled the hind on board and made off up the Channel", landing the animal at Etaples, France. Later the hunt master, Brigadier-General T S M

Pitt, would travel to France, intending to return the animal to England where it would be provided with a collar inscribed "Started in Kent ended in France". In the event the authorities would not release it and the deer remained in France until her death in September 1927. Angered by the lack of action against incidents such as this in which they could see neither the sport nor the fun, and realising that so long as the RSPCA remained the sole campaigning body nothing practical would be undertaken on behalf of animals involved in blood sports, a number of its members broke away to form their own organisation.

Later that same year, 1924, Henry Amos, and former Humanitarian League founding member Ernest Bell, launched the League for the Prohibition of Cruel Sports. Within weeks of its formation the League (which would later become the League Against Cruel Sports) had taken offices in Victoria Street, Westminster, and begun publication of the monthly journal *Cruel Sports. (Note 2)* The initial response to this first movement specifically to protect wild animals was encouraging, with such notaries as Edward Carpenter, Henry Salt and George Bernard Shaw rallying to the flag. The following year saw the League's inaugural meeting held at Church House, Westminster, which was immediately invaded by hunt supporters and, according to the *Daily Sketch* of 25th November 1925, the "speakers were noisily interrupted throughout the meeting" by "elegant hunting rowdies".

Within months of its foundation the League's priority target became stag hunting, with campaigning directed towards parliamentary abolition. Between 1924-1931 there would be attempts to outlaw carted deer hunting with the annual introduction of the *Protection of Animals Bill,* which was an attempt to repeal the 1921 clause to the *Protection of Animals Act 1911* which allowed for confined animals to be given a "reasonable chance of escape" prior to being hunted, with another clause which banned altogether the hunting of any animal previously kept in captivity.

This Bill was invariably introduced into the Commons by Isaac Foot, who stated "the object of the Bill was to repeal the Act of 1921 and substitute for it a simple straight-forward measure which would present no difficulties in the Courts. Under the Bill the penalty for the hunting or coursing of any animal which had been kept in captivity or confinement was a fine not exceeding £25, or alternatively, or in addition, a short term of imprisonment with or without hard labour." All these attempts were advanced as Private Members Bills, which ensured they would remain stillborn, for considering the entrenched opposition most were lucky to survive a First Reading. The 1925 attempt (introduced by Mr H Williams in the absence of Isaac Foot who was temporarily out of Parliament) did manage a short debate, while the 1930 Bill (again introduced by Isaac Foot) reached a Second Reading and was then referred to a Standing Committee.

March 1930 saw a new innovation in the debate with the introduction, under the Ten Minute Rule, of Lovat Fraser's *Protection of Animals (No.2) Bill* which, for the first time, attempted to legislate against wild deer hunting. What began as an internal poll of RSPCA members to determine their views on stag hunting led to a ballot showing that 3,125 favoured a ban, with 1,142 against, which in turn was directly responsible for the introduction of this Bill. The LACS (who were responsible for publishing this Bill) followed with a publicity campaign against the West Country deer hunts, which quickly escalated into an 85,000 signature petition in support of the Fraser Bill. The *Daily Herald, Daily Chronicle, Star,* and *Manchester Guardian* supported the Bill, while intellectuals such as Bertrand Russell, Robert Blatchford, C P Scott and the Chief Rabbi of the United Kingdom contributed to the National Appeal Against Staghunting. Regardless of the massive public support for a ban the Lovat Fraser Bill, after passing its First Reading, failed to make any further headway against the pro-hunt bloc in Parliament.

By now the alarm bells were ringing throughout the shires. On 22nd March 1930 the *West Somerset Free Press* reported: "Never before has a meeting of the Minehead branch of the Farmers' Union aroused such interest or attracted such an attendance as that held on Monday at the Plume of Feathers Hotel, when the subject of the campaign against stag hunting appeared on the agenda." On 29th March 1930 the same paper wrote: "The importance of the subject to be discussed – the proposed Bill to abolish stag hunting – brought together almost a record attendance of members at a special meeting of the Dulverton branch of the NFU...". The first speaker Philip Everard warmed up the audience by saying that the stag hunters had been silent in their own defence for far too long and that now was the time to impress the rest of England with public opinion. "We all know that," he continued, " it is carried on by public opinion, that if public opinion here in the West Country was against it, it would have been dropped long ago. We know that 99 out of every 100 here approve of it." He concluded his speech with the dire warning that the recent Bills to abolish carted deer hunting and rabbit coursing had both passed second readings, and that once a Bill got this far "it was as good as law". So if the Lovat Fraser Bill was to clear a Second Reading, "maybe not during this sitting of Parliament...but if this Government stays in it will quite possibly happen in the course of the next 18 months. That means that next season's stag hunting will be our last."

With attempts to stop carted deer hunting an annual event and now direct attacks against wild deer hunting in Parliament, members of the DSSH had started to panic. This soon gave way to a determination that the best form of defence was to attack the enemy with the "truth" about stag hunting. Such a move had become an obsession with Fred Beadle, a retired businessman from Kent in his early fifties who had moved to Exmoor to breed pedigree cattle and sheep. A fanatical follower of the stag hunt, who was related to the late Morland Greig (having been killed at Gallipoli in 1915), Beadle was convinced that the only salvation was to form a society composed of representatives from every branch of hunting that would become strong enough to protect blood sports as a whole.

The matter came to a head at the DSSH AGM at the Castle Hotel, Taunton, on 24th May 1930. In a meeting that was dominated by the perceived threat from Lovat Fraser's Bill, and which would prove to be the pivotal moment for the future protection of blood sports, Fred Beadle outlined the background to their present situation. In a long speech, which was reported in great detail by the *West Somerset Free Press* on 31st May, he explained how the current agitation had been "the work of a few frenzied fanatics, wrought up to their present pitch of indignation by inaccurate and misleading accounts circulated about stag hunting."

The RSPCA, he continued, which had been taken over by these "anti-sport fanatics", and was the main instigator of the Fraser Bill, was now hiding behind the Society for the Prohibition of Cruel Sports, which in turn had been created by "some of the more rabid of the anti-sport people" from that very organisation. There appeared not the slightest touch of irony when Beadle went on to explain:

> "Although it might be difficult to officially connect these two societies, there was ample proof that they were in close touch with one another and working together. It was hardly to be expected that the RSPCA, whose income was largely derived from sportsmen who subscribed the money for the prevention of wilful and deliberate cruelty, would admit that they used those funds for the suppression of the sport of the very people who found the money, and it was not until they came out into the open by promoting Bills for the suppression of stag hunting that it could be proved what was the policy of the RSPCA."

Now in his stride Fred Beadle thundered that these antis

> "had hesitated at nothing in charging sportsmen with every form of brutality and abominable conduct, and had created such an atmosphere among decent people not conversant with sport, that they really believed that any person who hunted a wild animal ranked with one who committed brutal and wanton cruelty, or with a native of some country where brutality to animals was proverbial."

"It could not be too widely realised," he concluded,

> "that the sole object of these societies was the suppression of all, as they termed them, 'Blood sports', and that if they were successful in suppressing one form of sport it could only be a question of a little time before they were all made illegal. It therefore behoved all interested in every form of sport to close

their ranks and to offer a united opposition to the insidious and lying propaganda with which the country was being flooded.

"To achieve this end the formation of a powerful and influential society was essential, because it had been practically impossible to get any reply refuting these charges published in the newspapers which made them, and even if published, a letter over the signature of an individual did not carry anything like the weight that a statement backed by the name of the RSPCA. If the suggested society becomes of sufficient importance, the Press and the public could not ignore its existence..."

At first he met with little enthusiasm beyond the confines of the DSSH, with newspapers such as the *Daily Mirror* reporting on 23rd September 1930 that little support had been gained amongst the hunting fellowship for a pro-stag hunting committee and that, in an informal vote that was taken at a private meeting of subscribers to a famous Leicestershire fox hunt, three-quarters of those present supported the resolution that "hunting a stag is not sport".

Though Beadle persisted, enlisting the aid of his younger brother John C, another fanatical deer hunter who was Chairman of the Mid-Kent Staghounds Committee, who harboured his own hatred of anti-hunt activists following personal clashes at his hunt. Together they continued pressing their cause, with the breakthrough coming when Froude Hancock, influential West Country brewer and acknowledged authority on deer hunting, threw his support behind the idea, enlisting the aid of J D Tapp, Harry Rawle and Tom Burnell, all serving committee members of the DSSH.

Sir Robert Sanders, later Lord Bayford, one time Master of the DSSH (1895-1907) and now an MP, was enlisted to keep tabs on any future anti-hunting bills. Then the 4th Earl Fortescue was approached, for as Lord Lieutenant of Devon and well known follower of hounds, his signature would add prestige to any future correspondence in the letters columns of the national press, from where most of Beadle's opening shots had been fired. The desired affect was achieved once Fortescue signed a letter to *The Times* promoting the concept that:

> "In view of the organised attempt which is being made to render illegal all forms of Field Sport, it was decided at the Annual Meeting of the Devon and Somerset Staghounds, held at Taunton, on Saturday May 24th, 1930, to support the suggested formation of a Society for the furtherance of all Field Sports."

On 4th December 1930, the first meeting of the British Field Sports Society was held at Caxton Hall, Westminster, bringing to fruition the dream of Fred Beadle. Within weeks London offices had been secured, key positions within the fledgling BFSS filled with some of the most prominent and influential hunting names in the country. Toby Fitzwilliam, whose qualifications included coming "from a well known sporting family...and could expect a welcome from most of the great houses in England", became the first full-time Secretary, with Kenneth Diplock (later to become Lord Diplock) acting as his assistant. The Duke of Beaufort agreed to become the Society's first President, thus assuring the complete affiliation of the entire fox hunting establishment.

Thus was born, from the ranks of the DSSH, the organisation which would defend blood sports with fanatical determination for nearly seventy years, ensuring that not one single piece of parliamentary legislation would ever reach the Statute Book. Only during the 1990s, following increasing public cynicism with regard to its blatant manipulation of the political system, and appearance of one-issue exclusivity, would the BFSS be forced to re-evaluate its public image. The answer was to extend the Society's range of concerns to include, not only the protection of blood sports, but wider rural issues such as local transport, post office closure and general farming issues. In that way did the BFSS complete the metamorphosis into what we know today as the Countryside Alliance.

In the year that the BFSS began to consolidate its position within Parliament, the LACS, frustrated by the lack of political success, decided to take the fight to the hunting field. In August 1931 the League would organise the first ever official picket against a stag hunt. The local press reported:

> "The possibility of a demonstration by supporters of the anti-hunting movement at the opening meet of the Devon and Somerset Staghounds at Cloutsham has arisen. There were rumours of such a demonstration prior to last year's meet, but it did not materialise. Recently, however, a circular, under the heading of the League for the Prohibition of Cruel Sports, has been issued which invites the co-operation of all members and friends in a League demonstration... . The circular states that 'return railway tickets available for five days will be issued free of charge on application to the secretary and that special motor-coaches will take members to the meet' from Minehead."

In the event, on 5th August 1931, the rumoured onslaught from hundreds of protestors failed to materialise, instead "at about half-past ten the arrival of a party of representatives of the League...was noticed" which consisted of "about thirty...of whom the majority were ladies". Of these about thirteen were from London including "Mrs. Walker King, who appeared to be in charge of the party", while other members "were Mrs. Leggatt, of Exeter, who it was stated formerly hunted; the Rev. Dr. Beadley, from Swindon, and Mr J. C. Sharpe, secretary of the League".

This lack of protagonists did not stop the *West Somerset Free Press* reporter from turning in a detailed and highly colourful account of the confrontation under the headline "ANTI-STAGHUNTERS ASSAIL CLOUTSHAM". In a taste of things to come, he described "on arriving at the spot where the crowd was thickest the League members unrolled banners to which the crowd was invited to pay attention". These banners bore such inscriptions as "Staghunting is not cricket", "Play the game", "See that your MP supports the anti-staghunting bill", and "Civilisation demands justice for animals", which soon led to the demonstrators becoming "subject to sarcastic and unsympathetic remarks, which were mingled with hunting cries, from the cosmopolitan assembly" at the meet.

The verbal abuse soon gave way to physical threats as the hunt supporters attempted to destroy the banners.

"A woman it was – an Exmoor farmer's wife – who captured the first banner. Grabbing it from one of the ladies of the party – there was a bit of a tussle for possession-she tore it fiercely to tatters and, amid the cheers of the crowd, trod the fragments in the road. Others strove to gain possession of banners, and in the midst of an excited mass the demonstrators struggled helplessly. Their banners were all destroyed, the women's umbrellas wrecked, the League literature ripped to fragments."

Otherwise, apart from local Dick Foster attempting to defend his garden fence, "nobody seemed to have been injured in the melee...though worse might have happened had not the police, who were reinforced for the occasion, taken steps to prevent any further disturbance". The police it seemed "handled the situation very tactfully...so much so, that when the demonstrators, who at last got clear of the crowd, were shepherded by constables down the slope from Cloutsham, cheers were raised for the police" by the hunters.

A certain Mr E A Hemingway

"now became the subject of attention...on the part of many of the crowd, and he, too, went down the steep with a posse of police about him. There were many in the crowd desirous, it seemed, of seeing him get an involuntary immersion in the stream below, but the presence of the police enabled him to escape a ducking. His camera, however, was thrown in the water and trodden on."

The Leaguers "on their way from Cloutsham to Webber's Post, where their motor-coach was parked, were subjected to a hostile reception... of cat-calls, jeers, and hunting cries from mounted and foot supporters" alike. Once aboard, mud was thrown at the coach, while riders continued to attempt intimidation of the protestors, finally when the coach moved off "escorting it for a considerable distance." The *Free Press* journalist concluded his report with praise for the League members, which would remain true for the long years of campaigning ahead, when he commented, "And it must be said that they did not flinch in the face of the demeanour of the crowd to the last..."

While this may have been the first confrontation at a stag hunt meet, it was by no means the first time the two sides had clashed. Previous confrontations between League members and stag hunt supporters, at public meetings usually held in response to especially notorious incidents such as when the DSSH sent a stag crashing to its death on the rocks 200ft below Countisbury Hill, near Lynton, had ended in uproar. When the League organised a public meeting following this incident, held in Lynton Town Hall on 27th August 1926, an account of which holds centre stage in Henry Williamson's book *The Wild Red Deer of Exmoor,* nearly five hundred stag hunters invaded the hall, spending over three hours shouting abuse, blowing their hunting horns and singing "John Peel". ***Note 3***

Violence was also becoming a regular feature of the anti-hunting scene. One man who knew all about this was the young Minehead freelance journalist Edward Hemingway. Following the publication of a number of his articles on stag hunting in the national press during 1927, he was assaulted by DSSH hunter Ernest Rawle. When the case went to court Dunster magistrates fined Rawle £5 and bound him over for six months. Worse was to come the next year when Hemingway was again attacked while attending a polo ball at the Metropole Hotel, Minehead. The *Daily Express* of 7th September 1928 would tell the full story:

> "The man was standing in a private part of the hotel when, without warning, a number of men, said to be prominent stag hunters, burst in, seized him, and, shouting at the tops of their voices and blowing hunting horns, dragged him by his arms and legs to the vestibule. They were joined by a crowd of shouting dancers, who followed the procession through the hotel grounds and across the road to the sea wall. The critic was then thrown five feet into deep water. He climbed to the breakwater when, it is alleged, one of the party shouted, 'Let's drown him again.' He threw the man into the water and tried to hold him under. Police are making enquiries."

Far from deterring Edward Hemingway, these attacks would force him into redoubling his opposition to stag hunting, a "pastime he viewed with utter disgust", finally leading to his becoming Chairman of the LACS.

Another knock-on effect of this violence was to create increasing media interest in the activities of the hunts, which in turn generated greater concerns as to the cruelty involved, causing public outrage on numerous occasions. The *Manchester Guardian* reported on 13th August 1932 how a few days previously a stag hunted by the DSSH from Hawkcombe Head

> "got away from the hounds at Watersmeet after being hunted about fourteen miles and went down Lyn Valley to Lynmouth where its flight was checked by a wall. In desperation, however, the stag leaped over the wall and fell down onto the rocks in the River Lyn several feet below. It broke its legs in falling and lay, quivering and helpless, tormented by the hounds for ten minutes until the hunters arrived to kill it. Meanwhile great anger was expressed by a large group of holiday makers who had gathered at the spot, and their feelings towards the stag hunters were so vigorously expressed that the latter deemed it prudent to withdraw from the scene as soon as they had secured the deer. Ever since this affair happened visitors have been protesting angrily about such things being allowed to continue."

The same paper reported an incident that occurred at Minehead on Wednesday, 26th October 1932, involving the QSH when

> "the stag suddenly jumped into the clay pits at the brick-fields and then ran down between the engine house and a mortar mill. It then jumped down into a pit, and was unable to get out again. Some men who were near held the exhausted animal, where it was imprisoned for about fifteen minutes until the hunters arrived to kill it. Sections of a crowd who watched raised angry shouts of protest."

Another piece of good news for the LACS during this time was the disbanding of the Sussex Staghounds. Formed in 1930, to hunt carted deer around Lewes and Haywards Heath, it was forced to close the following year after the Master, Tom Walls, sustained a serious injury after being thrown from his horse.

By now the increasingly radical tactics being used by the League were causing serious concerns amongst some of its more conservative members – as were the attacks against Royalty for its hunting activities, and Henry Amos's constant sniping against the RSPCA for its failure to come out against all blood sports. For while it was true that the RSPCA had thrown their weight behind the Lovat Fraser anti stag hunt bill, their attitude towards fox, hare and otter hunting was at best lukewarm. The first crack appeared in 1931 when the Hon Stephen Coleridge, the LACS's President, resigned over what he termed his "dissatisfaction with the conduct of some members of the League". His resignation was followed by that of the Treasurer and co-founder Ernest Bell, while July the following year saw Coleridge's successor as President, Lady Cory, also resign.

Pushed to attempt a compromise by his friends Henry Amos stood his ground. For him the answer was

> "whether the League shall continue to stand for the principles, the spirit, the method and the policy it was founded to promulgate, or whether it shall tone down the spirit and water down its policy and become, to all intents and purposes, a branch of the RSPCA, and thus be in the pocket of the fox-hunting party."

The point of no return had been crossed and it was evident that the inability of the personalities involved to reach an amicable settlement would force a split. For the first time, but not the last, the anti-hunting movement would divide against itself. On 8th July 1932 the LACS defectors held a meeting to form their own anti-hunting group the National Society for the Abolition of Cruel Sports (NSACS). They would have no truck with direct action or anti-establishment rhetoric, but would concentrate their activities through education and reasoned debate. Throughout its existence the NSACS has cultivated intellectuals, writers and academics, with Vice-Presidents who included Bertrand Russell, J B Priestly, H G Wells, Iris Murdoch and Patrick Moore. Though in reality, with the exception of a few interesting publications, the most notable of which was the 1965 book *Against Hunting*, coupled with its drafting of the 1948-49 anti-hunt bill, it has done little to advance the cause of blood sport abolition. From now until the early 1960s the main thrust of campaigning would remain with the LACS.

The remainder of this decade was a lean time for the opponents of deer hunting, with only a couple of forlorn attempts at parliamentary action. On 28th April 1937 Mr J Barr introduced his *Protection of Animals Bill*, which was similar to the Foot bills that aimed to prevent carted deer hunting. It received a First Reading, but got no further. Two years later, on 26th April 1939, Mr Lansbury brought in the *Protection of Animals (Prevention of Deer Hunting) Bill*, which was aimed at the West Country packs. During a short speech he gave as his main reason for introducing this Bill an incident occurring on 28th January that year when "a hunted hind took to the sea at Warren Point, near Minehead, followed by a calf. A follower of the hunt tried to shoot her from the shore, but in the face of hostility shown by the crowd, desisted. The hind eventually came ashore, but the calf was drowned, its body being later recovered from the water by a fisherman." Lansbury then read a short brief prepared by Sir Francis Acland, MP for North Cornwall, to the effect that all the witnesses to this incident were mistaken, and in fact the hunt officials were trying to save the hind and set it free once it regained land. In the event this Bill was given a First Reading and then disappeared without trace.

The outbreak of World War Two, in September 1939, put an end to any further attempts at legislation, though not stag hunting itself, which continued unabated throughout the war years. The BFSS stated its intention to cease operations for the duration, then changed its mind when it became apparent that the LACS would continue to operate. Though to be fair most of the League's wartime activities were left almost entirely in the hands of its Secretary, Joseph Sharp, who confined himself to writing letters to the press from his home in Kent.

On Exmoor, when not chasing deer or acting as the mounted division of the Home Guard, known locally as the "Exmoor Mounties", the DSSH co-operated with government agencies to organise deer drives which apparently impressed the Ministry of Agriculture. For in 1940 they reported that "despite the continuation of hunting, two-thirds of the deer killed on Exmoor during that year were shot". *Note 4*

The retort from anti-hunt factions was that deer hunting with hounds had been proved ineffectual, with the only reason for its continuance being that the Wartime Country Agriculture Committees were top-heavy with hunting types.

In Parliament occasional questions on the subject were raised. On 6th February 1941 Mr Leslie asked the Minister of Agriculture whether he would "consider prohibiting hunting of carted stags in view of the cruelty inflicted and the fact that the only damage to crops etc., was caused by the hunters." Passing the buck, the Minister, R S Hudson, replied that he "had no information that appreciable damage was done to crops or food production by stag hunting" and that "its prohibition was primarily a matter for the Home Secretary". The following year, on 5th May 1942, Mr W Leach raised the question of a recent stag hunt in North Devon during which he claimed: "There was ample testimony available to prove how cruel were the injuries inflicted on the stag…" He demanded an inquiry, but was told by L R Pym, Lord of the Treasury that "no useful purpose would be served…".

Only with the end of the war would the issue of stag hunting again be a serious political issue. When it came, the fallout from the ensuing confrontation would pre-determine the conscious thinking regarding blood sports for decades to come.

APPENDIX 2 offers a brief explanation of parliamentary procedure.

Note 1. Prior to 1703 there were two distinct branches of the Buckhounds. The Hereditary or Manorial Pack dating from 1362, and the Household or Privy Pack (circa: 1528) being the other one. In about 1703 these two packs merged to become the United Pack, better known as the Royal Buckhounds.

Note 2. The reason for the name change remained a mystery for many years until cleared up by LACS Research Officer Jess Barker in 2007. The name was changed from League for the Prohibition of Cruel Sports to League Against Cruel Sports in 1942. The reason being to avoid income tax – the word "prohibition" pointed to campaigning for legislation being its primary objective, meaning the League could not be considered a charity, and would therefore be liable for income tax. Fifty members were needed to pass the motion, but at the first AGM since the start of the war in 1942 too few people were able to attend, and the meeting was postponed until June, at a time so that members could get home before the black out.

All pre-1942 abbreviated references to the League for the Prohibition of Cruel Sports, which should read LPCS, will be cited as the post-1942 LACS to avoid unnecessary confusion in the text.

Note 3. This little book with the grand title of *The Wild Red Deer Of Exmoor: A Digression on the Logic and Ethics and Economics of Staghunting in England To-day* runs to a mere sixty-four pages, of which twenty-four are taken up with an account of the Lynton Town Hall meeting. This in turn is based on a report published in *The North Devon Herald* as Williamson claimed his notes on the meeting were "nearly all illegible".

Note 4. The proper name for the "Exmoor Mounties" was The Mounsey Hill (Mounted) Detachment of the Dulverton Company of the Local Defence Volunteers (LDV).

The first CO of the unit was Mr S Hancock, Master of the DSSH, and, when he left for army service, Bernard Waley-Cohen, one of the hunt's joint secretaries, took over. Government work took him away, and the third CO was Col Robert Dundas Alexander of Porlock, a 1914-18 Western Front veteran and former Master of the Exmoor Foxhounds. In the early days of the 'Mounties' Ernest Bawden, famous huntsman of the DSSH for twenty years, was a section commander.

Chapter Three

"Attila, or St Francis?"

THE CESSATION OF HOSTILITIES in May 1945, followed by the landslide Labour election victory on 5th July, convinced many abolitionists that at last their time had come. Though when it came, it was the NSACS, and not the LACS, who grasped the nettle. With the re-introduction of Private Members' time in 1948, which had been suspended for the duration of the war, Anthony Greenwood, a leading member and later President of the NSACS, persuaded Mr F Seymour Cocks (Labour MP for Broxtowe) to present a Bill drafted by the NSACS. This measure would abolish stag and otter hunting, hare coursing, plus the killing of badgers for sport.

The announcement of the impending debate for the *Protection of Animals (Hunting and Coursing Prohibition) Bill,* coupled with a similar *Prohibition of Foxhunting Bill,* to be introduced by Frank Fairhurst, was greeted with much anticipation in the abolitionist camp. They fully expected that the Labour government, which was widely seen as a truly reforming socialist administration, would give its full support to both the Bills. They reasoned that many Labour politicians, who throughout the 1920s-30s had either sponsored or supported anti-hunt measures, were now cabinet ministers with real power to do something positive. Had not the present Minister of Agriculture himself, Tom Williams, moved a motion at the 1928 Labour Party Conference to abolish blood sports? ***Note 1***

Unfortunately they were "counting their chickens" without giving due consideration to Labour's awakening realisation to the world of "realpolitik". Under pressure from the TUC, who opposed any move against hunting, followed by dire warnings from country landowners that any ban would be countered by severe disruption to food production, the Labourites were beginning to have serious doubts. When the BFSS began to mount a massive campaign, which brought hare coursing miners to Westminster and red-coated huntsmen riding through Regent Street and Piccadilly into Parliament Square (an incident which would enter hunting folklore as the Piccadilly Hunt, eventually commanding its own annual reunion) the government began to have grave misgivings, which soon turned to open hostility against both Bills. ***Note 2***

Just as in 1930 the West Country stag hunters were in the vanguard of protest. "In no uncertain manner," reported the *West Somerset Free Press* on 12th February,

> "the voice of people who do not want to see hunting abolished was raised at a mass meeting held in Dulverton last Saturday. All forces of opinion against prohibition in the Devon and Somerset country...were represented in the hundreds of people who packed the Town Hall, overflowed down the stairs, and crowded the street, to which the speeches from the platform were carried by loud speakers."

When the *Protection of Animals (Hunting and Coursing Prohibition) Bill* was debated at its Second Reading, on 25th February 1949, F Seymour Cocks made an eloquent and informed speech, much of it devoted to the pros and cons of Exmoor deer hunting. Ending the speech, Cocks made an emotional appeal to fellow MPs:

> "With every day that passes the future of civilisation is in process of formation. We ourselves are moulding the future of our country and our race. We are moulding it this afternoon. Shall we take as our pattern for the future the practices of Attila, the Hun and hunter, or the teachings of St Francis of Assisi? Attila, or St Francis? That is the choice I ask the House to make. That is the choice the House must make this afternoon..."

Opposition to the Bill came from Mr Manningham-Buller (Daventry) who believed that photographs alleged to show deer hunt outrages were taken in France, proving that abolitionists were unable to find evidence of cruelty in their own country. While Vernon Bartlett (Bridgwater) claimed to have received over 170 requests to oppose the Bill, while only 19 that he should support it, mainly from strange people such as the lady from Shoreham-on-Sea who started her letter by referring to him as a "spineless yellow rat…". Humour entered the debate when Earl Winterton (Horsham) replied that "the lady is a constituent of mine and I believe she is slightly mentally afflicted". Winterton then went on to assert that supporters of this Bill were "Bloomsbury Boys", who like their patron saint Oscar Wilde condemn manly field sports "because they are outdoor sports requiring courage, endurance, and physical fitness, every one of which qualities is anathema to them".

The Minister of Agriculture, Tom Williams, speaking for the government said that "to abolish hunting without providing an effective alternative…would mean there certainly would be more rather than less cruelty in the country". When pressed to explain his change of heart on the hunting issue, Williams replied, "One should never be ashamed to own that sometimes one may have got it wrong."

After five hours of such debate Anthony Greenwood summed up with a sad reproach to his government for urging their supporters to do, not what they knew to be right, but rather what was politically expedient. When the vote was taken the Bill was roundly defeated by 214 votes to 101.

Outraged at what they considered a sell-out to pressure from blood sport interests, over two hundred supporters of Seymour Cocks's Bill tabled a motion calling on the government to reconsider their attitude on the issue. Fearing a back bench revolt the government quickly offered to appoint a committee to enquire into the treatment of wild animals in Britain. On 2nd June 1949 the Home Secretary announced the formation of a committee under the chairmanship of Mr John Scott Henderson, KC.

When the credentials of the Scott Henderson Committee were scrutinised by the anti-hunt side they became less than optimistic regarding the possibility of a favourable outcome. Later comments from the BFSS's founder Fred Beadle that "it all depends who is put on the Committee as to what they will find out", confirmed suspicion as to who was setting the agenda. The Committee consisted of:

Miss Frances Pitt, Master of a Shropshire hunt, and Vice-President of the BFSS.
Major L P Pugh, FRCVS, Veterinary to the West Kent Foxhounds and Bolebrook Beagles.
Mr W J Brown, MC, interested in shooting and a well-known contributor to the hunting magazine *The Field.*
Dr H Burn-Murdoch, who was interested in fishing and was considered sympathetic to hunting interests.
Mr Charles Brandon, JP, Secretary of the Transport and General Workers Union, who was a supporter of the Labour Government, therefore totally opposed to any interference with hunting.
Professor P B Medawar, FRS, an expert zoologist, though a leading member of the Universities Federation For Animal Welfare, which was unwilling to support a ban on hunting.
Mr John Cripps, Editor of *The Countryman.*

By any standards the Scott Henderson Inquiry was biased in favour of the outcome requested by the government, with no inclusion from any animal welfare organisation, independent naturalist, or representative from farming interests. It was also widely thought that the RSPCA's exclusion from the committee was attributable to its support for the Cocks Bill.

When the one hundred-and-twenty-page long *Report of the Committee on Cruelty to Wild Animals* was published two years later in June 1951, the findings were predictable. All forms of hunting were found to be perfectly acceptable, offering little, if any, cruelty. *Note 3*

With regard to red deer hunting, the committee claimed that much of the evidence submitted by animal welfare societies "has been exaggerated." It continued that: "We do not think that this exaggeration has been malicious or intentional, but that it has been mainly due to a lack of understanding of what the eye-witnesses really saw, and also to the tendency to 'see the worst'." Its conclusions were simple enough: "In our view, therefore, the hunting of red deer is a useful and necessary form of control... . Inevitably, some suffering is involved, but it is no greater than that involved in any other practical method of control and does not justify legislative action to prohibit the sport. Hunting should...be allowed to continue as at present...".

Their response to New Forest fallow deer hunting was similar:

> "The only important difference seems to be that a fat fallow buck usually collapses at the end of a hunt, so that the huntsman can kill it... . As, however, the deer would in any case have been killed eventually, and there is no question of prolonged suffering being caused by exhaustion, we do not think that this adds appreciably to the suffering involved in this form of hunting. We do not think that hunting in this area (Hampshire) is so important...but nevertheless it is a useful method of control..."

For many though, the Scott Henderson findings concerning carted deer hunting summed up their views on blood sports generally: "We are not satisfied, from the evidence which we have received, that there is a sufficient degree of cruelty in this sport to justify legislation to prohibit it: and therefore, while we cannot say that it fulfils any useful function, other than the provision of recreation, we do not find it necessary to make any recommendation about it."

The NSACS and LACS attempted to extract crumbs of comfort from the report, with both expressing pleasure that the committee has stated: "The gin trap is a diabolical instrument which causes an incalculable amount of suffering" and "its sale and use in this country should be banned by law within a short period of time." The gin trap was outlawed in 1958. There was also approval of the recommendation that: "It should be made an offence to set a snare to catch a deer."

Surprise was also registered at a revolutionary recommendation by the committee which suggested that: "All wild animals should be brought within the provisions of the *Protection of Animals Act 1911*. This will make it possible for action to be taken against any person who causes or permits unnecessary suffering to a wild animal."

Unfortunately for the anti-hunters this idea was immediately followed by the inclusion of two clauses that read:

> "nothing in the Act should apply to the commission or omission of any act in the course of the hunting, pursuit, capture, destruction or attempted destruction of any wild animal unless such hunting, etc., was accompanied by the infliction of unnecessary suffering...
>
> subject to other provisions of the Act, the hunting, coursing, pursuit, capture, destruction or attempted destruction of any deer, fox, hare or otter for the purpose of sport shall be lawful while conducted under the approved rules of the sport..."

As far as the BFSS was concerned the report could not have turned out better. For the next forty odd years the Scott Henderson Report would form the bedrock for their defence of blood sports. Within months of the report's publication the Society had issued mass circulation pamphlets, such as *The Truth* and *Control Or Carnage?*, which presented edited highlights from "a committee of impartial people..." appointed "to inquire into cruelty to wild animals".

Not until the 1990s, when bodies such as the National Trust commissioned their own independent investigations into deer-hunt-related cruelty, were the biased findings of Scott Henderson finally put to rest.

Note 1. Frank Fairhurst's Prohibition of Foxhunting Bill was to have come up for debate on 11th March, but he agreed to withdraw it when it was announced that there would be an enquiry into the law relating to cruelty to wild animals.

Note 2. The 1949 Piccadilly Hunt was the last time a mounted hunt was seen in central London, although the capital was no stranger to the sound of the hunting horn. Deer hunting had been a regular feature of London life since medieval times, with the area around Soho obtaining its name after the huntsman's call "So ho" when hounds found a deer. Hyde Park was originally in the territory of the Berkeley Hunt, which started in the twelfth century and owned hunting country from Berkeley Castle in Gloucestershire to Berkeley Square in London.

According to the 1911 *History of the County of Middlesex: Vol 2*, during the 1820-30s the close proximity of London caused the Berkeley Staghounds to be attended with "amusing incidents" such as when a stag was run to bay in Lady Mary Hussey's drawing room at Hillingdon. On another occasion, after a stag entered the kitchen of a house, the angry owner of the house said in reply to Grantley Berkeley's apologies: "Your stag, sir, not content with walking through every office has been here, sir, here in my drawing room, sir, whence he proceeded upstairs to the nursery, and damn me, sir, he's now in Mrs.---'s boudoir."

The same source tells us:

> "One of the oddest scenes, however, caused by the vagaries of the stag, occurred when, after entering London by Regent's Park, a fine one covered with foam and stained with blood, and followed by two couple of hounds, one morning ran up the steps of No. 1 Montague Street, Russell Square. The efforts of Grantley Berkeley to persuade two young ladies who were looking out of the window to allow the stag to enter the hall in order to ensure his capture were rudely interrupted by their father, who, to the amusement of the other members of the hunt and the large crowd that had assembled, told him that if he did not instantly take 'his animal away' he would 'send for the beadle'. The stag was eventually captured by the aid of some friendly butcher boys."

The last time that a member of the Royal Family is believed to have hunted in London was on 2nd March 1848. The future Edward VII, then the Prince of Wales, rode out with the Royal Buckhounds from Denham in the Thames Valley into London, passing Wormwood Scrubs and finally taking a deer in the goods yard at Paddington Station.

Note 3. 1951 also saw the formation of the Masters of Deerhounds Association (MDHA), a self-governing body formed to regulate the activities of stag hunters. In practice it can adjudicate on any breach of rules brought to its attention, though in reality it exists to justify any incident that may have caused public controversy.

Chapter Four

"This wild stag was not a captive animal. It was only temporarily unable to get away."

THE PUBLICATION OF SCOTT Henderson's report in June 1951 was not the only blow suffered by the anti-hunt movement that year. For October would see the return of a Conservative government under Winston Churchill, consigning to a legislative wasteland any ambition concerning blood sport abolition. This administration, along with the succeeding ones of Eden, MacMillan and Alec Douglas-Home, would ensure that deer hunting would remain firmly at the bottom of any political agenda. Though these wilderness years, or "thirteen years of Tory misrule" as they came to be collectively known, would speed the end of the passive banner-waving protest mentality, bringing in its wake a new militancy that would foreshadow the direct action political activism of the "Swinging Sixties". In the vanguard would be none other than the LACS.

The first few years of the 1950s were a sorry time for the League. The return of the Tories meant that with hunting now a dead issue, the press lost interest in the LACS, considering it to be a spent force. In reality, the main thrust of campaigning was primarily undertaken by a small number of individuals, such as Gwen Barter, Vera Sheppard, Jean Pyke and Richard Hall, through the letters column of local newspapers. Occasionally an incident would occur to propel otherwise anonymous opponents of stag hunting into the spotlight, as in the case of Gladys Mantle. The *Daily Graphic* would tell how, on 8th March 1948,

"Mrs. Gladys Mantle, of Holford, near Bridgwater, Somerset, saved an exhausted hind which sought sanctuary in her garden... . The animal, hard pressed by the Quantock Staghounds, was followed into her garden by the hounds, horses and members of the hunt. 'I clung to its neck,' she said later. 'There was an awful melee...about the garden. I told those who were trying to drag the hind out, "Clear out!" and eventually they did.' "

This otherwise quiet and unassuming woman would receive over five hundred letters of support for her actions, a medal for bravery from the League, and heroine status within the anti ranks. From now on, in company with husband Lionel, she would become an ardent opponent of the QSH and would remain so until her death in the mid-1980s. In fact the situation was getting worse with deer hunting, for far from making any inroads against the existing six packs in the country a seventh was now added. In 1956 Lady Rosemary Brudenell Bruce re-formed the Savernake Staghounds (that had last hunted in 1900) to hunt the fallow deer around Marlborough, Wiltshire.

All this was to change in 1956 when Edward Hemingway became Chairman of the LACS. For Hemingway was not only a journalist by profession, but also a born self-publicist, who instinctively knew not only what made a good story, but how to capitalise on it with the media. His hatred of stag hunting, which stemmed from the attacks against him in the late 1920s, was heightened by a series of incidents, which determined him to turn the full attention of the League on the deer hunters.

On 6th March 1956, the DSSH drove a hunted hind over the quarry face at Holmingham near Bampton, killing both hind and two hounds after falling sixty feet. Next day, the *News Chronicle* reported one of the quarrymen who witnessed the incident as saying: "I wish some of the riders had gone over as well. That is what I think of staghunting." Eleven days later, on 17th March, the DSSH chased a deer from Alderman's Barrow, near Exford, forcing it into the sea, where it drowned. Again the same year, 22nd December, the *Exeter Express* reported that "a hind was driven into the sea, driven out again, dragged down by the hounds and slaughtered on the beach below Culbone Church, West Somerset, by the DSSH".

The following year, in February 1957, a hind was drowned near Dulverton. The RSPCA report into the incident stated:

> "The investigation showed that the hind, after being hunted for about five hours arrived at the swollen River Barle. With six hounds the hind was carried down river by the swift tide to the smaller of three river islands. At this stage the hind was washed ashore on the island, but the RSPCA is satisfied that it was then dead, having been drowned coming down river. Witnesses...were unanimous in their verdict that it was a most distressing sight to see the hind swimming frantically down river assailed by hounds. There is reason to believe at times some of the hounds were actually astride the hind's back as she threshed through the water."

The killing of this hind, when reported at length in the press, caused a public outcry, and several questions were asked in Parliament concerning the hunt's activities.

The threat to their image by this hind-killing controversy brought five members of the DSSH on "a special journey to attend a press conference in London" led by hunt chairman Sir Bernard Waley-Cohen – the main thrust of their argument being that "there had been a pernicious programme by anti-hunting bodies who had not stopped from supplying members of the press with inaccurate and distorted descriptions of stag hunting". At the same time "pictures had also been circulated of stag hunting abroad which had no bearing at all on stag hunting in this country", the "effect of this untrue propaganda was to work on the sensitiveness of people who knew nothing of the facts" and were "ready to accept those stories at their face value".

The following day Edward Hemingway held a press conference of his own during which he claimed that "the opposition to the sport was now so intense that the abolition of deer hunting was in the realm of practical politics". He then announced that the League intended "to appoint a special committee for the preparation of a Bill" for which "there would be powerful parliamentary support". The intention would be to "extend to deer the protection...provided by statute to other animals", while an "essential provision of the Bill would be to acquire the holdings of the Badgworthy Land Company and to vest the land in the Nature Conservancy for administration as a conservancy for wild deer". This radical suggestion, however remote the possibility of implementation, would send shock waves through the Exmoor hunting communities.

Early in March 1957 Edward Hemingway announced the formation of a separate group within the League, the National Committee for the Abolition of Deer Hunting (NCADH), to concentrate solely on the issue, with veteran League campaigner Joseph Sharp as Secretary. A £5,000 donation for the campaign enabled the placing of large adverts in newspapers circulating in stag hunt areas asking for public support "to help wipe the foul blot of stag hunting off the map of North Devon". This campaign launch would culminate with a noisy placard demonstration at the 7th August opening meet of the DSSH, at Cloutsham, when twenty protestors, led by League stalwarts Mrs Cicely Norman and her sister Mrs Florence Disney, were jostled and pushed by the mounted field. Later Mrs Norman would complain that "a horseman had cracked his whip dangerously near her". ***Note 1***

This meet was particularly newsworthy as it would be the first time that Mrs Nora Cox would act as sole DSSH Master following the suicide by shooting of her Joint Master husband, Captain Denys Cox, the previous July. Fully aware of her moment in history, Mrs Cox told the assembled meet: "I believe I am the first woman master of stag hounds for 400 years. I am conscious that if we are beaten, then all hunting in Britain would certainly end. It is a terrifying responsibility for a woman. But I am determined to carry on this season." ***Note 2***

The concerted effort to press for parliamentary legislation to ban the sport finally brought dividends at the beginning of 1958 when Labour MP for Tottenham, Sir Frederick Messer, was given leave to introduce his Private Member's *Protection of Deer (Hunting Abolition) Bill.* The reaction was predictable, if not somewhat over the top, with the DSSH calling a "public protest meeting" where "the Anti-stag hunting Bill must be defeated" at Dulverton Town Hall on 15th

February. Reporting on the night the *West Somerset Free Press* exclaimed, "It takes the local Pantomime Society to fill the Town Hall...and the local Carnival Society to fill the streets...but last Saturday one event did both." With the hall packed to capacity, many hundreds more outside listening "over amplifying apparatus", Taunton Tory MP Edward du Cann told them the "Bill would never see the light of day". He explained that "certain Members would ensure there was an awful lot of talk on the Bill that was coming up prior to it – a Bill about the compulsory purchase of land." This hint that the Bill would be "talked out of time" drew cheers from the crowd, while the North Devon MP James Lindsay attacked the proposed Bill by saying that hunting was "the price the deer has to pay for a painless death".

The only dissenting voices that evening came from the redoubtable sisters Cicely Norman and Florence Disney who had entered "the lion's den" to tell the assembled hunters that she (Cicely Norman) "had heard a lot of balderdash and drivel in her time, but nothing worse that she had been hearing at this meeting". On leaving the meeting the two sisters "found themselves in the midst of a crowd which kept up a derisive barrage of shouts...blasts on whistles, toots on hunting horns and plenty of boisterous chaff". Eventually the police moved the crowd, escorted the pair to their van and as it drove away "a hand was seen waving from the window". The following day it was the turn of Edward Hemingway to go over the top with a letter to the Home Secretary "demanding protection for members of the public in the Exmoor area" from "a frenzied mob of shouting...staghunt supporters amid a pandemonium of whistling, cat calls, and the blowing of hunting horns".

As predicted the Bill was killed without a Second Reading debate a few days later on 21st February 1958. The same Bill was reintroduced on 24th June 1959, again by Sir Frederick Messer, this time commanding a short debate on its First Reading, with opposition from Edward du Cann that basically quoted verbatim from the Scott Henderson report. The same Bill would be brought back during the 1959-60 Session of Parliament by Arthur Skeffington, though would not get beyond a formal First Reading. ***Note 3***

By the middle of 1958, aware that the political initiative was temporarily stalled, Hemingway began dropping broad hints via his friends in the press that the League had a "secret weapon", which would be used to disrupt the DSSH during the next seasons hunting. The plan was to "spoil the hunt by laying a false-scent trail of chemical to lead the hounds away from places where stags gather".

So concerned was Col Louis Murphy, who was starting his first season as master in August 1958, following the resignation of Nora Cox, that he called a press conference on the eve of the opening meet to explain just how "unconcerned" he was. There would be no change of policy or practice as a result of the threatened "stink layers" from the antis, while in fact the stag hunt was pleased with the publicity the issue had aroused as "it caused increased interest in the sport and brought…an enormous number of additional supporters". Just to be sure though he sent a telegram to NCADH Secretary Joseph Sharp warning, "There is a danger that stock grazing in the area will be contaminated by the chemical and that hounds will chase them. Should any damage by hounds to stock result from such an eventuality I shall hold your society responsible." Sharp was unmoved, remarking tartly that "…Murphy cannot intimidate us and we intend to continue with our plans. I regard his telegram as an admission that the hunt cannot control its dogs."

The day after this press conference, 6th August 1958, the very first "hunt saboteurs" went into action against the DSSH at their opening meet. The *Daily Telegraph's* man reported:

> "Members of the League were out early yesterday morning spraying the roads round Cloutsham…from which the hunt started. They used an anti-pest spray behind a Land Rover car. It rained after the first effort and they returned about an hour later and sprayed again. When I arrived two hours before the hunt started the 'secret' chemical smelled strongly of aniseed."

The League later claimed that special attention had been paid to William Harding, the hunt harbourer, by soaking the gateways, making it "impossible for him to leave his farm without getting some of the chemical on him". Louis Murphy laughed this off, saying that "Bill Harding was not staying at his farm last night". He continued that "the stag they found was a magnificent animal", adding that the reason the hunt failed to make a kill was nothing to do with antis, but rather that hunt supporters had chased the deer in their excitement and ruined the scent.

In the event Edward Hemingway was more than pleased at the outcome, saying "the fact that the hunt had to call off their hounds after they had lost a deer...shows only too well how thoroughly the League's volunteers had done their job... . We have telegraphed congratulations to our members who carried out this magnificent piece of work in the cause of animal welfare. This is only a beginning. We shall treat many other staghunts in the same way during the next few months."

True to his word, the League continued its attempts at hunt sabotage, turning its attention to the QSH. The *West Somerset Free Press* reported on 6th September 1958 that members of the League "laid false chemical trails on an extensive scale on the Quantock Hills" the previous Saturday, and that "reports indicate that the chemical trails have worked as successfully in ruining the hunting on the Quantocks...as they have been when they were laid on Exmoor". An explanation that "it was not until after 2 p.m. that the hunt got a stag on the run, but the hunt lost the scent two hours later and no kill was made" prompted master Sir Jeremy Boles to come up with a novel excuse for this failure. According to him the antis "made one big mistake. They went to one end of the hills, and we hunted at the other end, so we did not come into contact with any of their trails."

Two weeks after the "false scent campaign" Edward Hemingway was given another opportunity to exploit the media when the comedian Jimmy Edwards (a household name at that time for his popular TV show *Whacko*) hunted with the QSH and was blooded at the kill in what the League described as "a filthy rite". This publicity gave the LACS a much-needed boost, not to say enhanced radical image. Though for local participants of the League's hunt sabotage activities there would be a price to pay. For some there would be petty acts of revenge, while for others there would be retribution of a more official nature. Cicely Norman, one of the leading demonstrators, was also Chairman of the Ilfracombe branch of the RSPCA, and when her name was associated with the protests she was asked to resign. In a letter from Lady Williams, wife of Sir William Williams, Chairman of the RSPCA's North Devon branch, she was told that her actions "may antagonise supporters of the RSPCA who are not opposed to staghunting". Later Mrs Norman would be sacked from her job running an animal clinic in Ilfracombe, and the branch closed down.

Another issue tackled by Edward Hemimgway at this time was the serious lack of hard photographic evidence concerning the cruelties of deer hunting. For while there were many sworn statements by eye-witnesses, the only actual film consisted of a few feet of movie footage showing a hind brought down and savaged by the hounds taken in the 1920s. Likewise the photographs in existence were twenty to thirty years old, most having been taken by pro-hunter Alfred Vowles, while the odd few of unknown origin were dismissed by the BFSS as having been taken in France. ***Note 4***

A good example of this tactic was reported in the *West Somerset Free Press* during their 1949 campaign against the Seymour Cocks Bill when

> "Giving particulars of some of the methods by which the opposition had misled people who did not know much about hunting, Mr J W Fitzwilliam (BFSS secretary) mentioned that some of the petitions which the opposition had been sending round bore on the back a huge photo of a deer swimming in a river, pursued by hounds: on the bank was a man whose clothes looked extremely un-English. 'We managed to find the original of this photo...and discovered that it was taken in 1938 and showed a pack of deerhounds in France which hunted inside a walled park from which the deer could not escape. That is the way in which they are obtaining petitions for their campaign. I think it is a standing disgrace that the people of this country should be deluded in that way'."

To redress this problem the NCADH placed a large advert in the *Free Press* offering "A prize of £50 for the best new photograph, showing an incident of stag hunting cruelty." It was Louis Murphy who highlighted the League's dilemma, when commenting on this advert, saying that

> "considering that every Tom, Dick, and Harry today has a camera it is quite remarkable that the best photograph that the committee can put in their advertisement depicting stag hunting cruelty must be over thirty years old. There is a carthorse in the picture – a very rare sight these days, and neither farmhand shown is wearing gum boots. With all the attention they gave us last season, and with all the photographers, amateur photographers, and spies out in the field, it speaks well for stag hunting and the lack of cruelty in it that they weren't able to find a picture to show what cruel sport it is."

Even the authenticity of this picture was challenged by E R Lloyd who claimed there was "something fishy" in that it showed "one of the farmhands being on horseback as hounds are supposedly setting upon a fallen deer." He would pose the question: "Has anyone ever seen a West Country farm worker sitting on his horse while hounds catch a deer? That stinks. He would dismount to ward hounds off until the huntsman arrived. He would be trying to save the venison, not calmly sitting on his horse." So if the clothes didn't betray the unBritishness of the scene, the actions of some unsporting foreign Johnny obviously did!

This problem of photographic proof would continue to plague the abolitionists for many years to come. There would be pictures, but most taken at long-range, or just prior, or just after, the kill. Few would convey what many considered to be the full horror of the cruelty of deer hunting. Another problem would be proving the provenance of the image, as most donators wished to remain anonymous for fear of reprisals, or their identities lost with the passing years.

Such a situation caused a minor controversy during the mid-1980s when a West Country hunt supporter, Captain E A Bailey, spent considerable time and effort writing to myriad newspapers attacking the validity of a League stag hunting film. In letter after letter Captain Bailey disputed the authenticity of an old black and white sequence which showed hounds dragging down and mauling an exhausted stag. Using the standard arguments that it was either filmed in France, or was "pre-war, before the days when the practice of despatching the bayed-up deer by a shot at point blank range was introduced", he constantly harped that "the film is irrelevant to the present day when hounds are trained to 'stand back' when baying up a deer. It is maliciously misleading to show such a film as anti-hunting propaganda today." The LACS had great difficulty responding to these allegations as details of the film's origins were buried deep in the archives (for anyone who has visited these archives this will not appear surprising) and only came to light after a lengthy search revealed the source. It transpired that the sequence was in fact filmed on the Quantock Hills in the Spring of 1958 (twenty years after Captain Bailey claimed that hounds were trained not to attack the deer) by American photographer Russell W Fuller, who was picnicking in the area at the time. Not only that, but it was also discovered the *Daily Mirror* had reported the incident on 5th May 1958, reproducing stills from the film, alongside comments from Russell Fuller that "...this was the most outrageous form of brutality and medieval barbarism I have ever see. I was shocked that such unnecessary cruelty has been allowed to continue in a land whose reputation for kindness to animals is so well known."

Though no doubt the most innovative and far-reaching action undertaken by the LACS during this time was the purchase of the first "sanctuary". In 1957 Hemingway bought the small but strategically placed Slowley & Sidewoods on Exmoor, then made great play in the press that it was "out of bounds" to hunters. He followed this, each time the hunt was meeting in the area, with a telegram to the DSSH master warning that "immediate proceedings will be taken against you or any other persons responsible for trespass".

This sanctuary was quickly augmented by two more, the Baronsdown estate and the adjoining Barlynch Woods, both near Dulverton. There was a certain irony in the purchase of Baronsdown in that between 1818 and 1824 it had been not only the home of Mr Stucley Lucas,

1 (above)Henry Salt.
2 (centre) Joseph Sharp.
3 (below) Edward Hemingway.

4 GONE TO SEA! A stag boldly swimming across Porlock Bay, C1920.

5 *Spectator sport, 1926 style.*

6 STAG IN THE WIRE. C1950s. One of the most dramatic photographs ever taken of stag hunting. Blood sport supporters have long claimed it was taken in France, but the truth is no one knows its origin.

7 *WHAT ARE THEY LAUGHING ABOUT?* Daily Mirror *20th March 1957. The author's first experience of stag hunting. (Note the schoolboy peering from between the two characters on right of picture.)*

8 Guard of honour for a dead stag. Devon and Somerset Staghounds, 19th March 1957.

9 Protestor Cicely Norman at a meet of the DSSH, 19th March 1957.

Off The Map of North Devon
Will You Help

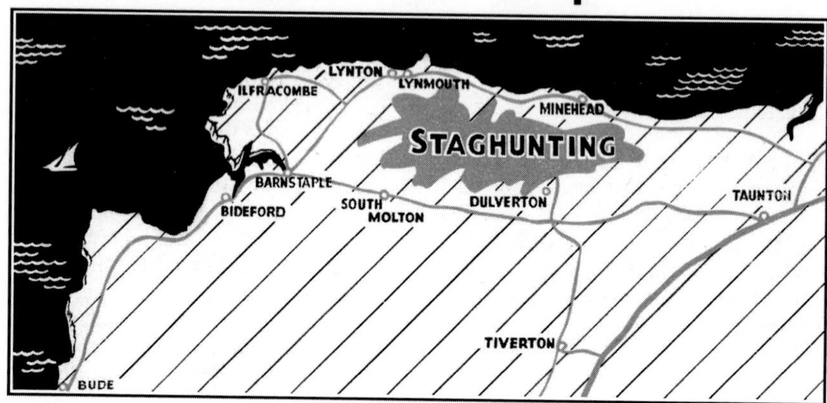

Urge Your M.P. To Support
The Bill To Stop
STAGHUNTING

All information from
The National Committee for the
Abolition of Deer Hunting
58 Maddox St. London W.1.
Tel: MAYfair 5538

SIGN OUR PARLIAMENTARY PETITION

P.T.O.

10 *1958 leaflet produced in support of Sir Frederick Messer's* Protection of Deer (Hunting Abolition) Bill.

Master of the North Devon Stag Hounds, but the hunt kennels as well. This hunt would of course, in 1837, become the DSSH. Then, in the autumn of 1959, just as Hemingway hoped it would, the inevitable happened, and the DSSH trespassed over it. The League's response was dramatic. First they demanded police protection, then sought redress with a High Court injunction, followed by the placing of armed guards around the "sanctuary".

While the League's main campaign against stag hunting would be directed through its sanctuaries, with further thought of action on the political front on hold, action of a different sort was beginning to take root that would eventually produce surprising results. For in the autumn of 1961 the last two Kent-based carted deer hunts would clash head-on with the redoubtable fifty-five year old Gwen Barter of Broadstairs. Already something of a *cause celebre* in the anti-hunt world for having been expelled from the RSPCA earlier in the year for attacking their hunting policy at the AGM, she would now find herself front-lined as a militant protestor.

As Gwen Barter would later explain, her involvement came about by default:

> "The beginning, for me, of worrying hunts was when my neighbour, Raymond Rowley, asked me to join a demonstration against Ashford Valley Foxhounds. He had told the local press of our intention to demonstrate and when we reached the pub chosen for the meet we were told that the hunt had been called off because of the cold weather.
>
> "A local reporter, from the *Kent Messenger*, asked us if we would like to go to another hunt, and led us to it! I didn't even know it was not a foxhunt but a 'carted' deer hunt, for it had moved off when we arrived at its venue. This accidental introduction to carted deer hunting got me involved against the sport, which I think I had not known about till then...
>
> "It took about two years to put an end to the Mid-Kent Staghounds and I then turned my attention to the Norwich

Staghounds, which was a much more solidly founded affair. I found a kindred spirit in Mrs Rash up there (better known as the novelist Doreen Wallace). We buckled down and she found some supporters. We leafleted a great deal (by post from the local telephone books) and managed to get the support of local societies. The photograph in the *Daily Herald* provided the *coup de grace* and the hunt ended for good."

Gwen Barter's simple telling belies a story of remarkable courage and perseverance during which she was physically threatened on many occasions. During the protest against the Mid-Kent Staghounds in November 1961 a potato was stuffed into the exhaust pipe of her car, the camera she was carrying was knocked from her hand and smashed, then eight hunt supporters "with me still sitting at the wheel…lifted my car onto the grass verge". The adverse publicity paid off when, in April 1962, the hunt closed down.

On 16th March 1962 the *East Anglian Daily Times* gave a half page report which read:

"A woman, carrying a protest placard and shouting 'Stop this cruel sport', suddenly jumped in front of a slowly moving vehicle pulling a trailer on which were crates containing deer for use at the meet of the Norwich Staghounds and the Easton Harriers at Saxstead Green, near Framlingham, yesterday.

"As the hunt was assembling in front of the Volunteer Inn, three cars covered with posters, and one equipped with a loud speaker made several slow journeys through the red and green coated riders and the big crowd of followers. Some of the posters stated: 'The cruel barbaric ritual of carted deer hunting must stop': 'Torment to tame deer is plain sadism': 'Hunting dumb animals is cruel': and 'Stop abusing and terrifying tame animals for amusement.'

"Just before the hunt was ready to move off Mr. Raymond Rowley…a member of the executive of the League, went to Lieut. Colonel Brian Gooch, Joint Master of the Norwich Staghounds, and loudly asked: 'As a sportsman, do you deny that hunting tame deer is cruel?'...

"Mr. Rowley then drew the attention of his twelve supporters to the two crates on the village green and when the trailer moved off with them, Miss Barter staged her own protest. Although the vehicle was only moving slowly the driver had to brake hard to avoid knocking her down. For some seconds she stood facing the driver, clutching her placard and urging for the hunt to be called off... . When the vehicle again moved forward slowly, Miss Barter twisted round, clutching the side mirrors and settled on the bumper. She lost her placard under the wheels. When the policemen asked her to get off she readily agreed.

"All the demonstrators then got into cars and followed the trailer about a mile and although they ran across fields they were too late to do anything more to prevent the release of one of the deer ten minutes ahead of the hunt.

"After being hunted for just over two hours over a wide area from Saxstead Green, the deer was caught and returned unharmed to its crate."

Not exactly headline-grabbing stuff by the standards of today's animal rights movement, but to the sedate world of early 1960s' animal welfare protest it was dynamic. Within weeks Gwen Barter was national news, with the *Daily Herald* launching its own campaign against carted deer hunting. When the *1963 Deer Bill* passed to the Lords for debate Labour peer Lord Crook forced through an amendment "to stop the scandal of carted deer". On 13th July 1963 the *Daily Herald* gave the story front-page coverage. Under the banner headline "Stop This Cruelty", accompanied by a photograph of a lassoed stag being dragged up the bank of a frozen stream after members of the hunt had struggled with it for fifteen minutes, it quoted the RSPCA as saying: "The *Daily Herald* can take credit for drawing public attention to this...the most reprehensible, odious and decadent of all forms of sport."

The amendment was defeated on the Bill's return to the House of Commons, but it made no difference. Gwen Barter's campaign had damaged, beyond all salvation, the image of carted deer hunting. On 20th September 1963 a public meeting was held in the Norfolk village of Diss, when over sixty locals supported a resolution deploring the sport. When local farmers then announced that they would no longer allow the hunt to cross their land the game was up. It is also very probable that "behind the scenes" pressure was brought to bear by the BFSS, who were now becoming very conscious of their public image, for the hunt to change direction. For even by the standards of 1960s animal welfare, the hunting of farm bred deer for fun was beginning to look somewhat "beyond the pale", in much the same way as the hunting of roe deer looks to the MDHA today. In the event there was certainly no vigorous defence of the sport launched by the BFSS, or anyone else.

On 20th October Brigadier H R Harris, the hunt chairman, announced that the Norwich Staghounds would cease operations, converting to a drag hunt. Trying to put a brave face on the situation he assured the press that "it is not because of the criticism…but because of financial reasons. We must cut expenses. Fewer people are following the hunt."

It made no difference what Brigadier Harris claimed, to many in the movement it was Gwen Barter, and Gwen Barter alone, who had brought about the end of carted deer hunting in England. During these three years, when she had also vigorously campaigned against fox hunting, on one occasion sitting on a fox earth to prevent it being dug out for which she received a bravery award from the LACS (in those days the League gave medals for individual acts of courage on behalf of hunted animals) Gwen Barter earned a reputation that would secure her place as the first true "hero" of the anti-blood-sport movement. She would subsequently become an LACS Executive Committee Member, finally resigning in 1980. For many more years she would continue to campaign against all forms of animal abuse through the columns of regional and national newspapers until her death, a few months short of her hundredth birthday, in 2005. To many her actions would give serious food for thought. If she could bring about the end of carted deer hunting with personal protest actions, when every form of peaceful persuasion had failed to make any impression on Parliament, why waste time trying to convert MPs to the cause. Would the time not be better spent taking the fight to the hunting field? ***Note 5***

As if to prove that not only were blood sports immune from political attack, but were also actively protected by the law, a court case had been played out during this time in Somerset which appeared to underscore the point. The case centred on an incident of 30th August 1962, when a hunted stag was pursued into the main street of Timberscombe village, slipped, then became wedged under a furniture van. It was dragged out by the antlers, then half carried, half pulled, twenty to twenty-five yards into the yard of the village hall, where its throat was slit by Louis Murphy. A subsequent legal challenge "of cruelly terrifying a stag contrary to Section One of the *Protection of Animals Act 1911*" was brought against Murphy by Edward Hemingway.

When the case was brought before Minehead Magistrates Court on 28th March 1963 the charges were dismissed by court chairman, Mr J Rawle, on the grounds "that the stag was not an animal within the meaning of the Act". For under the *1911 Act:* "If you have a captive stag you can hunt it and you can recapture it (as in carted deer hunting), but you must not ill-treat it in any way. This wild stag was not a captive animal. It was only temporarily unable to get away."

At the close of trial Mr Philip Stevens, Hemingway's defence, asked for a stated case on the magistrate's decision. "What is meant by a captive animal," he asked, "and what is meant by captivity is a matter of law which needs clarification. What is meant by captivity or close confinement?" The issue would now go before the High Court.

The High Court ruling, when it came, on 14th November 1963, was a classic of legal prevarication. The Lord Chief Justice, Lord Parker, in company with fellow judges Mr Justice Winn and Mr Justice Fenton Atkinson, ruled "that as the law now stands a wild animal in such circumstances is not entitled to protection from cruelty". They then continued "that a period of time must elapse before a captured wild animal can be considered to be 'captive' in law". So while Lord Parker and friends had been honest enough to admit that in reality *no* wild animal was protected from cruelty under English law unless subjected to captivity, they had singularly failed to specify the *length of confinement* required before that protection became available. As the LACS would later ask: "Did they have in mind 3 seconds, 3 minutes, 33 minutes, 3 hours, 3 days, or longer?" An attempt to have the issue taken to the House of Lords for adjudication failed when the three judges "refused an application for a certificate that the case involved a point of law of general public importance".

For the League, who were understandably upset by this judgement, the disappointment was overshadowed by the loss of its two leading figures. In a case of ironic coincidence, on the same day, 28th March 1963, that Louis Murphy was cleared of cruelty, Joseph Sharp (sixty-two) collapsed and died suddenly while on his way to the railway station from his home at Worthing, Sussex, to catch the train to his London office. Less than five weeks later, on 2nd May 1963, Edward Hemingway (sixty-one) died at his Minehead home after being taken ill at a London press conference the previous day. Tragic as these two deaths were for the League, the organisation was fortunate in that it had a strong individual at hand not only to step in and take the helm, but to carry on and expand the work started by Hemingway. Over the next fifteen years, the new Chairman, Raymond Rowley, would continue the purchase of deer sanctuaries, turning the LACS into one of the largest landowners on Exmoor, while at the same time waging a relentless campaign against the region's three stag hunts. *Note 6*

The past seven years of constant attack by the League had shaken the BFSS out of their complacency, forcing them at last to face the realisation that to most people they were viewed as a reactionary group of upper class defenders of traditional country sports. Decisions were taken that the image must change to one of being seen to actually promote the cause of conservation. It was at this time that the connection was forged between blood sports and political measures that could be seen to promote animal welfare. Against a backdrop of sustained attacks against carted deer hunting, mounting anger over hunt supporters controlling the RSPCA, and with the possibility of a Labour government at the next election, a suitable cause was sought which could get the ball rolling. The subject of wild deer protection seemed the natural choice, following growing concerns that deer poaching was reaching serious levels in some areas of the country, and would hopefully be seen as a counter balance for their constant defence of stag hunting.

By early 1963 the BFSS was ready for action. A Bill aimed at making deer poaching a criminal offence, limiting the type of weapon that could be used to kill a deer, and creating close seasons for deer killing was drafted by their parliamentary agent R Hancock. The *Deer Bill 1963* was introduced by Jasper More, a member of the BFSS General Purposes Committee, who then oversaw its passage through the House of Commons. During the Second Reading on 8th March the debate was dominated by More and Marcus Kimball, the latter who would later become Chairman of the BFSS, with the remaining speakers acting as a sort of impromptu supporters' club, compliments and praise flowing in profusion. Anthony Greenwood would voice concerns from the NSACS regarding the proposed dates for close seasons, but finished by saying that he would not oppose the Bill. The last but one remark came from Col Marcus Lipton who commented: "This Bill is not so admirable as has been suggested... . It seeks to prohibit all forms of cruelty to the deer, with the exception of the least excusable of all, namely, hunting with hounds for sport."

The final stages of the Bill would be cleared in record time, with a Lord's amendment to ban carted deer hunting removed on its return to the Commons, and received the Royal Assent on 31st July 1963. The *Deer Act 1963* would allow close seasons for red, fallow and sika stags and bucks from 1st May to 31st July inclusive. There was no close season for roe deer bucks (this would be rectified with the *Roe Deer {Close Seasons} Act* 1977 which added a close season from 1st November to 31st March). Red, fallow, sika and roe deer hinds were all granted close seasons from 1st March to 31st October. No protection under this Act was given to other species of alien deer that are now firmly established in a feral state in Britain – namely the muntjac and Chinese water-deer.

The Act also made illegal the shooting of deer at night, i.e. "between the expiration of the first hour after sunset and the commencement of the last hour before sunrise". However,

> "a diseased or wounded deer, or one marauding any cultivated land, pasture or enclosed woodland may be killed by any person at any time of day or night, or even during the recognised close season provided that he is the occupier of the land...or that he acted with the written authority of the occupier and that proof can be given that such action was necessary for the purpose of preventing serious damage to crops or property."

The Act further stated that it is unlawful to use "any net or snare, or any arrow, spear or similar missile" to kill deer, while under Schedule 2 Prohibited Firearms and Ammunition it banned:

Any smooth bore gun of less gauge than 12 bore.
Any rifle having a calibre of less than .240 inches or a muzzle velocity of less than 1700 foot pounds.
Any air gun, air rifle or air pistol.

The police were also given powers to arrest without warrant anyone suspected of having committed an offence and anyone convicted of an offence under this Act would be liable "to a fine not exceeding £20 or, in the case of a second or subsequent conviction, to a fine not exceeding £50 or to imprisonment for a term not exceeding three months, or to both such fine and imprisonment". Later, under the *Criminal Law Act 1977,* the maximum fine for an offence under the *Deer Act 1963* was increased to £500. While this legislation was undoubtedly much needed, it can be clearly seen that it was engineered in such a way as to give maximum protection to the interests of hunting, to the extent that the prevention of deer poaching in stag hunting areas became virtually impossible. It failed dismally, in fact didn't even attempt, to address the issue of shotguns as a method for killing deer. In reality, it legally sanctioned the shotgun, which most deer experts consider one of the cruellest methods for killing deer, to accommodate the secret deer drives of the DSSH. In fact, attempts in 1977 to amend this Act, when deer poaching had reached epidemic proportions, would force the BFSS to show its true colours while defending the interests of the stag hunters.

Both the LACS and NSACS saw this Act as nothing more than a blatant piece of blood sport window dressing, with the League's magazine *Cruel Sports* referring to it as "a prize piece of Parliamentary humbug", in which "those responsible for its guidance have astutely dodged all attempts to amend on real humanitarian grounds and employed every form of Parliamentary chicanery to ensure that it would receive the Royal Assent this Session".

The passage of this Bill, not to mention the methods used to fast-track it through, only served to reinforce for many the belief that any hope of worthwhile animal welfare legislation was little more than a pipe dream. The League's AGM on 15th May that year would act as a catalyst for some members of the audience when the former Conservative MP for Brighton, Kemptown, Howard Johnson, made an extraordinary speech. To a packed meeting in Caxton Hall he announced: "I have a vision in the coming stag and fox hunting season of whole numbers of you sitting in the roadway at meets of the hunt, doing exactly what the anti-nuclear demonstrators do." He continued with the warning that such actions could lead to arrest, adding that some members of the hunt might ride over demonstrators, maiming, wounding and possibly killing them. "I hope they don't," he concluded, "but if they do kill you, they will stand a very fine chance of hanging or imprisonment." It appears from the *Daily Telegraph* report of the meeting that Mr Johnson received a standing ovation from frustrated League activists.

Certainly the idea of direct action tactics appealed to the League's new Chairman, Raymond Rowley, elected at this meeting following the sudden death of Edward Hemingway. By early December 1963 newspaper reports were dropping broad hints that a new idea was afoot with the creation of something called "hunt saboteurs" which were in training with the LACS, who had made available "all the latest know-how on how to sabotage a hunt". While it was certainly true that the League had actively encouraged its members to use mildly disruptive tactics against their local fox hunts, with members such as Jean Pyke, Gwen Barter and Vera Sheppard becoming notorious in hunting circles, the emphasis had always been on passive poster demonstrations. All this would change with the formation of the Hunt Saboteurs Association. *Note 7*

Note 1. Mrs Cicely Norman was a well-known, long-standing, opponent of stag hunting with an impressive track record of physical demonstrations to her credit. The 7th August demo against the DSSH was only one of a number she organised to publicise the launch of the NCADH. In fact, it was one of her protests on 19th March 1957 that prompted the *Daily Mirror* to publish extensive coverage of stag hunting the following day, which included the double-page "What are they laughing about?" photograph that would leave such an impression with this author.

Note 2. Mrs Nora Cox did not last the season. She resigned in early February 1958, with the position taken by Col Louis Murphy. She would return as sole master during 1974-76, then joint master (with M E Robinson) from 1976 till mid-80s under the name Nora Harding.

Note 3. Sir Frederick Messer's *Protection of Deer (Hunting Abolition) Bill* was a far-ranging and innovative measure for its day, concerned not only with stag hunting, but deer welfare generally, as this report from the 8th February 1958 *West Somerset Free Press* shows:

> "It requires the Minister of Agriculture, or in Scotland the Secretary of State, to prepare for any necessary area a scheme to prevent by means of controlled shooting any substantial increase in the number of deer. Objections to any scheme may be made over a period of three months, and any order shall be subject to annulment by either House of Parliament.
>
> "The use of hounds may not be unlawful in the implementation of a scheme, but otherwise "if any person uses hounds for the purpose of hunting any deer, or assists at or takes part in any such hunting with the use of hounds, or sets or causes to be set any snare for the purpose of capturing or killing any deer" he shall be guilty of an offence.
>
> "Proposed penalties are a maximum of £50 for a first offence and up to £100, or three months imprisonment, or both, for a subsequent offence, and the confiscation of any snare, firearm, or other equipment used in committing the offence.

"The Bill further lays upon the Minister the duty to prescribe a close season during which it would be an offence for anyone to kill or attempt to kill any deer."

The BFSS, when drafting their *1963 Deer Act*, obviously poached the best bits of Messer's Bill, careful of course not to include a single word that would in any way endanger blood sports.

Note 4. Alfred Vowles was a prolific photographer of the Somerset scene from the early 1900s until the late 1940s. Among the thousands of images he took were many dealing with stag hunting. Of these a number showed deer in water pursued by hounds, stags at bay and various other hunting incidents, many of which were sold as postcards. A few of his pictures were used in anti-blood-sport literature, but for some reason not in any great number. He was the author of the 1920 book *Stag-hunting on Exmoor.*

Note 5. The celebrations of the demise of the Norwich Staghounds were a muted affair for Gwen Barter. Earlier that year (1963) "whilst on a visit to London she had met with a motor accident which resulted in the amputation of her foot". Regardless of her injury she would continue with over another forty years of active campaigning on behalf of animals.

Note 6. Something of the character of these two remarkable men, Joseph Sharp and Edward Hemingway, can be gleaned from the obituaries published in the LACS *Cruel Sports* January/March (Vol 5. No.1) & April/June (Vol 5. No.2) 1963.

"Mr. Joseph Clifford Sharp was a lifelong humanitarian and vegetarian, who had given 35 years devoted service to the work of the League in a never-ending endeavour to awaken the public conscience to the many unspeakable cruelties inflicted on wild animals in practices which cloak themselves under the name of sport.

"A Lancashire man by birth, Mr. Sharp attracted the attention of the late Mr. Henry B. Amos, the founder of the League, in the late 'twenties by the letters he contributed to North of England papers which forthrightly attacked the cruelties to wild animals which the pursuit of blood sports involved. He was invited by Mr. Amos to assist in the work of the League, and early in 1928 was appointed Assistant Organiser of the League, a post in which he quickly proved his value as a ready and forceful speaker at meetings held to further the activities of the League.

"When health reasons compelled the resignation of Mr. Amos from the General Secretaryship of the League in 1930, Mr. Sharp was appointed by the then Executive Committee of the League to succeed him. Those early years were trying times. The League was growing and vigorous, but not the powerful body with a well-defined policy that it is today. There were internecine factions which still had to work themselves out, and it is to Mr. Sharp's lasting credit that he weathered the storms successfully, and skilfully piloted the League to permanent solidarity through troublous days. In the 'thirties he had more than his share of rowdy meetings to handle, and demonstrations against hunting activities in various parts of the country where, owing to the belligerent nature of the hunting rowdies of the day, it was never certain whether the demonstrations or meetings might not end in a free fight, or some unseemly scuffle, which was certain to be reported in local newspapers to the disadvantage of the League. The way in which he avoided trouble in those early days and still stood his ground with quiet courage, earned him commendable praise which he fully deserved.

"When the war broke out in 1939, it seemed as though the League and its work would come to an end. The London offices were given up, but Mr. Sharp, with the backing of the then Executive Committee kept the League alive through the war years from his own home then in Sidcup in Kent.

"In 1946 the League returned to London, opening its present offices (58 Maddox Street, W.1) with Mr. Sharp in charge. From that point it has never looked back but has grown steadily in stature and importance, and so incidentally did the extent of Mr. Sharp's work and responsibility. In 1947 Mr. Sharp presented evidence on behalf of the League to a group of MPs which resulted in the Bill to abolish stag hunting, which the late Mr Seymour Cocks, MP, moved in Parliament. Though defeated on Second Reading, this Bill caused the setting up of the Committee on Cruelty to Wild Animals. There is no doubt that largely through the evidence Mr Sharp marshalled before the Committee, about the atrocities of deer hunting and fox hunting the Committee recommended in its Report that all animals should be brought within the *Protection of Animals Act 1911*.

"In 1957, Mr. Sharp was appointed Secretary of the National Committee for the Abolition of Deer Hunting, and took a prominent part in the intensified campaign against stag hunting, which resulted in a Bill to make the practice illegal being brought before Parliament by Sir Frederick Messer, MP.

"Mr. Sharp was a kindly, friendly man who had a happy gift of gaining the goodwill of both friends and opponents, and there is no doubt that the animal welfare movements generally will be the poorer for his death. He saw the campaign in which he stood in the forefront for 35 years become a public issue of importance, and though he did not live to see the cruel forms of sport he abhorred legally abolished he lived long enough to know that that day is not long delayed.

"In his private life he was a steadfast worker for the religious denomination to which he belonged, and his recreations included a love of music and singing. Also he was a skilful conjurer and puppet master, and when he could be prevailed upon to entertain a young audience with his mastery over these arts they were assured a delightful time. Mr. Sharp was married, with a grown-up daughter."

"Mr. Edward Alexander Hemingway, Chairman of the League, was a free-lance journalist of considerable skill and with a wide reputation, indeed his repute was not only nationwide but extended beyond these shores. He was frequently reported in the Foreign Press for his forthright and often outspoken views and criticisms of those who offended against the very high moral standards he had set himself, irrespective of the status or personality of those he criticised.

"As an agricultural journalist he was particularly knowledgeable and his services were frequently called upon by farming papers and periodicals. A number of daily newspapers relied upon Mr. Hemingway for minute by minute reports of events in the West Country and particularly in the field of what he termed so frequently 'real sport': football, rugby, cricket and other ball games.

"He was always the champion of the under-dog and never failed to turn the spotlight of the Press upon any act of injustice. Those who knew him well would often find him in the early hours of the morning working hard on the case of some 'unfortunate' who had become the victim of the 'bloated bureaucracy'. He cared not whom he had to hit, and his bitterest opponents knew that when he did so he hit hard. He seemed to gain most pleasure out of hearing officialdom climb down and apologise. His host of contacts in all walks of life enabled him almost to report or prepare for a situation before it actually occurred. He boasted to having his ear so close to the ground that he knew when his enemies stirred.

"Mr. Hemingway's work for the League can never be measured in words. He literally burnt himself out in the cause of animal welfare and particularly in the welfare of the wild and hunted creatures. He became Chairman of the LACS in 1956, before which he served on the Executive Committee for 24 years.

"For 10 years or so in the 1940s he was a member of the Minehead Urban Council and had been Chairman of its Finance Committee.

"Even though he had suffered failing health during the last 12 months of his life he never missed a League committee meeting. It was during an LACS press conference in London that he was taken ill. He was rushed by car to his home in Minehead where he died the following morning, 2nd May at 10.30am. He was buried with his mother and sister in the family grave at the village of Golcar, near Huddersfield. He left a wife and daughter."

Note 7. Legend has it that the HSA, like the LACS and BFSS, came into being as the result of a deer hunting incident. John Prestidge, a young Devon journalist, appalled when he found himself working on the story of a pregnant hind who had been driven into an Exmoor village and killed by the Devon and Somerset Staghounds, said to a colleague that "someone ought to sabotage the hunt". The rest, as they say, is history.

Chapter Five

"The HSA! Vot's the cap and vere's the country?"

THE HUNT SABOTEURS ASSOCIATION "officially" went into action for the first time on 10th January 1964 against the South Devon Foxhounds near Torquay. *Note 1*

The result brought "utter confusion to the hunt" after raw meat was thrown to the hounds, phantom fanfares on the hunting horn were used, and saboteurs blocked the lanes with their cars in an attempt to stop the riders moving off, forcing the hunt to break up early and return to kennels empty-handed. Nothing on quite this scale had ever been attempted before, and while the hunt were shocked, believing it "some kind of communist group out to overthrow the aristocracy", the press loved it. Within days both national and local newspapers were giving extensive coverage to the fledgling HSA, reports which captured the imagination of many aspiring anti-blood sport militants. The next few days would bring over 1,000 letters of support pouring into the saboteur leader's home. *Note 2*

The organiser of the protest was twenty-one year old John Prestidge, a freelance journalist from Brixham, Devon, who had contributed much of the "animal-loving copy" that filled the pages of the *Daily Mirror* at the time. Later mythology would claim that the formation of the HSA was inspired by League Chairman Raymond Rowley's desire to set up a more militant wing to operate separately, but in tandem, thus appeasing the more traditionalist LACS members. The short-lived 1958 "false trail campaign" certainly gave rise to such an assumption, but there seems little truth in this, though certainly at the time much was made in the press of John Prestidge travelling to London with other saboteurs "for instructions...so that trained action groups could be set up all over the country". Though according to both Prestidge and Rowley no formal meeting of the two groups ever took place. The traditional view was that as a journalist Prestidge was able to use his contacts to promote the hunt saboteurs, and that the concept was entirely his own. The truth no doubt lies somewhere between the two.

The reality was that by the middle of February 1964 the HSA was in action most weeks, with over 200 active members "signed-up". While

> "many were students and old Ban-The-Bomb activists...there was also a leavening of older people from all walks of life. Well known members included author Monica Hutchings and stargazer Patrick Moore, while there was even a Windsor Castle official, sixty-year-old Philip Cross, Keeper of the Curfew Tower."

An office had been opened in Fore Street, Brixham, with ex-Palladium dancer Joyce Greenaway as the first secretary. An annual membership fee of two shillings and six pence (12½p), with £10 life membership, was set, later augmented with two £500 donations from the former Liberal MP for West Ham Count Maurice de Bendern, and lifelong campaigner against hunting Claire Monk. The Brixham-based HQ boasted a seven-person committee which included the reformed former Joint Master of the South Shropshire Foxhounds Capt. Robert Churchward, "whose wildly enthusiastic tape recordings of horn calls, holloa's and 'tally ho's' had most novices in stitches at the first hearing, but were to prove invaluable in teaching saboteurs the tricks of the trade".

The tactics and primary tools of the trade developed at this time have changed little during the intervening forty years. Apart from the obvious use of the hunting horn, which can cause havoc in the hands of an adept saboteur, the *holloa*, which hunters use to call their hounds or each other, can be equally disruptive when a couple of well placed antis holloaing across a wood can keep the hunters galloping to and fro for most of the day. There was also the mysterious masking agent known to the press in these early days as Chemical X. Contrary to popular belief it had nothing to do with aniseed, but was a "concoction of amyl acetate (a paint stripper), Jeyes' fluid and water which is usually mixed in large cans with a pump attachment for spraying", and for years has been affectionately known as "Sab Special". Another alternative was *Antimate,* "a commercial product sold in aerosol cans from pet shops. Made of natural herbs, such as rosemary and thyme mixed with eucalyptus oil, it was designed to be sprayed on the hindquarters of bitches in heat to neutralise their distinctive smell and so avoid unwanted pregnancies". Both substances are sprayed on the ground before a hunt, or in front of the hounds to confuse their sense of smell at any convenient point throughout the day. Smoke bombs and rook scarers (rookies) were also used on occasion, though "experienced saboteurs will emphasise that a successful 'hit' is not a matter of confrontation (unless that was the avowed intention as was the case on occasions with the later Save Our Stags campaign) but a form of rural guerrilla warfare". In fact "three or four saboteurs who go out early in the morning, spraying the ground, then using the horn and holloa at strategic moments, can effectively abort a day's hunting without the hunters even realising they have been sabbed." ***See APPENDIX 3***

As early as March 1964 small groups of saboteurs were well organised in Street (Somerset), Weybridge (Surrey), Littlehampton (Sussex), Bristol, Northampton, and of course the Brixham HQ. On 15th February scuffles at a meet of the Chiddingfold Farmers Hunt at Ewhurst, Surrey, led to the HSA's first arrest when Littlehampton group leader Norman Redman was charged for using "insulting behaviour whereby a breach of the peace may be occasioned". He had "dashed among the hounds, throwing meat from a tin" in an attempt to gorge the hounds (this practice was discontinued by saboteurs soon afterwards) who are starved the night before a hunt. At Godalming County Magistrates Court the following week he was fined £15 and bound over to keep the peace for two years.

West Country saboteurs tackled their first stag hunt on 4th April, which the Association's first (and only) *News Bulletin* reported with true *Boy's Own* gusto:

"Fifteen hardy saboteurs should certainly be awarded medals for courage and devotion to duty for their tenacity and engagement.

"In the teeth of a Force 7 gale and surrounded by a swirling blizzard of snow, an advance guard of three HQ members spent all night at Dunkery Hill Gate – the highest point of bleak Exmoor. Their objective was to outwit the Devon and Somerset Staghounds by exposing their practice of 'harbouring' stags for the hunt in convenient coverts or woods.

"Intelligence sources had previously pin-pointed the likely hiding places, and the party spent all night visiting each spot. Using various explosive devices and a number of other strategies the party flushed the harboured stags out of the woods. To do this they had to out-manoeuvre sentries posted by the hunt, but, despite the wariness of the opposition, it would appear that the saboteurs were highly successful.

"Only one stag was spotted by the hunt. One saboteur got between the stag and the hounds and managed to lay a smoke screen. The stag got away and the hunt got nothing.

"Special mention must be made here of three HQ members who formed the advance guard – John Prestidge and his two able lieutenants, Barry West and Leo Lewis. Their exploits on Exmoor during their all night vigil in Arctic conditions are in the best 'Commando' tradition."

The publicity generated by this raid took the saboteurs by surprise, for it soon became apparent that while many pressmen were ambiguous regarding the cruelties inherent in fox hunting, few had the slightest sympathy for deer hunting. Typical of the coverage was the *Bristol Evening Post* that gave over its front page under the banner headline "HUNT SABOTEURS SET UP SMOKE SCREENS". To the graphic description of deer escaping under cover of dense red smoke were added tales that the saboteurs "would have been using a helicopter as a spotter had it not been for a raging blizzard which hit Exmoor today".

The *West Somerset Free Press* was equally colourful telling how

> "On Saturday morning, after a briefing session in a Dulverton café, the saboteurs, young men and girls, mostly wearing jeans and anoraks, drove to the meet, but did not attempt any diversions. Soon the 'field operation' was in full swing. Thunder flashes roared-one saboteur let one off in a tree as the Master passed the bottom of Eastwater – and there were intermittent counter-blasts on an alien hunting horn. When the hunted deer came round the bottom of Cloutsham with a lone hound in pursuit, the saboteurs were galvanised into feverish activity. One youth ran after the hound shouting, while another lit two flares that belched a billowing cloud of pink smoke. By the time the smokescreen had built up to its full strength both the stag and the lone hound had disappeared. But the 20 or so saboteurs were not to be deterred and some time later desultory bangs could be heard down in the Horner Valley."

A few weeks later another strike was made against the DSSH at Comers Gate. Attempts to flush the harboured stag had to be abandoned due to thick fog, which brought visibility down to around fifty yards. This also beat the hunt, which was called off. In the early morning murk a curious meeting then took place between a group of the saboteurs and the DSSH Joint Master Bob Nancekivell who agreed to take part in a public debate on stag hunting. Interviewed by the *Western Morning News* he said: "If it is to be a debate I shall ask my Joint Master, Major Nigel Hambro, to go – provided there is no rough house. We must conduct this on reasonable and proper lines." He then continued:

> "I shook hands with the saboteurs and I told them they would always be welcome at the meet. I agreed that they had a right to think as they did – provided they acknowledged my right to

think as I wished. The saboteurs seemed to be quite reasonable chaps. I think they want something to do to let off steam. My personal view is that they could not have behaved better."

This meeting would prove to be the precursor of a strange kind of chivalry between saboteur and huntsman, whereby each side would tolerate the presence of the other without recourse to violence, which lasted until Nancekivell's retirement as Master in 1974.

With fox and deer hunting at a close for the summer, Brixham HQ decided that the North Devon-based Culmstock Otterhounds would now become the focused target. On 2nd May nine saboteurs who attended a meet at Colyford were viciously attacked. Their vehicle was surrounded, windows smashed, tyres slashed and the occupants assaulted with otter poles and whips. Leo Lewis, the driver, was pulled from his car and beaten by four men who broke his jaw. Although seventy saboteurs turned out against the Culmstock a few weeks later in retaliation, routing the hunt, the damage inflicted by the subsequent court hearing would be far reaching.

On 29th September, at Axminster Court, hunt whipper-in Trevor Glasper "was fined £10 for assaulting Lewis and causing him actual bodily harm". Three other members of the hunt "were each fined £3 for common assault". The seven saboteurs also in court "were bound over for 12 months in the sum of £50 each" after being found guilty of "disturbing the peace". Even though a defence lawyer had been procured for the saboteurs by the LACS's Raymond Rowley, the prosecutor Lewis McCreery gave the game away when he told the court that: "These seven people are brought before you to try to ensure that there will be no similar occurrences." He was in fact giving notice that the full force of the legal system would be brought to bear against anyone who attempted to interfere with legitimate blood sports. It worked (binding over was treated far more seriously back in 1964 than it is today), taking the aggrieved seven (who included Leo Lewis and John Prestidge) so much by surprise that none of them ever took any further part in hunt sabotage.

The remainder of 1964 would see wild press stories such as that by the *Daily Express's* William Hickey which told how "hunt saboteurs, who have so far used aniseed, trails of meat and secret chemicals to distract hounds from their foxes, have devised a new plan. They are going to hire a helicopter, swoop down in front of the fleeing fox and rescue it in a net." Even the *Sunday Telegraph's* columnist Mandrake entered into the spirit of the occasion with a competition, offering a winning prize of £10 "for the best imaginary comment...on the hunt saboteurs from Jorrocks", that quintessential huntsman from the fertile pen of Surtees. The prize went to a Yorkshireman from Northallerton "for the marvellous Olympian incredulity with which he invests Jorrocks, in the concise comment: 'The HSA! Vot's the cap and vere's the country?'"

In November plans were announced by Prestidge "for a series of 'Commando' raids on fox farms in Oxford, where cubs are reared specially for hunting" which were triggered by a series of articles in the *Daily Mirror* by their newly appointed investigative journalist John Pilger. While Boxing Day meets would "find themselves hampered by chemical sprays, smoke screens, false hunting calls, padlocked gates and unofficial riders deliberately getting in their way" from the 700 saboteurs who would deliver the "biggest-ever blow at hunting". The action sounded good in the newspapers, but little of it transferred to the hunting field. Then early in the New Year John Prestidge resigned as chairman, the official reason given later was that he had "become disillusioned by the politicisation of HSA as a result of 'left wingers' joining the movement". By early 1965, the Brixham HQ had effectively ceased to exist, throwing the HSA, as a national organisation, into a state of chaos.

With no directions coming from HQ the emphasis momentarily shifted to the Surrey and Gloucestershire areas. Living in Gloucestershire, with the Duke of Beaufort's Foxhounds on my doorstep, it seemed logical that for the remaining 1964/65 hunting season the local saboteurs should concentrate their efforts here. No one anticipated the reaction of police and hunt supporters that would follow. On our first attempt we experienced constant threats and intimidation that forced us to call off our protest. On every subsequent occasion we were met with a large police presence that left us in no doubt that, to quote one police office, "you don't play silly buggers with one of the most prominent establishment figures in the country." The next few months would see pressure exerted against my family, with the most petty-minded example being the expulsion of my twelve-year-old sister from the Beaufort estate. Every year the Girl Guides, of which she was a member, would spend a week camping at Badminton. On this occasion an estate worker with a list in his hand was waiting when the party arrived, asking if Jane Pedler was related to the hunt saboteur Ian. When she replied that I was her brother he announced that he was under instructions to escort her from the estate.

Just after Christmas, at a meet held at Didmarton, a member of the hunt rode up to me and without the slightest provocation lashed me across the face with a riding crop, knocking out most of my front teeth. When asking the police about the possibility of criminal charges the reply was that the only concern to a Gloucestershire court would most probably be what damage had my teeth caused to the alleged gentleman's antique riding crop. The final straw, for my mother at least, came a few months later when the postman delivered a somewhat stained, rather soggy, brown paper parcel to our home. When opened, we found it contained the severed head of a fox.

From these early experiences (at the time I was eighteen years old) I learned two things that have held me in good stead for all of my active life as an opponent of blood sports. Firstly, never attempt to take on the establishment without expecting dire consequences to follow in the form of violence or intimidation. Secondly never anticipate redress from the legal system, because it just won't happen, so don't waste your time. My advice to any aspiring hunt saboteur, and the maxim by which I have always operated, is that if you are the recipient of injustice at the hands of these people then deal with it yourself, either at the point of impact, or at some later date.

About the only promising development around this time had been the 1964 October re-election of a Labour government under Harold Wilson that offered the possibility, at least in the foreseeable future, of new anti-hunting legislation. By April 1965 the Gloucestershire group had ceased to exist in all but name as a result of the constant violence, with Ray Sheppard's Bournemouth group suffering the same fate in February after attacks by axe-wielding supporters from the Sparkford Vale Harriers. That same month (10th February 1965) Marcus Lipton (Labour, Brixton) introduced his *Protection of Deer Bill* under the 10 Minute Rule, which was vigorously opposed by the North Devon Liberal Jeremy Thorpe, who based his argument on long quotes from the Scott Henderson Report. The Bill disappeared into the labyrinth of parliamentary procedure, as we all knew it would, but the fact that stag hunting was again an issue in a House of Commons broadly sympathetic to animal welfare was a great morale boost to the battered saboteurs. When a few of us were invited to the Commons the next month to meet with Marcus Lipton, who assured us that he would reintroduce his Bill at the first opportune moment, we came away believing that with MPs like him it would only be a matter of time before we saw the end of deer hunting.

The remainder of that year saw remnants of various West Country groups join forces to make valiant, but often inconclusive, forays against a collection of fox, hare, otter and, increasingly, stag hunts. Our most notable successes were against the Quantock Staghounds, which proved a much easier target then the DSSH, not only because the field was much smaller, the supporters tending to be less troublesome, but mainly because the area hunted over was nowhere near the size of Exmoor. *Note 3.* We also had a couple of saboteurs from Bridgwater, who not only knew the Quantock Hills intimately, but had a stag-hunt-hating uncle who was only too happy to loan us a Land Rover. For a short time it felt like saboteurs heaven. When we felt really adventurous occasional visits would be made to harry the New Forest Buckhounds in Hampshire, or attempt to find the elusive Savernake Staghounds, near Marlborough.

On a personal level I always felt happiest when out against the stag hunts, not that I didn't consider the other blood sports cruel, but because somehow I always found deer hunting "more" cruel. In part this may have derived from my childhood article in the *Daily Mirror.* Maybe it had something to do with the size of the animal, or that I found the natural grace and beauty of deer debased by seeing them harried across country by a pack of hounds. Bob Nancekivell always maintained that it came from too many viewings of *Bambi* as a child. Certainly the few deer kills (as opposed to the fox and hare kills) I witnessed during this time left a lasting impression that would instil in me a hatred of stag hunting far in excess of anything felt for other types of blood sports. It was from this time that the bulk of my energies in the hunting field would be directed towards coercing as many antis as possible to expend their efforts against deer hunting.

Nationally, the situation continued to deteriorate, with most HSA groups buckling under the continuous assaults of courts and "hunt heavies". In an age when shortage of private transport (few young people of saboteur age owned a car) was a serious problem and most people did not possess telephones in their home, the most common form of contact was by letter. This made it very difficult to organise successfully, considering the scattered locations of many remaining saboteurs. The April 1965 Norman Redman affair did not help either. Redman (the first ever saboteur to face arrest) was angered by John Prestidge's insistence that he should take no part in any sabotage activities until the terms of his binding-over had expired. Feeling "disowned" by the movement and "keen to get back at his old friends", Norman Redman accepted an invitation to ride with the Crawley and Horsham Foxhounds. The national press, for whom the HSA was still good copy, rushed to the meet to report him hold forth about "infantile hunt saboteurs". London and Littlehampton groups were able to mount a protest against their former comrade and had the satisfaction of seeing him fall headlong from his horse into a thorn bush. It was an episode the HSA could well have done without. Eager to capitalise on the situation, the BFSS tried to promote Redman as a pro-hunt speaker at numerous public debates, but thankfully he soon lost interest and quietly faded from the scene. ***Note 4***

During these two years, the LACS found themselves in something of a publicity wilderness, having been completely usurped by the saboteurs. For a time Raymond Rowley attempted to portray himself as a one-man HSA, the most amusing example being a double-page spread in the *Sunday Mirror* by James Pettigrew. Under the headline: "A very foxy fellow is Mr. Rowley, the terror of the tally-ho set", it printed six photographs of him in various disguises which he used to fool the hunt. The accompanying article told us that: "Every week, he loads up his eight-year-old battle-scarred Rover saloon with cine-cameras, raw meat and biscuits, bottles of aniseed, a selection of clothing disguises and a make-up kit. From Muswell Hill he drives to sabotage hunts held in counties as far apart as Somerset and Yorkshire."

Later the tack would change to talk of "secret weapons" about to finish off the DSSH. Explaining this miracle device in the *Sunday Mirror* of 25th October 1964 Raymond Rowley was quoted "...it did not need many people to put it into operation. I could almost do it by myself. It's not a false trail and scattering chemicals on the ground is not involved." So good was this device that he was confident that "...we're well on the way to knocking them down for good". Many hours of harmless fun were had by stag hunt saboteurs in idle speculation as to the composition of this creation, with the favoured option being some type of oscillator. Though in the end we decided that Rowley's secret weapon was the HSA!

By the autumn of 1965 the LACS was reverting back to its pre-war publicity spinner, the large public rally. One of the largest held was in the Regal cinema at Minehead on 14th August, when the film *Born to Suffer* was shown to a capacity audience of over four hundred. The actress June Thorburn, who would tragically die in a plane crash two years later, opened the meeting to the jeers and hunting horn calls of massed hunt supporters. Later the rally would nearly end in a free-for-all when DSSH Chairman Sir Bernard Waley-Cohen climbed onto the stage, attempting to hi-jack the proceedings. Fearful that future events could lead to violence, the LACS seriously curtailed their future plans to screen this film in other hunting areas.

The League would now turn away from confrontational rallies and flirtation with hunt sabotage, preferring instead to concentrate on securing for itself a solid image as a campaigning organisation with feet planted firmly in respectable legality. There was also a shift away from deer hunting, with much of its energies now concentrated towards the abolition of hare coursing. Led by the redoubtable Liverpool MP Eric Heffer, there were various attempts to outlaw this blood sport via Private Members' Bills, all of which failed. Though there was a real feeling that eventually the government would take up this measure and force it through as a Government Bill. With this in mind the League promoted many publicity initiatives to increase public awareness, while a heavily disguised Raymond Rowley stalked the coursing fields of Northern England, with camera hidden inside a pair of binoculars, looking for the evidence that would secure abolition.

While the start of 1966 saw the League's star in the ascendancy, the HSA's honeymoon period was definitely over. Hard pushed to raise double figures for an effective strike, the remaining West Country saboteurs turned ever more to undercover methods. We soon learned that the most effective tactic against stag hunting was to "flush" the woods on the evening and early morning prior to the meet, particularly against the QSH. Over the months we became extremely good at this stunt, with the published hunting reports telling of "blank days" and early "home was the order", giving us ever-growing confidence. Mostly these activities were relatively uneventful, although on odd occasions we would clash with hunt pickets or possible deer poachers (we never were sure), and then things could become a tad scary. The most memorable happened in Staple Plantation, near West Quantoxhead when, without warning, we were fired upon. For what seemed an age we back-tracked through the woods, attempting to reach our vehicle, while all the time tree branches and other assorted debris fell around our ears from repeated shotgun blasts. We replied with "rookie bombs" (made by removing the explosive from the string, tying three together and throwing) which made a tremendous noise, but achieved little else in the way of deterrent. Finally, as suddenly as it started, the firing stopped, to be followed by the loudest silence I can ever remember. Never were three young men to make a quicker exit in their lives.

The most active saboteurs at this time were Dave Wetton's London group, who were also shouldering an ever-increasing responsibility for the national organisation of HSA. The previous November A J Prestidge (John's father), who had temporarily taken over as chairman, wrote to both Dave Wetton and myself telling us that "it has been our wish for some time that each group should be completely self governing and self supporting…". He concluded by saying: "In order to help you attain complete independence we have agreed to donate from our fund the sum of £150" that "must be used to further the known aims of the society...". In effect, with the handing over of responsibility to regional group leaders the Association, as a national organisation, had ceased to exist.

From this time, until the major revival in 1972, the bulk of the work to keep the HSA alive as a player in the fight against blood sports was carried out by Dave Wetton. Without his tireless efforts over the next six or seven years, there would be no hunt saboteurs today. Even less would there be an "animal rights" movement, for it is undeniably true that the direct action approach of the HSA in these early years sowed the seeds of the uncompromising militancy that we now take for granted. ***Note 5***

The public debate between DSSH Joint Master Bob Nancekivell and the hunt saboteurs finally took place at Bristol's YMCA Hall in early February 1966. The Labour MP Marcus Lipton had initially agreed to take part, but was forced to cry off due to ill health. Raymond Rowley also pulled out, as by this time relations between our two organisations were beginning to deteriorate. In the end Dave Wetton and myself held our own quite well, with my father acting as "impartial" chairman. Later in the year I would visit Nancekivell's home at Cloud Farm, deep in the heart of the Doone Valley (feeling very much like Johnathan Harker entering Castle Dracula for the first time), followed by a rain-soaked day as a guest of the hunt. This was in response to an invitation "to see the sport from the other side", which achieved little other than to allow me to keep a promise made to Nancekivell during our public debate.

This ambiguous relationship that developed between Bob Nancekivell and myself, for it was certainly never a friendship, was a constant bone of contention among many of my saboteur contemporaries. In truth, I suppose that the man fascinated me, for in an age when most stag hunt officials were supercilious, colourless and mediocre, he appeared a larger-than-life character standing head and shoulders above the rest. Undoubtedly a first-rate self-publicist who, in his own mind, could justify any act of cruelty to wild deer that would leave most people aghast, it was nevertheless impossible to dislike the man on a personal level. Whatever may have lurked behind the public façade, on the surface he was always open-handed, gregarious and ready to debate the issues at length over a drink. It is certainly true that I learnt more about the intricacies of stag hunting from him than could be picked-up from a dozen books.

With little action coming from the hunt saboteurs (night raids to flush out the harboured deer does not make good copy), the press continued to front-page a catalogue of stag hunt "incidents" such as the stag shot in a factory after being chased through the streets of Barnstaple by the DSSH. A week later the same hunt found itself attacked by angry holidaymakers after killing a stag in Porlock's main street. A few months later the *Western Daily Press* reported an "exhausted stag finally took to the river pursued by the pack of hounds and as it tried to defend itself from the snarling dogs, it lashed out with its large antlers, killing one hound and injuring two more." The joint master of the QSH, Godfrey Peter Roffe-Silvester, was fined £10, with £21 costs, by a magistrates court in Minehead for killing a stag at bay on land owned by the National Trust, which in turn was rented out to well-known Holford village anti, Lionel Mantle. In his defence Roffe-Silvester claimed he "had a reasonable excuse to be on the land because he was engaged on a humanitarian purpose".

When a three-year-old pregnant hind was chased nearly ten miles, killed and the unborn fawn pulled from her stomach by huntsmen, Bob Nancekivell, replying to questions from the *Western Daily Press,* stated, "I didn't see if the deer was pregnant, but it wouldn't surprise me if it was. They are bound to be pregnant at this time of year, but the unborn fawn...would have been very small." The LACS, responding to these seemingly endless press reports, and no doubt as frustrated as the HSA at their inability to stem the tide, resorted to yet another "secret weapon". This time Raymond Rowley would claim that "a team of animal lovers are to be trained to snatch trapped deer from the huntsman's gun. They will have special equipment, including a Landrover and a winch, to rescue animals cornered at the bottom of a cliff or quarry. An ambulance will stand by to take the exhausted deer to their sanctuary at Baronsdown, near Dulverton... ." On the political front Marcus Lipton kept his word with the introduction on 14th May 1968 of another 10 Minute Rule *Stag-Hunting with hounds (Abolition) Bill.* After an attempt by BFSS boss Marcus Kimball to "object" the Bill disappeared as usual.

The following month, on 26th June, uproar broke out during the RSPCA's AGM when the annual report was rejected, for the first time in the society's history, by 448 votes to 197. The large pro-blood sport membership, objecting to the society's revised policy on hunting, which stated that the RSPCA "is opposed to all hunting for sport of foxes, deer, hares and otters...", voted down the report. Within weeks a vicious internal battle was raging between pro and anti-hunting factions that would tear the RSPCA apart for years to come. Among the many casualties forced to resign over the coming months would be Lady Brook-Popham who found herself seriously compromised by the policy change due to her duel commitments as Vice-President of the South Somerset branch of the RSPCA, and Chairman of the Quantock Staghounds.

Unbeknown to many of us at the time this conflict was the first real challenge to the perceived status quo within the animal welfare movement. The reality was that most activists well knew that the RSPCA and LACS, while being the leading exponents in their field and extremely wealthy, were both equally useless from a direct action perspective due to the ruling committees that controlled their policy. The RSPCA was, up to 1968, directly influenced by BFSS interests maintained by grass roots pressure from large numbers of pro-hunt supporters who had been encouraged to join the Society for that very reason. Whereas the League had gradually distanced itself from any pro-active stance to the point where policy was dictated more or less at the discretion of Raymond Rowley, with the committee acting merely to "rubber stamp" his decisions. The revolt of anti-blood sport activity at the June 1968 RSPCA AGM would set in motion a process that would ultimately see militants take control of all the leading animal welfare organisations. In the years to follow a new breed would rise to the surface, activists such as Richard Ryder, John Bryant and Richard Course, who had joined HSA only to find that their talents were better suited to battling blood sports in the committee rooms with "points of order" rather than in the field with anti-mate and smoke bombs. This process would also sound the death knell of "animal welfare", for from now on the "animal rights movement" was coming of age.

For those of us in the field, who still saw success in less grandiose terms than "regime change", there was a gratifying little Christmas present on which to close 1968. On 20th December, at Minehead Magistrates Court, Bob Nancekivell was fined £5, with £15 costs, for the "technical assault" of twenty-one year-old anti-hunt protestor Ann Sizer during a kill earlier in the year. He was also suspended from his position as Chairman of Lynton Magistrates for one year. It seemed for a moment that maybe, just maybe, there was some small measure of justice after all.

Note 1. There has long been confusion as to which date actually constitutes the first "official" HSA action, with the passing of well over forty years adding to the mythology of the event. While the April 1964 HSA *News Bulletin* states 10th January as the first time, it is certainly true that John Prestidge and a small group of saboteurs attempted to disrupt the same hunt, the South Devon Foxhounds, on Boxing Day 1963. Of that day John Prestidge would remember: "We did so well that they cancelled the hunt. The local butcher gave us fifty pounds of meat and we fed it to the hounds. We used hunting horns. Nothing like it had ever really happened before and it caused absolute chaos!"

The Boxing Day sabotage was something of a dry-run, with Prestidge, according to later reports in the *Guardian,* having only "picked the first of his supporters" the previous 15th December 1963. At this date the HSA did not have a distinct identity of its own, with the press still reporting the activities "of hunt saboteurs from the League Against Cruel Sports". The waters were further muddied with the LACS Chairman Raymond Rowley reported as taking "one hundred activists on a 'dawn attack' with 'secret chemicals' against the Old Berkeley Foxhounds Boxing Day meet at Amersham, in Buckinghamshire".

It was certainly the case at this time that the LACS not only flirted with direct action tactics, but publicly promoted the concept as well. In fact as late as 1966 Rowley was merely "expressing his 'regret' at the HSA's 'independent' development from the League".

So while John Prestidge may have led his first hunt saboteurs into action on Boxing Day 1963, the bounds of probability are that the first time they were "officially" in action as the Hunt Saboteurs Association was the 10th January 1964.

Note 2. It is hard now to comprehend the impact that the formation of HSA, with its concept of non-violent direct action, had on a society that had been structured to respect authority on all levels. With the exception of the Campaign for Nuclear Disarmament (CND) that sprang up in the 1950s most protest was of a passive and genteel nature (euphemistically known as "civil disobedience"), so the radicalism of the hunt saboteurs that advocated "in your face" physical confrontation was seen in some quarters as quite shocking.

An amusing example being my dear old granny, for whom I could do no wrong, who would send me to Coventry for weeks after catching sight of my throwing a smoke bomb in the general direction of the local aristocracy on the evening news. Even though she came from a solidly Labour background, married to a trade union activist who had been arrested during the 1926 General Strike, it was still considered not the done thing to assault "your betters". For her it was still very much a time of "knowing your place".

It is certainly true that the direct action tactics that are now so much a part of political and social protest today had their beginnings with the birth of animal rights in 1963. The uncompromising militancy of such groups as ALF and Stop Huntingdon Animal Cruelty (SHAC) can be directly traced back to the days of the first hunt saboteurs. For it soon became evident to those of us in the front-line back in the early 1960s that the forces of law and order had no intention of acting even-handedly, preferring instead to adopt Draconian measures in the hope of breaking our spirit. Much the same approach was evident from governments of all political persuasions with weasel words and false promises covering up the reality that they would not, or could not, confront the many cruelties perpetrated by the more influential elements in society who derived their pleasures from killing for fun. It was but a small step to take the fight from just blood sports and encompass all types of animal abuse, be it vivisection, factory farming, commercial sealing and whaling, the fur trade and a hundred other atrocities against our fellow travellers on this sad little planet.

So with the passage of over forty years the end result has been that politicians, and the concept of humane political change are now viewed by many activists with contempt, forcing ever-increasing numbers to campaign outside the law under the adage "never mind what's legal, do what's right".

Note 3. During this period, when Bob Nancekivell was Master of the DSSH, there was seldom any violence. The problem for the saboteurs was that the hunt supporters were constantly in attendance, ostensibly wanting to engage in conversation and explain the finer points of their sport, but in reality making sure we didn't disrupt it.

Note 4. In 1965 this author drafted an HSA "Manifesto" (back then a "must have" item for any self-respecting aspiring radical group) which contained a statement that has come back to haunt me many times thanks to numerous re-printings in the HSA magazine *HOWL*. After a brief history of the preceding two years of the saboteurs I made the statement that: "There have been many incidents – too many to name here. But some day, when we have won, someone will write a book telling of all that has happened."

Little did I think at the time that I might be that "someone". For while no stretch of the imagination can term this book a definitive history of the HSA, it is certainly the first to give the Association its rightful place in the story of blood sport abolition. The full story has yet to be written, so come on, Dave!

Note 5. Dave Wetton would continue to be one of the leading hunt saboteurs and animal rights activists for many years to come. After the 1972 revival he would become Secretary of the HSA, then later an EC Member of the LACS until the mid-1980s. Like many animal rights campaigners he was also heavily into "human rights", involved in such issues as genocide in the former Yugoslavia, abuses in Indonesia, or the brutal Chinese occupation of Tibet. It was as the result of a one-man protest against China's President Jiang Zemin during his state visit in October 1999 that cost Dave Wetton his job. Working as a quantity surveyor on London underground's Jubilee Line Extension he took the chance during a lunch break to run in front of the president's cavalcade shouting "Free Tibet, Free Tibet". For this he was at first suspended, then dismissed, by his employers.

Chapter Six

"a bunch of yobs and unwashed squatter types"

THE NEW YEAR OF 1969 got under way with yet another pregnant hind killed by the DSSH after being chased for over three hours, followed by the standard defence from Bob Nancekivell that "most hinds are pregnant at this time of year, but you cannot tell from the outside if they are or not". The Quantock Staghounds acquired a new Master in the form of consultant physician's wife Ruth Thrower, who confided to *Western Daily Press* columnist Helen Reid that, "Perhaps I shouldn't say this, but sometimes I'm secretly pleased when the stag gets away." In the House of Commons Marcus Lipton pressed the Attorney-General, Sir Elwyn Jones, to remove Bob Nancekivell from the list of magistrates following his conviction for assault on Ann Sizer. In reply he was told that "the Lord Chancellor took the view that after the dust had settled, Mr. Nancekivell, who had served well as a magistrate for twenty years, should continue to act as a JP..." though he would remain suspended for twelve months. "Is not this an unusual procedure?" responded the caustic Lipton. "If a man is not fit to serve as a JP for twelve months, what is going to happen in that time which will make him fit after twelve months?" Another parliamentary stunt was pulled on 17th June when, undercover of most "sporting" Tories absent from the Commons attending Royal Ascot, Ben Whitaker (Lab: Hampstead) introduced *The Protection of Animals Bill,* which was intended to bring all hunted animals in line with the *1911 Act.* Admitting to the *Sun* that this Bill had little chance of becoming law

Whitaker added that his main hope was that "it may be used as a model for future Government legislation".

The LACS began the serious acquisition of land across Exmoor with the purchase of the seventeen-acre Whitley Meadows near Barnstaple in August, followed by the purchase of thirty-six-acre St Nicholas Priory Estate, near Dulverton, the next month. In the summer of 1970 two more were acquired, Brook Wood and Hakeford, adding another ninety acres of hunt free land to the tally. By the end of 1973 the number of sanctuaries had risen to thirteen, increasing to twenty-five by 1976. When the League ended the sanctuary buying policy in the early 1990s the final count would be thirty-five, comprising a total holding in excess of 2,500 acres, making it one of the largest private landowners in the West Country.

As the acreage increased, so the problem of trespass became more acute for the DSSH. For while it is relatively easy for a hunt to avoid a small isolated piece of land, it becomes extremely difficult when there are numerous small pieces all congregated in roughly the same place. The Exmoor hunts proclaimed publicly that these sanctuaries were of little consequence, but privately admitted to their constant nuisance value. They did not relish the ever-present threat of publicity from repeated trespass action brought by the League, nor the fact that so many hunts had to be aborted when deer entered a sanctuary. Needless to say the idea caught the imagination of the ordinary rank and file membership, with much of the financial stability enjoyed by the League during these years directly attributable to Raymond Rowley's deer sanctuaries initiative.

The HSA continued to survive thanks to Dave Wetton, who found new members by placing small adverts in *Private Eye, The Vegetarian* and *New Musical Express*. The lack of central co-ordination led to the formation of splinter groups around the country such as Direct Action Against Bloodsports, and the Dorset-based Campaign for the Relief of Wildlife (CROW). The RSPCA AGM on 25th June 1969 again ended in uproar with allegations that the Society's council had entered into secret negotiations with the BFSS to replace the existing Chairman Lt Col John Lockwood, with the allegedly pro-hunt Bath businessman John Hobhouse. In turn, Hobhouse threatened to sue

Raymond Rowley over the allegations, which later turned out to be true when an RSPCA spokesman admitted "that talks had been going on with the BFSS" but they "were not clandestine...and they were not yet really under way". What this meeting did achieve was to consolidate the thinking of a number of ordinary members who now believed that in its present state the RSPCA was beyond salvation, and that the only remedy was radical reform from within.

The long awaited political breakthrough arrived on 26th November 1969 when Arnold Shaw (Labour: Ilford) secured the First Reading of his *Deer Hunting and Hare Coursing (Abolition) Bill.* The introduction of this Bill had been in direct response to massive publicity generated by a number of emotional letters published in the national press from a reformed former stag hunter. On 5th November *The Times* gave centre stage on its letters page to Richard O Hall who, drawing on many years' personal experience on the hunting field, told how

> "on one occasion a stag's right eye was shot out and it hung down its face; it turned away and trotted down the road to a stream, crying as it went. The pack of hounds were uncontrollable and got past the hunt servants and boiled over the stag ravaging it all the time until whipped-off and a second shot killed it."

He continued by explaining that:

> "In late February a hind will be carrying a small perfectly formed live calf. After chasing a pregnant hind all day, until it can no longer run any farther, it ultimately gets killed. It is then cut open and the entrails are taken out together with the live calf still concealed in the uterus and now covered with the intestines. This sorry heap is fed to the hounds."

The editorial, under the headline "Outdated: Objectionable", gave *The Times'* judgement that: "Deer hunting...with all that it involves, is clearly an affront to British taste today."

The following day *The Times* gave equally prominent space to a reply from DSSH Chairman Sir Bernard Waley-Cohen who thought "it is high time that some of the heat was taken out of the subject of field sports generally and staghunting in particular, and the subject considered unemotionally and dispassionately". He then launched into a spirited defence of his sport based primarily on a reiteration of the findings of the 1951 Scott Henderson Report. The *Daily Mirror* meanwhile had taken the unprecedented step of giving over the whole of its front page to a reprinting of Richard Hall's letter under the heading: "Remorse of a stag hunter". The following day, 7th November, the *Daily Mirror* again devoted its entire front page to the issue, explaining how Labour MP Arnold Shaw, on drawing tenth place in the Commons ballot for priority to introduce private members' measures had decided to use his option on deer hunting after reading Richard Hall's letter.

On Friday 13th December 1969, when Arnold Shaw's Bill was scheduled for a Second Reading, due to one of the most blatant acts of filibustering ever seen in the House of Commons it failed to reach debate. The previous Bill, John Temple's *Conservation of Seals Bill,* was used by pro-blood sport Tory MPs to prolong pointless debate on an uncontroversial issue in an attempt to deny time to discuss the stag hunt measure. When a vote was taken the *Seals Bill* was passed by 105 votes to 5, with two of the opponents being the BFSS's Jasper More and Marcus Kimball. Kimball's next act was to shout "Object" when the Speaker called Shaw's Bill, thus ending any chance for debate. The outcry from angry Labour back-benchers was predictable, with Ian Mikardo going so far as to threaten that these same tactics would be used against any Tory-sponsored Private Members Bill for the rest of the session. The next few months would see a major campaign launched to persuade the Labour government to grant time for a full debate and a free vote. The LACS commissioned a Gallup Poll that found sixty-five per cent questioned wanted stag hunting abolished, with sixty per cent in favour of ending hare coursing. The League also led a march of over 1,000 to Downing Street, handing in a letter asking Harold Wilson to persuade the Cabinet to make time available for Arnold Shaw's Bill. By the end of February inside sources were dropping broad hints that the government intended to introduce its own Bill along similar lines to Shaw's.

In the West Country, panicked by the growing momentum against their sport, the three packs of staghounds called a combined meet at the Quantock village of Crowcombe. On 10th March 1970 some 300 riders, including Master of the New Forest Buckhounds Don Egremont, supported by over 2,000 foot-followers and spectators, gathered to hear Sir Bernard Waley-Cohen preach to the converted. Shouting through a microphone he informed the crowd: "These people," referring to the antis, "seek to make out that this whole neighbourhood consists of a mob of uncivilised barbarians. But we give unanswerable evidence today of the sort of people we are – country folk, animal lovers in practice and not just in theory, and people of strong principles." Later, when asked by *Somerset County Gazette* reporter Peter Hesp if he was surprised that there had been no counter-demonstration by hunt saboteurs Waley-Cohen replied: "Not in the least. They know very well what happens to them down here. They know that if they come and try to make a nuisance of themselves by one of those indecent and undesirable hullabaloos, very short shrift will be given them." In fact a few saboteurs were at the meet, having spent the early morning hours attempting to flush the woods, but unfortunately after a short two-hour hunt they managed to kill a young stag.

A few weeks later, on 19th March, the government announced that it intended to introduce a Bill to abolish hare coursing. The "official" reason given for dropping deer hunting was that "ministers take the view that the barbarity of hare coursing is made worse by the betting on dogs taking part, making the sport akin to bear-baiting and cockfighting". Vague promises were made that a Bill to abolish deer hunting would follow at some later date, but few MPs were convinced. Obviously the Crowcombe meet, having failed to impress the antis had certainly frightened Harold Wilson, as a gloating Sir Bernard Waley-Cohen explained to the DSSH AGM in July. Addressing the Exford gathering he told them, "I am informed by my friends at Westminster that this great manifestation of support for stag hunting impressed the government, and made them think long and hard before giving time to any Bill designed to interfere with our sport." John Ellis, Labour MP for Bristol North-West, put a brave face on his disappointment by declaring his intention to introduce another deer hunting bill as soon as possible, but in the end it all became academic. The *Hare Coursing Bill*, debated on 15th May 1970, with a majority of 133, failed to make it to the Statute Book due to the calling of a General Election. Subsequent attempts to abolish coursing between 1970-79 (and there were many) all failed as a result of fanatical opposition from BFSS-supporting Tories, while the election of Margaret Thatcher saw the end of any realistic possibility for reformist animal legislation.

The 1970 RSPCA AGM again ended in scuffles following attempts to evict LACS member Vera Sheppard after she announced from the platform that the election of John Hobhouse as Chairman "marks the end of a 10-years campaign for the control of the association for the interests of bloodsportsmen". In the weeks following a splinter group of disaffected members would meet to form the RSPCA Reform Group which, under its Chairman John Bryant, would wage an internal battle in the years ahead to reverse BFSS control of the Society.

In contrast to the RSPCA, the fortunes of the HSA were on the turn. Increased membership over the past few years, thanks to the continued dogged determination of Dave Wetton, had enabled the disruption of ever more hunts around the country. July 1971 would see the first recorded AGM held in London, with an attendance of twenty-five, during which the core of the HSA's constitution (according to legend initially written on the back of a cigarette packet) was approved. The first real breakthrough came on 3rd July the following year when the *Guardian* journalist Jill Tweedie wrote a long sympathetic article on the hunt saboteurs after accompanying them on an otter hunt. ***Note 1***

In the months that followed the Association's membership would rise to over 1,000, and the end of 1972 would see seventeen active groups, with fifty-eight "potential" groups of two or more people. Three years later, 22nd November 1975, an even better recruiting ground arrived in the form of a BBC TV access programme called *Open Door*. This twenty-minute long show, which enabled pressure groups to present their case on national television, would prove to be the major turning point in the Association's history. Fronted by the three hunt saboteur veterans Sue Hough, Dave Wetton and Iain McNay, such was the impact of this programme that within days over 3,000 viewers responded, of which most later joined up, turning the HSA into a force to be reckoned with.

If proof were needed as to the impact that the HSA would have on the hunting world from this time then no better, or more gratifying, confirmation could have been forthcoming than the compliment published in the 1978-79 edition of the blood sport bible *Baily's Hunting Directory*. Writing in the introduction Douglas Leslie would say:

> "I feel bound to mention for yet another year, the undesirable activities of the self-styled 'Hunt Saboteurs', who still persist in defiling the countryside wherein we enjoy our sport. Their record throughout the year has been quite deplorable, and although many of them are now living behind prison bars at the rate payer's expense, their very presence at a meet is sufficient to ruin a day in the minds of many who love the country for what it is."

Not only had the fortunes changed, so had the tactics. The increasing number of new recruits, some proving to be first-rate saboteurs, now enabled the HSA to concentrate on specific issues. The first, which would turn out to be one of its most successful campaigns, was the sabotage of the annual common seal cull in the Wash during the summer of 1973. Hunt saboteurs, co-ordinated by Northampton group leader Rorke Garfield, under the umbrella Save Our Seals Campaign, placed themselves between the seals and the hunters' guns for over two weeks. The excellent press coverage and overwhelming support received from the general public forced an early end to the killing. The following year, just a few days before the cull was due to start again, the Home Secretary, Roy Jenkins, announced that hunting licenses would not be issued that year. No reasons were forthcoming but the HSA believed that public support for its actions the previous year played a large part in the decision.

It was the success of the seals' campaign, coupled with some "friendly" persuasion from Rorke Garfield while sat on a Lincolnshire sandbank waiting for the seal killers to arrive, that prompted this author to follow through on an idea that had been a long-running ambition: to set up a splinter group within HSA that would concentrate solely on the issue of deer hunting. For while it was true that this was the most disliked of blood sports, by both press and public alike, it was also the least understood, and certainly the one which received the smallest share of attention publicity-wise. The reasons for this were obvious in that with only four deer hunts in the country (the Savernake Buckhounds had disbanded in 1965) and some 200 fox hunts nation-wide the press tended to concentrate on the bigger picture. The only exception being the photographs of stag hunting taken by the LACS's Raymond Rowley that always commanded front-page coverage, although they were few and far between. There was also the problem that hunt saboteurs would concentrate on local targets in preference to travelling across country in an attempt to disrupt a form of hunting of which they understood little, conducted over terrain that appeared daunting to say the least, and carried out by people who were believed to be extremely violent. What was needed was a group with a remit to operate full-time against stag hunting that could co-ordinate direct action with other national groups, coupled with polite pressure to encourage the national press into giving the subject substantial and in-depth coverage.

The experience gained against stag hunting over the previous seasons had given the local saboteurs extensive knowledge of not only the best disruptive tactics, but also the Exmoor and Quantock country. While most actions still centred around attempts to rouse the harboured stag the night before a hunt, increased numbers had enabled the disruption of more hind hunts. Occasionally, when numbers did not permit open confrontation, we perfected a form of hit-and-run that drove them to distraction. Central was the use of "marine distress flares" (smoke bombs) which, after reconnoitring the meet, would be released at the most appropriate spot. There was no question that this in any way helped to save the life of a hunted deer, but was merely to "show the flag", to let them know we were around, and with red, yellow or white smoke spewing forth in every direction to make a serious dent in the huntsman's dignity.

Having registered our protest, we would depart with all speed, although one Boxing Day things didn't go to plan. Having driven through the QSH meet at Crowcombe in an old van, driven by my late friend Sue Smith, which had a sliding panel rigged in the floor through which we poured our "Sab Special", followed by three smoke bombs, we made a hasty exit. We later pulled the same stunt at a foxhunt a few miles away. With bravado now the better part of valour it was decided to try for a third. This time (it was a beagle pack) a couple of the local red coats decided to exchange hare for hunt saboteur. A most exciting car chase ensued, which at times reached speeds of seventy to eighty miles around the country lanes. With Sue at the wheel, driving like a demented banshee, I busied myself lobbing smoke and rookie bombs from the back of the van, none of which dented our pursuers' enthusiasm, tending in fact to increase their desire to "account" for us all the more, and we only managed to lose them in the back streets of Yeovil nearly an hour later. To this day I remember the enthusiasm with which they tried to catch us and often wonder who they were. Of such memorable runs are sporting memories made!

The HSA was extremely positive about the stag hunt project, with the promise of all possible help from their end, including the use of the Association's magazine (which had seen its first issue that summer of 1973) *HOWL (Hounds off Our Wildlife)* to promote the campaign once it got underway. A number of meetings were held with saboteur groups throughout the West Country, with an inaugural meeting in Crewkerne to elect a committee, and finalise plans for the launching of what we had decided to call the Save Our Stags Campaign. ***Note 2***

At the time we had no way of knowing that SOS would achieve something of a "cult status" among the animal rights movement, with the offers of assistance quite often outweighing our ability to co-ordinate them. Over the next fourteen years there would be hundreds of official, and unofficial, actions taken by antis against the stag hunters, ranging from mass saboteur strikes to individual acts of sabotage against hunt-related property and vehicles. At times the SOS committee became very concerned about the levels of "commercial damage" taking place, actions that we never condoned, although we somehow felt responsible.

Television always found our actions rather photogenic, giving the demonstrations extensive news coverage, followed by a number of in-depth documentaries on deer hunting. All this tended to give us a sense of localised, small-time celebrity status, which was all very well until the next time you arrived at a meet to be greeted by a small herd of very angry hunt supporters racing in your direction, led by one built after the fashion of a rather large brick toilet shouting, "Get that lanky sod in front, he's the one who started all this!"

The press also entered into the spirit of things with a constant stream of excellent copy front-lining the stag hunting issue. In fact the *Sunday Mirror* (11th March 1973) complimented the launching of SOS with a front and centre page spread headlined "DEER HUNT HORROR" by staff reporter Peter Seeds, detailing the killing of a stag in the village of Williton after a twelve-mile chase across the Quantock Hills. Local newspapers could be relied upon to cover specific incidents in depth, whereas the national press tended to go for more sensational coverage, often sending some of their best journalists to spend the weekend with us on all-expenses-paid jaunts, during which Exmoor's hoteliers must have made a fortune. The tabloids were evenly split on how they wanted to cover the issue, some wanting the Boy's Own derring-do hunt saboteur angle, while others preferred the shock, horror, stag hunting in all its gory detail version.

We always tried to accommodate all tastes, with two outstanding examples of the genre being a full-page 1975 *Daily Mirror* article by veteran journalist Donald Gomery under the headline "The stag that got away" that gave gung-ho tales of mid-night rookie raids, throwaway comments that likened hunt sabotage to a "giant game of chess", and every cliché in the book. By contrast the *Daily Star* centre spread article of 9th October 1979, under the banner "BARBARIC: Children watch an animal being butchered – all in the name of sport" was accompanied by some of the most graphic photographs, taken by Douglas Doig, to appear in the popular press before or since. These photographs, illustrating the involvement of very young children during the disembowelling of a stag at the end of a hunt, are still used today as examples of perceived blood sport callousness. Of the two types of story SOS always preferred to work on articles that exposed the practice of deer hunting, rather than the glorification of the people who opposed it. While it was momentarily gratifying to the ego to see your actions portrayed in heroic fashion it was a distraction from the real issues that the campaign had been founded to propound, not to mention leaving us wide open to accusations of "glory hunting". It was also considerably easier to arrange for one or two SOS operatives to escort a journalist around the moors for the day, acting as guide and interpreter, than to attempt a large-scale sabotage at short notice.

The minus side to all this frenetic SOS activity was that many West Country saboteurs tended to lose sight of the bigger picture. For on a national level, mindful of the fact that the main political thrust throughout the mid-1970s was the abolition of hare coursing, the HSA tended to direct much of its major activities towards this particular blood sport. Coursing events up and down the country were frequent targets for large-scale sabotage strikes, with the Waterloo Cup (the major coursing event of the year) given particular attention. The pitched battles fought out across the Sefton Estate during this three-day event in February between the saboteurs and mass ranks of the National Coursing Club, aided by the mounted division of the Liverpool police, became an annual media event. It was something of an in-joke during this time that the only time the HSA got together as an organisation was for weddings, court cases and the Waterloo Cup.

This period also saw the widening split between animal rights militants and the more traditionalist elements of animal welfare become ever more bitter. For while the internal battle for the soul of the RSPCA continued, the battleground had now spread to the LACS. The failure of legislative attempts against hare coursing, coupled with increasing disquiet felt by many of the membership towards Raymond Rowley's autocratic style, particularly the continued purchase of deer sanctuaries in preference to political donations, which some thought was a defeatist step, forced a leadership challenge at the May 1977 AGM. For the first time in fourteen years Rowley found his control of the League threatened when former Miss Australia, Jan Rennison, attempted to force the issue to a vote. The meeting ended in uproar with Rowley screaming that his opponents were "a bunch of yobs and unwashed squatter types" and Rennison retorting that he was nothing but "a little dictator".

An EGM was held in November, when the issue again remained unresolved, though both candidates agreed to withdraw until a compromise could be found that was acceptable to both parties. In order to resolve the crisis Lord Soper, the League's President, was able to persuade Lord Houghton, the seventy-nine year old ex-Chairman of the Parliamentary Labour Party, to stand as an alternative to Rowley, while Jan Rennison agreed to withdraw her candidacy. Houghton was elected unopposed at the reconvened AGM in December, then re-elected at the 1978 AGM. Raymond Rowley was placated with the specially created non-Executive Committee post of Sanctuaries Consultant.

While the League was tearing itself apart internally SOS found itself embroiled in a controversy that very nearly branded it as "a racist organisation". In May 1977 it was announced by the Somerset-based travel firm Our World Travel that they had concluded a deal with the German travel firm Pegasus to offer £400 a week package holidays to hunt the Exmoor red deer. The scheme raised a storm of protest, with SOS leading the opposition with threats of massive disruption, which were countered by stag hunt supporters claiming that our reaction was based more on anti-German sentiment than animal welfare.

Stories that "singing saboteurs" would follow the Germans with a rendition of Deutschland uber Exmoor, some dressed in SS or Wehrmacht uniforms, complete with swastika armbands, began to gain credence. While still wilder stories that the LACS were buying a fleet of Land Rovers to specifically disrupt the German hunters drew swift condemnation, not only of the package holiday plan generally, but the SOS saboteurs actions specifically, from Raymond Rowley. In fact the League had always been a little edgy on matters concerning blood sports and Germans due to constant reminders from the BFSS to a telegram of congratulations sent to a certain Adolf Hitler following their abolition by the Nazi Party in 1936. The fact that most of these stories were believed in hunting circles, also by the more politically correct animal rightists, only served to make the campaign ever more successful. The letter columns of the local press also began to fill nicely with references such as "if the usual Teutonic thoroughness is applied to stag hunting our own hunters will be left at the post", or suggestions that maybe the Germans should be encouraged to stalk the deer "with flame throwers", adding the realisation that many ordinary West Country residents, not just abolitionists, were totally opposed to this holiday plan.

When reports of the publicity spread back to Germany a re-think was ordered, leading to an announcement in October that the deal was scrapped. In reality, SOS, nor any other anti-hunt group, ever indulged in serious anti-German rhetoric, or threatened to mount any demonstration containing a Nazi-type theme. We merely played along with the hunter's perception that this was what we would do, by simply using the expedient of replying "no comment" to countless press questions on the subject.

Just as the dust was settling over the non-appearance of the German tourists an issue arose concerning the deer sanctuaries that would attempt to question the League's image, both as conservationists and responsible landowners. On 25th January 1978 a letter was sent to Lord Houghton by two Exmoor farmers, Ken Christopher and W J Pugsley, who, writing on behalf of a further twenty-six farmers in the Dulverton area, claimed that "the acquisition by the League of these small areas makes it impossible to control the numbers of deer and foxes in the manner which has been accepted as satisfactory by landowners and farmers for more than 100 years".

They further asserted that "the interruption of this control has resulted in the increase in numbers of deer and foxes to the extent that they now present an intolerable threat to agricultural production and the livelihood of the farming community". Continuing that the "League's responsibility to its neighbours for damage to crops, fences and livestock cannot be shirked by declaring small areas to be sanctuaries" and suggesting "that it must also concern itself in the wider issues of ecology, conservation and efficient land use", the letter concluded with a request to either allow the DSSH to enter League property, or allow the farmers themselves to enter for the purpose of shooting the deer.

At first the League took the letter seriously, stating that they would undertake an independent survey of the area to verify the levels of damage. In early March they employed the services of Professor T H Clutton-Brock, from the Cambridge-based Wildlife Consultants Ltd, who spent a day on Exmoor touring the farms in question. His finished report stated that "deer damage is heavily localised", although many fields "showed little sign of deer presence…". In one particular instance the "deer had been using a larch plantation heavily, had barked a number of trees and had clearly been feeding extensively in the surrounding area", but the report failed to substantiate the claims that sanctuaries had made local farming "intolerable".

The report also contained a number of suggestions for dealing with the problem, the most practical being the formation of a joint committee made up of farmers and League appointees to determine the exact number of deer in the affected area, to agree the size of a sustainable herd and "arrange with the farmers for a specified number of deer to be culled…by a professional hunter using a rifle".

The farmers were happy to sign up for the committee idea, but not until they had seen a copy of the Clutton-Brock report. The problem was that the League, having initially agreed to do so, now adamantly refused to let them see the report. Thus was set in motion a controversy that would rage for over four years, with ever-increasing bitterness on both sides. During these years the local press would fill with acrimonious reports that only served to widen the divide, while the hunting press in general, and the *Shooting Times* in particular, fuelled the row with a constant stream of "deer damage exposé" articles that highlighted the League's alleged intransigence. By the time that the two sides finally met face to face in March 1979, the damage was done and a wonderful opportunity to advance the cause of deer management from the abolitionist standpoint had been thrown away.

The negotiations would drag on for another two years, only to end in stalemate when the League proposed "a two-year survey using independent researchers to advise on the scale…of deer damage in the Dulverton area", during which time they would be willing to "compensate any farmers in the defined area for proven deer damage".

The condition attached to this offer was that all twenty-six signatories of the original letter agree to sign individual legal contracts with the LACS otherwise there was no deal. The farmers claimed that this was nothing short of a face-saving opt-out for the League, who responded that it was a safeguard against hunt related manipulation of the situation. The issue remained unresolved, but would simmer intermittently for years to come.

Note 1. Within a few years of this article otter hunting would be suspended for the very simple reason that the hunts could not find any otters left in the wild to kill. The "official" blood sport version of events was told in the 2004 book *Endangered Species: Foxhunting – the History, the Passion and the Fight for Survival* written by Michael Clayton, a hunting enthusiast and former editor of *Horse & Hound:*

> "Scott Henderson approved otter hunting with reservations, but the sport was to be abandoned voluntarily by otter hunters from an entirely correct sporting perspective: the quarry species was not sustainable; a cull was not appropriate.
>
> "Not due to hunting, but man's toxic pollution of rivers, otters were becoming extinct in England and Wales in the 1960s. Urban pollution poisoned otters; rural use of rivers for chemical sheep dips in some cases made otters infertile. Led by Capt Ronnie Wallace, one of the leading Masters of Otter Hounds (Hawkstone 1946-68) as well as of Foxhounds, the sport of otter hunting with hounds voluntarily closed down, or switched to mink hunting, well before otters were made a protected species in 1978."

The truth is somewhat different. The decline of the otter was noted by naturalists from the 1950s onwards. How did the otter hunting hierarchy react? For a start they carried on hunting and killing otters. From 1958 to 1963 the eleven otter hunt packs in England and Wales, according to their own records, killed 1,065 otters between them.Then their allies in the hunting media denied there was a problem. The following example is an extract from an editorial about otter hunting entitled "Hounds of Summer" in *The Shooting Times and Country Magazine* of 14th May 1964:

> "Nor should the notion be allowed to gain ground that the otter is a

rare creature. It has always had its 'ups and downs' if one may judge by old records, rather in the same way as the partridge, though with longer cycles. In this year of scientific destruction it is possible, almost certain, that some have perished from the poisons that are poured on to the land, but there are still many of its kind."

Similarly the following is taken from an editorial in the *Shooting Times* of 8th September 1966:

"Exaggerated rumours are creeping into the press in respect of the otter. According to a report in the *Daily Telegraph* of 29th August, 'The wild otter may well become extinct in Britain unless resolute action is taken now to protect it from persecution, says the League Against Cruel Sports.' If it is meant to suggest that the few otter hound packs in this country are in any way menacing the otter population of Great Britain, this statement is patently nonsense. But is there, in fact, any worthwhile evidence to suggest any serious decline in the population of an animal which, almost wholly nocturnal in its habits, is probably commoner than is generally supposed? To say that the otter is in danger of extinction is claptrap."

The managing editor of the *Shooting Times* during part of this time (1960-1964) was Leslie Pine. Following a day out with the Courtenay Tracy Otterhounds in Wiltshire, he was presented with the severed head of a dead otter as a trophy for being an honoured guest. It was this act that led Pine to resign from the magazine, change sides and write the blood sport exposé *After Their Blood.*

An attempt was made on 13th May 1968, by MP Edwin Brooks (Labour: Bebington) to introduce a Private Member's Bill to protect the otter, but stalled after a First Reading. This prompted Henry Williamson, author of the classic pro-hunt *Tarka the Otter*, to write in the *Daily Express* the following day:

"And now – what of otters today, and their one-time protectors, the otter hunts? No longer are they patriarchal, that age has gone with the wind of change. Fishing is almost big business. The community must protect otters from fishermen as well as the many other declining old-time protectors, the hunts.

"The law must assume responsibility. No otters should be hunted. No otter shot or trapped. The wildlings of our small island are in desperate need of help by homo sapiens. It is a matter of noblesse oblige – every man to assume a noble responsibility – or annihilation of our inheritance."

A few years on, when it became increasingly obvious that the otter was declining towards extinction it is true that some hunts, who found very few otters anyway, claimed to be only trying to locate otters, not hunt them. But by the mid-1970s there was growing pressure for Parliament to take action on the issue, which prompted the BFFS Chairman, Marcus Kimball, to write on 8th November 1976: "Speaking personally, I would never give up a field sport without using every device to protect and retain it. We expect to have quite a battle on otter hunting in the next session of Parliament and we shall have to play that as best we can..."

The following year, while addressing the Otter Conference held by the Joint Otter Group on 22nd June 1977 Kimball spelt out his intentions: "Let me warn you if any attempt is made to add the otter to the list of protected animals, my friends and I in Parliament will argue every clause in the Bill over and over again and add every other animal and extraneous reforms so that the proposal will eventually be talked out."

Despite all the bluster and threat from the blood sports brigade the otter achieved a degree of protection in 1978 when it was placed on Schedule 1 of the *Conservation of Wild Creatures and Wild Plants Act (1975)* and it became illegal to kill the animal. Significantly, it was not illegal to hunt the otter and this anomaly allowed the alternative summer hound sports of mink hunting and in East Anglia coypu hunting to flourish. The hunts merely changed names and the same people hunted the same rivers from the same meets with the same dogs, but they assured the nation that they were hunting mink or coypu, not otters. Mink hunting did little but spread the species further afield. Coypu hunting disrupted genuine efforts to control this introduced species. Both pastimes further imperilled the otter.

The arrival of the *1981 Wildlife and Countryside Act* should have secured even greater protection for the otter. It became an offence to disturb the known resting or breeding place of an otter, but in practice no one has paid much heed and the summer hunts have been allowed to do more or less as they like for the intervening years.

With thanks to the ANIMAL WELFARE INFORMATION SERVICE for much of the above information.

Note 2. The original committee consisted of Brian Roach, Sue Smith, Marley Jones, Patrick Hirst (who acted as liaison officer with the HSA) and myself. The inclusion of Sue and Marley on the committee would cause a few laughs in the years to come. For when stopped by the police for "acting in a suspicious manner" and asked to identify yourselves try convincing them that you are Smith & Jones!

Chapter Seven

"deer must be made a protected species..."

ALTHOUGH THE BFSS-SPONSORED *1963 Deer Act* had undoubtedly given the deer in England and Wales some measure of protection the passage of thirteen years had shown it to be woefully inadequate in dealing with the massive increase of deer poaching which, in some areas of the country, had reached epidemic proportions by the late 1970s. It was evident to anyone with a serious involvement with deer-related issues that something needed to be done that would redress the issue, for there was seldom a week that went by without a new deer-poaching atrocity making the headlines. The hunting press, in particular the *Shooting Times,* would front-line the issue on a regular basis and for once the stag hunt saboteurs, who often found the butchered remains of the poacher's work scattered around the deeper recesses of the Quantock and Exmoor woodlands, found common cause with their habitual foe.

So derisory were the fines imposed under the *1963 Deer Act* (£20 maximum for a first offence, regardless of the number of deer killed during that offence) compared to the profits to be made from the sale of illegal venison (£65 for a roe buck, rising to £150 for a red deer stag) that vast profits could be made with little fear of legal interference. The methods used by the poachers were designed to ensure speed of operation, with no thought given to the suffering caused to the animals. Snaring, cross bows, dogs and shotguns were the usual tools of the trade. The shotgun tended to cause the maximum suffering because once the poacher had transfixed a number of deer with a powerful light they would be peppered with buckshot, causing maybe a couple to be killed outright, with considerably more to flee wounded, or blinded. It is possible that the more seriously injured would be followed and killed, but the remainder would escape to die of their wounds. During my time in animal rights I had occasion to call in the services of trained marksmen to finish off some twenty deer crippled in this way, with the most pitiful being a young stag that had its complete lower jaw shot away.

Occasionally the appalling scale and cruelty of deer poaching would come to light following the rare instance of an offender being brought to court. When Geoffrey Battams was convicted in August 1974 for killing 180 deer on the Woburn Abbey estate he gave a rare insight into the poachers' methods when he stated "...one day I went to the park and my dog pulled down a buck. I pulled it to the side of the road and cut its throat, but it kicked me so I ran the car over its head to finish it off." He also claimed that "...my dog is able to kill the smaller (deer) but needs some help with the larger ones. I do that by breaking their necks or cutting their throats to stop them squealing." Two years later, in June 1978, the killer of over 200 deer, David Woodhouse, told much the same story when describing a typical night's slaughter.

> "We arrive at the scene about midnight and hang about to see that there's no one around and then we use lamps to show the dogs the deer. Once the dogs have got their teeth into a deer, we have to get there quick and hold its jaws shut to stop it making a noise. Then we break its neck or slit its throat."

At the same time as Woodhouse was boasting of his prowess in killing deer, the callous nature of deer poaching was brought home to the general public in an emotive story that would turn an orphaned roe deer into a national icon. Journalist Alan Gordon, writing in the *Daily Mirror* on 31st May 1978, told how:

> "A baby deer named Bambi was safe and well...a living example of man's cruelty—and his kindness. Bambi's mother was near to giving birth when she was spotted by poachers. They strung

piano wire between two trees, then mercilessly drove her into the deadly trap at speed. The terrified deer slammed into the wire and received a massive cut round her neck. But she untangled herself and plunged on pouring blood...driven on by the thought of her approaching baby. Somehow she managed to shake off the poachers who haunt the woods at Cranbourne, Dorset. Then she dropped exhausted in a glade. And there Bambi was born. With her last ounce of strength the deer bit through the umbilical cord and licked her son clean before she died. Bambi was helpless. He stood for hours on his shaky legs beside his dead mother."

The young deer was saved after it was spotted by a local walker, who took it to the RSPCA. In the weeks that followed photographs of Bambi would appear in the press, with constant updates on his progress back to health, and eventual return to the wild.

So serious was the situation by the early 1970s that the British Deer Society (BDS) estimated that the national deer population had dropped by about twenty-five per cent due to poaching, while in several counties of England the deer had been virtually wiped out. The first attempt to amend the *1963 Deer Act* came in June 1974 when Labour MP Peter Hardy, in company with a number of others, made an unsuccessful approach to Home Secretary Roy Jenkins with a request to increase the ludicrously low fines possible under the *Act.* By late 1976 the failure of the Labour government to take any action prompted Lord Northfield to announce his intention to introduce a Bill into the Lords that would increase the fines to £500, order the confiscation of all poaching equipment including vehicles, make it an offence to sell venison except to a licensed game dealer, give greater power to the police for stop and search of suspected poachers and ban the use of shotguns as a weapon to kill deer.

What happened later is best described in a letter from Peter Baillie, Chairman of the British Deer Society, which was printed in the *Shooting Times:*

"On 25 January (1977) Lord Northfield introduced the *Deer Bill* in the House of Lords. On the very same day, Mr. Jasper

More (Conservative MP for Ludlow and vice-chairman of the British Field Sports Society) presented no less than three *Deer Bills* in the House of Commons, covering ground already covered by Lord Northfield's Bill.

"From the outset, the Northfield Bill met particular opposition on two counts. First, the Devon and Somerset Staghounds, represented by the BFSS, disliked the section aimed at curbing the prevalent widespread deer poaching. A re-drafted, though less effective, provision was eventually agreed.

"Secondly, the Devon and Somerset Staghounds and the National Farmers' Union objected to the proposals dealing with the use of shotguns on deer. The former continue to drive red deer to shotguns, a practice deplored by most informed people. The latter, stoutly supported by certain elements in the BFSS, demanded the almost unconditional right to shotgun all species of deer, however inefficient and cruel this might be. Again a very one-sided compromise was reached.

"Nevertheless, the Bill successfully completed all stages in the Lords and was sent to the Commons (to be introduced by John Farr) where, on Second Reading on 15 July, it was 'objected to' by Mr. Nigel Forman (Conservative MP for Sutton Carshalton). On being asked why, he confessed that he had been requested to object by Mr. Marcus Kimball (Conservative MP for Gainsborough and chairman of the BFSS) who admitted that the NFU wanted the Bill blocked; it appears that they were not anxious that this should be known."

The failure of Northfield's Bill showed the lengths to which blood sport supporters were willing to go in order to protect their interests. What also soon became apparent was the wide gulf that existed between deer control experts from groups such as the British Deer Society, and those "experts" whose only real concern in deer hinged on hunting for sport. The one aspect of the Bill that caused the most division between the two sides was the use of shotguns as a method for killing deer. An interesting exchange of views took place in the *Shooting Times* which, apart from exposing these differences, cast serious doubt on the claims that hunting with hounds was the only means of deer control across Exmoor and the Quantocks.

Writing on 3rd March 1977 Kenneth Whitehead, undoubtedly one of Britain's leading experts, had this to say:

> "Apart from the poacher, and perhaps the farmer anxious to protect his crops, the only people who still regularly use a shotgun on red deer are members of the Devon and Somerset Staghounds, who from time to time organise deer drives to cull, principally, surplus hinds as hunting alone does not seem able to kill sufficient. When approached on the subject, the hunt maintain that these shotgun deer drives are the only effective method of deer control and claim that all wounded deer are always followed up by hounds and accounted for. With the banning of shotguns on red deer, the Devon and Somerset Staghounds will now have to make other arrangements for culling surplus deer, and as I have several times suggested to them, a solution could be to appoint one or two suitably trained forest rangers, who during the autumn staghunting season could act as harbourer, whilst during the winter hind hunting season could selectively kill surplus hinds in those areas where stocks were too high. A comparison can surely be made with the manner in which the Forestry Commission now go about deer control. At one time it was the practice to drive deer to men armed with shotguns, but now the rifle has replaced the gun, and quite apart from being more humane, far better results are being achieved. A quarter of a century ago the Scott Henderson Committee made a thorough examination into the question of cruelty to wild animals and their report was that 'the shooting of deer with shotguns must inevitably be accompanied by a great deal of suffering.' Twenty-six years has not made the shotgun any less cruel."

Major T F Trollope-Bellew, careful to conceal the fact that he was

Chairman of the QSH, was quick to repudiate Whitehead when, replying on 21st April he stated:

> "The Deer Act 1963 has worked well. The only alteration which is required is to increase the fines to take account of the changed value of the pound.
>
> "The consequences of the new Bill becoming law would be disastrous. While there can be no guarantee that the increased use of rifles would result in less wounded deer it might well have just the reverse effect; it would certainly be the cause of greatly increased danger to people and livestock. It would also lead to an increased demand for rifles, which the police would doubtless resist.
>
> "May I say that as chairman of the Exmoor National Park Committee I most strongly deplore the idea of turning Exmoor into a 'cervicidal Bisley'. Conditions on Exmoor and the Quantocks are so totally different from those on a Scottish deer forest that to attempt to introduce the methods of one to the other would be disastrous.
>
> "It is perfectly possible to kill red deer humanely with shotguns, provided the right calibre of gun and correct shot size are used and the range is not too great. This being so, it seems farcical to suggest that rifles must be used for lesser breeds of deer. If it is made compulsory to use rifles to shoot anything so small as a muntjac, the next thing is that it will be suggested that only rifles should be used to kill hares.
>
> "But quite apart from the attempt to make rifles compulsory, the Bill contains many absurdities and every effort should be made to prevent it becoming an act."

In a reply that was printed on 12th May Whitehead again registered his objections to the stag hunts deer drives:

"I was surprised to see that Major T.F. Trollope-Bellew should recommend the use of shotguns on red deer, for surely, with his military training, he must realise that it is advisable to use the right weapon for the job and since the whole reason for deer drives in south-west England is to reduce the number of deer, surely the quickest, simplest, and most humane way to accomplish this would be to use a weapon that is capable of doing the job at ranges of up to 100-150 yards rather than having to have the deer driven to concealed guns so that they pass within the lethal range of that weapon, namely not more than 20 yards for the shot to be effective, *provided* the shot is correctly placed. A head shot is useless and will only blind the animal.

"No one would disagree with him that 'it is perfectly possible to kill red deer with shotguns provided...the range is not too great.' It is, therefore, all a question of range and unless you have an army of guns placed at more than 40 to 50 yards apart, how often can a deer be driven to within that range so that it can be cleanly killed?

"I appreciate that hounds are always in attendance at these drives in order to follow up wounded deer and whilst that may be good training practice for hounds it is not the most humane way of going about deer control.

"In support of using shotguns in south-west England, Major Trollope-Bellew states that 'conditions on Exmoor and the Quantocks are so totally different from those on a Scottish deer forest that to attempt to introduce the methods of one to the other would be disastrous.

"It may interest him to know that in the Lake District where conditions are not 'so totally different' from those on Exmoor and the Quantocks and, indeed, the human population per acre may well be higher, the National Trust employs a man to control both red and roe deer with a rifle, and I see no reason whatsoever why a similar method of control should not be used in south-west England."

This correspondence, along with much more of a similar nature, between the two sections of deer control within the "sporting fraternity" underscored the polarised viewpoints of those involved. The one striving to create a structured, legally enforceable system of management that would safeguard the interests of deer nationally, with the other concerned solely with protecting the rights of stag hunters, while maintaining the illusion that it was the only practical form of control possible in the West Country. The most gratifying aspect of this exchange of views, which when advocated by abolitionists were dismissed in hunting circles as the ranting of "ignorant animal rightists" were here proposed by some of the most respected experts as the natural extension of deer control methods already in operation throughout the rest of the country.

When the *Deer Bill* was reintroduced into the Commons on 5th May 1978 this time it was killed by left-wing Labour MP Ian Mikardo, who opposed it on the grounds that it was not an anti-stag hunting measure. The Bill was again "objected to" by Miss Jo Richardson (Labour: Barking) when it came before the Commons again in July 1978. Her reasons were that the Bill "still allowed for the killing of deer (culling, licensed marksmen and the continuation of hunting with hounds) and until a Bill was brought forward that banned the killing of all deer, she would not support it."

While the anti-hunt lobby was now busily engaged in making sure that even limited protection for deer was denied Guy Somerset, Chairman of the Exmoor Society, was making a public plea that "deer must be made a protected species if they are to survive in any great numbers". His reason was that "deer belong to whoever's land they happen to be on and the owner is perfectly within his rights to shoot them. With carcasses now fetching more than £200 each there has been a dramatic increase in legalised shooting and herds are being seriously affected. This is wrong."

On Thursday, 30th November 1978, Lord Northfield introduced a revised *Deer Bill* into the House of Lords It had been radically redrafted after consultation with the Home Office in an attempt to appease the pro-hunt lobby, the anti-hunt lobby, the shotgun lobby, the NFU and Deer Farmers Association. In truth there was little left of the original Bill other than a severely watered-down version of the anti-poaching clauses, but it was hoped that this would enable it to clear the Commons. It didn't.

When Peter Hardy moved for the Second Reading in the Commons on 23rd February 1979, the Conservative member for Tiverton, Robin Maxwell-Hyslop took objection. The reason he had obstructed was "because of one clause which might have led to a ban on the use of shotguns by farmers protecting their crops", even though that clause had already been accepted by the NFU. The Bill was again scrutinised to double-check that nothing else could be found which might offend someone else.

The Bill returned for a sixth attempt in March 1979 when it was again blocked by Arnold Shaw. This was the same MP who in 1969 had introduced the *Deer Hunting and Hare Coursing (Abolition) Bill,* who now killed this one because in his opinion it "would formalise and institutionalise" stag hunting. It transpired that Shaw, who was himself a member of the LACS executive committee, had killed the Bill at the behest of certain elements within the League, even though it was in direct opposition to the wishes of its Chairman, Lord Houghton, who wished to see the Bill become law. A new date of 30th March was given for the Bill to be presented yet again, but owing to the calling of the General Election this had to be abandoned.

The Bill again came before the Commons in June 1979, winding its way through the seemingly never-ending parliamentary process until finally clearing the last hurdle on 7th July 1980, when it went through to the House of Lords. The final success of the *Deer Bill* was due to John Farr, MP for Harborough, who piloted the Bill through all its stages, although "he had taken good care to eliminate all foreseeable forms of opposition by tabling 85 amendments which had the effect of drastically reducing the scope of the Bill" even further. It cleared the Lords, then returning to the Commons it received the Royal Assent on Friday, 8th August 1980.

The *Deer Act 1980* came into force during late November, to be greeted with general scepticism from most quarters, with the *Shooting Times* perhaps saying it best:

> "The long-awaited deer bill becomes law this month but we fear, as indeed do many deer experts, that it will not do enough to help deer, particularly where poachers are concerned. Over the past few years we have frequently returned to the horrific cruelty inflicted by unscrupulous poachers on the deer population, and often we have been able to report on successful prosecutions. Sometimes a fine, or even imprisonment, however, has not deterred the more cunning members of that invidious fraternity and sometimes – more often than not, we fear – they continue their revolting crimes uninterrupted.
>
> "Will the new *Deer Act* work? The new maximum fine of £500 or three month's imprisonment is a mere gesture in the right direction. Disposing of carcasses becomes more difficult for poachers with stricter licensing of dealers and their obligation to keep strict records. Searching or pursuing deer with intent to take, kill or injure becomes an offence, as does removing a carcass without authority. But we fear that...only intensive policing of the (poaching) area is going to stop them now."

The *Deer Act* would again be amended in 1991, but little would change. The level of fines would increase in line with inflation, but the use of shotguns to kill wild deer would still remain legal and a determined poacher could still operate more or less unhindered, even when the deer were given the much vaunted protection of the stag hunts.

Nothing better illustrated this point than the killing of the nationally renowned white hind of the Quantocks. For nineteen years the near-Albino hind Snowy had roamed the hills around Bagborough, safe under the "special protection" of the QSH until early in 1993 when she was killed by a poacher; the local grapevine claiming she was brought down by a lurcher, with the head subsequently found in the Bridgwater Canal and the pelt at a house in South Somerset. Even though the police carried out extensive enquiries including the close questioning of a local from the Holford area, no charges were ever brought. Although it was reliably reported in the press that the QSH were "very upset" at her demise, it was evident from their inability to protect the West Country's most famous deer that their claim to be a deterrent against the poacher was something of a sham.

Chapter Eight

"a giant game of chess"

THE JULY 1978 LACS AGM cemented the "take-over" with, not only the re-election of Lord Houghton as Chairman, but also the first radical to sit on the Executive Committee in the form of John Bryant, fresh from his battles to reform the RSPCA. It also gave Lord Houghton a sympathetic animal rights power base that could be used as a springboard with which to pursue his long-term aim of making animal welfare a serious political issue. In May of that year over sixty animal welfare organisations had banded together under the collective title of the General Election Co-ordinating Committee for Animal Protection (GECCAP) with the remit to extract Manifesto commitments from the main parties prior to the expected General Election. The hunting issue would come to dominate the proceedings as much of the groundwork had been laid by another RSPCA "reformer" Richard Course, whose name would become synonymous with blood sports over the coming years, coupled with the fact that Houghton was not only Chairman of the League, but also Chairman of GECCAP.

It appeared that initial approaches from GECCAP would prove successful when the policy-making national executive of the Labour Party voted in early June to include a Manifesto pledge to abolish blood sports, only to be over-ruled on the direct orders of Prime Minister James Callaghan. His decision was taken after pressure from back bench MPs with low majorities who feared that such a move would lead to defeat in rural constituencies. The following announcement from the LACS that it would concentrate all of its resources on persuading the Labour Party to change the decision (which was partially successful with a commitment to abolish deer hunting and hare coursing) prompted the inevitable backlash from the anti-Houghton faction.

Led by former Coldstream Guards officer Peter Kerr, a campaign was orchestrated to discredit the League Executive Committee as having "been taken over by extremists from the Hunt Saboteurs Association" who were "prejudiced in favour of those who wish to pursue class warfare under the guise of protecting deer...". Peter Kerr felt his suspicions were confirmed early in 1979 with not only the election of Richard Course to the committee, but also the donation of £80,000 to Labour's General Election campaign.

Infuriated by the donation, Kerr demanded an Extraordinary General Meeting in an attempt to overturn the decision, which when held in July 1979, voted by 224 to 71 in favour of the donation. When this failed to quieten the dissenters, a postal ballot was held which supported the actions of the EC by 2,492 in favour, with 1,959 against. The subsequent slaughter of the Labour Party at the polls brought fresh attacks against the EC which were accompanied with rumours that an attempt was to be made which would return Raymond Rowley as Chairman. To crank this move, Richard Course revealed to the press that Rowley had secured for himself a fifty-year lease on the St Nicholas Priory deer sanctuary, near Dulverton, at £1 a year. With this revelation the heat went out of the controversy, followed by the resignation of the remaining pro-Rowley faction with the rebuke that the way was now open for the "small group of militant left wing extremists" who now dominated the LACS.

It was certainly true that over the next few years HSA activists would come to play an increasingly high profile role in the running of the League. Though with the benefit of hindsight it is obvious that this role was purely academic given that the politics of this country would be dominated for the next eighteen years by Margaret Thatcher's brand of conservatism. In some respects the League would revert to the introspective attitudes of the last period of wilderness years during the 1950s and early '60s, when its constant inability to influence political decision making would lead to personality clashes and petty bickering. Taken over by the militants it may have been, but in reality it was a neutered beast now that the doors of Parliament were closed.

The real change would come from the grass roots of animal rights, where a realisation that the so-called democratic options no longer existed would foster a belief that the only way forward lay with ever increasing militant extra-parliamentary direct action. Nowhere was this attitude more keenly felt than in the ranks of SOS, where a serious increase in violence against the saboteurs during the 1978/79 season had led to a radical rethink concerning future tactics.

The scene had been set during one of the last hunts of the season (28th April 1979) when, during the seven-hour chase of a spring stag, hunt riders had continually ridden down and whipped saboteurs, rammed anti-hunt vehicles, blocked roads so as to systematically attack the trapped cars, and instigated three pitched battles that resulted in fifteen cases needing hospital treatment. The stag itself, which had been found at 12.45 and finally brought to bay at four minutes to eight that evening, also met a particularly bloody end that was witnessed by a saboteur who claimed that after three attempts to shoot it the animal was finally killed by having its throat slit. The LACS were so outraged that they demanded a Home Office enquiry into the incident, while QSH Master Walner Robins, rattled by the ensuing publicity, took the unprecedented step of attempting a damage limitation exercise with lengthy letters of denial to the local press.

Revenge of a sort was enacted when ten saboteurs stormed the QSH AGM on the 14th July at Taunton's Castle Hotel, releasing stink bombs and smoke flares. After scuffles with hunt members, hotel staff and police, all the raiders escaped without arrest. Two weeks later at the HSA AGM in Bristol, SOS committee members detailed the escalating violence from the stag hunts, explained that for the past three years the financial state of the QSH had steadily deteriorated due in part to constant attention from saboteurs, leading to the point where it was now operating on overdraft facilities, and then announced their intention to make an all-out attempt to finish off the hunt.

There were some on HSA's national committee who expressed their concern that ad-hoc attacks against individual hunts was one thing, but to turn up repeatedly week after week at the same hunt, especially now that the intention to force it to disband was public knowledge, would lead to unacceptable levels of violence. Though the mood of the general membership was one of overwhelming support for the idea, partly because SOS had obtained something of a cult status, but mainly because the Labour election defeat of a few weeks previously was still raw, with many now feeling that with no chance of parliamentary action here was a real chance at least to finish off one stag hunt themselves.

From the start of the 1979/80 season, SOS met with violence from the hunt supporters, though at first it was mainly directed against our vehicles. Tyres were slashed and nails hammered into them, windscreens were smashed, while on a number of occasions brake pipes were cut and sugar poured into petrol tanks. Retaliation was swift. Every vehicle found to have connections to the hunt (many displayed QSH supporter stickers on the windows) was attacked and damaged. We later learned that much of this damage had been the work of the Animal Liberation Front (ALF) who, while certainly not acting on direct instructions from SOS, were responding to our general appeal for help in putting this hunt out of action.

We also had the good fortune to include in our ranks a coach driver whose boss collected vintage or unusual vehicles, one of which was an old Welsh mines rescue vehicle. About the size of a coach, armoured-plated, with the lifting-gear removed and replaced with seating for about forty, it made the ideal saboteur "battle-bus". He agreed that we could have the use of it whenever required, thus removing the fear of finding ourselves blocked in, for all we needed to do was push the obstructions out of the way. If memory serves me well I think the maximum number of cars shunted at any one time was six. Another toy played with during this period was a land rover that had been fitted with a ramming-bar. With two sockets welded each side of the bonnet, complimented with a V-shaped contraption similar in shape to the cow-pushers familiar on early American trains, which could be slotted into place whenever needed, it made a fearsome weapon. It was only used twice, then abandoned on the advice of the police

11–13 Three stills from the 1958 Russell W Fuller footage, with one showing the deer being dragged down by hounds from the Quantock Staghounds.

14 Gwen Barter at the Norwich Staghounds, 15th March 1962.
15 Raymond Rowley with hunt master Col Brian Gooch at the Norwich Staghounds, 15th March 1962.

THE END OF A "CARTED" DEER HUNT BY THE NORWICH STAGHOUNDS ON DEC. 10th, 1962

(This animal was alive and was re-crated and taken "home" to be used again another day)

16 A lassoed stag is dragged up the bank of a frozen stream. A leaflet produced by Gwen Barter as part of her campaign against the Norwich Staghounds.

17 *A stag held by DSSH hunt supporters in the River Yeo prior to being shot. One of a number of such pictures taken by Raymond Rowley over the years. This one gaining front-page national coverage on 21st October 1966.*

18 Twenty years of service to the deer. The woman with her sleeves rolled up in this 1950s' photograph is Mrs Nora Cox, master of the DSSH.

19 The woman in hunting gear to the right of this picture taken in 1979 is Mrs Nora Harding, master of the DSSH. Same woman. Different name. Over twenty years apart. Note the huntsman holding the deer's heart.

20 Young supporters accept their souvenir of the kill. DSSH October 1979.

21 Save Our Stags Class of 1980. Off to a demo in the big city.

who gently pointed out something along the lines of "next time" and "throw the key away".

The LACS meanwhile, having determined to attempt a combination of total commitment to securing a future Labour government, coupled with covert support for the direct action tactics of HSA, set about a re-vamp of its image. To accomplish the first, following the single largest legacy in its history a move was made to its present Union Street offices in Southwark, where additional staff, drawn mainly from the ranks of the hunt saboteurs, were employed. The next phase, to include leading saboteurs on the committee, was partially completed in December 1979 with the election of HSA Press Officer Chris Williamson and myself to the EC. Though it soon became apparent the inclusion of saboteurs was considered by many committee members as a necessary evil to be tolerated as the price that had to be paid for their help in removing the old guard. Arnold Shaw, who was acting as Executive Director following his defeat in the 1979 election, certainly felt this way, while the real "power behind the throne", Richard Course, made no secret that his intention was to utilise the League's resources to obtain a Labour Party commitment to abolish blood sports in time for the next General Election.

The appointment, in early 1980, of Maeve Denby to the post of Executive Director was seen as a move in the right direction, coming as she did with close connections to the Labour Party, having fought as a candidate in three general elections. On the other hand Lord Houghton, now viewing many of the League's activities with growing concern, was considered a liability. He was ousted as Chairman in an office "coup", with the official reason given as "resigning due to pressure of work within the House of Lords", the position being filled by a "reluctant" Richard Course.

The next twelve months would see a situation develop between Denby and Course that threatened to tear the League apart, which culminated in a February 1981 resolution from Course that "Maeve Denby has not met the expectations of the EC" and her "immediate resignation...is requested" with a £5,000 settlement if she agrees. Reluctantly, I seconded Course's motion, a decision that still haunts me today, in the mistaken belief that this was the best solution for the long-term well being of the League. The subsequent press release stated "that Maeve Denby resigned her position for personal reasons". Within a couple of months a "reluctant" Richard Course had agreed to fill the position of executive director.

Back on the Quantocks the violence was beginning to escalate out of control. Led by three individuals, two of which were nicknamed the Mong Brothers (in a very un-pc reference to their appearance bearing the hallmarks of rural inbreeding), with the third affectionately known as Fungus in honour of his striking similarity to the hero of the Raymond Briggs book *Fungus the Bogeyman*, which was popular at the time, a systematic policy of attacking saboteurs was begun by hunt supporters. The brothers would career around the hills on motorbikes looking for the saboteurs; once located, they would alert Fungus and his heavies, relaying our position (in a pre mobile phone era) by walkie-talkie. This led to vicious fighting on every occasion the saboteurs turned up, with both sides soon armed with walking sticks, pickaxe handles and fence stakes as a matter of course. As the hunt swelled its numbers with support from neighbouring packs, so SOS increased with saboteurs pouring in from across the country. At some point during this period virtually every major HSA group took some part in the campaign. ***Note 1***

There would seldom be a week between the start of the 1979 season, until well into 1983, when SOS saboteurs did not make some attempt to disrupt at least one meet of the QSH. Quite often this would entail one small group flushing the woods during the night, while another would take over to ply their trade of horn and false scent during the day. The mass strikes would be arranged every four to six weeks, when dozens of "sabmobiles" would rendezvous at Bridgwater's Salmon Parade, alongside the River Parrett, then drive in convoy onto the Quantock Hills. Many of the HSA groups would travel through the night to help out, with some like the Merseyside and West Midlands making repeated visits.

Again it was the last meet of the season (26th April 1980) outside the Travellers Rest, Enmore, that proved the most violent. After drawing off the pack four times during the day tempers flared out of control around two o'clock, when the better part of 150 supporters and saboteurs pitched into each other for a chaotic twenty-minute fight. When it was over both sides had many injured, including the Mong Brothers and Fungus, who were taken to hospital, in company with three HSA group leaders.

The strange thing regarding this violence was that neither side ever made serious recourse to the police. The QSH always played it down, along with the effectiveness of the saboteurs, whereas SOS never requested police intervention as a matter of principle, preferring to deal with it in their own way. The police for their part seldom pushed the issue, with the Bridgwater force broadly sympathetic to the antis, while the Taunton police tended to think that dealing with brawling blood sport factions somewhat beneath their dignity.

An added bonus never to be missed were the impromptu press statements of hunt master Walner Robins who, with the usual dismissive comments regarding the day's activities, could always be relied upon to spice them up with a touch of pure comic genius. One of the better examples, appearing in the *Somerset County Gazette* after a successful SOS raid at which the hunt had failed to kill read:

> "Hunt saboteurs were out in force, blowing horns and spraying strong-smelling chemicals, when the Quantock Staghounds visited Exmoor for their Easter Monday meet.
>
> "They claimed they had split up the pack of hounds and disrupted hunting, but Hunt Master Walner Robins, who farms near Selworthy, said: 'They were a nuisance, nothing more.'
>
> "He spoke of a magnificent run, 15 miles as the crow flies, from the meet at Lowtrow Cross on the Brendons right across Exmoor and into Devon. The spring stag they were hunting got away and the hunt was called off near Witheridge in Devon about 6:30 pm.
>
> "Mr. Robins also denied that the hounds had been split up or the hunt disrupted, and said the saboteurs only succeeded in making a nuisance of themselves among hunt followers and spectators.

" 'Their language at times was disgusting,' he said. 'I can sympathise with anyone who is genuinely against stag hunting, but a lot of these are nothing better than hooligans. I am convinced they couldn't care less about cruelty to animals; what is more cruel than spraying chemicals on hounds *or catching a hind and spraying it before the hunt, which is what they have been known to do.* (author's italics)

" 'Many of these people are students who are just out for kicks. It's a known fact that some are paid for what they do. The last I heard was they were being offered £5 and an evening meal – I can't say by whom because I don't know.' "

The inherent silliness of most "I know it for a fact but can't supply any evidence to prove it" pro-hunt arguments are self-evident from the above statements, but the one regarding payment from mysterious sources has given many years of harmless fun to hunt saboteurs. First muted in the 1960s, this story had us paid by the Kremlin in an attempt to destabilise the ruling class as part of the ongoing Cold War. When confronted with this accusation during a TV talk show in 1967, far from denying it, I actually went for total wind-up by admitting that it was true, further pointing out that our biggest problem was obtaining a decent rate of exchange for the roubles!

Though the inference that hunt saboteurs were "just out for kicks" was wide of the mark, it would certainly be untrue to claim that many of us did not derive great excitement from the dangers inherent in direct action activities. Whereas hunters consider it courageous to band together in hundreds, augmented with hundreds more in vehicles of every description, to pursue one terrified deer that has not the slightest chance of presenting the remotest danger to a single hunt supporter, we did not. For many in SOS the thrill was to pit oneself against the ultimate quarry, often out-numbered four, five or six to one, with the very real possibility of serious injury ever present. Some saw the disruption of stag hunting as a sport, or as I was once quoted "a giant game of chess", with the life of a living animal as the ultimate prize. Others, such as my late friend Sue Smith, preferred covert to confrontational, becoming expert at creeping through the woods in dead of night "flushing out" the harboured stag, with the odd kennel raid thrown in for good measure.

It would be equally untrue to claim that all hunt saboteurs felt this way, for I remember numerous occasions on the Quantocks when the level of violence encountered caused some to be physically sick, but certainly there were others who loved the adrenaline rush. It is also worth remembering that while SOS was fortunate not to lose anyone to permanent disablement, the HSA nationally has had two members killed, with many others suffering long-term injuries.

The difference between the opposing factions is best understood by their respective attitude towards what constitutes a memorable day on the hunting field. For the hunter, as explained by Walner Robins above, it is such events as the tormenting of an animal for periods of six hours or more, over a distance of fifteen miles, hopefully ending in its death to please those riders obsessed enough to stay the course. Now contrast that to the reply given by SOS activist Marley Jones to the question, "Is there any one memorable experience in particular which stands out in your mind as being especially gratifying?", which appeared as part of a question and answer interview for the American magazine *Agenda:*

> "The most exhilarating moment I had was on January 1st, 1981, during a meet of the Quantock Staghounds. We saw hounds and riders streaming past us over the brow of a hill in fast pursuit of a red deer hind.
>
> "We were able to circle the hill and race on foot into the combe where we thought she was heading, and arrived just in time to see her coming towards us at full speed. She was covered in sweat, out of breath, her tongue hanging to one side. We froze until she passed, and then we saw the hounds almost upon her. We charged behind her, covering the ground with false scent and at the same time pushing the hounds back with our hands.
>
> "At this point the hunt master and a number of riders appeared

and we were forced to retreat. But the hind was safe! I think that as long as I live the elation felt by all of us will stay with me."

Incidents and emotions such as that were what made it all worthwhile, for though it was certainly true that for many hunt saboteurs the excitement, danger, camaraderie and overwhelming sense of pleasure derived from "pissing off the red bellies" were a large part of the attraction, nothing ever compared to the end of a hunt that had resulted in the escape of the deer. Straggling down off the Quantock Hills on a cold, damp winter's evening, past the disconsolate groups of riders was a pleasure to be savoured.

By comparison, the radical approach anticipated from the LACS had failed to materialise, with most of its energies now directed towards attaining the political respectability demanded by Richard Course. Initiatives were undertaken on behalf of deer that included offering a £1,000 reward for information leading to the arrest and conviction of deer poachers, with the ultimate irony being that the first claimant was a Hampshire gamekeeper! One of the last major sanctuaries was purchased during this period, with £50,000 paid for the magnificent sixty-acre Alfoxton Wood, at Holford on the Quantocks, along with substantial financial assistance to the first animal rights movie ever made. *Note 2. APPENDIX 4*

In early 1980 the American film director Victor Schonfeld approached numerous animal welfare organisations in Britain to help fund the completion of *The Animals Film*, an explicit documentary detailing animal abuses around the world. Most, including initially the League, turned him down, though seeing the potential in such a movie I did a deal with him to the effect that if I coerced the LACS committee into funding the venture he would guarantee prominent coverage of stag hunting. The money secured, our next problem was gaining the confidence of a stag hunt that would enable him to obtain the required footage, the planning of which fell to devious minds within SOS. We eventually convinced the DSSH that Schonfeld was filming a documentary on British hunting for a US television sports channel and that the finished programme would never be screened in this country. Sue Smith, whose face was not well known due to her penchant for night-time activities, was recruited into acting as the film unit's Exmoor guide to make sure that the full reality was filmed, not the usual sanitised version as occasionally appeared on the BBC.

On completion *The Animals Film,* containing the most explicit scenes of deer hunt kills so far shown, plus bonus footage of SOS saboteurs in action, won critical praise following its world premiere at the London Film Festival in November 1981. Unfortunately it later met with limited distribution, due in part to its uncompromising portrayal of horrific cruelties which Victor Schonfeld refused to edit for cinema release, though ironically he did agree to cutting scenes dealing with the Animal Liberation Front (ALF) so as to qualify for screening on Channel 4. The cuts were demanded by nervous television executives who feared that scenes showing an ALF raid against vivisection establishments had been undertaken at the behest of Schonfeld's film company Slick Pics International, thus laying Channel 4 open to the charge "of promoting the commission of an illegal act".

Another filming operation that *was* enthusiastically embraced by Richard Course concerned the employment by the League of the remarkable young hunt saboteur Mike Huskisson. Already something of an icon within the animal rights movement for having masterminded the high profile 1975 rescue of two "smoking beagles" from ICI, Huskisson would spend two years operating jointly as LACS Press Officer Mike Wilkins, while working deep undercover in hunting circles as Michael Wright. Starting in April 1981 he would infiltrate many of the leading hunts in the country, including notching up fifty-nine visits to the three West Country deer hunts. By the time he was finally exposed by the *Sunday Telegraph* in late May 1983 he had amassed over 5,000 stills and nearly 2,000ft of movie footage.

The one thing that always amazed me, which was to leave a lasting admiration for Mike Huskisson, was that his total hatred of blood sports would allow him to treat his personal safety with cavalier indifference. Not content with returning week after week to stay silent while witnessing scenes which were anathema to his soul, while under constant threat of exposure from suspicious hunters or over-familiar saboteurs (for though he was well known in animal rights circles few knew of his triple life) he would even allow his photographs to be published during the period he was undercover rather than miss an opportunity to promote the cause. The most striking example appeared on 24th January 1982, when a five-page article on stag hunting by Ena Kendall, accompanied by ten of his pictures, appeared as a cover feature in the *Observer* colour magazine. Taken only a few months earlier (22nd August & 8th October 1981) two of the photographs were given such prominence, splashed over three pages, that it was incredible no hunting enthusiast questioned the source, prematurely ending the operation with a severe beating. When he was finally exposed seventeen months later Huskisson would tell the full story in *Outfoxed*, arguably one of the finest books to come from the anti camp.

Courage of a different kind was exhibited in early 1981 when two leading members of SOS, Marley Jones and Mandy Dawes, volunteered to help crew an American anti-whaling ship. The background to this fascinating episode is best told quoting from an article that I wrote while aboard the ship at the time:

> "On the morning of 16th July 1979, the illegal pirate whaling ship *Sierra* was rammed off the coast of Portugal and forced to limp into harbour with damage valued at more than £250,000. Her insurance company, Lloyds of London, refused to pay as she was improperly registered as a fishing boat, and her Japanese backers had to foot the bill.
>
> "Seven months later she was completely repaired and preparing to put to sea, to resume her slaughter of the last of the great whales. She never made it. At 6.17 a.m. on 6th February 1980 a 10ft wide hole was blown in her side and she sank at her berth in Lisbon harbour. The destruction of the *Sierra*, murderer of 25,000 whales, was the work of a small group of direct action environmentalists collectively called Sea Shepherd Conservation. *Note 3*
>
> "Unfortunately, shortly after the initial ramming, the vessel *Sea Shepherd*, base ship of the group, was arrested by the authorities

and held in Lisbon. Following the final sinking of the *Sierra*, the Portuguese announced their intention to sell *Sea Shepherd* and hand over the proceeds to the whaling company. Rather than allow this to happen, three crew members returned to Portugal, boarded their ship at night, and scuttled her. Thus ended the life of the first ship – but almost at once the hunt began for a new one.

"After much searching it was decided to purchase the *St Giles*, a 178ft, 657-ton former Hull trawler, at a cost of £50,000. A further £50,000 was needed to fit out the ship as a conservation vessel. This was to prove a long and tedious job necessitating the ship remaining at Greenock in Scotland for six long months."

It was while *Sea Shepherd II* remained stranded at Greenock that I was approached by her Canadian captain, Paul Watson, with a request for financial help. It transpired that he had used up all available funds to purchase the ship, with no chance of raising the money for major repairs, or even to pay for fuel to get the ship to America. Most of the major animal welfare organisations in Britain had declined to help for, while privately sympathetic to his actions, they were reluctant to be seen publicly funding such a radical enterprise.

In my capacity as a committee member I then approached Richard Course about the possibility of help from the League. He left me in no doubt that paying out money to help save whales, when there were Labour politicians who needed funding to fight elections, was not something that he intended to sanction. So being of a devious disposition I resorted to plan B. Sounding out the individual committee members I soon discovered that it was a fifty/fifty split, with those against solidly from the "old guard" who, as luck would have it, always left the Saturday committee meetings early to catch their trains home.

The rest was easy. I placed a late motion on the agenda, making sure I still had a quorum, that "the LACS make an unconditional donation of £10,000 to purchase fuel which will allow *Sea Shepherd*

II to reach America and complete fund raising in time to campaign against the Russian whaling fleet in July."

The ship sailed on 25th April 1981 for Alexandria, Virginia, where major repairs to engine and radar were undertaken, then through the Panama Canal, up the West Coast of America, via Los Angeles and Vancouver, finally to confront the Russians in the Bering Sea, off the Alaskan coast. Of the two SOS activists, Mandy was forced to return home from Washington DC, soon after the ship arrived, due to ill health, while Marley Jones remained until the end of the mission. As we watched the progress of *Sea Shepherd II* it was a comforting thought that not only was "one of our own taking part", but that this small West Country campaign to save the red deer had been indirectly responsible in helping to save some of the last great whales. ***Note 4***

Back on terra firma, things took a violent turn during the QSH Easter Monday (20th April 1981) meet. Having been forced to switch their annual holiday venue from the Quantock Hills to the middle of Exmoor in an attempt to avoid the saboteurs, the hunt was in an angry mood from the start. The subsequent three-hour harassment which resulted in the pack being split, with over half the hounds being drawn away and not recovered until late in the evening, brought their temper to boiling point. The final straw came when about thirty riders were photographed riding across the League's Gilmore Farm sanctuary, near Dulverton.

After attempting to smash the camera, the hunters harried the saboteurs for nearly two miles, slashing at them with riding crops and bullwhips. Both sides then collided with another fight underway between antis and hunt heavies who had smashed the windscreen of a transit van attempting to bring reinforcements to the first fight. The ensuing battle became extremely vicious, during which a number of riders were dragged from their horses and seriously hurt, with the violence only ending with the arrival of the police.

The spin-off from this trespass onto League land was to expose the surprising revelation that practically every member of the executive committee did not know where Gilmore Farm was. It also transpired that with the exception of a few major sanctuaries such as St Nicolas Priory and Baronsdown, they had little idea how many properties were actually owned across Exmoor. The follow up was that the LACS EC initiated the first sanctuary survey. This survey would also expose the unpalatable fact that due to lack of management or adequate patrolling during hunting days they were proving quite worthless as a refuge for red deer.

The issue came to a head when an internal report on the sanctuaries by Richard Course was leaked to the press. In this report Course made no secret that in his view "the sanctuaries had done nothing to reduce the number of deer killed in the area" and "that at best the land offered only an irritation to local stag hunters and did not play a major role in the fight against blood sports". He concluded that "the sanctuaries have only one purpose – to attract money from people who believe animals live in them 'in a kind of Utopian dream world' and to use the cash to promote anti-hunting legislation."

The *Times* journalist Craig Seton was right when he wrote on 24th July 1982: "Ironically, Mr. Course's doubts about the sanctuaries and the embarrassment the public disclosure of his views caused has probably meant that they will now undergo several years of comparatively expensive development – just what he did not want."

This was exactly what appeared to happen with the appointment of former hunt saboteur John Hicks to the position of sanctuaries manager, who immediately requested £60,000 to be invested in the properties over the coming four years. With his special interest in nature conservation and experience in woodland management, plus a no-nonsense approach to bureaucracy, it at last seemed that a new era was about to dawn for the League in the West Country.

Note 1. The most prominent groups included John Hale and Miriam Hollis from the West Midlands, Dave Callender's Merseyside group, Steve Brimble from Luton, Jeanette Jones and her people, Ralph Cook's Exeter group, and the Western Federation (a collection of West Country based animal rights groups) which was mobilised on a regular basis by HSA Tactics Officer Flod Pamment. Rorke Garfield's National Animal Rescue Association (NARA) also helped out on many occasions. Most of the HSA committee came individually, or with their local groups, including:

Bob August (Chairperson), Sue Hough (Treasurer), Bob Deacon (Contacts Liaison), Chris Williamson (Press Officer).

Special mention must be made of an amusing incident concerning HSA committee member, and legendary saboteur, Aubrey Thomas. Something of a loner, Aubrey was well known in anti circles for disrupting his local hunts on an individual basis (i.e. sabbing alone) and thought he would try it against the QSH. Dressed in T-shirt, shorts and trainers (he was incredibly fit and kept abreast of the hunt on foot) he arrived at the meet and inquired why all the local sabs appeared to be just waiting around. When it was explained that little could be achieved until the tufters had roused the stag, with much of the action not taking place until later, he replied with his customary, "Sod that," and vanished afoot into the Quantock Hills. That was the last anyone saw of Aubrey until well after dark that night, when search parties had scoured the hills looking for him, amid a growing chorus of consensus that he should be left to the elements, finally brought him to bay. Not the least abashed, he admitted that he had seen little of the hunt, adding cheerfully, "You can get a damn good run around here."

Another individual who stands out during this time was the young Bristol saboteur Ian Nunnerley (affectionately know to us all as "Magic") who was fearless in his defence of friends during the violent confrontations. Careering around the countryside in a battered old silver MKII Cortina, with the bonnet emblazoned with a huge yellow sticker proclaiming "Nuclear Power No Thanks", his hair a mass of curly frizz, he embodied the youthful enthusiasm of the dedicated animal rights campaigner of the 1970s and '80s. Often drawing unwanted attention from the hunt heavies for his striking appearance, he was never known to back off and remained one of the last SOS campaigners to quit the field after the final pitched battles of 14th April 1984.

Note 2. Although the purchase of sixty-acre Alfoxton Wood served its initial purpose of preventing both the QSH and Somerset West Vale Foxhounds from hunting through it, it failed to offer the desired protection for the red deer that lived within it. The reason being that the neighbouring pro-hunt farmer would plant kale, or root crops, in the surrounding fields, which of course enticed the deer, who in turn were regularly shot. This changed in 1987 when the said farmer was obliged, by mounting debts, to sell forty-five acres to the LACS at a cost of £70,000. This large sanctuary is now home to one of the best herds of deer on the Quantocks, with this author counting in excess of 130 during the 2006 rut.

Note 3. Paul Watson is still one of the most active, and colourful, characters within the international animal rights movement. A founder member of Greenpeace, he was expelled after a campaign against the Canadian seal cull during which he threw sealer's clubs and pelts into the sea, temporarily costing Greenpeace its tax-exemption status in the US. The Sea Shepherd Conservation Society was formed following his expulsion in 1977 and has chalked up one of the most impressive tally sheets of any direct action movement on record. Following the sinking of *Sierra* two other whaling vessels, *Ibsa I* and *Ibsa II*, were sunk in the Spanish harbour of Viga during 1981. Two more whaling ships were sunk in Reykjavik, Iceland, along with substantial damage to the nearby processing station, during 1986, while 1992 saw considerable damage caused to the minke whaling vessel *Nybraena*, following a scuttling attempt at her moorings in the Lofoten Islands. A similar action was carried out the following year (1993), south of Fredrikstad, against the Norwegian whaling ship *Senet*.

Paul Watson is still going strong, with his violent confrontations against the factory whaling ship *Nisshin Maru*, during the 2008 Japanese Antarctica humpback whale slaughter, making compulsive viewing on the television news bulletins. Within weeks of this action Watson was sailing back to the Gulf of St Lawrence and the Atlantic coast of Newfoundland in an attempt to sabotage the legalised Canadian annual slaughter of 275,000 harp seals and 8,200 hooded seals.

The full story of this remarkable organisation can be found in Paul Watson's book *Ocean Warrior: My Battle to End the Illegal Slaughter on the High Seas*.

Note 4. It would be another five years before we were to see *Sea Shepherd II* again. In August 1986 she would limp into port at my home city of Bristol, spattered with bullet holes, following a violent confrontation with Faeroese navel vessels during an attempt to disrupt the annual Faeroe Islands pilot whale slaughter.

Chapter Nine

"I did not find her a reliable witness..."

THE ISSUE OF DEER poaching had occupied the attention of SOS nearly as much as the private war against the QSH. In fact we had been operating anti-poaching patrols since the mid-1970s, with varying degrees of success. The most notable concerned a well-organised gang that were based in the Midlands, but carried out most of their poaching activities in Kent, Dorset and large parts of the West Country. They used an expensive Bedford van fitted with a refrigerated unit that could accommodate up to thirty carcasses. Working closely with other deer related groups we were able to keep tabs on this vehicle for over nine months, until one night information was received that it was operating on the Quantock Hills. Before dawn the van caught fire and was totally destroyed. There were some who thought arson was to blame, while others merely shrugged their shoulders and thought so what, deer were worth gestures like that!

What had been obvious for a long time was the connection between poachers and deer hunters. The poacher in his role of hunt supporter would follow the hounds to confirm the location of suitable targets, then once the killings had taken place would arrange with local farmers for transport out of the area. It transpired that the most common method used was to hide the carcass under lorry loads of swedes and turnips that were destined for London's Smithfield Market. Much of the venison then found its way onto continental dinner tables, with the favourite destinations in France, Belgium and Germany.

While it was extremely difficult to prove the connection, the allegations being vehemently denied by the hunting lobby, occasionally the curtain was raised, as the result of a 1988 court case would prove. This instance concerned DSSH supporter Simon David, whose father operated an abattoir, in partnership with family employee Martin Willis. Driving around the moors in his father's four-wheel drive Subaru truck David would blast away at the deer with waxed shotgun pellets, while Willis would use the abattoir to butcher the carcasses. One of the interesting sidelights of the subsequent trial, during which the pair were fined over £2,000, was a letter from the hunt giving David a glowing character reference. His father had written to the DSSH apologising for any adverse publicity or embarrassment that the case might bring upon them, and a letter had been received in reply stating that they would be welcome to return to the hunt. Some months later David appealed against his fine, but instead found himself in prison. At Wells Crown Court, Judge Joy Ann Bracewell sentenced him to one month in a detention centre.

Stag hunters also played a pivotal role in protecting the poacher by constantly playing down the seriousness of the poaching problem so as not to compromise their credibility as the *only* true protector of the deer. When the situation on the Quantocks appeared to be nearing crisis levels in January 1982, and serious attempts were made to co-ordinate a coalition to deal with the situation comprising the LACS, RSPCA, British Deer Society, Forestry Commission and Somerset Trust for Nature Conversation, the QSH attempted to torpedo the initiative from the start.

Hunt master Walner Robins countered by claiming that the outcry against poaching on the Quantocks was nothing more than "a cry of frustration" brought about because the LACS "is angry because neighbouring farmers occasionally shoot deer which stray on to their fields from the Alfoxton sanctuary." He did concede that "we know there are a few genuine poachers but they are not a problem". Yet by October of the same year, when the proposed coalition had failed to materialise and any involvement against poaching by anti-hunt factions had been neutralised, Walner Robins suddenly discovered "evil and despicable" poachers were roaming the Quantock Hills. His sudden interest had been occasioned by the discovery of three deer near the village of Holford which had been "peppered with pellets" after having been blasted by shotguns at long range. My "cry of frustration" had arisen from a similar incident near Spaxton, when I had to arrange the humane destruction of three hinds in a similar condition.

It would take another four years for the declining numbers of deer on the Quantock Hills to be taken seriously, but by February 1986, under the auspices of the Somerset Trust for Nature Conservation, the Quantock Deer Forum was born. Its remit was to conduct a detailed survey of deer numbers, which would be conducted annually, co-ordinate the activities of over fifty voluntary wardens on the hills, and formulate a general policy to deal with the threat from poachers. On the surface it looked good, but there were those whose suspicions were roused by the composition of the Deer Forum's membership, especially when one of its main spokesmen turned out to be Major Thomas Trollope-Bellew. His statement that "everything that can be done is being done to stamp out poaching" tended to ring hollow when people began to wonder if he could be related to the same Major Trollope-Bellew who had, on behalf of stag hunt interests, so vigorously opposed the attempts to amend the *1963 Deer Act.*

County councillor Mal Treharne would cut his teeth as a blood sport apologist while acting as the Somerset County Council's liaison officer, later becoming one of the most vociferous pro-deer hunting voices within the Countryside Alliance. The example set by the Quantock Deer Forum would be followed by hunting interests in other areas, with an "independent" report produced by the Devon Trust for Nature Conservation leading to the formation of a similar forum on Exmoor with Tom Yandle, vice chairman of the DSSH as its chairman. This report entitled *Exmoor Red Deer Survey 1981-82* was both "naïve and inconsistent" according to the LACS's wildlife officer John Bryant.

In a review for the magazine *Wildlife Guardian* he slated the report saying, "Quite frankly I am amazed that such unscientific conclusions can be reached from the painstaking investigations undertaken by the Survey Team." He went on to illustrate his point by writing:

> "For instance, the report states in one paragraph: 'It is important to appreciate the nature of culling deer with hounds and the importance of the hunt within a community that successfully

integrates the activities of farmers, foresters etc.' but in an earlier paragraph it states that one of the most serious threats to the continued existence of red deer on Exmoor is 'habitat loss being caused by Exmoor landowners, farmers and foresters who are clearing woodland, gorse and bracken to improve pasture for sheep and cattle.'

"The report also seeks to discredit the League's view that where necessary, the deer can be controlled by qualified marksmen, by citing one case where a deer was wounded by an unidentified shooter. The report's authors fail to report the views of the British Deer Society or the Deer Management Society of Devon who both cull deer with rifles in the same way as the Forestry Commission, and also fail to discuss the point that in order to maintain the Exmoor herd at around 1,000 deer, 300 of the animals must be culled each year, whereas the hunt only kills about 55, leaving the other 250 to be shot."

The SOS war of attrition with the QSH continued unabated throughout 1982 with the frequency and intensity of the violence increasing with every meet that we attended. As there were few weeks that we failed to put in an appearance the casualty list began to look quite frightening. As most of the saboteurs had full time jobs it was fairly difficult to arrange mid-week hits with numbers higher than four or five, which of course opened them to severe risk of a serious beating with no chance of back up. Activities during the week were mainly confined to flushing the woods of deer (at least during the stag hunting season) and ever-increasing acts of economic sabotage against hunt vehicles and property. This included pubs, hotels and any and every commercial interest that supported deer hunting, though it must be stressed that it was not SOS policy to commit serious damage. The isolated acts that resulted in severely damaged or destroyed vehicles were the work of extreme animal rights splinter groups such as the Animal Liberation Front or the Hunt Retribution Squad who, even though we made repeated requests for them to stop, were convinced that they were doing us a favour.

In fact these actions made our position even more precarious when confronted by very angry hunt supporters at the next meet we attended following one of these attacks.

It was such a situation that led to a particularly vicious pitched battle waged across the village green and adjacent woodland at Holford in early October. In a fight that lasted for the better part of an hour, with enraged hunt supporters pouring in from every direction, the local residents inevitably became caught in the middle. It was partly as a result of this incident, plus a growing anger at the high-handed attitude of the QSH in general, that prompted a number of Holford parish councillors to organise a referendum asking the entire village whether the hunt was still welcome. As if to rub salt in the wounds, on 30th October members of the QSH trespassed onto land belonging to Holford resident David Fineberg, from which they had previously been banned, where they killed a stag. At a secret ballot the villagers voted by a majority of three to one telling the hunt to keep away from Holford. At subsequent meetings with the Holford residents officials of the QSH agreed to stay out of the village. Another astonishing decision taken by the hunt was to abandon Saturday meets altogether, with the "official" excuse that it was "a bid to cut disruption caused by hunt followers" on the Quantock Hills. Many of us thought it more likely a bid "to cut disruption caused by hunt saboteurs"!

When the QSH began ad-hoc Saturday hunting on Exmoor at the invitation of the DSSH it did not take long for trouble to follow. The first serious encounter came on 15th January 1983 during a meet near Dulverton when, after continuous scuffles throughout the day, hounds were drawn away by the saboteurs, causing violent reactions from hunt staff. The League's sanctuaries manager John Hicks was attacked, later prompting Dick Course to angrily retort, "From now on all our staff will be accompanied by minders from the East End."

The fact that 1983 was election year prompted all kinds of speculation that the Labour Party would make the abolition of blood sports a Manifesto commitment. In an attempt to pre-empt such a move, Tory MP Humphrey Atkin, in the sure knowledge "that much of the anti-blood sport agitation is by Left-wing troublemakers", launched the Campaign for Country Sports. Though not much of a campaign, being primarily comprised of expensive-looking leaflets extolling the virtues of deer hunting (and other assorted sports) as the only practical means of control, it did convey the fact that hunting as a political issue was firmly back on the agenda. The antis countered by reviving the General Election Co-ordinating Committee for Animal Protection (GECCAP) with extensive canvassing of all the main parties. In the event left-wing Labour leader Michael Foot committed his party to the abolition of all hunting with dogs, but it all proved academic for the Labour Party again went down to crushing defeat at the polls.

With the prospect of another five years of the Thatcher government, many accepted without question that any attempt at political initiatives was a non-starter, turning instead to ever more desperate direct action tactics. Even the LACS, while making the right noises publicly and filling the pages of their magazine *Cruel Sports* with endless reports of pointless private members' motions at Westminster, were beginning to feel the strain. An increasingly frustrated Richard Course, fearful that the League would revert back to its relegated status of the 1950s, desperately looked around for publicity that would keep its name in lights and at the same time frustrate the hunters. New sanctuaries were purchased, with £60,000 paid for a 200-acre farm on the middle of Exmoor, while a campaign was launched to encourage county councils across the country to ban hunting on their land, along with the similar Co-op (Land) Campaign.

To clear the decks and cement the League's "respectable political credentials" with the Labour Party, Richard Course now also judged the time right to rid him-self of the troublesome and generally apolitical hunt saboteurs who had been so instrumental in securing his control of the LACS. Latching onto a decision to employ direct action tactics against angling, made at the HSA's 1983 AGM, Course branded them a "bunch of lunatics" and demanded that the decision be reversed. When the saboteurs politely declined his request, the LACS adopted a policy of non-co-operation with the HSA. The annual goodwill donation of £1,000 to HSA funds was cut, while spiteful attacks were launched against the saboteurs at public meetings and in the press. This sorry state of affairs would sour the next five years until the resignation of Richard Course as League Executive Director in 1988.

The chance to haul the hunting fraternity before the courts was grabbed at every opportunity by the LACS, but was fraught with the very real possibility of failure, as was proved when an attempt to prosecute the QSH for armed trespass was thrown out by Minehead magistrates. Following the killing of a stag on David Fineberg's Holford property the previous year the League brought a prosecution against three hunt members under the *1980 Deer Act.* In June 1983 John Fewings was charged with armed trespass and unlawfully killing the animal, and hunt master Walner Robins and hunt chairman Roly Ford with aiding and abetting him.

As most of the case rested on clauses within the *Deer Act* the defence solicitor Jo Collins was able to convince the court that hunting representatives were assured that this Act was not intended to be used against them. She concluded her case by stating,

> "When they (Parliament) framed this statute they did not for one moment anticipate that the actions of staghunters were going to be subject to litigation in this field. They were not poaching. They were hunting. What are the League doing if they think that every time anybody crosses a piece of land and they are hunting, they commit a criminal offence by this Act?"

In September 1983 a new front was opened in Hampshire when a host of celebrities from stage and screen including Peter Cushing, James Mason, David Jacobs, Katie Boyle, Sir Henry Moore, Richard Adams, Beryl Reid, Bill Travers, Virginia McKenna and the Bishop of Salisbury agreed to act as patrons in a bid to stop fallow deer hunting. They had responded to calls from Southampton based photographer Chris Belcombe who had recently formed The New Forest Deerhunt Abolition Alliance. The launch of this group closed a gap in campaigns against deer hunting, for the New Forest Buckhounds had somehow escaped serious opposition for many years. While it was true that SOS had made occasional visits and the LACS had made passing reference over the years, their activities had been completely overshadowed by the West Country stag hunts.

Now the NFDAA would concentrate on attempting to get the

licence needed to operate a hunt in the forest revoked. As the New Forest is termed a "State Forest" it is managed by the Forestry Commission, who in all their woodlands employ the services of professional marksmen to control the deer numbers. Such was the case in the New Forest, where all species of deer, including fallow, were managed in that way. The exception being that a discretionary licence was granted to the NFB for purely recreational reasons. It may have been true that only around ten bucks were killed annually, with maybe another hundred harried around the forest throughout the hunting season, but logic dictated that if the majority could be controlled by forestry marksmen then so could these additional ten. The Alliance planned to monitor each hunt, photograph kills and related acts of cruelty, while keeping the killing of fallow deer for sport firmly in the public gaze.

At the time SOS committee members contemplated turning themselves into a similar monitor-mode, but rejected the idea as the long-term aim could in no way resemble those of the NFDAA. For whereas they were working towards a single-issue plan for the rejection of a hunting licence, as no such licence system operated in relation to West Country stag hunting, our efforts could only duplicate the recording of hunt incidents which had been carried out by the LACS for years with no discernible success. So a decision was taken in late October to continue with the disruption of deer hunting, at least for the remainder of the 1983/1984 season, then, depending on the violence encountered to evaluate the situation the following year.

As it turned out the next six months proved some of the most violent that SOS would encounter. The QSH on the days they hunted across Exmoor were augmented by large numbers of extremely aggressive DSSH supporters who, at the first sight of saboteurs, would rush to the attack. Another problem was that a number of seasoned SOS veterans had given up, tired of being constantly injured, with many of the new recruits cowed at the unexpected levels of violence encountered. The final full-scale attempt to disrupt a stag hunt came on 14th April 1984 against the DSSH. From the moment the hunt moved off from the meet at Brendon Two Gates, near Simonsbath, there was fighting. During the day ten people were injured, with some needing hospital treatment. At one point the Devon and Cornwall Police used a helicopter to track saboteurs, while police on the ground attempted to arrest the leaders.

The end came some miles from the meet, near the village of Winsford, when the entire mounted field charged the saboteurs. Most antis remained in their vehicles while riders lashed out with their crops. Angry and frustrated, I stood my ground and started lashing back with the battered walking stick that had been my constant companion throughout the SOS campaign. I would be joined by a solitary saboteur (a magnificent fellow with a bright yellow Mohican haircut I was later informed answered to the name Sunflower) and we maintained a "back to back" until the last rider had passed. This "last stand" had proved prophetic, for it confirmed what we had known for some time: the day of the stag hunt saboteur was over, but it had allowed us to bow out in style. The good news, we learned later, was that, thanks to the previous night's flushing, the deer were so scattered that even though the hunt found two stags they had failed to make a kill. From now on SOS members would continue to flush the harboured deer on the nights prior to hunting, tactics that continued until 1987, but there would be no more daylight confrontations.

During this time the LACS had been gearing itself for a mammoth legal battle with the DSSH. The story went back to 1982 when the hunt had allowed their hounds to enter five different sanctuaries on seven separate occasions. The League had attempted to prosecute over the years with little real success because the law on hound trespass had not been defined, some County Court Judges had ruled that hound entry on prohibited land was not trespass, while other County Court Judges had ruled that it was. The decision was taken to try for a legal definition that would be binding in law, which could only be obtained by taking the case before a high court judge, whose ruling would be binding on all county court judges.

After a statement of claim for damages by trespass was issued to the hunt, the League applied to the High Court for an interim injunction in March 1983. Such applications are a short matter – the Judge simply examines the *prima facie* evidence without witnesses and lengthy submissions by lawyers. However, if a contested interim injunction is granted there is no turning back – a full blown trial has to go ahead regardless of costs or consequences.

The injunction was granted and the three Joint Masters of the DSSH (Nora Harding, Maurice Scott and Michael Robinson) were ordered by Mr Justice Staughton to ensure that their hounds were kept off the five named sanctuaries. As Contempt of Court is classed as a serious criminal matter, failure to comply with the ruling could have resulted in a prison sentence. The hunt could have, and should have accepted the injunction, especially as they had admitted that their hounds had entered League land, but they chose to contest it. So a lengthy and expensive high court case became inevitable.

For the next two years the League's Sanctuaries Manager John Hicks, supported by his wife Jo and a small army of volunteers, carefully monitored the hunt every time it went out. Now and again they went fairly close to the sanctuaries named in the interim injunction and they also went close to some of the other twenty-eight sanctuaries, but not once in two years did one hound put as much as one paw on any of the League's properties.

This was just what the LACS were praying for. It was conclusive evidence that an injunction worked – for it proved that the hunt could control their hounds. It was now shown that their previous written undertakings to keep hounds out of the sanctuaries were a sham that they had no intention of keeping. But, most of all, it justified to the League's EC that, where derisory £25 fines for trespass, promises and written undertakings were no deterrent, the threat of prison appeared to do the trick.

The hunt appointed Mr Edward Cazalet QC to defend them. This meant that the League could also raise the stakes to QC level. Up to then, Mr Paul Darlow, a Bristol barrister had handled the case, but he agreed that a more experienced and senior Counsel should be appointed. The League's solicitor, Mr Tom Hart of Powells in Weston-Super-Mare recommended the very best, Mr Louis Blom-Cooper. It was also decided, due to the complexity of the case, to appoint a second barrister, Mr Jonathan Fisher.

And so on Tuesday 26th February 1985 at Bristol High Court the Honourable Justice Park, resplendent in red and black robes opened the trial. Mr Louis Blom-Cooper, surrounded by books, papers, two barristers and a solicitor rose to his feet to open the most significant court case in the League's long battle with the stag hunters. The trial would last for twelve days, during which time claim and counter-claim would resound throughout the court, with reputations left in ruins and a final decision that left few abolitionists in any doubt as to the justification of their cause. John Hicks would be termed "...a fair-minded and reliable witness", while the judge's view of hunt master Nora Harding was that, "I did not find her a reliable witness, and I am not able to attach any weight to her evidence." The astounding ignorance of deer control methods on Exmoor which was shown by the DSSH's "expert" witness Richard Prior moved Justice Park "to the conclusion that the hunt's expert evidence of the consequences of the hunt's inability to hunt deer in any given area, seemed to me to be somewhat exaggerated." ***APPENDIX 5***

The case ended on 13th March 1985, with a further three weeks for the judge to review the evidence. On 2nd April Justice Park recalled everyone to Bristol for his judgement. He took two hours to deliver some fifty-seven pages, which found all seven entries to be trespass but gave an injunction to Pitleigh with these words: "For the three trespasses at Pitleigh the damages will be £25, £25 and £50. There will also be an injunction restraining the Defendants by themselves, their servants and agents, or mounted followers, from causing or permitting hounds to enter or cross the property." In conclusion he ruled (thereby making conviction at County Court level mandatory) that:

> "Where a Master of Staghounds takes out a pack of hounds and deliberately sets them in pursuit of a stag or hind, knowing that there is a real risk that, in the pursuit, hounds may enter or cross prohibited land, the Master will be liable for trespass if he intended to cause hounds to enter such land, or, if by his failure to exercise proper control over them, he caused them to enter such land..."

In simple language it meant that each and every time one or more hounds enter property without permission it will be deemed as intentional or negligent-and thus trespass. With costs awarded to the League in excess of £70,000 it was a very expensive lesson for the hunt to learn that the days of feudal privilege were over and that they did not possess the God-given right to ride roughshod over anyone who happened to disagree with them. The knock-on effect of this ruling was that unprecedented numbers of farmers and landowners contacted the League for assistance in keeping hunts off their land. When the League placed adverts in the press explaining "Hound Entry *is* Trespass" the BFSS complained to the Advertising Standards Authority that the wording was misleading. The complaint was rejected. In a last desperate bid to avoid falling foul of the injunction, Nora Harding announced that the only means by which trespass could be avoided was to erect a six foot high wire mesh fence around the Pitleigh sanctuary. The intervention of the Exmoor National Park Authority, on the grounds that such a fence conflicted with the moor's visual appeal, temporarily prevented its erection. Though later, no doubt as a result of "influence in high places" they did erect their fence around Pitleigh. Due to an oversight, namely the fact that the hunt had neglected to tell the neighbouring farmer on whose land the fence was erected, they were ordered by the furious owner to remove a sixty metre section. The effect of this was that deer chased by the hounds could go into the sanctuary through the gap, but because most of it was still fenced, the animal could not get out the other side. The hunt was unable to chase it back out through the gap for fear of trespassing, so as long as the deer stayed put it was safe. The fencing off of sanctuaries by the DSSH (there were others apart from Pitleigh) was an expensive drain on their resources that offered limited success, but certainly conveyed the message as to the lengths to which they were willing to go in an attempt to protect their right to hunt unhindered.

The fallow buck hunters of Hampshire also found themselves under increased pressure following the publicity generated by the New Forest Deerhunt Abolition Alliance (NFDAA). In fact, so successful had they been in exposing the cruelties of this hunt, the RSPCA, Animal Aid and the LACS decided to join forces and finish them off. A major new campaign was launched at the end of July 1985 under the umbrella title of the New Forest Deer Protection Council. The new group would be led by long-time local opponent of the hunt Graham Sirl, while the well known local wildlife photographer and film maker Eric Ashby, would act as the Council's technical adviser.

The League continued to purchase ever more land with additional woodland at Chelfham bringing that sanctuary to over thirty acres. This was followed by another twenty-two acres near East Anstey. The DSSH did their best to impress the Devon town of South Molton by chasing a terrified stag into the town centre, cornering it in the Co-op car park in full view of numerous shoppers, then blasting it to death at close range with a shotgun. Nora Harding had the perfect excuse, shifting the blame on to the unfortunate animal by claiming: "It has done this sort of thing before. I think it may have had an urban mentality." The pro-blood sport, former *Daily Telegraph* editor, Max Hastings was not so impressed when writing in *The Field.* For him: "The stag hunt which pursued its beast into the middle of a Devon town a few weeks ago did not only shame itself, it inflicted a bitter blow to the image of field sports. Yet when these incidents take place (as, every season, several do) there is no attempt by the relevant field sports body to impose sanctions or even publicly condemn their conduct."

On 15th January 1986 Labour MP Harry Cohen introduced a Ten Minute Rule Bill on the subject of cruelty to animals, which included the abolition of stag hunting. A similar measure was tried the following month (12th February) when Kevin McNamara (Labour) introduced his *1986 Amendment Bill to the 1911 Protection of Animals Act* under the same Ten Minute Rule. The intention was to add the words "wild animals" to the original 1911 Act, thus bringing hunted animals under legal protection. The Bill, which in reality was nothing more than an attempt to enable Honourable Members to make a pronouncement on the issue, got no further than an initial vote of 133-0 in favour, though McNamara was "delighted" with the result, claiming that: "This is the first time that Parliament has agreed in principle to prohibit all forms of hunting… . We now need the election of a Labour Government committed to this matter, to get the time needed to pursue the Bill."

This was not to be as the Labour Party again went down to crushing electoral defeat on 11th June 1987. For many it was abundantly clear that the Labour Party was unelectable and would remain so for the foreseeable future. While it was understandable to some that the LACS should continue to advocate continued pressure within the political system, there were many others who had had their fill of pointless Early Day Motions, Ten Minute Rule and Private Member's Bills and the attendant waffle that was the stock in trade of Westminster. And the fact that all of it was conducted under the auspices of a Tory government that, in the words of Norman Tebbit, "...has always taken the view that the question of field sports is a matter for the individual conscience...and would not try to prevent people from taking part in the sporting activities which they enjoy" only reinforced the futility of political campaigning at this point in time.

Truth to tell by the late 1980s there were many in animal rights for whom the very concept of a political solution to the blood sport issue had become something of a myth. All the evidence pointed unequivocally to the fact that successive Labour governments, with the 1949 Attlee sell-out the prime example, had no real intention of introducing legislation should they return to power. While it was certainly true that all attempts via back bench methods had been from Labour MPs, invariably from the Party's left-wing, it was equally true that once in office the Labour Party had singularly failed to make the subject a priority, or make serious attempts to promote government Bills. There were in fact many within the Labour Party's ruling elite who viewed the constant harping by these left-wingers as a serious irritant, fearing that their attacks against "privileged sports" would be construed as a class issue. The fact that both Michael Foot and Neil Kinnock had endorsed a Manifesto commitment to ban hunting was seen more as a desperate measure by a moribund party to solicit a few desperately needed votes than as any serious commitment to address animal cruelty. It was certainly felt that any future Labour government would have to be dragged screaming to the cause of abolition.

With the demise of Save Our Stags, the heat went out of the deer hunting agenda in the West Country. It was certainly true that the

LACS kept hammering away at the three packs, with the £70,000 purchase of a further forty-five acres in Holford which, together with the adjacent sixty-acre Alfoxton Park woodlands, made this part of the Quantocks a virtual no-go area for the hunt. On Exmoor an ever-vigilant John Hicks was working around the clock making sure that to trespass on the sanctuaries was becoming ever more difficult, but all of this made little difference to the bigger picture. The hunts still managed to spend their days virtually unhindered, while filling the press with shocking incidents. A pregnant hind, after having been chased through the village of Porlock by the DSSH, was shot and wounded. Bleeding profusely, it staggered down to the sea where it tried to escape the hunters by swimming out to sea. The villagers watched from the beach as the deer eventually drowned. ***APPENDIX 6***

The same hunt chased and killed a young stag in front of a group of Girl Guides at a weekend camp in the Horner Woods, near Porlock. The following morning the same guides found another stag lying half-submerged in the river. It was still alive, but in a terrible state of exhaustion and unable to move. The animal was taken to a Minehead vet, but was later to die. A local deer expert explained:

> "That the hunt was responsible for the death of the second stag is in no doubt… and here's how it probably happened. A splinter pack would have left the main group of hounds under a new scent. As we've heard the main group and the huntsmen accounted for the first stag by the campsite. The splinter pack on their own, meanwhile chased the second stag to water. And that is how he eventually escaped them.
>
> The hunt will deny that they ever lose control of their hounds but it happens all the time. The stag would have taken to water to elude the hounds. Having…done so it would have dropped from sheer exhaustion. I don't know if you have ever seen a deer who's managed to escape the hunt – they will lie up for hours and hours before they move again. You can see that their muscles get all cramped up. This one, in the cold water, didn't stand a chance."

Not to be outdone the QSH managed a few headline-grabbing stunts as well. A young hind was chased into the holiday village of Doniford, from where it fled into the sea. Construction workers at the site managed to close the gates and forced the hunt to ride away empty handed. The hind waited in the shallows before escaping back to the hills under cover of darkness. The photograph that accompanied the press story, showing the vulnerable little animal terrified and bewildered standing at the water's edge, was perhaps one of the most pathetic deer hunting images ever published.

A similar incident happened when a four-year old stag was chased into the sea near St Audries and rescued by three volunteer coastguards. One of the rescuers warmed the shivering animal by rubbing it with his hands and wrapping his own clothes around it while waiting for a coastguard Landrover to take it to a vet in Williton. The vet, who gave the stag three injections, said that it was very exhausted and in danger of developing pneumonia, which confirmed the opinion of its saviours who were convinced that "...he would not have lived long without help". In contrast to the attitude of QSH Joint Master Bill Fewings who retorted: "It may well have been our stag, but it was half an hour ahead of us all the time and I called off before we got anywhere near the beach. I don't doubt it went into the sea, but I'm sure it would have been alright without help. He would have gone back to the hills on his own if he had been left alone."

These types of incidents are commonplace during an average stag hunting year and it must be remembered that while many make the press there are considerably more that do not. Of the ones that are publicised, maybe one in ten are accompanied by photographs, which in the main fail to convey the true nature of the incident under discussion. Very occasionally one will appear which will prove the old adage that "one photograph is worth a thousand words". Never in their wildest dreams could the DSSS have imagined that when they moved off from their meet at Aldermans Barrow on 10th October 1987 such a picture would be splashed across the front page of numerous national newspapers within a few days. Following an otherwise unmemorable hunt, they managed to chase their stag onto the roof of a cottage in Porlock. Having been driven from the woodland it fled through the village streets, then onto a lean-to, and then on the roof, where it became trapped when the slates gave way under its weight. While locals argued with huntsmen who were attempting to shoot it, another local, Bill Cavanagh, photographed the terrified animal. The resulting pictures released a wave of revulsion from the general public, followed within days by a renewed effort to promote legislation outlawing stag hunting. ***Note 1***

Derbyshire North East Labour MP Harry Barnes tabled an Early Day Motion reading:

> "That this House deplores the increasing frequency of incidents and damage arising from the hunting of deer with packs of dogs; notes the overwhelming public opinion in support of the abolition of this unnecessary practice; and calls upon Her Majesty's Government to introduce early legislation to give deer the same protection from cruelty as domestic and captive animals currently receive under the terms of the *1911 Protection of Animals Act.*"

Not surprisingly, even though seventy-four MPs signed within days, the government ignored the plea. Though what did prove interesting was that the frequency of these deer hunting incidents were increasingly bringing them into conflict with other blood sport interests. It became commonplace to hear fox hunters bemoaning the fact that horrific stag hunting publicity was placing the spotlight on *all* hunting and it soon became evident that many would be willing to "sacrifice" stag hunting to protect their own sport.

Though back in the real world a Tory Somerset County Councillor Mrs Diana Wilson, in company with friends Doreen Cronin and Richard and Daisy Hall, incensed by this latest outrage, decided they would form a local based group to campaign on a local level. The Devon and Somerset Residents Association for Deer Protection was formed and over the following years would cause immeasurable damage to stag hunting interests.

Similar moves were afoot in the New Forest following the publication of a draft report by the New Forest Review Group, a body of representatives from various organisations set up by the Forestry

Commissioners to consider the effects of environmental pressures on the Forest which threatened its character and wildlife. Included in this 181-page report were various recommendations for curtailing some of the worst excesses of the various hunts operating in the Forest, but the report concluded that hunting would be allowed to continue as "...it is a legal activity unless or until Parliament decides otherwise". In a move to force a change of heart on the Forestry Commission the New Forest Deer Protection Council, New Forest Animal Protection Group, and LACS joined forces in a coalition calling itself Hounds off the New Forest. Fronted by wildlife photographer Eric Ashby and author Monica Coleman the new campaign was launched on Boxing Day 1987 with the avowed intention of raising a 50,000 signature petition to be sent to the Minister of Agriculture, urging him, as the Minister responsible for the Forestry Commission, to ban all hunting in the New Forest.

During this time the external image of the LACS as a professional public relations machine belied an internal structure that was sliding into chaos. Central to the problem was the increasingly dictatorial attitude of its director Richard Course. Unable to brook criticism or delegate responsibility for the running of the organisation he was constantly at odds with other staff members. The situation reached crisis point during February 1988 when he blew an undercover operation to *The Sunday Times* that included a dog fighting ring, the *News of the World*, and a member of the League's staff planted as a mole within the ring. His reason for doing this was that he wanted a more upmarket paper to cover the story. Subsequent actions against what he considered disloyal elements led to a request from Lords Houghton and Soper (LACS President and Vice President) for a full report on the situation. After failing to receive the Executive Committee's support, Course resigned on 23rd April 1988.

After his departure the League journal *Wildlife Guardian*, in a terse one-paragraph announcement, concluded by saying: "When the history of the abolition of hunting is written, Richard Course will undoubtedly feature prominently in those annals." Richard Course went on to try and form a new LACS. He believed that his charisma and contacts would make this possible but, in these situations, members tend to remain loyal to the organisation they know rather then to the individuals within it. Consequently he failed and the resulting bitterness would lead him down another road. Within weeks he was telling the press: "I have come to despise the League Against Cruel Sports, even though I was its Chairman and Chief Executive, simply because these people know as well as I do that the abolition of hunting will not make any difference to the welfare of foxes, hares or deer." The offer of a new home with the hunting fraternity was not long in coming.

By the Autumn of 1988 the first shots, in what would ultimately prove to be one of the most decisive battles against stag hunting, were fired when sixteen members of the National Trust (NT) submitted an AGM motion calling for all hunting of fox, deer, hare and mink to be prohibited on Trust land. Their intention was to instigate a ban based on a series of the NT's own bye-laws, which stated that:

> 1: "No unauthorised person shall cause or allow any dog…belonging to him or in his charge to enter or remain on any Trust Property to which entry is allowed unless such dog…is under proper control and is effectually restrained…from injuring, annoying or disturbing any…animal."
>
> 2: "No unauthorised person shall on Trust Property knowingly take, molest or wilfully disturb, injure or destroy any living creature…"
>
> 3: "No unauthorised person shall ride a horse on any part of Trust Property where horse-riding is likely to result in damage to Trust Property whether prohibited by notice or not."
>
> 4: "No person shall ride a horse to the danger or annoyance of or without due consideration for other persons resorting to Trust Property."

The Trust's Ruling Council, which opposed the motion, were obliged to distribute it to all one and a half million members for a ballot, with the resulting votes added to those cast at the AGM later in the year. In the subsequent postal ballot of Trust members less than five per cent voted, with many outraged members later complaining that they had known nothing of the ballot. In response the Trust officials acknowledged that the ballot papers had been unclear and inadequately identified. In the event the 29th October AGM vote would prove a watershed, for even though the resolution was defeated by 46,248 to 29,345, the Ruling Council could see a tidal wave of controversy approaching that threatened to tear the Trust apart.

Desperately looking for measures to head off the inevitable, the Council of the NT set up a Working Party under the Chairmanship of Sir John Quicke in March 1989 to study the practices of the Trust relating to hunting within the general policy agreed by the Council. The remit neither included a review of that policy, nor considered the moral issues of hunting. ***APPENDIX*** 7

When the Quicke Working Party reported back to the Council in June the primary recommendation was that a system of annual licences be introduced as the principle means of regulating all hunting on Trust properties. It was also suggested that under the terms of the *1981 Wildlife and Countryside Act* it might be possible to limit certain hunting activities by listing them as Potentially Damaging Operations (PDOs) on Sites of Special Scientific Interest (SSSIs). While this did not necessarily mean that these activities would be forbidden on sensitive sites, it did mean that permission for them to continue must be obtained from English Nature (formally the Nature Conservancy Council) thus passing the buck and relieving the pressure from the NT. The Council adopted the report.

In conclusion, the Working Party admitted that, from the start of their study, they had been hampered by a lack of knowledge on the numbers of deer and the structure of the population (the only such research to date had been the 1981-82 report undertaken by the Devon Trust for Nature Conservation of which John Bryant had been so scathing), coupled with a similar ignorance concerning the social and economic significance of deer hunting in the West Country. They therefore decided to commission two independent surveys to rectify the problem. The Deer Management Research Group of Southampton University was asked to produce a report on the conservation and management of deer on Exmoor and the Quantocks. The Centre for Rural Studies of the Royal Agricultural College, Cirencester was asked to produce a similar study concerning the economic and social aspects of deer hunting in the same area. Both reports to be complete within two years.

During this period, when the Trust's Ruling Council was doing everything it could to placate blood sport interests, it seemed to many ordinary members that the QSH was deliberately trying to make the job as difficult as possible with a series of headline-grabbing incidents. On 20th February 1989 the hunt chased a hind into the grounds of Halsway Manor, near Crowcombe, which was being used as a conference centre by employees of Clarks the shoemakers, who were on a management-training course. When the animal collapsed against the wall of a flowerbed in the eighteenth-century manor the QSH Chairman Anthony Trollope-Bellew arrived asking permission to enter the grounds so that he could kill the "sick" creature. The trainee managers took a quick vote electing instead to call in Bridgwater vet Michael Adamson who pronounced that the hind was not ill "merely exhausted and terrified". After being given an antibiotic injection, the deer was left in peace to find its own way back onto the Quantock Hills – which it did a few hours later.

Exactly two months later, on 20th April, the QSH topped their previous effort with a show of callousness on NT land that was filmed by the LACS's John Hicks. This remarkable film shows a lone pricket (a young male deer growing its first antlers and not quite two years old) being chased across the Quantock Hills towards excited hunt followers, who then take chase on horseback and in vehicles. Then it shows the deer collapsed in the heather from exhaustion and fear. Riders are within feet of it, and the deer could easily have been shot to put it out of its misery, but instead horsemen charged it with whips and crops to make it run further. But after another 150 yards it collapsed again. The film continues with the deer being forced to run again while huntsmen pursue it screaming and cracking whips.

A third time it collapsed. Again riders forced it to run, only to collapse thirty yards further on. The fourth time it went down the gun was sent for, but the Hunt Master said it hadn't been given a good enough run, and that it should be given "another chance". All this was taking place within yards of the League's Alfoxton Wood. As the hunters formed a line to stop the animal reaching safety the hunt saboteur in John Hicks over-rode the detached observer and he ran shouting at the deer. The startled creature turned and dashed through the line of riders into the sanctuary. A copy of the film was sent to the Quicke inquiry.

The DSSH meanwhile, in retaliation for the constant criticism of their activities coming from Porlock residents, erected a two-metre high deer-proof fence costing thousands of pounds around the village in early 1989. The Chairman of the Exmoor Society, though powerless to prevent the fence, described it as "...a hideous thing" and "an expensive price to pay for hunting". If "the iron curtain", as it soon became known, was meant to keep their actions away from public view it failed miserably. On 10th October 1989, exactly two years to the day after the "stag on the roof" incident, the hunt again killed in Porlock, after a stag made it through to the village side of the fence. For what it was worth the locals were enraged, while the press had a field day.

Just over two months later, on 18th December, shortly before the Christmas Parliamentary recess, six MPs (Harry Barnes (Lab), Andrew Bowden (Con), George Buckley (Lab), Frank Cook (Lab), Alan Meale (Lab) and Sir Teddy Taylor (Con) tabled yet another Early Day Motion. It read: "That this House believes that deer hunting with packs of dogs is an obscenity and should be abolished." On the first day the Motion gained the support of 151 MPs-a phenomenal number for the first day of any EDM. By the middle of the following year the number of signatories had risen to over 230, well over one third of the House of Commons. This prompted Jeremy Corbyn (Lab: Islington North) to introduce a Ten Minute Rule Bill against deer hunting. On Friday, 22nd June 1990, when the Bill had its Second Reading it was deferred on the simple objection of Sir Nicholas Bonsor (Con: Upminster), Chairman of the BFSS. Though an event of much greater significance was about to engulf that much loved British institution: the National Trust.

The continuing intransigence of the Ruling Council on the issue of blood sports was about to dominate the forthcoming AGM once again when two controversial motions were submitted. One, from Paul Sheldon, called for the NT "...to ban the hunting of foxes, hares and mink with hounds and the associated activity of 'digging out' and terrier work...". The other, less wide-ranging, though ultimately to prove far more contentious demanded: "This meeting recommends that...wherever the Trust has the right to decide whether or not hunting should be permitted on land it owns, the hunting of deer with hounds should be prohibited from 1st August 1991...". The motion was jointly proposed by Doreen Cronin and Diana Wilson of the Devon and Somerset Residents' Association for Deer Protection. Neither of them could have had the slightest notion that the resulting furore would change forever not only the conscious thinking of the NT, but would place in question the very future of stag hunting. ***APPENDIX 8***

Note 1. The lack of antlers on the animal in the Bill Cavanagh photograph would indicate that it was a nott stag – West Country term for a male red deer that never produces antlers. This was probably the reason he was being hunted that day, as nott stags are not considered good breeding stock.

Chapter Ten

"...go out as apostles into the world and support this war"

AT APPROXIMATELY 7:15 PM on 3rd November 1990, in the Conference Hall at Llandudno amid television lights, cameras and thrusting microphones, the vote on the resolution to ban the hunting of deer with hounds on Trust land was finally announced: FOR 68,679, AGAINST 63,985.

On one of the extremely rare occasions, in almost 100 years of its existence, the membership of the NT had defied a Council recommendation that members should vote against a motion. Even though the companion motion from Paul Sheldon, to ban the hunting of fox, hare and mink, was defeated by a similar majority, the Trust now had a moral obligation to implement the wishes of its members with regard to stag hunting. The Ruling Council though had no intention of doing this, announcing instead that they would convene a meeting on 13th December to review the situation. The implication of this vote for the future of deer hunting sent shock waves across Exmoor and the Quantocks. Weeks of frantic activity ensued in an attempt to persuade the NT to reject the ban, culminating in a mass meeting at Brushford's Carnarvon Arms Hotel organised by the BFSS. The turnout was so great that the meeting had to be moved outside into the hotel's courtyard where they heard former LACS director Richard Course, cementing his new-found alliance to the blood sport lobby, tell them that: "What I find sick and perverse and downright dishonest is that all these people who oppose the hunt know as well as I do that if hunting was abolished the deer would disappear from the hills." Though the best line of the night went to BFSS director John Hopkinson who told his audience to "go out as apostles into the world and support this war".

The subsequent revelation that the Trust's outgoing Chairman Dame Jennifer Jenkins (wife of former SDP leader Roy Jenkins) had used between 30,000 and 40,000 proxy votes in an attempt to defeat both motions did nothing to allay the anger felt by the general membership when the Council's decision was finally announced. There would be no implementation of a ban, but rather the setting up of another "working party" to investigate the implications of a ban. This would be conducted over the next two years and completed by March 1993, at which time the issue would again be discussed at the following AGM.

The composition of this new Working Party soon began to raise serious concerns amongst the proponents of a ban when, contrary to repeated assurances of impartiality by the Council, it became evident that it was heavily biased in favour of hunting interests. Of the five person team Mr D Pearce (farmer and nominee of the Royal Agricultural Society) had spoken out strongly against Doreen Cronin's motion at the 1990 AGM and made it clear that he considered individuals should be free to hunt if they wished. Mrs Ruth Blok (nominee of the Council for the Protection of Rural England), in summing up for the Council on the fox hunting resolution at the AGM, argued that the question of banning hunting was a matter that should only be decided by Parliament and that "the Trust...should not be held captive to single pressure groups".

Mr Richard Steele, who had not expressed a personal view on the hunting issue, was the nominee of the government-controlled Nature Conservancy Council (now English Nature) and had been its Director-General from 1980-1987, so was expected to support its line. The NCC had been the subject of fierce debate some months earlier, during Nicholas Ridley's time as Secretary of State for the Environment, because of its declared policy of withholding grants to applicants who indicated their intention to ban hunting from their land. At the time of this controversy it was stated that of the fifteen-member (government-appointed) NCC at least half took part in one kind of blood sport or another, with the Vice-Chairman being a Master of Foxhounds.

The Chairman of the Working Party, Professor R J G Savage, was something of an unknown quantity. For as a founder member of the Somerset Trust for Nature Conservation (which has its headquarters on Trust land near Bridgwater in Somerset) it was feared that he may have held the same opinions as the STNC's Director, Roger Martin, who had vigorously opposed the stag hunt ban at the AGM. The last member of the team was Mr S Ponder who appeared to have no direct or indirect blood sport connections, though as an elected member of the NT's Ruling Council it was supposed he would support the general policy of no ban.

It did not take long for the ripples of this snub to the members' wishes to spread beyond the confines of NT committee rooms. In fact blood sport magazines such as *Horse & Hound* and *Shooting Times*, at the behest of the BFSS, had been calling for their supporters to join the Trust since before the first vote on the issue in 1988. The LACS had deliberately stood back from the issue for as John Bryant explained they were "opposed in principle to the tactics of infiltration and entryism on a single issue". Now they felt unable to "stand idly by and allow such undemocratic decisions to dictate the fate of wildlife".

The League now set about seeking the co-operation of other animal welfare organisations in mounting a campaign that would alert the members to the truth of the situation and persuade them to demand the end of hunting on NT land. The campaign would include the mass leafleting of all Trust's properties nation-wide in order to build up a huge anti-hunt block vote in order to overturn any future pro-hunt decisions of the Ruling Council. The QSH meanwhile, the deer hunt with the most to lose from a ban, was frantically collecting signatures throughout the South West for a pro-hunt petition. Anthony Trollope-Bellew, chairman of the hunt, with wife Annabel in tow, resplendent in full hunting regalia, mounted astride their hunters, would personally deliver it to Trust headquarters in London.

The new chairman of the NT, Lord Chorley, in one of his first statements on taking office confirmed in the eyes of many that this new working party was nothing short of a sham. His January 1991 statement that: "They (the deer) do a lot of damage which the farmers put up with because they enjoy hunting" and "if they are not allowed to hunt they would shoot the deer" did rather pre-empt the future report's conclusion. In fact, not only was the biased nature of the working party under intense scrutiny from the Devon and Somerset Residents' Association for Deer Protection (DSRADP), but so also was the very structure of the ruling council and the power wielded by the chairman within it.

For under Trust rules it was permissible for the chairman to be given tens of thousands of proxy votes not only to use to vote for or oppose resolutions at his absolute discretion, but also to secure the election to the Council of persons he personally favoured. Therefore, as pointed out by Doreen Cronin, it was possible that these "votes could so weight the voting for council members as to set up a permanent oligarchy under the Chairman's personal patronage". ***Note 1***

In an attempt to redress this feudal state of affairs the DSRADP decided not only to float a resolution to change the proxy voting systems, but also to stand seven candidates at the 1991 AGM. Doreen Cronin, along with Diana Wilson, Ron Barnes and Geoff Southall of DSRADP, in company with Richard Ryder, John Hicks and John Bryant duly put their names forward. There were no surprises when their resolution and candidates were all defeated in November following the chairman's use of the proxy system against them. It was estimated that Lord Chorley used 40,000 discretionary votes against the resolution and 40,000 by nine to elect nine persons of his own choice to the Council. One side effect of this was that the NT, now viewed with extreme cynicism by many members, decided to set up yet another "Working Party". This one, under the patronage of Lord Oliver of Aylmerton, would be asked to review the Trust's constitution.

The decision by the DSRADP to suspend attempts at constitutional and procedural change within the Trust while awaiting the publication of the Savage Working Party Report did not mean a lessening of action on the home front. The constant round of committee and public meetings, fund-raising events, letters to the press and confrontations with the stag hunts continued. The occasional incident such as on 21st January 1992 when the QSH chased a pregnant hind to her death after falling forty feet into Triscombe Quarry on the Quantocks, would enable the DSRADP to elicit the most incredible show of indifference from the Trust's hierarchy. Writing to Lord Chorley, asking why this incident did not warrant the suspension of the hunt, they were informed that after a full investigation "there were not sufficient grounds for withdrawing the Quantock Staghounds licence, *especially as it appeared from a number of similar incidents in the past that this is a general, but happily an infrequent, problem*". (author's italics)

In preparation for the controversy expected to erupt following the publication of the Savage Working Party Report in a few months time DSRADP, along with the International Fund for Animal Welfare (IFAW) and International Animal Rescue (IAR), commissioned a Gallup Poll in November 1992 asking the question, "Do you agree or disagree that the National Trust should honour the successful resolution of its members and ban deer hunting with hounds on its land?" There was no doubt of public support with eighty per cent in agreement, ten per cent against and ten per cent Don't Knows.

Subsequently a number of MPs put down an EDM in Parliament that read:

> "That this House welcomes the exceptionally high percentage of public support indicated within a recent Gallup Poll for the successful members resolution to ban deer hunting...and awaits with eager anticipation the Trust's recognition of that public expression of view regarding an activity on land they hold in keeping for the nation."

The NT response when it came, on 20th April 1993, was a surprise to no one. The Ruling Council announced that it had accepted the recommendations of the Savage Working Party not to implement a ban on deer hunting. The very last paragraph of the forty-two page report summed up its priorities precisely: "A ban on hunting would destroy confidence and goodwill and would cause many people to see the Trust as an antagonist, not a friend, of the countryside and its needs. *We regard this as the most serious implication of a ban by the Trust on hunting.*" (author's italics)

The Savage Report was accompanied by the two professional reports that had been commissioned in 1989 following the Quicke Working Party Report. Both these reports, Southampton University's *Conservation and Management of Deer on Exmoor and the Quantocks* and Cirencester College's *Economic and Social Aspects of Deer Hunting on Exmoor and the Quantocks,* were largely ignored within the main Savage Report. The reasons for this was quite simple, these two extremely detailed documents were at considerable variance with the Trust's own Report.

For instance, the NT Press Release had told the world that Savage had concluded that "to achieve the necessary active co-operation from landowners and farmers which is essential to the welfare of the deer, the role of the hunt is of critical importance". Whereas the Southampton Report stated in relation to the programme operating on the Quantocks: "There is no reason to believe that, given a ban on hunting, such co-operative management would not continue if hunting were no longer part of the management." It further declared:

> "A decision on whether hunting should form part of future management or not will need to be made largely on grounds of ethics, animal welfare… . Thus, the current, relatively small contribution of hunting to the total cull does not suggest to us that the mere presence or absence of hunting will make overall management of the population impossible to achieve."

The Southampton Report qualified its assertion that hunting was basically irrelevant as a serious form of deer control by highlighting the contribution made by the three West Country packs. Concluding that there were approximately 7,000 red deer (though this figure was contested by the hunters) occupying Exmoor, the Quantocks and surrounding areas, with a need to cull around 1,000 each year, the total killed by hunting appeared to be no more than 130. It seemed perfectly reasonable to assume this number could be added to the remaining 870 already culled relatively humanely by marksmen.

The Cirencester Report did a similar demolition job on the economic and social implications of a deer hunting ban. Instead of indicating dire consequences for the local economy, which had been predicted by the hunts, they estimated that just a tiny one per cent of a very localised workforce would be affected – and that even this could be avoided if drag hunting took the place of chasing a live quarry. They concluded: "Suffice it to say that in comparison to the tourist economy of Devon and Somerset, the hunting economy of Exmoor pales into insignificance."

The immediate reaction of many following the Council's decision was to resign their membership of the Trust, a situation which prompted Lord Soper, LACS President and NT member, to propose his own motion to be placed before the forthcoming November AGM. The motion, supported by 875 signatories, proposed:

> "This AGM notes with concern the Trust's public acknowledgement that thousands of members have resigned...following its refusal to implement a ban on hunting deer with hounds on its property on Exmoor and the Quantocks and that the Working Party failed to address the issue of cruelty and animal welfare referred to by the movers of the resolution. We therefore call upon the Trust to set up a balanced Working Party of members of the Council who are both supporters and opponents of hunting, to examine those aspects of management not addressed by Professor Savage's Working Party, i.e. issues related to cruelty and animal welfare."

When the ballot paper for the pending AGM was sent out to the membership many found it utterly confusing, with some convinced that the Council had rigged it this way in a deliberate attempt to defeat Lord Soper's motion by default. The LACS, alerted by many angry Trust members, now took the unprecedented step of demanding a high court ruling on the issue. When it was heard in late October before His Honour Judge Hallgarten, after hearing all the arguments, he declared for the League, saying "that the Trust had failed in its statutory duty to compile agenda documents so as to avoid any real risk of confusion to its voting members and that there was therefore a real risk that a significant number of reasonable lay members would be induced to vote the wrong way."

The League's new Executive Director, James Barrington, and solicitor Gerald Shamash then met with NT Chairman Lord Chorley, Director General Angus Stirling and David Pullen, solicitor for the Trust to formulate a statement to be read out at the AGM. The Trust's membership were informed of the legal action and the intention to reconvene the meeting after due notice at a suitable date, likely to be in the Spring. Lord Soper, who attended the 6th November 1993 AGM, agreed to the adjournment in relation to his motion.

However, the NT Council subsequently met on 16th December and resolved not to reconvene the meeting in the Spring for the purpose of considering his motion. Instead, it was decided to hold the meeting on the morning of the next AGM, which was due on 29th October 1994, thereby effectively delaying the debate of this motion for a full year. Following further legal advice, the LACS decided to demand that the Trust call an Extraordinary General Meeting to address Lord Soper's motion, plus a further motion calling for a postal ballot of all Trust members to ask whether or not deer hunting should be permitted to continue on its land.

Finally, under intense pressure from over 1,400 members, far more than the 1,000 required to demand an EGM, the Trust backed down and announced that a meeting to discuss the ban would be held at the Central Hall, Westminster, on Saturday 16th July 1994. The success of this decision was entirely due to the optimism of Dr Peter Jackson, one of only two dissident voices on the Ruling Council to support a ban, who had bolstered the flagging spirits of the pro-ban lobby by telling them repeatedly that they could carry the resolutions at the EGM. For many believed that with an estimated 40,000 resignations as a result of the Trust's attitude, plus the unknown number of hunting supporters who had joined at the instigation of the BFSS, not to mention thousands of discretionary proxy votes at Lord Chorley's disposal, success did look something of a forlorn hope.

The League's Jim Barrington, as a member of the Trust, got the meeting off to a fine start by proposing the first resolution, while Dr Jackson delivered the second. When the votes were finally announced many in the hall, including Doreen Cronin, "listened open-mouthed and almost unbelieving" as the significance of their victory sank in. The first motion calling for a "balanced Working Party to be convened to consider the aspects of cruelty and welfare that were ignored previously" was carried by 114,857 votes to 99,607. While the second asking that "a postal ballot to be conducted following the report by this Working Party, which will avoid the proxy voting problems, and give a true reflection of the members feelings" was passed by 117,920 votes to 96,613.

After the meeting Lord Chorley expressed his "disappointment" at the way the voting had gone, the Ruling Council having opposed both motions, nor did he feel that the Trust was bound by the demands of its members. Though he did concede that the result was a "significant expression of members' feeling on the specific matters contained in the resolutions" and that a decision would be made, with the result announced at the next AGM in October.

When the decision finally came it met with a mixed reaction from many by now jaundiced NT members. For, while reluctantly agreeing to implement yet another Working Party to look at deer hunting, the Ruling Council rejected the resolution that succeeded by an even larger majority to hold a postal referendum following the completion of the Working Party's enquiry. Not until April 1995, some ten months after the original EGM resolution, would the Council invite Patrick Bateson, Professor of Ethology at the University of Cambridge, to conduct a two-year scientific study with the following terms of reference:

> "To study suffering as a welfare factor in the management of red deer on National Trust properties on Exmoor and the Quantock Hills having regard...to the scientific evidence on stress induced in deer by hunting with hounds and by other culling methods, animal welfare legislation, and the likely effects, in so far as they can be estimated, of a hunting ban on suffering among deer."

Though there were "one or two reservations" surrounding the appointment of Professor Bateson following sensational press reports which tended to give the impression that the ultimate outcome of the study was already pre-empted, the general feeling amongst advocates of a ban were geared towards "keeping an open mind". Bateson himself was in no doubt of the difficulties he faced. Writing two years later in the introduction to the finished report he would say:

> "The problem for my team and myself was not simply working in a highly charged atmosphere in which our arrival was inevitably regarded with suspicion by both sides. Studying animal welfare scientifically is still in its early stages and very little work has been done in the field on what happens to animals that have been hunted. We had to develop many of the methods that we used with very little to guide us. We also had to work quickly. Two years from conceiving a scientific project to producing a final report may seem a long time to the layman. But in practice it was a tough assignment to gather the necessary data and analyse what we obtained in the time that was available to us. I believe, however, that we have obtained a clear result."

During those two years Professor Bateson, in company with a sixteen-person team, studied a plethora of previously published material, attended hunts with LACS monitors and DSSH supporters, conducted scientific studies on both deer killed by hunting and shooting, culminating in the seventy-seven page report entitled *The Behavioural and Physiological Effects of Culling Red Deer*, which was presented to the NT on 9th March 1997. The report's findings stunned both anti- and pro-hunters alike with the damning condemnation of the cruelties that had now been scientifically proved inherent in the "sport" of deer hunting. Page after page resonated with statements such as:

> "The study produced clear-cut results. These show that lengthy hunts with hounds impose extreme stress on red deer and are likely to cause them great suffering. The hunts force them to experience conditions far outside the normal limits for their species...at least at the same level as for severely injured deer and usually last for hours in the case of deer which are killed

and much longer in those that escape... . Moreover, the potential for such suffering occurs with every hunt."

This was in turn qualified by the statement:

"I acknowledge that the degree of suffering, which I regard as unacceptable, may not occur in every deer that is hunted. Even so, it is not possible to say in advance of a hunt whether an acceptable level of stress is likely to occur. It is therefore necessary to act on the basis that *the potential for an unacceptable level of suffering arises in any hunt.*" (author's italics)

There was no mistaking the final judgement on the issue when Professor Bateson concluded

"that the level of total suffering would be markedly reduced if hunting with hounds were ended. Hunting with hounds can no longer be justified on welfare grounds. What was previously debatable about suffering is now clear and those who hunt, and others concerned with animal welfare, will need to take the evidence into account."

Apart from the report's unequivocal assertion that stag hunting was inherently cruel, based on the findings of meticulous scientific research, the report also contained detailed eye-witness evidence that not only trashed the concept of a "clean kill" at the end of every hunt, but clearly illustrated the callous nature of deer hunting itself. The report read:

"Of the four kills which were either witnessed by ourselves or videoed, deer were not killed instantaneously when shot on half the occasions. On the 25th April 1996 a stag was shot in the left hand side of the head from close range (approximately 5-10 m) after it had lain down in deep bracken, following a chase of approximately 23 km over four hours. The shot broke the upper, vertical section of the lower jaw. The stag immediately leapt to its feet and ran off into nearby woodland. It was killed with a second shot (from a humane killer) about 10-15 minutes later. On 9th September 1996 a stag was shot in the head, from a distance of about 10m, again after lying down in bracken following a hunt of over 10km. The stag did not get to its feet but was still moving, and we believe that a humane killer was then used. The stag was immediately bled out, with blood samples being collected in the usual way. The stag then tried to get to its feet, but was held down by three men. It struggled and bleated intermittently, and responded to touches on the eyeball by jerking away sharply, until its death 5 minutes after the first shot. All that we can conclude from these observations is that some hunted deer are wounded at the kill; we cannot give a reliable estimate of how often this happens." *See APPENDIX 9*

So horrified was the NT with the findings of the Bateson Report that on 10th April, the day after it was presented to them, the forty-four members of the Ruling Council who convened decided unanimously that licences to hunt on Trust land would not be renewed following the end of that season on 30th April 1997. The seven-year campaign instigated by Doreen Cronin and the Devon and Somerset Resident's Association for Deer Protection had won a remarkable victory against overwhelming odds that many had thought impossible. Maybe the League summed it up best when it said:

"The only shame…is that the Trust demanded hard scientific evidence to prove what anyone with a grain of common sense would say, and indeed what the LACS has been saying since it formed in 1924! Had the NT accepted its own members' vote in 1990 and banned hunting on its land, both the red deer of the West Country and the Trust itself would have been spared a great deal of trauma!"

While it was true that for the opponents of stag hunting the battle for the heart and soul of the NT was over, for the supporters of blood sports it was only just beginning. An initially stunned hunting fraternity, unsure of how to respond to such a damming condemnation of their activities, bought time by feigning "moral dilemma" as a result of Bateson's findings. The ebullient Janet George, Chief Press Officer for the BFSS, initially claimed on 10th April that:

> "the report is much more damning and much more conclusive than we thought it would be. A lot of people who are keen stag hunters may not want to continue in the light of it. To enjoy a field sport, you have to feel reasonably confident that you are not causing undue suffering. As a society, we don't have the power to stop any field sports, but we will have to decide now whether we can continue to support it."

By 16th April Janet George's flirtation with reality had degenerated into:

> "This science is crap – the way in which blood samples were taken alone should make this report worthless-never mind the crazy assumptions, but it's manna from heaven for the anti brigade. It is very junk science – but it could help dig our grave- and certainly will finish off the Quantock Staghounds if we can't turn it over on 'scientific grounds'."

Having now recovered from their initial shock, and, resorting to the tried and tested adage that if it is not of their opinion it must be flawed, the BFSS began the counter attack. Their first move was the commissioning of a critique by Lord Soulsby, which attempted to demolish the findings of the Bateson Report. In the event, when Soulsby's paper was published on 1st August it was so transparently pro-hunt that its primary impact served only to strengthen Bateson's findings. The wide range of blood sport publications available to the hunting set were pressed into service to, not only trash the Report, but Professor Bateson's reputation as well. Led by the May 1997 issue of the prestigious *Hunting* magazine, a plethora of one-sided pseudo-scientific articles were rushed into print with the intention that "with icy politeness, men of authority expose the flaws in context and procedure of a document sunk by its own ineptitude...". Running in tandem was a BFSS-inspired move, fronted by six people representing West Country hunts and NT tenants, seeking a judicial review on the Trust's decision to ban hunting, coupled with a demand that in the interim the 10th April decision be quashed, with stag hunting restored in the meantime.

But when the application for a judicial review was presented in court, Mr Justice Robert Tucker said that he did not have jurisdiction to hear such an application which should first be taken to the Charity Commission (in view of the NT's charity status), asking for permission for the stag hunters' case to be heard. He further ruled that their case was not strong enough to warrant an injunction being granted to allow hunting to continue pending a full hearing. He then awarded costs estimated at between £15,000 and £20,000 against the co-applicants for this abortive attempt.

On taking their request for a judicial review to the Charity Commission, that body, in granting permission, stressed that this did not indicate their support for the hunt's view. When this application was heard on 21st August 1997, before Mr Justice Robert Walker, the hunters failed to win a high court injunction suspending the ban, but were granted leave to seek a further hearing. Lord Justice Walker advised the NT to reconsider the ban, although he made it clear that he was not ordering them to do so. The judge said that the deer hunters "had an arguable but not a strong case". His primary criticism of the Trust concerned the speed with which their decision was made, but said that the question of whether the ban was lawful would be for a full trial to decide, should the plaintiffs choose to pursue the matter.

With the full Council of the NT due to meet on 2nd October, intensive pressure was exerted by the blood sport lobby to force a change of heart in an attempt to avert a costly legal battle. It is estimated that the hunts spent further thousands of pounds hiring professional lobbyists and sending out glossy information packs, including a fifty-page dossier outlining the reasons why the ban should be lifted to all fifty-two members of the Trust's Council. The DSRADP countered by sending a resumé of the history of the debate stressing that, contrary to the view of certain tenant farmers that they had not been consulted, the consultation had been ongoing throughout the seven years since the original successful resolution of 1990 and that tenant farmers had attended and spoken at AGMs and EGMs putting forward their views.

After more than four hours of discussion behind closed doors on 2nd October, the forty-two Council members present reaffirmed their original decision that the ban should stay on the 900 acres of the Quantock Hills and 12,000 acres on Exmoor. The QSH bitterly announced that as a result of this decision they may be forced to disband, while the DSSH bemoaned loudly that they had lost twenty-five per cent of their territory. More bad news was to follow on 27th November when the Forestry Commission (FC), following an enquiry held at their Edinburgh HQ in the light of the Bateson Report, announced that stag hunting would be banned on their land.

With discretion now becoming the better part of valour with the realisation that maybe they were not going to receive the "justice" due them in the courts of law, the hunters cast around for another way to impose their will on the NT. But first they must prove exactly what they were capable of should the antis get their way. This proof came loud and clear in early February 1998 when two members of the QSH, the harbourer Robert Rowe and former vice-chairman Ben Bartlett, publicly boasted that between them they had shot over 100 deer on the Quantock Hills. The killing was easy they claimed: "We shoot them in the evening and the early morning and very often, because they are so tame, during the day." Both men would openly admit in the local press that their reason for shooting the deer was because they could no longer be hunted effectively.

Throughout this period shadowy meetings between desperate hunt supporters had been taking place to determine what form the intended infiltration of the NT should take. Finally it was agreed that an all-out attempt should be made at the 7th November 1998 AGM in Cardiff to fill the eight vacancies on the Ruling Council with pro-stag hunt candidates. To consolidate the effort, a body calling itself Friends of the National Trust (FONT), with its real purpose disguised as a group pledged to change Trust policy on access to the countryside and the defence of village life, began recruiting supporters for its real aims at country fairs throughout Britain. It also conducted numerous secret meetings with the Countryside Alliance (CA), which had recently transformed itself from the BFSS, who in reality were the real power, considering that CA President Baroness Ann Mallalieu and QSH members Charles and Jo Collins were its founding members. The plan was simple enough, to recruit eight candidates who would stand independently for election at the forthcoming Trust AGM, while concealing their connections with stag hunting interests. ***APPENDIX 10***

The first indication that the general public had that something untoward was happening came when the right-wing journalist Auberon Waugh published a ranting attack against the NT in his weekly *Daily Telegraph* column on 10th August 1998. " The Trust's committee has been taken over by a group of urban animal activists," he screamed, "whose rhetoric is full of Left-wing implications." But not to worry he continued, because, "It is good news that concerned members have formed a group, to be called Friends of the National Trust, to rescue the committee from these bossy Left-wing power maniacs and animal fetishists." After explaining that FONT were fielding candidates, though failing to mention Ann Mallalieu or the hunting connection, he stressed that more support was needed in the fight to liberate the Trust from the animal rights fanatics, ending his article by providing the names, address and fax number at Crowcombe (heartland of the QSH) of the principal organisers Jo and Charles Collins.

The LACS, now fully alerted to the situation, organised a "sting" operation. One of their writers from *Wildlife Guardian*, who wrote under the pseudonym The Owl on the Prowl, contacted the Collins' posing as a hunting vicar who was incensed at the Trust stag hunt ban. A number of calls later, with tape recorder rolling on each occasion, he soon amassed the evidence proving that FONT was a front for the hunting lobby, set up with the assistance of the CA to conduct an orchestrated campaign to overturn the NT ban. The Owl then took the liberty of ensuring that media organisations were in possession of the tapes. The *Today* programme, Radio Four's current affairs flagship, subsequently quizzed Charles Collins on his intentions whilst the *Guardian, Independent* and *Daily Mirror* furnished their readers with The Owl's evidence. The BBC's *Countryfile* also gave Ann Mallalieu the fourth degree, during which she adamantly claimed she did "not even know half the names" on the list of FONT candidates. As a result of The Owl's exposé, just one of FONT's eight candidates, Hugh Van Cutsem, scraped onto the Council in eighth place. Three motions proposed by FONT attacking the leadership of the Trust were also comprehensively rejected by the membership. After their total failure at the AGM Charles Nunnely, Chairman of the Trust, termed FONT "a bunch of whingers who talk nonsense...", then added that the stag hunt ban, based as it is on sound science, was here to stay.

The comments from Charles Nunnely were no doubt the result of the recent decision of the NT Council to reaffirm its ban on deer hunting, which had been taken in light of yet another report, which appeared to indicate unacceptable cruelty. In early October 1998, the initial findings of a report known as *The Joint Universities Study on Deer Hunting* (JUS), headed by Dr Roger Harris were reported verbally to the NT. There appeared to be common ground at the time with the findings of the Bateson Report in that "the data from both studies suggested that deer experience suffering as the result of being hunted and that at least some experience a high level of suffering". The JUS conclusions, at that time, suggested that, "Attempts should be made to find ways in which the suffering involved in hunting may be reduced while maintaining hunting", which, similarly, seemed to confirm that the suffering existed. It was as a result of this report, apparently supporting Bateson, that the NT Council made its decision to uphold the ban.

Almost a year later, a written copy of the JUS Report surfaced via hunting circles causing wide-spread confusion in both local and national press who, in some instances, assumed that it was "a new report". The confusion was understandable as Dr Harris now appeared to have committed a 100 per cent turnaround by claiming that hunting did not compromise animal welfare. Though little surprise was registered when it was eventually discovered that the JUS Report had been funded entirely by the Countryside Alliance.

The 1999 NT AGM again saw FONT attempt to infiltrate the Council with a raft of seven more of its own candidates, all deliberately concealing the fact that each of them was actively involved in the defence of blood sports and all failing to gain election. From now on this would become an annual event, though occasionally adding a touch of humour to what was otherwise a mundane exercise in "spot the stag hunter". The best example being when Clarissa Dickson Wright, celebrity chef of television's *Two Fat Ladies* fame and prominent blood sport advocate, stood for election in 2001. While admitting that, "I am pro-hunting. I believe in the holy triangle of farming, field sports and conservation," she stressed that her real reason for standing was "to improve the food in National Trust cafes and restaurants".

The NT Council met on 27th January 2000 to again re-evaluate its decision on the ban in response to pressure from hunting interests that they consider the findings of the *written* JUS Report. The Council also discussed a supplementary paper submitted by Bateson answering the criticisms of his work by Dr Roger Harris, which was supported by some of the finest scientific brains in Britain. More than a dozen academic heavyweights in the field of animal physiology, including Professor John Krebs and Professor Sir Richard Southwood, one of the foremost zoologists in the country, all gave their unqualified backing to Bateson's original research. ***Note 2***

All of them stressed that the JUS Report, which hunters now claimed invalidated much of Professor Bateson's research, in fact mirrored many of his scientific findings as to the levels of stress and muscle damage caused to animals as they are chased for miles. The only difference between the two reports lies in the interpretation that is being put on the results. The Council once again announced its intention to keep the ban in place.

During the nearly three years since the report was first published Professor Bateson had not only to undergo the most extreme scrutiny of his work, but had experienced almost constant attacks against both his character and professional integrity. From the initial accusations of "junk science" and "Micky Mouse research" from BFSS/CA activists, through spiteful and disingenuous articles in the hunting press, culminating in attempts to destroy his academic career. One of his sternest critics, the Cambridge colleague and veterinary scientist Douglas Wise, was so incensed by the stag hunting report that he attempted to have Bateson removed from his university post, while attempts to seek his dismissal from the post of biological secretary to the Royal Society were also tried.

Interviewed in *The Times* on 3rd January 2000 Bateson admitted:

> "I didn't expect any of this, I thought I could probably develop the argument as I had done in considering the work on experiments on animals. ***Note 3.*** I thought there would be some balanced position to preserve some aspects and yet minimise the welfare costs. But the issues are now so highly charged it is impossible to engage in rational debate."

At this time it appeared that the NT, regardless of the fanatical attempts to force a change of policy, would remain true to their original decision and retain the stag hunt ban indefinitely. The future was to prove that the tenacity of the blood sports lobby should never be underestimated.

As for the three Ds, Diana Wilson, Daisy Hall and Doreen Cronin, who were all party to the formation of the Devon and Somerset Residents' Association for Deer Protection following the 1987 "stag on the roof" incident, and whose 1990 resolution at the NT AGM was to deal such a moral blow to stag hunting, they all resigned from active campaigning at the DSRADP AGM on 18th July 1999. They cited "advancing years", and the need "for others with the energy of youth on their side to carry on the fight". The DSRADP wound up its activities in April 2000 when it was absorbed into the newly formed South West Deer Protection (SWDP). In the following few years this new group, chaired by the IFAW hunt monitor Kevin Hill, would capture on camera what the Bateson Report had so conclusively proved with science.

Note 1. The pro-hunt writer and FONT nominee Robin Page (who was elected to the NT Council in 2003) would later write "at that time National Trust elections resembled the warped democracy of Eastern Europe before the fall of the Berlin

Wall. The chairman had the privilege of dispensing proxy votes to his favoured candidates and many of those elected received many thousands of gifted votes." (*Daily Telegraph* 2nd December 2006)

Note 2. The full list of Bateson supporters was:

Professor N J Mackintosh, FRS, Chairman of the School of Biological Sciences, University of Cambridge.

Professor Sir Richard Southwood, FRS, Department of Zoology, University of Oxford.

Dame Anne McLaren, FRS, Wellcome/CRC Institute, Cambridge. Past President of the British Association for the Advancement of Science.

Professor Sir John Krebs, FRS, Department of Zoology, University of Oxford. Former Chief Executive of NERC.

Professor Donald Broom, Department of Clinical Veterinary Medicine, University of Cambridge.

Professor Morris Gosling, Department of Psychology, University of Newcastle (former Scientific Director, Institute of Zoology, Zoological Society of London.

Professor R McNeill Alexander, FRS, School of Biology, University of Leeds.

Professor T Clutton-Brock, FRS, Department of Zoology, University of Cambridge.

Dr Roger Ewbank, Former Director of the Universities Federation for Animal Welfare.

Professor Stan Lindstedt, Department of Biology, Northern Arizona University.

Professor A J Webster, School of Veterinary Science, University of Bristol.

Professor Knut Schmidt-Nielsen, Member of the US National Academy of Sciences, Foreign Member of the Royal Society, Department of Zoology, Duke University.

Dr John Fletcher, Deer Farmer, Auchtermuchty, Fife.

Note 3. Professor Bateson's 1991 "Assessment of pain in animals" published in the journal *Animal Behaviour.*

Chapter Eleven

"Let him walk"

DUE TO THE VOTE by NT members, the issue of deer hunting probably received more publicity nation-wide at that time than during any other period. The three West Country red deer packs gained the bulk of this attention, with much also focused on the fourth pack in England, the fallow deer hunting New Forest Buckhounds, while no mention was made of the recently formed scratch packs that hunted the roe deer. There was, however, another type of deer hunting that persisted, though admittedly not on the British mainland. The "sport" of carted deer hunting, which though still legal in Britain and ended in 1963 through public opinion, was still practised in both the Republic of and Northern Ireland. The County Down Staghounds operated in the North, while the Ward Union Staghounds hunted the country around Dublin.

It was to follow, film and experience the carted deer hunt, at the invitation of the Irish Council Against Blood Sports, that League director Jim Barrington and John Hicks went in early 1991. The subsequent article written by Jim Barrington gave a fascinating insight into one of the more curious forms of human enjoyment at the expense of animals:

> "The meet of the Ward Union Staghounds was advertised as taking place at Naul, a small village north of Dublin. Outside the pub, where most of the riders and supporters had gathered, was the tell-tale sign of this particular hunt – a small green trailer in which the day's quarry was transported to the meet. Unlike

ordinary stag hunting, carted deer hunting provides its own deer from a herd held at the kennels. Photographs and video film of the nervous beast were unobtrusively taken through the slats on the side of the trailer. What was not known at the time was that there were *two* stags in the relatively tiny cart.

"Looking, though perhaps not sounding, like Irish stag hunters, we mingled with the supporters and were allowed to photograph the release of the deer just prior to the hunt. Upon release of the stag the sheer size of the animal became obvious. The antlers had been sawn off to prevent damage to other deer back in the herd and for easy handling in the cart. Two lumps on its head remained where the animal's magnificent antlers would (and should) have been. Two riders flanked the cart while the main field was held back, some 300 yards. Giving the stag a few minutes grace, the pack was then set on and the hunt began.

"In another section of the cart a second stag waited, brought along in case the first deer was caught too quickly or would not run at all. It is debatable which deer suffered most, for while running from a pack of hounds inevitably causes distress, the second animal is forced to remain in the small trailer, bumped around narrow country lanes, with the sounds and smells of its pursuers all around.

" I was told that the hunted deer was a good 'three hour' stag, this being the duration he was expected to run. Normally when brought to bay, I was informed, 'a few of the bigger lads' go in and wrestle him back into the trailer. Occasionally, a deer will not be caught and this becomes an 'outlier'. It may be hunted on a subsequent day or darted and taken back to the kennels. If it is not a havier (castrated deer) it could be shot to prevent it breeding with other wild deer. On this day, the pack strayed off after an outlier and as a consequence neither deer were caught.

"The whole activity of carted stag hunting raises questions about its validity as a so-called sport. Though the hunters claim that their activity is humane (after all they do not kill the deer or at least do not intend to), deer are put through an ordeal which cannot be justified, least of all in the name of sport. Deer are sometimes attacked by the hounds and this is always a possibility when the stag's main weapons of defence, its antlers, are removed. Hinds, which are also used in carted deer hunting, of course constantly face this problem.

"Myopathy, the stress induced condition brought about by a prolonged chase, may affect the deer as it can in other forms of stag hunting. Captivity itself brings further stresses – the removal of the antlers, castration and close proximity to hounds all add to an activity which has had its day."

On his return to London Jim Barrington would offer the full support of the LACS resources to his Irish counterparts, with gratifying results.

The summer of 1991 saw former Beatle Paul McCartney, along with first wife Linda, buy the eighty-four-acre St John's Wood, near Dulverton, for a price in excess of £100,000. The purchase came about after John Hicks had assured the McCartneys that this woodland, when joined with four existing sanctuaries in the area, would create a huge block of more than 200 acres of hunt-free land. This same period saw the LACS transform their Voluntary Warden scheme, which had patrolled the sanctuaries on an ad-hoc basis, into the official Sanctuary Ranger unit which, supplied with video equipment, would not only start to record the acts of trespass, but ever-increasing footage of hunt cruelties. Meanwhile the Quantock Hills Joint Liaison Group was so desperate to catch the growing number of poachers that they approached the army to help. 40 Commando at Norton Manor Camp was asked "about the possibility of Marines being used in surveillance. They could spot the poachers during their night time exercises on the hills."

The main concern for QSH Master Bill Fewings right now was that someone kept stealing his hounds. They had been repeatedly taken off the hills during hunting days, as had hounds from the Tiverton

Staghounds. When a number were found wandering near the M5 motorway he offered a £500 reward to catch the culprits. The BFSS of course needed no such prompting as "they had positively identified two animal rights activists who had been seen handling the animals" during a hunt. No arrests were ever made. 14th February 1992 saw the failure of Kevin McNamara's Private Member's *Wild Mammals (Protection) Bill* to obtain a Second Reading by 175 in favour to 187 against. On 9th April 1992 the Conservatives won their fourth consecutive General Election victory, thus neutralising for another five years any possibility of anti-hunting legislation. On Exmoor John Hicks left the League to set up his own venture, International Animal Rescue, while Graham Sirl, transferring from his campaign against the New Forest Buckhounds, was appointed in his place as Head of West Country Operations.

The publication in July 1992 of a report by The Somerset Trust for Nature Conservation, co-authored by Frances Winder and Paul Chanin, was interesting not for what it said – which in truth was very little – but because it challenged the hunt's estimate of deer numbers and thereby re-opened the whole question of hunting as a valid management control method. The report's findings, after four years of research, suggested that there were between 800-900 red deer on the Quantock Hills and that even this figure could be regarded as a conservative estimate. The figures were arrived at by using a system of dung pellet counts, the reliability of which had been challenged in a number of recent scientific papers. More importantly, the questions that most needed answers were not even touched upon, i.e. providing a breakdown of the estimated total into age groups or the ratio of stags to hinds.

However, despite its deficiencies the survey did seem to confirm what many non-hunting deer enthusiasts had suspected for a long time – that the total number of deer was high. Indeed, John Hicks was frequently ridiculed by the hunt when he consistently took this view because it suited them to project a low figure so that the annual number of deer taken by the hunt appeared to be a serious culling contribution. ***See APPENDIX 11***

The QSH killed a total of forty-two deer during the 1991-92 season comprised of nine autumn stags, twenty hinds and thirteen spring stags. Road casualties and poachers were said to have been responsible for a further fifty-six deaths. Allowing for others shot by farmers/landowners, an approximate overall total of 150 deaths from all causes were said to have occurred. But this report suggested that, based on an overall figure of 900, an annual cull of up to 300 deer would be required. There was also a general consensus amongst the non-hunters, although unconfirmed by this report, that there were a disproportionate number of hinds to stags. Yet the QSH total of forty-two was made up of twenty-two stags and twenty hinds. This all seemed to confirm what the antis had been saying for years, for if a total cull of 300 was required who needed the hunt to kill a mere forty-two with all the consequent cruelty, general disruption and damage by vehicles, etc. to the environment? The net result of this report would be the formation of the Quantock Deer Management Group, which in reality turned out to be nothing more than an extension of the QSH.

While on Exmoor the autumn of 1992 would bring "one of the most harrowing visions" volunteer monitor Kevin Hill would ever see, images that would haunt him for years to come. In a submission years later to the Burns Inquiry he would write:

> "a stag, hunted by the DSSH, was cornered in a garden near Winsford. The stag made a last attempt to escape by pushing through a hedge. He then found himself behind a building and momentarily stood still. Hunt followers at the scene immediately held the stag. A member of the hunt staff then shot the stag. The stag slumped to the ground and all present, including a monitor working undercover, presumed the stag to be dead. To everyone's amazement the stag laboured to his feet. He had his head lowered and his back arched. The undercover monitor expected the stag to be shot again immediately to prevent even further suffering. This was not the case; a follower was heard to say, 'Let him walk'. With hunt followers surrounding the stag and one leading him by his antlers he was guided up a bank. When at the top the followers forced him to the ground and he was shot again, this time fatally. His throat was cut and after

a short time he was dragged down the other side of the bank, thrown over a fence, and dragged to a Land Rover."

These actions were made all the more poignant a few minutes later by one of the hunt followers who commented that the deer should never have been made to walk up the bank, not for reasons of compassion but because there were recognisable anti-hunt campaigners in the area.

On 1st February 1993 the LACS would appoint this remarkable man, Kevin Hill, as their new Sanctuaries Officer. His expertise with a camera, coupled with more than his fair share of courage, would go on to provide some of the most damning evidence against deer hunting ever committed to film. Just three months later, on 22nd May, he captured footage of a horrifying scene in which a hunter sat on a tiny roe deer while it slowly bled to death. The deer had been hunted for some hours before making towards St Johns Wood, the sanctuary bought by Paul and Linda McCartney. The deer attempted to jump the six-foot fence that the DSSH had erected around the wood to prevent hunted deer escaping, but was left dangling from the fence by its antlers. Jeromy Gibbs, a member of the newly formed Cheldon Buckhounds, pulled it off the fence, cut its throat and then sat on it for a full *fifteen* minutes. A land rover then pulled up and the unfortunate animal was thrown in the back while still alive and taken away to be finished off. What Kevin Hill had filmed was the first public exposé of a new type of deer hunting that was becoming fashionable in the West Country. ***Note 1***

Formed in the summer 1990 by Hunt Master David Ford (ex-whipper-in Tiverton Staghounds and ex-kennelman Cambridgeshire Foxhounds) the Cheldon Buckhounds, with a mixed pack of fox hounds, basset hounds and beagles, had revived the blood sport of roe deer hunting, not seen in Britain since 1914. Also formed the same year was Mr Lawrence Clark's Buckhounds, with the Isle Valley Buckhounds coming along in 1992, with their hunting season set between September through to the following May.

All three packs, accepting their status as an unrecognised blood sport, approached the Masters of Deerhounds Association (MDHA), asking for affiliation. Even though Dick Lloyd, the association's chairman thought,"It is a perfectly fair sport and the hunts are well supported, mainly on foot," outright membership was refused, but the hunts were given probationary status. Problems arose immediately the press story broke of Kevin Hill's film, for fearing public distaste the MDHA suspended the Cheldon and ordered an investigation into the incident. The subsequent inquiry exonerated the hunt, the suspension was lifted and the probationary status restored.

Apparently still concerned at the possibility of public outrage over the creation of an entirely new blood sport, the MDHA decided to set up a working party to examine the future implications of roe deer hunting, with a remit to report back in 1995. Public opinion was also uppermost in the minds of the Masters of Foxhounds Association when they swiftly ordered an embargo on the drafting of foxhounds to be used by roe deer packs, fearing that the reputation of their "sport" could be tarnished by too close an association with this new venture. *Countryweek Hunting* magazine summed up the feelings of many hunting enthusiasts in an editorial on the subject:

> "The 197 packs of foxhounds, 22 of harriers and 75 of beagles, would fall under suspicion in the public mind of complicity by association in an activity from which the public would surely recoil...that the hunting of some former quarries no longer stands up to the criteria of what now constitutes sport is already accepted by pro-hunting opinion."

The editorial then proceeded to extol the virtues of former otter hunters for bringing this species back from the brink of extinction and then emphasised that the public would not tolerate a resumption of the hunting of this animal. It concluded by saying that:

> "...roe deer are seen just as much as public martyrs now as otters were then. The Bambi complex and revulsion against the freebooters who course roe deer with oversize lurchers in southern England are examples of that. The reaction to pursuit of roe deer take them, in modern motorised Britain, out of the sporting

agenda. It would be impossible to condone such a practice, and difficult to limit the damage it would do to the repute of hunting as a whole."

What all this meant was that many fox hunters found it extremely difficult to justify the brutalities inherent in stag hunting, wishing that the controversial issue would just fade away. However, they also realised that abolition would be the "thin edge of the wedge" for their sport, and found the possibility of being publicly allied to a new type of deer hunting a terrifying prospect.

This situation also caused something of a dilemma for the antis in so much that official recognition of roe deer hunting by the MDHA would be the legitimatisation of the "sport" that would put back the abolitionist cause by decades. For, having failed to outlaw one single blood sport, we would have found ourselves confronted with the reality of a whole range of new ones to deal with. The fear was that if the hunting of roe deer were to become widely accepted (bearing in mind that there were fifty odd such hunts in France and half a dozen in Belgium) there would be nothing to stop any would-be sportsman from starting his own pack in Britain. It was also worrying that as roe deer could be found in reasonable numbers in most counties of Britain, the problem would not remain in the West Country, but would spread nationwide.

As things turned out, thanks entirely to Kevin Hill's film, the MDHA's working party reported back that "roe deer hunting was not a legitimate field sport", which was upheld by the BFSS, and the packs were expelled. Undeterred by the fact that they were considered too dirty by hunting's official bodies, they went on to form their own Master of Buck Hounds Association. Their activities continued, albeit in a shadowy and secretive fashion, for they do not advertise meets, no reports of their actions are published, no official hunting organisation or publication will acknowledge their existence and only rarely does the public continue to hear of them.

Such an occasion was recorded in the February 1999 issue of the localised Newsletter *The Polden Post:*

"On Saturday, 16th January, the quiet lanes of Bawdrip (near Bridgwater) were filled with 80 followers of the Cheldon Buckhounds...ready to spend the day chasing roe deer who reside in Pen Woods and on North Moor. The hunt had been invited by Percy Norman from King's Farm. The deer had been doing damage on the farm and he wished to 'shake them up a bit'. Adding 'We all had a most enjoyable day, starting with a stirrup cup made from whisky, sloe gin and port through to catching a deer at 4.00pm,' while failing to mention the deer which limped away with a broken leg."

The local residents had a different story with one, Jim Earnshaw, writing to *The Bridgwater Mercury* with a letter which is worth quoting in full as it gave a rare snapshot of what was no doubt a typical roe deer hunt. He wrote:

"God's in his heaven and all's right with the world – or so I thought on Saturday 16th January as my wife and I prepared to take advantage of the fresh, shining day with a brisk walk. As we set off down the lane in Bawdrip there were clouds of brightly coloured finches swooping overhead and the long tailed tits were a magic sight. Perhaps today we would see the little herd of deer which bound across the water logged meadows and give pure delight to all who see them.

"Yes indeed we did! The sound of baying hounds and horns of a hunt echoed across the fields as we left the shelter of the village and looked over the hedge towards Pendon Hill where we were presented with a scene of indescribable savagery. An imported deer hunt from Tiverton were chasing the little pack of deer in an uncontrolled frenzy. The deer zigzagged back and forth; horsemen charged up and down the lane spattering us with mud. One of the local farmers screamed about on his quad preventing the deer from finding sanctuary. What was indescribably awful was the excited braying laughter and cheering coming from savagely excited hunt followers as a deer was turned and nearly caught. The hounds streamed through a field full of sheep which scattered in great distress and the deer and the hunt disappeared towards Pendon Hill leaving the world in silence and we were left sadly to reflect on parents who had brought their children to see such slaughter as an enjoyable spectacle and as part of our traditional way of life.

"No doubt the deer eat some of the farmers' crops which we the general public pay them great subsidies to grow to add to the European cereal mountain. I do not argue whether it is necessary or not to cull them. The enjoyment and pleasure which some people seem to get from the wicked torture of innocent and helpless animals is the abiding memory left as I write this letter."

One side effect of the controversy caused by Kevin Hill's film was to heighten the campaign within Somerset County Council (SCC) to force through a deer hunting ban on their land. Somerset would be the latest in an ever-increasing list of councils across the country that had responded to the LACS campaign, started in 1983, which now totalled 154 local councils, including 35 County Councils. Amid angry demonstrations outside SCC's County Hall, in Taunton, on a wet and windy 4th August 1993, the debate began when Liberal Democrat Council Leader Chris Clarke moved the motion, seconded by deputy leader Jackie Ballard. ***Note 2***. After one of the most heated debates on record the final vote gave a conclusive 28 – 22 in favour of a ban. The implications for the QSH were devastating, for the ban on the Council's 140 acres included Over Stowey Customs Common which is a narrow strip of land running along the top of the Quantock Hills that virtually cuts them in two. After threatening to ignore the ban, shoot all the deer they could find and set fire to the Quantock Hills, the hunt finally settled for the strategy of setting up a fighting fund so as to challenge the council decision in the Courts.

When the Judicial Review of the ban was heard on 27th/28th January 1994 Mr Justice Laws adjudged that SCC was wrong to ban primarily on moral grounds. In making his judgement, Justice Laws quoted from a book on administrative law that said:

> "The powers of public authorities are…essentially different from those of private persons…a private person has absolute power to allow whom he likes to use his land…regardless of his motives. But a public authority may do none of these things unless it acts reasonably and in good faith and upon lawful and relevant grounds of public interest."

He then posed the question whether or not "the councillors' moral objections to the practice of hunting are capable of justifying the prohibition as a measure which conduces to the benefit, improvement or development of their area within the Local Government Act of 1972". He concluded that in his view the decision was "taken because those in favour of the ban thought hunting to be morally repulsive and on no other basis". Therefore

> "Section 120 (1) (b) confers no entitlement on a local authority to impose its opinions about the morals of hunting on the neighbourhood. In the present state of the law those opinions, however sincerely felt, have their proper place only in the private conscience of those who entertain them. The Council has been given no authority by Parliament to translate such views into public actions…"

Mr Justice Laws did, however, when giving his judgement, immediately grant leave to appeal, which some saw as an indication that he accepted that other legal opinions might well be different from his own.

The Council immediately lifted the ban while deciding whether or not to appeal, with much raising of glasses and a ceremonial crossing of Over Stowey Customs Common by the QSH. The LACS meanwhile sought advice from some of the country's most eminent barristers, Sir Louis Blom-Cooper QC, Mr David Pannick QC and Mr David Bean, an expert on local government law. It was their unanimous view that Mr Justice Laws had reached the wrong conclusion in relation to the powers that local authorities can exercise. Although councils are bound by public law, they can exercise private law rights and indeed do so in relation to certain aspects of their work. It was felt by the three counsels that the prohibition of hunting on land owned or controlled by a local authority was a perfectly legitimate stand to take and was legal under the authority's private law rights. In their written opinion they stated: "The exercise of the attributes of ownership of land, whether by a private citizen or a local authority, likewise sounds in private law. The court has no jurisdiction to entertain an application for judicial review in respect of a local authority's decision to ban hunting from land owned by it – subject always to the private law right being exercised without malice or bad faith." Further, the Counsels felt that the 1972 Local Government Act, section 120, applied to the acquisition of land and not the management, regulation or control of that land owned by the local authority.

At the full council meeting on 18th May, following these encouraging legal Opinions, it was decided by 32 votes to 13 with 6 abstentions to proceed with a formal appeal. A fighting fund was launched by the council to raise the money needed to pursue it, a clear legal decision needed as other local councils that had banned hunting were coming under pressure to reverse their decisions following a concerted campaign from the hunting set. Within weeks a substantial sum in the region of £75,000 had been raised, which included donations from many other councils, along with £10,000 from the International Fund for Animal Welfare and £5,000 from the LACS, who also footed the entire cost of the legal opinions.

Kevin Hill was back in the news during September when he filmed a kill by the DSSH in the River Barle, near Dulverton. The deer was surrounded by screaming hunt supporters and baying hounds, then shot at four times with a shotgun. Wounded and terrified, the animal plunged up and down the river until it was finally leapt upon by hunt officials who, wrestling it by the antlers, held it underwater until it died. In an attempt to prevent the filming of the incident Kevin Hill was repeatedly punched in the face, his arms pinioned behind his back and the camera lens smeared with mud. Remarkably, he escaped with the film intact, which when shown to local representatives of the British Deer Society caused such outrage that they demanded an immediate inquiry by the MDHA. The subsequent enquiry, chaired by BFSS

Vice-Chairman Lord Mancroft, instantly slapped a five-week ban on the hunt.

However, Lord Mancroft stated that the stag had eventually been killed with a humane killer and the allegation that the animal had been drowned "was not corroborated by the video". By that time the lens was covered in mud and Kevin Hill was being held with arms twisted behind his back to prevent filming, but neither he nor the camera's microphone picked up any sound which might have been the report of a humane killer. At the MDHA enquiry, hunt officials presented the head of the dead stag, with a neat bullet wound in the head, but no postmortem evidence was submitted to show whether the shot was fired before or after death. The enquiry also concluded with the ridiculous claim that Kevin Hill was partly to blame for the botched kill. According to Mancroft, "...difficult circumstances were exacerbated by a few unruly hunt followers and Mr Hill himself, whose attempts to film the scene handicapped the marksmen from making this humane kill," even though the footage clearly showed that he was nowhere near the two gunmen attempting to shoot the animal from the river bank. The film was given extensive TV coverage, with the "Oscar" going to local BFSS representative Rosie Pocock for her appearance on *Good Morning Television,* during which she claimed that the animal had been dealt with "efficiently" although it was "unfortunate that the stag took six minutes to die".

The Court of Appeal finally met on 7th/8th March 1995 to render its verdict on the SCC hunting ban. The Master of the Rolls, Sir Thomas Bingham, in company with Lord Justice Simon Brown and Lord Justice Swinton Thomas rejected the council's appeal by a majority of two to one. In a judgement that turned on the ethical issue of a councillor's legal right to ban an activity which they found morally unacceptable the findings were anything but straightforward. In a rather tongue-in-cheek article for *The Times,* David Pannick QC, one of the three who supplied opinions for the LACS, gave his verdict on the case:

> "On the issue of principle, then, one judge regarded the ethical considerations as necessarily relevant; one judge thought that

> such factors were necessarily irrelevant; and the Master of the Rolls confined himself to saying that such matters were not *necessarily* irrelevant. This makes it unnecessarily difficult for councillors, and their legal advisers, to understand the law.
>
> "In the light of the Court of Appeal judgement, local councillors should be advised that the law (probably) is, and (certainly) should be, that if local councillors ask themselves the question posed by the relevant statutory test, a discretionary decision under general criteria may be influenced (even decisively) by ethical considerations, so long as all other relevant factors are taken into account.
>
> "Any other conclusion would unjustifiably inhibit the function of local government to provide an opportunity for elected representatives of the community to decide (so far as they are given general discretion by Parliament) what is right and proper for their area."

Though on three other points their lordships were specific. This "decision" applied *only* to the SCC case and must not be considered a general judgement on other council hunt ban cases, that permission was granted to appeal the decision to the House of Lords, and that costs would be awarded against the council. When SCC decided not to take the matter to the Lords and the case was effectively closed, the QSH's bill amounted to a quarter of a million pounds, which included the invoice of a psychiatrist for treating hunt members who were "stressed out".

There was a little addendum to this story. Not content with their victory in the Court of Appeal the hunters then took the vindictive step of trying to get those councillors who had voted for the ban disqualified from office. Their tactic was to complain to the District Auditor that the councillors should be surcharged for the cost of taking the case to the Appeal Court. If successful this would almost certainly have resulted in some of the councillors being declared bankrupt and banned from office. However, the Auditor ruled that the course of action taken by SCC was legal, with the costs ultimately paid from public funds.

As if to complement the farce taking place in the Court of Appeal the House of Commons was enacting a farce of its own. On 3rd March 1995 the *Wild Mammals (Protection) Bill*, presented by Dumbarton Labour MP John McFall, was given an unopposed Second Reading of 253 – 0. The Bill, which was similar in scope to Kevin McNamara's that was defeated by only twelve votes on Valentine's Day 1992, was intended to amend the *Protection of Animals Act 1911*. This Bill would make it a criminal offence to "cruelly kick, beat, impale, crush, burn, drown or torture" any wild mammal. These were offences included in the *1911 Act* which protected domestic and captive animals, but which had on occasion been inflicted on animals such as hedgehogs, squirrels and foxes without any possibility of securing a conviction because wild animals were specifically excluded from the *1911 Act*. This Bill was supported by both police and the RSPCA following a number of recent cases where hedgehogs had been kicked to death by drunken thugs or thrown alive onto fires, while squirrels and foxes had been nailed alive to trees and even burned to death after being doused in petrol.

The problem was that McFall's Bill also included a clause which would make it an offence to "wilfully cause any dog to kill, injure, pursue or attack" any wild mammal. So the fact that this Bill received an unopposed Second Reading was nothing to do with altruistic motives on the part of pro-hunt Tory MPs, but all to do with the fact that these MPs were under the impression that McFall's Bill would never make it to the Committee Stage. To make sure of this they engineered every delaying tactic in the parliamentary book. With only four days to go before the last possible day for the Bill to pass its Third Reading in the House of Commons, MPs sympathetic to blood sports were still filibustering other Bills in the queue before the *Wild Mammals Bill*. They had talked for hours on the *Dog Fouling Bill* and submitted dozens of amendments to a non-controversial *Charities (Amendment) Bill* in an attempt to ensure that McFall's Bill ran out of time.

However, the astute and determined McFall had spotted that a Government Bill in another Committee had been completed a week early. Being aware that when such a vacant Committee slot appears, the sponsor of another Bill can apply for that space, he neatly guided his Bill into this vacancy. When the MPs on the other Committees realised that their efforts had been negated, they withdrew the delaying amendments and the *Charities (Amendment) Bill* completed its Committee Stage. Despite this, the *Wild Mammals (Protection) Bill* had to be passed in only two short Committee sessions if it was to be returned to the Commons on Friday 14th July. With time now so short, pro-hunters could easily "talk-out" or "object" to it at the final Report Stage and Third Reading. John McFall and the Bill's other sponsors, as well as the RSPCA, LACS and IFAW, had quietly agreed weeks earlier, that the anti-hunting and snaring clauses should be withdrawn, to call the pro-hunt lobby's bluff on clause one – "cruelly kicking, beating and torturing".

When the hunting lobby now objected to the word "torture", on the grounds that the courts might be persuaded that such a term could apply to hound hunting and snaring, hasty negotiations outside the Committee took place with assistance from the Home Office lawyers offered by Minister Nicholas Baker. Finally, it was agreed that the Bill would make it an offence to "cruelly kick, beat, impale, crush, burn or drown any wild mammal", but certainly not "torture", and the amended Bill was passed by the Committee. The next day, 14th July 1995 the Bill was passed by the Commons without objection, and then sent to the House of Lords.

Angela Smith, LACS Head of Political and Public Relations, echoed the thoughts of many in the animals rights movement when she wrote: "This will be the most important legislation for British wildlife ever. Never before have all wild mammals been protected from such a wide range of cruel practices. It is a shame that hunting and snaring are not included, but thanks to John McFall, we have a least salvaged what is still a ground-breaking Bill." In reality the BFSS cabal in the Commons had never intended that this Bill should reach the Statute Book, only agreeing to its passage through the Commons in the sure knowledge that their counterparts in the Upper Chamber would wreck it.

Three months later, on 16th October, in the House of Lords, Lord Mancroft and other BFSS Peers insisted on another eight amendments

– all of which were superfluous. They knew full well any amendment adopted in the Lords would cause the Bill to go back to the Commons for approval and that there was no time for such a procedure. In fact the Bill could still have become law, despite these wrecking tactics, if John Major's government had allowed a few minutes for the amended Bill to be given the final approval. Shadow Leader of the House, Ann Taylor, appealed to the government to co-operate, but the Leader of the House, Tony Newton, refused. Elliot Morley, Labour animal welfare spokesman, was right when he said: "It does seem that there is an element of buffers and duffers in the Lords who are never going to let that measure go through unless the Government gives it time." How right was proved three months later when the same *Wild Mammals (Protection) Bill*, this time presented by Alan Meale (Lab. Mansfield), was again before the House of Commons.

Following a debate of only one and three-quarter hours, on 26th January 1996, the Bill passed its Second Reading, Committee Stage, Report Stage and Third Reading in a matter of minutes and was passed to the Lords the same day. The difference was that this Bill had government support, primarily due to intense "behind the scenes pressure" following the debacle of McFall's measure. Fearful that public perception of Tory attitudes to animal welfare could prove a turn-off at the next election, which was due at the latest within eighteen months, the Major government felt obliged to offer a sop to the animal welfare lobby.

Intense negotiations between the LACS, RSPCA, BFSS and government eventually resulted in complete agreement on the Bill's wording. The "deal" consisted of the League and RSPCA agreeing to the concept of "intent" being incorporated into the Bill, in return for a longer list of offences than had been in the previous version. There had been stiff opposition from the BFSS on various definitions of cruelty such as "mutilates" and "drags", all of which were thought to compromise many of the "legal" activities practised by hunters and gamekeepers, the latter which of course slaughtered every species of animal and bird as a matter of course in an attempt to protect game birds for the shoot.

As with John McFall's Bill when it emerged from the House of

Commons last time, the "Meale" Bill contained no measure against lawful hunting, shooting or "pest control", but did, for the first time ever, enable prosecutions to be mounted against anyone who "mutilates, kicks, beats, nails or otherwise impales, stabs, drags, stones, burns, crushes, drowns, drags or asphyxiates any wild mammal, with intent to inflict unnecessary suffering". Clearing the House of Lords on 14th February after a short debate without objection, the Bill returned to the Commons, becoming law on 30th April 1996. So, eighty-five years after the *1911 Act* which gave legal protection from cruelty to domestic animals the *Wild Mammals (Protection) Act* now gave the same protection to all wild animals from the tiniest shrew to the largest red deer. ***Note 3***

Save Our Stags made a comeback in early 1996, though in no way connected to the West Country hunt saboteurs. This group was formed in Northern Ireland to spearhead a campaign against carted deer hunting, following public disgust after press and television front-lined the issue. It began when Brian Black, an environmental reporter with *Ulster Television,* accidentally came across the County Down Staghounds whilst out on a boating trip. Using his initiative Black took out his camera and filmed the hunt in action. A terrified stag was seen running for its life as around thirty riders charged into a Department of the Environment nature reserve and, in a desperate attempt to escape the pursuing hounds, the deer tried to swim Strangford Lough only to become trapped at the shore. The stag, clearly exhausted, sank helplessly into thick mud and was eventually dragged out by huntsmen and returned to the kennels to be hunted another day.

The video footage was shown on Ulster's *Live At Six* news programme. The backlash from stunned viewers took the TV station by surprise, with the switchboard jammed for hours. Northern Ireland's press took up the story with banner headlines such as "Beyond Belief", "This practice must be banned", and "Saddened and disgusted…we must change the law". For weeks the story continued with letter pages filled by expressions of outrage, horror and disgust, many with the common theme that "…this must be stopped, we have enough violence over here without involving animals".

The Ulster Society for the Prevention of Cruelty to Animals when pressed to seek a prosecution declined due to the vagaries of the law. Northern Irish law is separate from the *Protection of Animals Act 1911* but in some ways was ahead of the UK, or was until the recent emergence of the *Wild Mammals (Protection) Act.* Animals in Northern Ireland, including all wild animals (mammals, fish and birds), are protected by the *Welfare of Animals Act (Northern Ireland) 1972.* Sadly hunting enjoys an exemption under this law, thus wild animals are protected from cruelty unless it is inflicted for "sport". The LACS, on the other hand, decided to challenge the issue, for the *Welfare of Animals Act (Northern Ireland),* unlike the *1911 Protection of Animals Act,* does not recognise the definition of "captive" animals, only "wild" or "domesticated". Wild animals can be hunted, domesticated cannot. The question for the League was whether or not a deer, which is bred by the hunt and kept in a paddock, can be deemed domesticated or a captive wild animal. If it could be proved in law that it was domesticated there could well be grounds for a prosecution and the possibility of banning the practice of carted deer hunting.

Though the League would pursue this particular "sport" without the assistance of the man who had kick-started the campaign against carted deer hunting following his 1991 trip to Ireland. For the previous December (1995) its director, Jim Barrington, had decided to travel the same road as his predecessor, and offered his services to the blood sport camp. Months of secret meetings with prominent hunters culminated in an article for *The Field,* in which Barrington claimed hunting had "culture" and its participants were "pillars of society" whom he did not wish to see "criminalised". When forced to resign he left the League bitterly alleging that he had been driven out by "extremists", taking with him a number of other prominent League officials, including the former chairman and long-time veteran Mark Davies. Soon after, Barrington formed the group, Wildlife Network, which would promote the cause of hunting through a series of publications advocating the "middle way". To be fair this group maintained an opposition to stag hunting, stating in its publication *The Hunt At Bay,* "the hunting of deer using dogs should be made illegal, either by an amendment to the *1991 Deer Act* or by a separate Act of Parliament".

This group would join forces with other pro-hunt parliamentary centred campaigns that had sprung up in the wake of the Labour Party promise of a free vote on hunting should they win the next election. It was destined to play a central role in the Commons opposition to a total ban that was fronted by Lib-Dem MP Lembit Opik.

After years of intensive lobbying, the animal welfare movement, now united under the general title Campaign for the Protection of Hunted Animals (CPHA: launched on 24th July 1996 and comprising the LACS, RSPCA and IFAW) had secured a firm promise of abolition from a possible future Labour government. Panic-stricken that their natural Tory allies would almost certainly lose the next election the blood sport fraternity set about a massive image clean-up. The haughty BFSS would eventually turn itself into the "friendly" Countryside Alliance (CA), now concerned not only with killing for sport, but a whole raft of very dubious country issues ranging from post office closures to affordable housing. Though of course in reality it was the same old gang beating the same tired drum. In fact, as early as December 1996, BFSS Chief Press Officer Janet George was giving notice that if a future Labour government permitted a debate on hunting they would "...cause chaos on the motorways" and "...bring central London to a standstill with horse boxes and tractors".

The few blood sport-supporting Labourites in Parliament, such as Baroness Anne Mallalieu, now found their services to the cause at a premium. Desperate to perpetrate the myth that hunting was a non-political, all party issue, they formed the Leave Country Sports Alone group to campaign actively against Labour policy from within. Only too keen to assist as their "official advisor" was Labour Councillor for Enfield and former LACS director Richard Course.

1997 kicked off with the first three prosecutions under the Act that the BFSS had fought so hard to keep from the Statute Book. On 23rd January a gamekeeper was convicted of "asphyxiating three fox cubs (gassed with cyanide) with intent to cause unnecessary suffering" and fined £350, while the same day saw a sixteen year-old convicted of kicking, beating and stabbing a hedgehog. The third case under the *Wild Mammals (Protection) Act* found twenty-year-olds Richard Smith and Paul West remanded for pre-sentence reports after using "an aerosol as a blowtorch to set fire to the hedgehog, which they then kicked around the garden like a ball".

What had begun in 1983 as a campaign by the New Forest Deerhunt Abolition Alliance to press for the revoking of Forestry Commission licences to hunt the fallow deer was now reaching its end game, with over 900 years of deer hunting tradition about to end. The 93,000 acre New Forest in Hampshire had been a centre for deer hunting since it was decreed as a royal forest by William the Conqueror in 1079. For centuries the monarch's right to hunt took precedence over all other activities, and any lesser mortals hunting animals to feed their families could expect the death penalty. In the fourteenth century the infamous King John hunted deer in the New Forest and local Commoners only had the right to graze their livestock and collect firewood. King William set up special courts to enforce the harsh forest laws and the Verderers' Court still survives today to supervise commoners' animals and collect payment for animals grazing the forest. Charles II was the last monarch to use the Forest as his private hunting ground, as by the late 1660s the provision of oak timber for shipbuilding had taken priority. It was only during the 1800s that the badly depleted woodlands began to benefit from extensive oak planting programmes. In 1924 the New Forest was taken into state ownership and administered on the nation's behalf by the Forestry Commission (FC).

Deer hunting, in one form or another, had been more or less continuous since Norman times, with hunting as we know it today starting in 1854 with private packs mastered by Buckworth Powell (1854-1858) and Francis Lovell (1858-1883). The New Forest Deerhounds were formed in 1883, still with Francis Lovell as master, not becoming the New Forest Buckhounds until 1914. It was the descendants of this pack that had been the recipient of constant attention from LACS and New Forest Animal Protection Group (NFAPG) monitors, and hunt saboteurs, since 1983. During the intervening years a mass of evidence, coupled with countless acts of savage violence, had been collected by the abolitionists, with all of it ignored or dismissed by the FC.

In November 1987 the Deer Protection Council called on the FC to investigate the hunt after a buck was whipped on to provide further sport when it stopped, exhausted, after a two and a half-hour chase. The terrified animal was pursued for another two hours before it was killed. In October 1988 the hunt was "reprimanded" by the FC after furious complaints from the public following the invasion of Sethorns campsite in the Forest. March 1991 saw Huntsman John Stride jump from his horse onto a fleeing buck and wrestle it to the ground. Hunt saboteurs, who attempted to intervene were beaten up by hunt staff, while Stride then shot the deer, holding the gun less than a foot from a saboteur's head. The FC did nothing about the breach of firearms regulations. By April 1991 the New Forest District Council called on the FC to ban the hunt, but the request was ignored.

On 1st January 1992 fifteen supporters from the hunt beat up a lone saboteur who was taken to hospital by ambulance where he received emergency treatment for severe head injuries. In fact the NFB was known to be an extremely vicious hunt, though not one that would face the saboteurs man to man, preferring the mob attack against lone individuals. During the 1970s, when SOS made the occasional visit to the buckhounds, similar incidents were also the norm. In June 1992 Southampton Itchen MP John Denham, presented to the House of Commons a petition signed by 36,563 residents of the New Forest calling on the government to ban deer hunting. August 1992 saw John Stride convicted of assault and criminal damage at Lymington Magistrates Court following the attack on a saboteur in November 1991. On 21st September the NFB invaded an animal sanctuary run by the seventy-four year-old wildlife photographer Eric Ashby. In March 1993 they were among several hunts exposed by the LACS as participating in a tax fiddle involving huntsmen selling carcasses of dead animals in cash-only deals without declaring the profits to the Inland Revenue. Another hunt saboteur was attacked, causing serious head injuries leading to loss of hearing, in September 1994.

The decision by both the League and NFAPG, in late 1994, to have hunt monitors at every meet soon began to pay dividends. In November members of the hunt were filmed sitting on a terrified deer while they waited for the huntsman to arrive with a gun. On 13th January 1995, following a six-mile chase, a fallow buck was brought to bay in a stream. The Hunt Master, David Marshall, was then filmed holding the animal's head under water with his foot. By the time huntsman John Stride arrives with the gun, it had stopped struggling and is believed to have drowned. The Joint Master Peter Barfoot later told the *Lymington Advertiser*, "Everything was exactly as it should have been...as far as I'm concerned that film is representative of what we do when we go hunting." He added as a rider, "The Forestry Commission keeper was happy with the kill."

The reason for that became obvious on 29th November 1996 when hunt monitors Peter White and Joe Hashman, who operated under the name of Wildlife Action, again filmed an exhausted buck coming to a standstill in the middle of a river. A fourteen-year-old hunter dismounted from his horse, leapt onto the deer and thrust the gasping animal's head under water. The huntsman, aware that the incident was being filmed, shouted to the boy to stop, then waded in and shot the deer. The fourteen-year-old turned out to be the son of the Forestry Commission Keeper!

Footage of these incidents, along with numerous others, a couple of which had prompted Arthur Barlow, Deputy Surveyor of the FC, to order paltry one and three-day hunting suspensions, were to make the NFB a byword for callous cruelty. The exposure of their activities on national TV and in the press made their name not only anathema to the general public, but had begun to cause serious concerns among their peers. Some indication of how they were viewed came when the Cinema Advertising Association (CAA) ruled that film of a fallow buck being "humanely" destroyed at the end of a hunt was too distressing and shocking to be seen in cinemas, even with an "18" certificate.

The footage was of John Stride trying to load his gun whilst holding the buck's head partly under water, then shooting it through the top of the head. The film was to have been part of the Ministry of Sound's "Use Your Vote" advertising campaign which was aimed at encouraging young people to vote at the forthcoming election. A letter from the CAA stated that, in their opinion, the footage breached the British Codes of Advertising and Sales Promotion Code 9.1 (fear and distress). The letter went on to explain that: "The Panel has borne in mind that for good or ill, relatively few people in this country have ever seen such vivid documentary images of animals being slaughtered by humans. The latent power of such an image to distress and shock is therefore considerable."

The end came in 1997. Early in June the hunt had submitted its application for the renewal of their licence. When the FC dragged its feet the hunt then appealed to the Verderers' Court (who still have a major say in the running of the forest) for the re-issue of the licence. What then happened behind the scenes is unsure, but at the end of July the NFB announced that "with regret" they would not hunt fallow bucks this season and that "it is unlikely that they will hunt again in the future". They claimed that the decision was taken because of the "increasing demands upon the forest made by the urbanisation of its fringes and millions of visitors each year". Ken James, founder of the NFAPG, no doubt had the real reason when he stated, "The hunt's excuses are simply a load of old nonsense, as usual. They had been forced into a position where deer hunting was impossible as they were highly unlikely to receive a licence."

In fact it was quite clear the hunt had "jumped before it was pushed". Years of relentless opposition from hunt saboteurs, LACS and NFAPG activists had so sullied the image of the buck hounds that finally public opinion had demanded an end to their reign in the forest, in much the same way that Gwen Barter's campaign in the early 1960s had brought about the end of carted deer hunting in England. The other factor was that no doubt the publication, in March of this year, of Professor Bateson's NT report (which confirmed that his findings could also encompass fallow deer) had given the FC a golden opportunity to end a practice that had become an open embarrassment to them. The NFB were simply the first victims of a FC policy change that would see all deer hunting banned on their land by November.

Even though their passing was greeted with elation its significance was submerged within the greater euphoria felt in the anti camp at the arrival, three months earlier, of the ultimate dream ticket. A Labour government had been elected to power, with an overwhelming majority in the House of Commons, bringing with it, in the baggage of its Manifesto, an ambiguous statement which read: "We will ensure greater protection for wildlife. We have advocated new measures to promote animal welfare, including a free vote in Parliament on whether hunting with hounds should be banned."

Note 1. Jeromy Gibbs always maintained that he had never slit the deer's throat.
Note 2. Jackie Ballard would later become a Lib-Dem MP, who would lose her seat during the 2001 General Election following a concerted campaign by pro-stag hunt interest to unseat her. She would go on to become RSPCA Executive Director.
Note 3. All this would appear at odds with the sad distortion of the truth now promulgated by the former LACS director, now turned blood sport apologist, James Barrington. According to him the "official" version now reads that "...anti hunting groups did not support a proposed Bill to protect all wild animals from undue suffering, whereas the countryside organisations did support such a measure. It's perhaps the clearest indication yet that the obsession to ban hunting with dogs is far more important in the minds of the politically correct than putting in place a genuine animal welfare law."

In fact the animal rights movement has long since ceased to be surprised by anything said by Jim Barrington, having been aware for years that his so-called "impartial" Wildlife Network is nothing other than a front for the CA. The truth of this situation was revealed in the *Observer* of 15th August 1999 by journalists Anthony Barnett and Mark Honigsbaum who wrote:

> "A parliamentary group founded by Sports Minister Kate Hoey to seek a 'middle way' on fox hunting is a front for the pro-hunting countryside lobby. Minutes of a meeting of the Countryside Alliance obtained by the *Observer* show that country landowners campaigning against the Government's proposed ban on hunting with hounds secretly channelled £46,000 to the Middle Way Group.
>
> "The funds were paid via the Wildlife Network, an animal welfare organisation, to cover the group's running costs and a stand at last year's Labour Party conference in Bournemouth, where the Wildlife Network promoted the Middle Way's call for stricter controls on hunts in preference to an outright ban. According to the minutes of the Alliance's hunting committee in June last year, the Middle Way, the brainchild of Hoey and former anti-hunting activist Jim Barrington, was 'a very useful group'."

The item, headed "Middle Way Group and Wildlife Network", continues: "Their financial requirements was for £25,000 for running costs and a further £21,500 to cover conference costs…We should endorse Kate Hoey's group and use it as a vehicle to educate potential Labour sympathisers who might find it acceptable to join."

Brian Fanshawe, the director of the Alliance's Campaign for Hunting, confirmed he subsequently met Barrington and authorised the payments, claiming the money went to the Wildlife Network, not the Middle Way Group. "I have no problem funding the Wildlife Network but we don't fund parliamentarians," added Fanshawe.

Chapter Twelve

"This has always been treated by the Labour Party as a private members' measure"

THE LABOUR PARTY VICTORY, on 1st May 1997, was like a breath of fresh air to the animal rights movement. After eighteen years it was evident to even the most casual political observer that the Conservative Party had long since passed its sell-by date, though the scale of Labour's success left just about everyone stunned. While every LACS member and hunt saboteur raised a glass in celebration there were a few who still doubted that much would change on the hunting legislation front. It was certainly true that Labour's leadership had declared their opposition to blood sports, with heartfelt pledges given to League delegates at Party conferences to vote the right way when the time came, but still there were nagging doubts. For some, the pseudo-socialism of Neil Kinnock and John Smith had given way to the neo-conservatism of Tony Blair's New Labour, bringing with it the view that, for many on the front bench, the haunting spectre that the hoary old issue of hunting would be seen as a throw-back to the bad old days of "class war".

The New Labour commitment to a "free vote" on hunting had come as the result of intense lobbying from the League and IFAW, in fact so effective were they that their joint stand won first prize at the 1996 TUC, Labour and Liberal Democrat conferences, while they were banned from exhibiting at the Conservative conference. Photographs of Tony and Cherie Blair, John Prescott, Jack Straw and attendant Labour grandees, in company with League Head of Political Affairs David Coulthread and Graham Sirl (acting director since Barrington's defection) filled the pages of *Wildlife Guardian,* conveying the impression to expectant readers that abolition was all but "in the bag".

The first move came when newly elected Basildon MP Angela Smith (former LACS Head of Political and Public Relations) submitted the first EDM on the issue demanding the "immediate outlawing of hunting wild animals with hounds". Then, on 16th June, Michael Foster (Labour: Worcester), having drawn first place in the first ballot for Private Members' Bills after the election, announced his intention to introduce the *Wild Mammals (Hunting with Dogs) Bill,* which would outlaw fox, hare, deer and mink hunting. The CPHA swung into action at once with their publicity campaign to promote this Bill, culminating in a double-decker red bus emblazoned with painted fox, hare and deer sent on tour around the country. The National Anti-Hunt Campaign (NAHC), formed in the summer of 1993 by the charismatic Neil Hansen, also took to the road with a mixture of street theatre and petition politics. With the intention of raising a million signature petition against blood sports, Hansen would embark on a one-man campaign tour that would take in most of the major towns and cities in Britain, where he would prowl tirelessly with megaphone in hand until his self-appointed task was accomplished.

The hunters' reaction was immediate, with threats forming an integral part of the debate. Michael Foster soon began to receive death threats which described how "his entrails would be ripped out and fed to the hounds" and that "he would not live to see this Bill become law" if he didn't drop the issue immediately. By 10th July the BFSS/CA had organised an 80,000 strong "Country Rally" in Hyde Park, which was fired up by speaker after speaker, starting with Conservative Party leader William Hague, telling them that this was the start of a fight to the end. Another speaker compared the rally to the beginning of the 1775 American Revolution, while *Daily Telegraph* columnist Auberon Waugh even suggested the idea of poisoning water supplies in protest at the ban! The Labour peer Baroness Anne Mallalieu best summed up the fanatical obsession felt by many there towards blood sports when she said, "Hunting is our music. It is our poetry. It is our art. It is our pleasure. It is our community. It is our whole way of life." The spirit of the rally was sealed in blood later that night when a couple of unwary hunt saboteurs, who had been observing the proceedings, were severely beaten and thrown under the wheels of a moving taxi. They were both treated in hospital for broken bones and other injuries.

At 9.38a.m.on Friday 28th November 1997 Michael Foster rose to move the Second Reading of his *Wild Mammals (Hunting with Dogs) Bill.* Five hours later, after a full debate, the Speaker called for the vote: Ayes 411, Noes 151. The biggest ever vote, and largest ever majority for a Private Members' Bill in history! The House of Commons erupted into unprecedented cheers and even clapping – a matter that was later branded as "un-parliamentary behaviour". The victorious Michael Foster then held a brief press conference and made his way out through the St Stephen's entrance of the Commons to be greeted with a thunderous cheer from a huge crowd waiting outside. Many, including hundreds of long-standing animal welfare campaigners, were overcome with the emotion of the moment. It would take the cold dawn of tomorrow's editorials, predicting that the government would not support the Bill, to wake them to the reality that something was not quite right.

The key lay with George Howarth, Parliamentary Under Secretary of State for the Home Department who, speaking for the government during the debate said, "We made a manifesto commitment that there would be a vote on banning fox-hunting, and that it would be a free vote. That manifesto commitment will be met today... ." When Howarth was pushed, first by Liberal Democrat Simon Hughes, and later by Conservative Ann Widdecombe, to state whether or not the government would give the Bill extra time he evaded the question, pointing out instead that there was no time limit for the Bill's Committee Stage, and no reason why it should not successfully progress through its Report Stage and Third Reading and on into the House of Lords. The sting came in the warning that if the Bill were to be thwarted or delayed in the Commons or the Lords, then that would be the fault of Opposition Members or the unelected House. The implications were obvious: the Bill would stand or fall as a Private Member's measure and would receive no support from the government. The green light had been given to the Bill's opponents and they would take full advantage of it.

The Committee Stage of the Bill began in a convivial mood with the Chair stating, "It is important we conduct our affairs in the highest possible traditions of debate in the House." The five (out of nineteen) committee members opposing the Bill all echoed the sentiments of Tory MP Owen Paterson that "the eyes of the country are on us and that we should consider the matter with all seriousness and not play parliamentary games". So when the Committee returned for its second session in January it came as a surprise to find that all the amendments to the Bill submitted by the Bill's opponents had been withdrawn. In fact, with the exception of one opponent, Liberal Democrat Lembit Opik, they did not vote or speak for the next two months, except to criticise the conduct of the Bill's supporters.

What they were trying to do was rush the Bill through the Committee as quickly as possible so that they could get other Private Members' Bills through to the next stage of parliamentary procedure. They knew that it would be extremely easy to block the Foster Bill at Report Stage by tabling a lot of amendments and then talking for hours. This would mean the Bill had to come back for further Report Stage debates but could not be debated until all the other Bills which had also completed their Committee Stage had received a Report Stage debate first.

In order to counter this, by ensuring that the *Wild Mammals (Hunting with Dogs) Bill* stayed in Committee until the week before the first Friday available for Private Members' Bills to receive their Report Stage debate, the supporters of the Bill ensured that there were no other Bills waiting to be debated after this one was talked out on Friday 6th March. The tactic succeeded brilliantly, ensuring that Foster's Bill secured at least two days of debate at Report Stage.

On the morning of the last day of the Committee, Wednesday 25th February, the defenders of hunting finally decided to submit a number of amendments to the Bill. For the first time since the Committee's initial meeting in December, pro-hunt MPs began to contribute to the debate about the Bill. Having failed to get it through Committee as quickly as possible by not participating in the debate, they now attempted to wreck it by speaking at length on the amendments they had failed to submit during the previous two months. Having failed to prevent the Bill's appearance on 6th March with their first tactic, they now gave this one their best shot.

However, Foster's supporters reacted quickly and, when the Committee returned to meet later that day, declared their intention to meet overnight through to 1 p.m. the following afternoon and if necessary to return a few hours later at 4:30 p.m. and meet for another night through to 1 p.m. the next day. They were prepared to meet and debate with the Bill's opponents right through from Wednesday morning to Friday afternoon – a marathon final session of over fifty hours. Once they realised their bluff had been called the hunters enthusiasm to filibuster evaporated and the Bill completed its Committee stage in a few hours. Though in reality they were not that concerned, knowing as they did that the Bill could still be wrecked during the Report Stage debate, if in a somewhat more public way than the preferred option of closed Committee sessions. Immediately all blood sport MPs were contacted and a concerted filibuster was organised.

Throughout the ensuing two Report debates, on 6th and 13th March, taking up some ten hours of parliamentary time, the defenders of hunting talked and talked about silly points of order, stupid technical points and insulted Michael Foster, purely to frustrate the democratic process. For example, every time a defender of hunting stood up to speak they were immediately asked to accept "points of order" from fellow pro-hunt MPs. These were made to assist the MP speaking to drag out the time taken on the amendments under discussion. Another tactic used was the insistence on a full division of the House (i.e. when all Members of Parliament must have their vote on an amendment recorded by passing through the lobby for the "Ayes" and "Noes") and then walking as slowly through the lobby as they could without risking the ire of the Speaker. This disgraceful charade continued until the debate was adjourned until the following week. The hunters had no doubt been encouraged in their actions by a front page article in the 6th March *Times,* which spelt out the government's position. Home Secretary Jack Straw had rebuffed the anti-hunting lobby by stating that the government should not push through a law banning the "pursuit". He went on, "We do not have a mandate for it… ." When asked whether he ever saw a role for the government in passing an anti-hunt Bill he answered, "No. Of course I cannot say what will happen in fifty years. But you ask my opinion which is that I do not see a role… . This has always been treated by the Labour Party as a private members' measure."

On Friday 20th March 1998 the hunting set now showed considerable interest in Marsha Singh's *Community Care (Residential Accommodation) Bill.* Even the reports on BBC Radio 4 the following day stated that the long speeches and numerous amendments tabled to this non-controversial Bill were made to prevent Foster's Bill being allowed further debate. Now there was no more time left, and without government support the *Wild Mammals (Hunting with Dogs) Bill* was dead. In the following weeks Michael Foster would have numerous meetings with Home Secretary Jack Straw in an attempt to gain support, but to no avail. In May he conceded defeat and formally withdrew his Bill, fearful that its continued appearance on the parliamentary order paper might prevent the progress of another Bill that would make puppy farming illegal.

The failure of the Foster Bill now brought into sharp focus the dilemma facing the Blair government. It became obvious that while paying lip service to the cause of abolition, the political will, or serious desire, to confront the issue head-on was not there at ministerial level. It was equally obvious that an overwhelming number of MPs fully intended to keep the ministers to what had been perceived as a firm promise to stop hunting. The government soon realised that this issue had the potential to cause serious backbench unrest, and would hang around their neck like the proverbial albatross until the matter was resolved.

An indication of the impression that the Bill had upon the government came on the morning on which it had been withdrawn. Jack Straw now appeared to climb down from his previous position when, speaking on Radio 4, he revealed that he would continue to work with Michael Foster to "try to find some way through this". A few days later Straw met with 163 Labour MPs who left him in no doubt of how seriously they viewed the government's failure to support Foster's Bill, forcing the Home Secretary to say that he would take their concerns to the Cabinet and consider the next move forward – one MP, Paul Flynn, even claiming that Straw had scribbled the words "I surrender" on a piece of paper before leaving the meeting. By mid-June *The Times* broke the story that the government, in an attempt to avoid making a direct decision, was going to propose

> "that county councils or some other layer of local government should be given the power to license or not license local hunts, possibly after holding referendums of all voters in their regions. The plan would mean hunting being stopped in areas with particularly strong local feelings against it, but the Government would not necessarily be blamed."

With predictable derision from the back bench the idea remained still-born and now a full year would pass before the government presented a new strategy.

The only good news would come from across the Irish Sea with the announcement from the Northern Ireland Department of Agriculture that "having taken professional and legal advice, we have concluded that hunting the carted stag is arguably an act of cruelty under the *1972 Welfare of Animals Act,* and we have advised the hunt that we may have to take action to prevent future breaches of the Act, or ask the DPP to prosecute those responsible". The fate of this form of hunting had rested on one crucial question – were the deer used in carted deer hunting wild or tame? Government vets called in to investigate confirmed what was obvious to many – the deer used were indeed tame.

When the Department of Agriculture spokesman stated, "It is arguable that the deer being used in this activity are being tamed by their semi-intensive rearing system. That being the case, we have concluded that they may indeed be regarded as domestic animals," the game was up. The public outcry following the televising of Brian

Black's film of the County Down Staghounds tormenting a tame deer two years' earlier, turned into a national campaign by Save Our Stags and ICABS, coupled with the legal challenge mounted by the LACS, had finally brought this 117-year-old hunt to bay. Or so they thought. ***Note 1, APPENDIX 12***

In the West Country QSH Joint Master Bill Fewings was proving that even for stag hunters money talked louder than principles. He would resign just days before the start of the 1998/99 hunting season after a falling-out with supporters following his sale of a 100-acre field to the NT! The hunt monitors continued to catalogue an ever-increasing number of incidents and acts of trespass on NT land. One of the worst occurred on 3rd April 1999, when a stag hunted by the DSSH in the Barle Valley became trapped in a hedge near the town of Dulverton. The hounds were inches behind the stag as he entered the hedge. Turning to face the hounds he was instantly attacked and pulled down by the head, while his front legs buckled under the onslaught. Hunt followers dived in trying to stop the attack, one grabbing the antlers and spinning the stag around. But this did not stop the attacking hounds, which then began biting the rear of the deer. The "Marsh Bridge incident", as it later became known was filmed by members of the recently formed group Protect Our Wild Animals (POWA), and was subsequently given wide TV and press coverage. ***Note 2***

The contribution made by the various monitoring groups, albeit from the LACS, SWDP, POWA, NFAPG and IFAW (who would gather most of the footage between 1998 and 2002) cannot be over-emphasised. It is very probable that the mass of evidence accumulated by these people has done more to highlight the cruelties of stag hunting than any other single factor during more than a hundred years of campaigning. It is also worth remembering that, unlike hunt saboteurs, who attend these events to prevent the killing of an animal, monitors are there to record specifically not only the death of the animals, but the attendant cruelty. Added to which the saboteurs are fully prepared to fight back when attacked, whereas the monitors must always remain passive under the most intimidating circumstances. At the kill, often the most serious flash point at any hunt, the saboteurs can relieve the frustration of failure engendered by the baiting from hunt supporters by engaging in retaliatory "non-violent direct action", while the monitors must stand and take it.

Some indication of the ups and downs of a hunt monitor can be gleaned from the detailed reports of Kevin Hill. The following are from the 1998/99 season:

> "On 12th August a stag being chased by the DSSH from near the meet at the Exmoor Showground tried in vain to escape to sanctuary land. The stag took a route down the Exe Valley passing Winsford and Bridgetown. The numbers of followers present meant the stag was never able to move undetected. Eventually he ran down towards the League sanctuary at Baronsdown. He was running on the very uneven river bed of the Exe. Again with help from monitors Ken James and his partner from the New Forest we had four cameras in the area. The road we were positioned on was about seventy-five yards from the stag at bay in the river. We tried unsuccessfully to record what was happening in the river, but were stopped because of the actions of hunt followers.
>
> "Complaints were made by myself and my colleague, Peter White, to the police, which included a report of assault. I received a number of bruises and Peter was threatened with being pulled off the roof of our vehicle where he was filming. However, our discomfort was nothing compared with what the stag was enduring in the river.
>
> "The baying of hounds when a stag can no longer run I can tell you is spine-chilling. It reaches new heights in both loudness and the constant pitch. It seemed an age before a huntsman arrived and shot the deer. The stress this stag had to endure during the chase and at the end is difficult to describe. For us it was made even worse because he was killed only a few yards from sanctuary land.

"At the next meet of the QSH publicised as near Aisholt, but in fact at Crowcombe Park Gate, a stag was hunted north of Forestry land and then south. The hunt pursued this stag to within four miles of Kingston St Mary. Together with Arminel Scott, a regular monitor and Secretary of the SWDP, we managed to get ourselves into a position to film the stag towards the end of the hunt. The stag crossed the road not far from Kingston St Mary near Taunton. Clearly under stress the stag jumped into a shallow stream next to the road. He seemed oblivious to humans nearby and actually ran in the stream towards us and a few hunt followers. He lay down in the stream ten feet from us. Paddy Groves, the QSH Master, unaware of the situation, rode by and quipped, 'What do you see there then?' With some embarrassment he had to be called back by his followers. The stag remained lying in the stream with all this noise going on. Groves returned to the scene and ordered the hunt gunman to shoot the deer. This was somewhat unexpected as Arminel and I were both there with video cameras filming. The gunman loaded a cartridge into his shotgun and stepped…into the stream just feet from the stag. As the gunman moved the vegetation to get a better aim, the stag, in a desperate bid to escape, jumped out of the stream and struggled up the hill toward Broomfield. Hounds were brought to the line of the stag and continued to hunt.

"There often comes a time during the latter stages of a hunt where it is clear a stag will not escape. It fills all of us monitoring with a feeling of sadness and disillusionment. There is no sanctuary to run to, no banned land to lie down to recover on. Except for the monitors present the hunted animal has no friends in the immediate situation. A short while later this stag was killed. Clearly a stag prepared to lie down in a stream while hunters were shouting only a few feet away has a stress problem. Deer with their shy nature do not like people or vehicles in the near vicinity and would normally run away. I believe there comes a time when, probably through being terrified, they will behave in an unnatural way. This is what drives them to run through gardens and streets or attempt to jump a fence which they have no chance of clearing. Or simply lie down in a stream with hunters close by..."

The first indication of a new government initiative on the hunting front came on 5th July 1999 when unconfirmed reports appeared in the press that an announcement could be expected shortly. The articles speculated that Jack Straw would outline proposals for a complete ban on all blood sports with dogs, to be phased in over two or three years. However, it seemed possible that stag hunting could be the exception, with a ban coming into force immediately. Just three days later on 8th July, during BBC 1's *Question Time*, Prime Minister Tony Blair appeared to confirm the speculation when in reply to a question from the audience he stated, "It will be banned. We will get the vote to ban as soon as we possibly can."

This statement sent the CA into a flurry of activity, culminating in a mass march and picket of the Labour Party Conference at Bournemouth. Chairman of the CA's Campaign for Hunting, Sam Butler, made rather a fool of himself that day by bellowing to the crowd, "Our forefathers didn't fight Hitler to have this lot take away our liberties." It soon became public knowledge that one of Butler's forefathers was "Rab" Butler, who certainly didn't fight Hitler. He was one of the leading Tory appeasers throughout the '30s and then aided Lord Halifax's manoeuvres that attempted to force Churchill into bringing about a negotiated surrender in 1940.

The expectation was that a Government Bill was in the offing and would be announced during the Queen's Speech that autumn. That did not materialise and once again it looked like abolition was at the mercy of the draw for a sympathetic MP to introduce another Private Member's Bill. Ken Livingstone had tried this earlier in the year, with the reintroduction of the *Wild Mammals (Hunting with Dogs) Bill,* though the attempt had only been to ensure that momentum to the cause continued, not with any serious hope of success. It was whilst waiting for that ballot, on 11th November 1999, when in answer to a Parliamentary Question, the Home Secretary announced the establishment of an inquiry into hunting.

After explaining that the government would offer "drafting assistance for this issue to be considered by the House of Commons through a Private Member's Bill on a free vote", Jack Straw continued that "the inquiry will be put in place to inform the debate". It "will look at the practical issues in hunting with dogs, how a ban could be implemented and what the consequences of a ban would be. It will provide an opportunity for the facts about hunting properly to be considered." Furthermore, "It will enable an examination of the effect on the rural economy, agriculture and pest control, the social and cultural life of particular areas of the countryside, the management and conservation of wildlife and animal welfare of hunting and if hunting were to be banned. The inquiry will take evidence from all interested parties." In conclusion he said, "The inquiry will be chaired by Lord Burns. It will be asked to report by the late spring next year. The names of the other members...will be announced as soon as possible."

When the Home Secretary announced the Inquiry's membership on 9th December there was more than a whiff of *déjà vu* in the air, with the spectre of the 1951 Scott Henderson Report looming large. For apart from Lord Burns, a former permanent Treasury secretary, all the others were either linked to institutions that supported hunting, or were supporters themselves. The most controversial appointment was that of Lord Soulsby of Swaffham, the same Lord Soulsby who had penned the BFSS sponsored critique which attempted to trash the Bateson Report. Two others had strong connections with the Royal Agriculture College in Cirencester, which had its own beagle pack that would be banned under any future legislation. They were Michael Winter, the college's former director of rural studies, and Victoria Edwards, a member of the college advisory board. The fourth was Sir John Marsh, former director for agricultural strategy at Reading University, which was a member of the Standing Conference on Country Sports. This was a think-tank that met twice a year and, according to its own literature, has as its sole objective the task of "maintaining countryside sports as an integral part of the national way of life".

Equally disquieting was the list of "neutral" nominees who had been rejected by Jack Straw. According to a Home Office memo they were A J F Webster, a vet at a research institute working in the division of animal husbandry at Bristol, Piran White, a lecturer in environmental studies at York University, Donald Broom, a professor in animal welfare at St Catherine's College, Cambridge, Stephen Harris, a professor of environmental science based at Bristol University, and Baroness Young, Chairwoman of English Nature. The LACS Chairman, John Cooper, spoke for just about everyone on the anti side when he remarked: "Our supporters, including many backbench MPs, will see this as an attempt to stitch up the animal welfare movement."

In fairness to the Burns team the accumulation of evidence over the next six months was exhaustive. They commissioned studies – most notably into the economic impact of hunting and any ban – saw the hounds in action, toured the country and held meetings with people from both sides, took written evidence and heard orally from everyone who had anything to say about the subject, from the Lords who own the kennels to individual hunt saboteurs. Though it was interesting to note that the HSA proper, with more than thirty-five years experience of hunting in the raw, was specifically omitted from the list of organisations asked to contribute evidence. In a complex, emotional and often paradoxical argument, it dissected the issues surrounding blood sports as no other inquiry had done before. It was without question the most authoritative investigation into how British people use dogs to kill other animals for sport in over fifty years. Although as a benchmark document, which incidentally came with a £700,000 price tag, it had a fundamental flaw: it did not say whether hunting with dogs was right or wrong, or whether it should be banned. This "all things to all men" approach tended to negate seriously the impact of the finished Report (*Report of the Committee of Inquiry into Hunting with Dogs in England & Wales)* when it was published in June 2000. Not surprisingly it was immediately seized upon by both sides as a vindication of their respective viewpoints. In fact, when speaking in the House of Lords on 12th October 2004, Lord Burns expressed his opposition to an outright hunting ban "in circumstances where there is no clear scientific support for the animal welfare implications of a ban". The reason he gave was: "There is insufficient verifiable evidence to reach views about cruelty one way or the other, and our committee came to that conclusion."

When the report was boiled down the contribution to the stag hunt debate was very little, with what it did say summarised in a few paragraphs. On the point of deer hunting as an effective control form it merely stated the obvious by saying:

> "It is generally accepted that red deer numbers in Devon and Somerset need to be controlled. Hunting with dogs presently accounts for about fifteen per cent of the annual cull needed to maintain the population at its present level. However, because of the widespread support which it enjoys, and consequent tolerance by farmers of deer, hunting at present makes a significant contribution to management of the deer population in this area. In the event of a ban, some overall reduction in total deer numbers might occur unless an effective deer management strategy was implemented, which was capable of promoting the present collective interest in the management of deer and harnessing such interest into sound conservation management."

In plain English a common sense argument that if you stop hunting an alternative, that has the support of the locals, must replace it.

On the fact that deer hunting was cruel, which was the sole reason why so many people opposed it, the Burns Report said:

> "Although there are still substantial areas of disagreement, there is now a better understanding of the physiological changes which occur when a deer is hunted. Most scientists agree that deer are likely to suffer in the final stages of hunting. The available evidence does not enable us to resolve the disagreement about the point at which, during the hunt, the welfare of the deer becomes seriously compromised. There is also a lack of firm information about what happens to deer that escape, although the available research suggests that they are likely to recover."

22 John Hicks.

23 Lashings of fun on the Quantocks. Saboteur on the run 1st January 1981.

24 Close to the end. DSSH 22nd August 1981.

25 & 26 Two stills from a 8mm cine film that was shot by Mike Huskisson at the DSSH on 22nd October 1981. The second one shows hounds attacking the beaten stag.

27 The Doniford hind standing at the water's edge after escaping from the Quantock Staghounds.

28 Bill Cavanagh's famous 10th October 1987 "stag on a roof" photograph.

29 "LET HIM WALK" *Autumn 1992. Having already been shot, this stag was made to walk up a steep slope, where he would be shot again.*

30 Left to right: IFAW monitors Kevin Hill and Peter White.

31 Nowhere left to run.

As for the alternative:

> "Stalking, if carried out to a high standard and with the availability of a dog or dogs to help find any wounded deer that escape, is in principle the better method of culling deer from an animal welfare perspective. In particular, it obviates the need to chase the deer in the way which occurs in hunting."

In effect this was a reaffirmation of the findings of the Bateson Report.

On 12th June 2000 Jack Straw announced that MPs would be given a free vote during the next session of Parliament on whether or not to ban hunting. This was days before the "official release" of the Burns Report (which would not be debated in the House of Commons until 7th July) and prompted a furious attack from DSSH Joint Master Diana Scott. Speaking to the *Mid Devon Gazette* she said, "People are absolutely disgusted and outraged that any Prime Minister should commission a report such as the Burns Report and not have the courtesy to read it before leaking the fact that there is going to be legislation to ban hunting."

More leaks came in August with news that the proposed anti-hunt Bill would include three options:

Total Hunt Ban – the banning of fox, deer, hare and mink hunting with dogs, plus the end of terrier-work and hare coursing. This was the preferred option of Deadline 2000, a coalition of the LACS, RSPCA, and CPHA. Formed on 30th November 1998 their aim was to ensure that hunting would not survive into the next millennium.

Middle Way – hunting with dogs retained, with some minor changes such as an amendment to end terrier-work. They also favoured some form of licence system (to be administered by an independent authority), much as the Forestry Commission and NT had operated on their land. The Middle Way Group of Parliamentarians claimed to be looking for the "middle way" in the hunting debate. While posing as "non-partisan" they were something of a smoke-screen for the CA, who paid out over £40,000, mainly via Jim Barrington's Wildlife Network, to support the Group.

Limited Change (Self-Regulation) – This was the CA's preferred option, with an "independent" supervisory body to be appointed by the blood sport lobby itself.

The guessing game was finally ended during the Queen's speech on 6th December with the statement: "A Bill will be introduced to enable a free vote to take place on the future of hunting with dogs." The First Reading of the Bill followed the next week, with the Second Reading on 20th December 2000. Jack Straw opened the debate by saying that since the election over 100,000 letters on hunting had been received by the Home Office and that there had been twenty-two Private Members' Bills on the subject during the past twenty years. He then continued that "although the Bill is a Government Bill, its content has not been determined principally by the government; rather, it contains three separate and exclusive options suggested by three different interest groups." He ended his speech by saying that he intended to vote for the Middle Way. Whereas Mike O'Brian, Home Office minister in charge of the Hunting Bill, during his speech to close the debate said that after having studied the Burns Report he would vote for a total ban. The vote that the Bill "be now read a second time" was Ayes 373, Noes 158.

The Bill then went to Committee, which at first stage comprised the whole House. They voted on 17th January 2001 as follows:

Option 1 (The Countryside Alliance) for self-regulation: For 155 Against 399

Option 2 (The Middle Way Group) for hunting by licence: For 182 Against 382

Option 3 (Deadline 2000) for a total ban: For 387 Against 174

The Bill then went to a committee selected from the House of thirty-two MPs, cross party and different preferences on the options. Their job was to thrash out the details of the Bill, to fine tune it and make it workable. On the same day as the vote (17th Jan) an article appeared by the *Guardian's* Westminster correspondent David Henckle which explained:

> "The Tories will...start a guerrilla campaign to make the Government's Hunting Bill 'as flawed and as sloppy as possible'

> with the aim of ensuring a fox hunting ban is unenforceable when the new law is implemented… . The Shadow Cabinet is expecting the Government to get a big majority…but has given the nod to a detailed parliamentary strategy to hide faults in the legislation with the aim of making the ban impossible to police.
>
> "Details of the strategy have been given and revealed in a confidential email sent to the pro-hunting Countryside Alliance. It was written by David MacLean, Conservative MP for Penrith and the Borders, the backbencher in charge of co-ordinating opposition to the ban. Shadow Cabinet sources said…that Mr MacLean was in charge of tactics to undermine the Bill – while David Lidington, a Home Office front bench spokesman, was making the public case against the ban."

The article ended with the telling quote from Mr MacLean's memo: "It is absolutely vital that the legislation is as flawed and sloppy as possible…I want every inconsistency, every dubiety, every ambiguity left in. If the law is clear then we are finished because most of us will not break the law."

Regardless of these dirty tricks, plus serious tinkering from Jack Straw during the Committee Stage, the Bill finally arrived back in the Commons on 27th February for a vote on the Report Stage, which was passed by 319 to 140 in favour of a total ban. The Bill now went to the House of Lords, where the process started all over again. Following the Second Reading debate on 12th March the *Times* Matthew Harris predicted that the noble Lords would vote against a ban because "many are barons and used to hunt". Such a vote, he argued, would also serve to save the government's face as

> "It (the three options vote) also ensures that the manner of the ban's death follows the Prime Minister's sneaking preference. The ban will be sacrificed to a 'Third Way' licensing system. Abolitionists will be elbowed by the procedure into a choice between licensing and no legal restrictions at all. Thus will Tony

Blair have his cake – no ban – and eat it: blaming the upper chamber."

But he was wrong. When the final Lords' vote was taken on 26th March the result was:

Option 1 for a total ban: For 68 Against 317

Option 2 for the Middle Way: For 122 Against 202

Option 3 to maintain the status quo: For 249 Against 108

The Lords had effectively destroyed the Middle Way option by voting so heavily in favour of keeping hunting without reform. The scale of the opposition to the Middle Way meant that the antis were now in a much stronger position to lobby the government into making a firm commitment for a total ban in the election manifesto. The concept that hunting could be regulated had been rejected by all but a few from the very start, including the CA. They constantly said that to be regulated by an outside body would be an infringement of their civil liberty. Groups opposed to blood sports felt with one voice that cruelty cannot be regulated. It is certain with the benefit of hindsight that this vote *gave the appearance* of bringing about the beginning of the end for hunting. The Middle Way MP Llin Golding, speaking on BBC Radio 4's *Today* program the morning after the vote, could see the writing on the wall. She thought that the Lords had shot themselves in the foot and that this vote would result in the abolition of hunting!

It was evident a few days later that the CA had also realised the seriousness of what the Lords had done. Their stag hunting President Baroness Mallalieu attempted to limit the damage with amendments to the CA's option of self-regulation, undoubtedly hoping to head off a Labour Manifesto pledge. There was also the hope that this new found willingness to compromise could form the basis for a future deal with Downing Street. For it was now obvious that Tony Blair did not want a hunting ban, favouring instead the Middle Way, and became dismayed when the peers threw out not just a ban, but also any form of independent regulation. There was one other reason why hunting peers had given second thoughts to regulation that, while posing no immediate threat, had certainly set alarm bells ringing in the upper chamber. The frustration felt by many backbenchers, such as Tony Banks and Sir Gerald Kaufman, to the intransigence exhibited by the Lords was at boiling point, bringing ever-increasing threats that the only way to resolve the issue was to use the parliamentary nuclear option: the Parliament Act.

So now the CA gave its backing to Mallalieu's concept of an independent statutory body to oversee the future of hunting. This body would have powers to fine hunts and individuals if they breached an agreed code, as well as a duty to investigate any complaints against hunts or individuals. These new proposals were now added to another animal bill that was winding its way through the House of Lords. On 9th March 2001 the House had passed the Second Reading of Labour peer Lord Donoughue's *Wild Mammals (Protection) (Amendment) Bill,* which sought to remove the existing exemption for foxes from cruelty and hunt supporters from prosecution to be found in the *Wild Mammals (Protection) Act 1996.* In effect this Bill, now that it contained the amendments for independent regulation, was an attempt to supplant the total ban favoured by the Commons with the Middle Way option now supported by the CA via the back door. As things turned out it all came to naught.

On 7th June 2001 the Labour Party was returned to power for a second term. In the manifesto was another ambiguously worded promise which read:

> "The House of Commons elected in 1997 made its wish clear to ban fox-hunting. The House of Lords took a different view and reform was blocked. Such issues are rightly a matter for a free vote and we will give the new House of Commons an early opportunity to express its views. We will then enable Parliament to reach a conclusion on the issue. If the issue continues to be blocked we will look at how the disagreement can be resolved."

Not exactly the heartfelt commitment wanted by the die-hard abolitionists both in and out of Parliament, but commitment enough to set them on the path of make or break for a total ban.

The Queen's speech on 20th June reiterated the manifesto promise with the one line statement: "My Government will enable a free vote on the future of hunting with dogs." The pressure was now on the government, with Greg Pope (Labour, Hyndburn) crystallising the sentiments of most when he said, "...that a free vote is one thing, but once such a vote has occurred, a Bill must be introduced at an early opportunity. They must have the political will and courage to use the Parliament Act to force through the will of the House of Commons on foxhunting." The day following the Queen's speech Robin Cook, the new leader of the Commons, confirmed the government's intention that the issue would "be resolved in the current Session" of Parliament.

Then the subject went very quiet, but in all fairness the government had a far more serious issue to resolve in the countryside. The start of the year had seen an outbreak of foot and mouth disease on a scale not seen since the 1960s. By February 2001 the situation was reaching crisis levels, forcing the Department for Environment, Food and Rural Affairs (DEFRA) to exercise powers under the *Foot and Mouth Disease Order 1983* which, amongst other things, declared that "hunting and stalking are prohibited". The epidemic would continue unabated throughout most of the year, with large swathes of the countryside turned into a huge funeral pyre as millions of carcasses were incinerated in an attempt to halt the spread.

The LACS also had problems of its own. Going back to 1997 and the Foster Bill there had been internal disagreements regarding the future direction of the League. The rump of the "old guard" wanted a campaigning agenda that included the financing of political initiatives, but not at the expense of its other commitments. Whereas the newcomers wanted to concentrate resources on securing parliamentary abolition, even to the point of selling West Country deer sanctuaries to finance the campaign. One of the first casualties of this ideological split was Chief Officer and *Wildlife Guardian* editor John Bryant, who after fifteen years left in September 1997, later working as an advisor to the CPHA. The turmoil within the League began to be resolved with the appointment in April 1999 of a new chief executive, Douglas Batchelor, who in a very short space of time would turn the League into a first-rate PR machine that could rival the CA blow for blow.

Though rumblings of discontent were never far away, the few remaining "old timers" feeling bitter at the new order: the issue coming to a head in May 2001 when Graham Sirl resigned his position as Head of West Country Operations. Unfortunately he then sent a long letter to the local press, smelling more of sour grapes than defection, apparently attesting to his conversion to stag hunting. In actual fact he was promoting the argument that many, including Lord Burns, had proffered, namely that if deer hunting was abolished by Parliament without a structured control policy in place "the deer population will be decimated". Whatever may have been Sirl's motives the result was a propaganda coup for the CA, with his views promoted alongside other turncoats from the anti side. ***Note 3. APPENDIX 13***

For much of 2001, rumours, and rumours of rumours, continued to speculate as to the possibility, or not, of a future hunting ban. By early November reports were being drip-fed via several newspapers that the Hunting Bill was definitely dead. The ongoing foot and mouth crisis, plus the need for emergency anti-terrorist legislation following the attacks on New York's Trade Towers on 11th September, was given as the reason. Then on 16th November Robin Cook made the surprise announcement that MPs *would* get their free vote, but not until sometime in the New Year. He also lifted the foot and mouth ban, telling fox hunters throughout most of Britain they could resume on 17th December in time for the big Boxing Day meets, although stag hunting would remain banned until further notice.

The 13th February 2002 saw Scottish MSPs vote overwhelmingly in favour of introducing a ban on hunting with dogs in Scotland, ending a process that had begun just over two years earlier. The total ban on foxhunts, hare coursing and fox baiting would come into force during autumn 2002. As a result of this news, MPs Tony Banks (Labour), Ann Widdecombe (Conservative) and Norman Baker (Lib Dem) sent a message to Tony Blair urging him to honour the government's pledge to hold the free vote as promised. The message read: "Scotland 1, England 0 – Come on Mr. Blair, even the score." Deputy Prime Minister John Prescott is then reported to have promised backbenchers he would raise the matter in Cabinet, telling them he felt the reintroduction of the anti-hunt Bill was "an issue of credibility".

Back came Robin Cook on 27th February to tell MPs that they would be given another free vote the following month, fixed for 18th March, with the House of Lords voting the following day. ***Note 4.*** Again, this vote would be for a choice of three options; an outright ban, no change to the current status quo, or the so-called "Middle Way" option of hunting with some type of regulation. After a debate lasting nearly five hours the 18th March vote was:

For a total ban: 386 Against 175

For the status quo: 154 Against 401

For the Middle Way: 169 Against 371

The Middle Way option had no doubt been included once again in the hope that backbenchers had lost some of their enthusiasm for a total ban. The fact that the Lords were now in favour of Middle Way, following the Mallalieu amendments, gave government ministers renewed hope that this watered-down version of hunting would enable a compromise that could allow the issue to be laid to rest with the minimum of fuss. As the vote showed the Commons was having none of it, for after decades of frustration from the Lords they could smell victory. From now on they would demand nothing less of Downing Street than unconditional surrender. The following day's vote (19th March) in the Lords was as expected:

For a total ban: 74 Against 331

For the status quo: 97 Against 147

For the Middle Way: 366 Against 59

Then on 21st March came a new shock when DEFRA Minister Alun Michael, now in charge of the Hunting Bill, announced there would be a further consultation period lasting no more than six months before legislating on the issue. He promised that the Parliament Act would be used to force through a Bill if the Lords continued to oppose it, while pledging that the Bill would deal with the issue "effectively once and for all" and would be framed with the principles of "cruelty and utility" in mind – in line with recommendations of the Burns Report.

On 10th April DEFRA released a letter to all interested parties asking for "comments or suggestions to help to establish the widest possible common ground" as "the legislation must be practical and robust...". Not surprisingly, as there was precious little common ground left, the MPs, peers, hunters, hunt saboteurs, animal welfare organisations, along with Uncle Tom Cobleigh and all merely reiterated their consistent positions, in a virtual replay of the Burns Inquiry. The only thing that would prove beneficial about this new exercise (it became known as the Portcullis Inquiry) was that it allowed for a subtle shift in emphasis with regard to the ethos of the hunting ban.

For some time a small number of leading advocates of the ban, the most prominent being the LACS director Douglas Batchelor, had been concerned that while the main thrust for abolition was undoubtedly the cruelty issue, this alone was proving difficult to sustain with some MPs who possessed little practical experience of the cruelties inherent in hunting. For while it was true that mountains of evidence existed to reinforce the argument that a ban *was* justified on grounds of cruelty alone, there were some who hesitated, swayed by the thought planted by the blood sport lobby that "what may appear cruel to one man may just as easily prove perfectly acceptable in the name of sport to another".

The following few months would see the transition from "what is legally permissible with regard to cruelty, or rather where does a legitimate sporting activity cross the line into unacceptable behaviour" to "is it *morally* acceptable that the law should condone the tormenting and killing of a sentient creature simply to provide amusement in the first instance?" The inclusion of the moral argument into the debate would be seen by some antis as a defining moment for the cause, that would predetermine the outcome of the titanic effort now required to secure abolition.

The CA, now in no doubt that the end game was in sight, took their campaign for "Liberty and Livelihood" onto the streets with a high profile series of stunts and demonstrations that they claimed would be its "Summer of Discontent", that would culminate in the largest march and rally Britain had ever seen. The fun and games was launched when members of the QSH, in company with five assorted fox hunt packs gathered, with horses and hounds, in Horse Guards Parade close to 10 Downing Street blowing hunting horns at 6:30 in the morning to deliver a "wake-up call" to Tony Blair.

The DSSH, back hunting since 11th February when the foot and mouth restrictions had been lifted, made their contribution to the campaign by arranging an incident that was guaranteed to remind antis and public alike of why there was such pressure for a stag hunting ban. From their meet at Mounsey Hill Gate on 3rd August 2002 the hunters pursued a magnificent red deer stag into the town centre at Dulverton. While only yards from the Exmoor National Park Offices, in full view of locals and tourists, the animal was seen swimming in the Barle River, pursued by five or six hounds. The hunt gunmen were scrambling along the weir attempting to shoot it. This was followed by hunt supporters wading waist deep into the river and grabbing the stag, which was then pulled across the river with baying hounds trying to attack the by now dead deer. Not content with impressing hundreds of holiday-makers, the incident went on to impress millions of television viewers – as Kevin Hill and Peter White had managed to capture the entire sorry show on camera.

Note 1. Regardless of all this effort, the County Down Staghounds remains in operation and retains a listing in Baily's Hunting Directory. The difference now is that they no longer chase tame carted deer, but apparently chase the local wild deer all over the countryside. See APPENDIX 12.

Note 2. Protect Our Wild Animals (POWA) was formed by John Bryant when he left the LACS in 1997. John is now an animal welfare consultant specialising in helping urban dwellers find humane solutions to problems with wildlife, particularly foxes. He is also the author of two books: *Animal Sanctuary* and *Living with Urban Wildlife*.

Note 3. Graham Sirl would later offer his total commitment to the blood sport cause. In a spiteful attack against the LACS in general, and hunt monitor Kevin Hill in particular, that was published in the 16th February 2006 issue of *Horse & Hound*, he stated, "I despise the people who put the Hunting Act forward, I despise those organisations (LACS, RSPCA and IFAW) that threw money at that campaign for an end that was absolutely zero. As far as I'm concerned, I wasted twenty years."

Note 4. The need for this second free vote was caused by the revised line-up of MPs following the June 2001 election.

Chapter Thirteen

"I read these messages; I don't understand them"

THE SUMMER OF 2002 progressed slowly with endless submissions and public hearings to facilitate DEFRA's new consultation exercise. Though much of the evidence had all been heard before, there were moments of light relief when Professor Andrew Linzey, banging the drum on behalf of "morality", compared hunting with child abuse, rape and torture. In his evidence to the Portcullis Inquiry Professor Linzey, who holds the world's first post in ethics, theology and animal welfare, said that "licensed hunting" was unacceptable because "we do not speak of 'necessary rape' or 'necessary torture' or 'necessary child abuse', and neither should we do so in the case of deliberate infliction of suffering on animals."

The CA's Summer of Discontent went largely unnoticed by the public at large, who probably saw more of National Anti Hunt Campaign boss Neil Hansen who had embarked on another marathon tour of the country to promote his No Hunting, No Compromise campaign. Although it was impossible to ignore the much heralded Liberty and Livelihood Rally. On Sunday, 22nd September, over 407,000 wax-jacketed and tweed-bedecked supporters of blood sports streamed through the streets of London in what was termed the largest outpouring of righteous anger since the Tolpuddle Martyrs were transported to Australia in 1834. Billed by the CA as a demonstration on behalf of countryside issues ranging from affordable housing to post office closures, the casual observer would have been hard pressed to discern a single placard advocating anything other than the right to kill for sport. But even this simple fact appeared an illusion to the marchers. For no longer was the issue about cruelty, now it had become a crusade by an endangered minority under attack from faceless bureaucracy bent on removing the freedoms of generations. Stag hunters, fox hunters, hare coursers and everyone else with a love of killing cloaked themselves in the mantle of the civil rights movement of 1960s' America, or indeed any other historical analogy that sprang to mind, declaring they were now the vanguard of the fight to preserve the liberties of free-born Englishmen. The transition from blood sport promoter to rural freedom fighter was complete. By Monday they were all back at home and the march, like all such marches before, had achieved very little. For the object of their wrath, the backbenchers in Parliament, knew that they held the moral high ground, and no amount of moral posturing from country cousin would convince them otherwise. Though unlike most marches this one came with an eight-page souvenir supplement courtesy of the *Daily Telegraph.*

The worst fears of these marchers were realised on 13th November 2002, during the Queen's Speech, when she announced, "A Bill will be introduced to enable Parliament to reach a conclusion on hunting with dogs." When the Bill was introduced into the House of Commons, on 3rd December, a nasty shock awaited the antis. For though it went for the total abolition of deer hunting and hare coursing, the hunting of fox, hare and mink would be subject to a registration system. These hunts would have to apply to an independent tribunal, not DEFRA, and satisfy "tests of utility and cruelty", which meant they must prove the need to kill wild animals and that chasing them with hounds was the least cruel method. Tony Banks, far from happy with this compromise, worded an EDM reading: "That this House notes the publication of a Bill to reach a conclusion on the hunting of wild mammals with dogs: and believes that only a total ban on hunting will be acceptable to this House and the public at large." The Bill passed its Second Reading debate, on 16th December, with a 368 – 155 vote for it to proceed, MPs having agreed in advance that the necessary changes to a total-ban Bill could be thrashed out during the following committee hearings.

Across the country, demonstrations kicked off, culminating in a string of beacons set alight throughout England and Wales, in protest against the proposed ban. On Exmoor the QSH, DSSH, Dulverton West and Exmoor Foxhounds held a combined meet in a show of solidarity, while the more militant stag hunters resorted to vandalism to make their point. Ancient oak trees, bridges and signs in the NT's Horner Wood were daubed with obscene slogans, while a couple of months later the NT's Bronze Age memorial cairn which tops the highest point on Exmoor, Dunkery Beacon, was spray-painted with pro-hunt graffiti reading "no hunt – no deer".

Between 7th January and 13th February 2003, the Hunting Bill Committee, meeting twice a week, debated and voted on many amendments. It eventually evolved to include an outright ban on all hare hunting and terrier work, but a ban on fox and mink hunting was not achieved. The Committee Stage was completed just as war was looming in Iraq, therefore it was agreed by anti-hunt MPs that the Bill should be "parked" for the time being rather than "further antagonise hunting groups, which included many military families".

As spring slipped into summer, the issue remained unresolved, but continued to simmer with the only available information coming via snippets of news in the national press. In May the Cabinet warned backbenchers that if they insisted on pushing for a total ban the government might withdraw the backing essential to the Bill's ultimate success. John Reid, leader of the Commons, hinted at growing coolness towards the controversy when he told reporters at Westminster that the government's "pretty crowded programme" might not allow time for the Bill to be debated. Meanwhile supporters of the Bill, such as Gerald Kaufman and Tony Banks, remained optimistic that the Bill would clear Report and Third Reading debates in time to reach the Lords in late June or early July.

The Report Stage debate finally arrived on 30th June 2003, when very early in the proceedings Gerald Kaufman asked whether a vote for an amendment tabled by Tony Banks (Clause 11 – demanding a total ban) would mean that the Bill would be doomed to failure as had been suggested in the press. Alun Michael's reply appeared to suggest that he was not sure how this amendment would affect the

Bill's chances, but stressed that *his* new amendment (Clause 13), which tightened the Bill even further to ban all hare hunting and terrier work associated with hunting would, if voted for, ensure the Bill's Third Reading and eventual passage into law. This was clearly unsatisfactory to Tony Banks, who continued to press for a straight answer to the question – if his amendment was successfully voted on, would the use of the Parliament Act still apply? Clerks were sent scurrying away to consult the rule books, while a new argument broke out between ministers and backbenchers when it was discovered that the programming for the day's debate had put the government's amendment, Clause 13, before Tony Bank's Clause 11. This meant that if Clause 13 was voted for, then 11, for a complete ban, would fall automatically.

Eventually, after much coming and going from the chamber, it was confirmed that if the Bill was amended to include Tony Banks' Clause 11 the Parliament Act could still be used to force it through the Lords. As the debate continued, speakers who had signed the government amendment, Clause 13, explained that they could see the strength in it but that in light of the assertion that government support would be given to a Bill amended to include Clause 11, that they would no longer give their support to it. A total ban was their preferred option. Alun Michael then disappeared from the chamber, asking advice on what to do, as it was now evident that MPs were not going to compromise and vote for his clause. On return he simply withdrew his Clause 13, leaving the way clear for a vote on the Banks amendment.

After a debate lasting five and a half hours the vote on what would be known as the Banks Bill was 362 for a complete ban on hunting, with 154 against. A separate clause, number 14, had also been added for a ban on mink hunting. The vote here was 341 in favour, with 160 against.

The very real possibility of a total ban now sent the hunting fraternity into a frenzy of threats, moral self-justification and propaganda overdrive. Pro-hunting North Wilts MP Charles Gray spelt out how the Bill would be killed in the Lords. The Bill would not be thrown out, but due to the "hundreds of amendments posted" by the peers, plus only two days allocated for debate, would be "timed out". Therefore ensuring that because the Bill failed through lack of time and not because the Lords threw it out, the government would find it very difficult to force through legislation under the Parliament Act. Though as Mr Gray was well known in anti-hunting circles as a man who often made predictions of which the opposite came true, there were many who kept their fingers crossed.

The CA wheeled out Jim Barrington to pound the line that the issue was not about cruelty, rather that "prejudice motivated" antis were more concerned in "thinking of red coats, plummy accents and toffs on horses". Hundreds of column inches were devoted in the national and local press to the defence of fox hunting, but strangely enough practically nothing appeared in defence of hare coursing or stag hunting. It was not surprising considering that most of the national press were now supporting the blood sport agenda, albeit hidden behind wordy editorials defending the rights of "endangered minorities" against "class-ridden" attacks, while the threat to use the Parliament Act was considered nothing short of the realisation of George Orwell's worst nightmares. The only honourable exception to this trend was a four-page spread in the *Independent* that allowed Kevin Hill to explain in some detail the real reasons why most Labour MPs had voted for an outright ban.

Another trend that started to take off was fading celebrities suddenly signing up to "fight for freedom". The best example of the genre being Noel Edmonds, of Mr Blobby fame, who of course, like most of these self-styled democrats, went to great lengths to distance themselves from the actions of which they now appeared so keen to defend. In an interview with *Horse & Hound* he explained, "I don't hunt. I have never hunted. I have no intention of hunting in the future. Indeed, I struggle to understand the appeal of hunting. However, I totally oppose a ban on hunting." So, in the name of Liberty and Livelihood, he had no choice but "to saddle up and be there at my local Devon meet. I shall be a Freedom Rider!"

Thousands of placards bearing the statement "59% of the public say KEEP HUNTING" appeared throughout the countryside on anything where it was possible to nail a placard. The only problem being that the statement was a lie. After the LACS made a complaint to the Advertising Standards Authority, pointing out that this figure of fifty-nine per cent had been reached by the manipulation of adding various opinion poll figures together, the CA was ordered to cease their use forthwith. ***APPENDIX 14***

During the 16th September Second Reading of the Bill, Baroness Mallalieu spelled out the Lords' intention to "set about unravelling the current mess – line by line". When the Bill was again debated, on 21st October 2003, against the advice of Labour Environment Minister Lord Whitty that they would create a constitutional crisis if they ignored the judgement of the Commons, peers votes by 261 to 49 for a return to licensed hunting. Then, just as Mr Gray said they would, the House of Lords ran out of time and there the Bill remained.

Within days the new leader of the Commons, Peter Hain, announced that the Lords would not be allowed to block this legislation. He was unequivocal, saying:

> "We have seen the most flagrant abuse of the House of Lords' power to destroy a Bill, massively voted for in the House of Commons, successively endorsed in our general election manifestos. That is the real choice here. Can we continue to allow the House of Lords to defy the House of Commons and the will of the people who voted this Labour government in with a mandate to ban cruelty to animals? We will have to find a way of ensuring that a ban on cruelty to animals, which was what the Commons voted for overwhelmingly and what the people supported in two general elections, is implemented."

The understanding now was that the government would introduce a Bill for a total ban to be included in the Queen's Speech on 26th November. Tony Banks echoed every anti's hope when he said, "The pro-hunting campaigners will be stuffed."

The 1st November was now designated Declaration Day, with a 37,000-strong army of hunters across the country vowing to pursue a campaign of "lawlessness and civil disobedience" if their sport was banned. Their commitment was sealed with the signing of the Hunting

Declaration, the brainchild of West Country philosopher Roger Scruton, which pledged them to "disobey...any law purporting to ban hunting". Their reasons were of the highest order: "Throughout history our citizens have put their personal freedom in the balance to resist oppression and ill-considered laws. We intend to follow in this honourable tradition of civil disobedience."

The Tory peer and CA director Lord Mancroft, speaking to one of the largest rallies that day in Honiton was full of freedom's fire, crying out to the crowd, "We are fighting for the inalienable right of human kind – to be free. Free to be you, so long as being you does not impair the freedom of others. That's what we're fighting for. And that's a battle worth fighting." Not to be outdone a representative offering solidarity from the USA's 170 hunts, Carla Hawkinson, sparked roars from the crowd at the same meeting when she compared the civil unrest promised by the hunters to the actions of American guerrillas during the 1776 revolution. Though if memories of revolution were to be invoked a better example for these mawkish proceedings may well have been the final words of Madame Roland, who on facing the guillotine during the French Revolution, cried, "Oh, Liberty! What crimes are committed in thy name!" There was certainly no doubt that the hunters now intended to use every metaphor in the English language to turn what was essentially a side issue about their right to chase small bundles of russet fur across the countryside in the name of sport into a crusade that ranked alongside the epoch-making moments of history.

From Exmoor now came yet another "independent" report, which concluded that any ban of the three stag hunt packs would cost the region a staggering £9.5 million in lost revenue, which was more to the CA's liking than the 1993 Cirencester Report that had suggested a negligible impact. ***Note 1.*** This new report was soon forgotten when a war of words broke out between the various protagonists as to the sums of money spent to secure a hunting ban. The Middle Way Group claimed that a "vast, wasted fortune" of over £30 million had been expended, with the RSPCA splashing out £15 million since Labour came to power in 1997, with IFAW a good second at £8 million, closely followed by the LACS at £6million. Liberal Democrat blood sport apologist Lembit Opik berated this spending by claiming: "A simple trawl through the list of causes seeking funds shows overseas projects for the protection of endangered species like mountain gorillas, rhinos and wolves… . Imagine what these groups could do with a fraction of £30 million." All went very quiet when similar figures were bandied about regarding the vast sums poured into campaigns to protect hunting.

The posturing and bickering continued until late November, when the Hunting Bill failed to materialise in the Queen's Speech, sending both sides into a new frenzy of speculation, fuelled as ever by the mandatory press "inside tips". One story gave out that Downing Street intended to soften the blow by promising to back a new Private Member's Bill the following year. Another claimed that a Parliamentary cross-bench Human Rights Committee, which had the job of making sure every piece of new legislation conformed to European law, had pronounced that the Bill breached the *Human Rights Act* on two counts. Firstly because no compensation was proposed for hunt workers left unemployed by a ban, and secondly because it infringed a farmer's right to choose the method of pest control on his own land. The Government Bill could not be amended to include these rights, because doing so would make the use of the Parliament Act invalid, as such legislation pushed through under this Act must have been rejected unchanged twice by the Lords. This was given as the real reason no mention of hunting had surfaced in the Queen's Speech, with the added information that a two-year wait was now on the cards while the government went through the entire Hunting Bill procedure again.

Appearing on GMTV, Peter Hain scotched the rumours that Labour had abandoned the Bill, saying that it was the Lords which had done this without any serious intent to amend it. He was emphatic "this cannot be allowed to continue. It needs to be resolved – we need closure on it – and we are seeking to work out how we can achieve this. Just abandoning a Bill…is a situation which is unprecedented and cannot be allowed to stand still." What Hain did not confirm was any indication of a timescale, which still meant to most antis that any proposed ban remained a distant dream. The CA thought much the same, only in their case that abolition was now becoming a remote possibility. They continued to promote Lord Donoughue's *Wild Mammals Protection Bill*, which had recently completed its passage through the Lords, as a way out of Labour's hunting dilemma. While their publicity stunts became ever more bizarre with the issue of a playing card set labelled Pack of Prejudice, featuring fifty-four MPs claimed to be the most dangerous opponents of blood sports.

By the early part of January 2004 the rumours had a Hunting Bill returning to Parliament in February or March. This would give MPs the chance to vote for a complete ban by Easter, with a delay on its introduction into the Lords until after the summer. This was to prevent peers spending so much time discussing the Bill that they deliberately wrecked the progress of other bills on the government's agenda. When nothing had materialised by late April, and their morale boosted by a legal opinion which suggested a ban would not go against human rights, 212 MPs signed an EDM "demanding that Tony Blair fulfils his pledge to end blood sports". Back came the assurance from ministers, only too aware that this had now become a serious "matter of trust" between Blair and the backbench, that a Bill would be introduced at the end of May.

By mid-July, with no Bill in sight, Deputy Prime Minister John Prescott now indicated that the Bill might not be reintroduced until the next Queen's Speech in November. A wave of anger erupted from the backbenchers, as this further delay could mean that the government would not be able to use the Parliament Act to force it onto the Statute Book, the arcane rules of Parliament dictating that the Act cannot be imposed unless a Bill has been held up in two successive sessions of the Lords. As Parliament prepared for the summer recess, on 23rd July, the Leader of the Commons, Peter Hain, appeared to confirm Prescott's statement, even hinting that the government might be having second thoughts about outlawing hunting before the next election, which was not due until sometime in 2005.

Gerald Kaufman pressed the government not to delay, saying that a total hunting ban would be a "splendid present" for the summer. Peter Hain replied in a curious statement, the significance of which would only become apparent the following September: "When I was a boy I always looked forward to Christmas, rather than the summer, for splendid presents, and I would advise him to bear that in mind."

The first indication that something big was about to happen came with a front-page "exclusive" in the *Mail on Sunday.* "LABOUR TO BAN HUNTING WITHIN WEEKS" screamed a banner headline on 5th September. The accompanying story explained that in a bid to head off Cabinet resignations and backbench rebellion, plus distancing the Prime Minister personally from any fallout, Downing Street had asked Commons Speaker Michael Martin to invoke the Parliament Act to quash expected opposition from the Lords. The first official announcement came on 9th September when Peter Hain told the Commons that the following Wednesday, 15th September 2004, had been set aside for a specially extended sitting in order to deal with all stages of the Hunting Bill in a single day – a procedure normally reserved for emergency legislation, such as anti-terrorist laws. The accelerated timetable meant that the Bill could be sent to the Lords in time for it to be forced into law within this session of Parliament.

The only problem for some MPs was Hain's confirmation that the government would press for a two-year delay in implementing the ban. He said that the delay, which would see hunting continue until November 2006, would allow time for the re-homing or "humane disposal" of thousands of hunting hounds, alongside time for people who might lose jobs to "refocus" their lives. Though other MPs did not see this as a serious problem, feeling that it could be possible for the government to lose this motion at next week's vote, leading to a ban as early as February 2005. ***Note 2***

On the morning of Wednesday, 15th September 2004, an estimated 20,000 pro-hunt demonstrators began pouring into central London from all corners of Britain, in response to a call from the CA. By mid-day Parliament Square was a seething mass of humanity, their temper inflamed by emotional rhetoric supplied from a large stage containing the heavyweights of the hunting world. Confronting this crowd was a solid wall of 1,300 police around the House of Commons, many in full riot gear, while mounted police patrolled the approach roads, and helicopters hovered overhead. For the few hunt saboteurs brave enough, or foolhardy enough to venture through this mêlée it was heart warming to realise that this overwhelming police presence was for once not in their honour.

At 12.39 p.m. the focus of their rage, the final series of debates to seal the fate of blood sports, began with the opening speech from Rural Affairs Minister Alun Michael. Over the next two and a half hours the *Hunting Bill (Procedure),* or First Reading, would again go over the well-worn ground of human rights violation, suppression of minority rights, legitimacy of using the Parliament Act, and the weary old issue that opposition to hunting was not about cruelty but class warfare. Perhaps the best lines of the day went to Tony Banks who stressed, "If this is a class issue, it is a middle class issue – a middle England issue. The profile of the passionate anti-hunter – which I know because I get thousands of letters from them – is a middle class white woman living in the home counties, or a county town or village, who reads the *Daily Mail.*" ***Note 3.*** When the debate came to a vote at 3.00 p.m. there was an overwhelming majority, of 310 in favour to 158 against, for the Bill to proceed.

At the same time, outside on Parliament Square, the demonstration had exploded into violent pitched battles as blooded protesters hurled themselves against police officers, in a vain attempt to breach the metal barriers erected to seal off the Commons. As a protest singer on the platform sang the refrain, "Fight, fight for your rights, the war has begun," smoke bombs, rook scarers, shotgun cartridges, bottles and coins were hurled at the police, who repeatedly charged with batons drawn. As ever more battered and bleeding hunters were carried back into the crowd, the ferocity of the attempts to storm Parliament increased. The small garden around Westminster Abbey was soon turned into a first aid station, while the square and lower end of Whitehall filled with acrid red, white and blue smoke from hundreds of distress flares thrown by the mob. The few hunt saboteurs on hand to witness this riot had little sympathy, with years of violence from the hunt under their belts, it felt good to stand back and watch the opposition on the receiving end for a change. ***Note 4***

Back inside the Commons the debate on the *Hunting Bill (Second Reading)* began at 3.47 p.m., again with Alun Michael opening the proceedings. The same arguments continued as before, until 4.22 p.m., when one of the most audacious breaches of parliamentary security in living memory brought the sitting to an abrupt halt. Five protestors, led by the young fox hunt master Otis Ferry, son of millionaire rock singer Brian Ferry, stormed the floor of the chamber. With elaborate inside knowledge of the Commons layout they had managed to evade armed police and footmen in tights to reach the "inner sanctum", where they then became lost for words. According to the *Guardian's* Simon Hoggart:

> "They were bending and twisting with hatred. But in spite of having crafted brilliant and successful plans to get past the security system, they hadn't quite worked out what to say. They had the world to address, but they had nothing historic, nothing memorable to hand. One of them merely shouted: 'It's totally unjust!' Another...yelled, 'This government! There's no democracy. You've mucked up pensions, you've mucked up everything!' It wasn't quite Oliver Cromwell dismissing the Rump Parliament..."

With the excitement over, and the threat to democracy safely in the cells for the night, the debate resumed, to rumble on to the decisive vote that would consign blood sports to the dustbin of history. At 5.38 p.m. the House divided again, to vote 356 in favour, 166 against, for a total ban on the hunting of wild animals with hounds. It was done.

A howl of impotent rage echoed across Parliament Square as the remnants of the demonstration, long since subdued by the police, were told the vote. Die-hard elements on the platform began a howling chant of "No Ban, No Ban", but mainly they had long since begun to drift away home, with a few slowly coming to accept that their time was all but up. The House of Commons still had the formalities of parliamentary procedure to complete. Another three hours of debate followed (Committee Stage), during which the time-scale of the ban was debated. The original three months after the ban period, the two-year delay on implementation preferred by the government, or Tony Banks, amendment for an eighteen-month delay, coming into effect on 31st July 2006. At 8.57 p.m. the vote carried the Banks amendment 342 for, 15 against. The final formality of the day, the vote on the Bill's Third Reading, was taken at 9.53 p.m. with a majority of 339 for, 155 against. The *Hunting Bill* would now be sent to the House of Lords one last time. If they refused to comply, compromise, or attempt some form of acceptable amendment, they now knew that the Parliament Act would be invoked to force it into law.

The following morning's newspapers ran predictably sensational headlines, with the *Daily Mail's* two-page photo montage of blooded hunters under the heading "The English Civil War" the best of the crop. While the same paper's Stephen Glover predicted: "This explosion of rage by those who wouldn't normally dream of breaking the law will be the defining event of the Blair State as the poll tax riots were for Mrs. Thatcher…" The saddest fact about the many editorials that day was not that they lauded these rioters as some type of champions for democracy, or even, as *The Times* wrote, that the issue was "a perfect example of the tyranny of the majority" over the minority, but that the central reason for this political and violent situation, that hunting was about cruelty, did not appear to rate a mention. Unlike their opposition to stag hunting in 1969, which they termed "outdated", "objectionable" and " an affront to British taste", *The Times* no longer saw cruelty as an issue, thinking now that attempts to outlaw the "sport" meant that "human tolerance is the loser in the…debate".

The simple truth about the press's attitude throughout the run-up to abolition was their total failure to address the real facts about blood sports. Hundreds of column inches had been devoted to everything from pro-hunt protests to the constitutional implications of using the Parliament Act, many illustrated with the Christmas card image of the traditional hunting scene. All of them giving credence to the *Evening Standard's* opinion that "it is characteristic of a liberal society to accommodate traditions and views that the majority may not share, and by any such standard this ban is wholly illiberal". Nowhere did you find reportage of the truth behind the glossy image, much less a photograph of the terrified stag at bay.

The weeks that followed saw an almost endless barrage of self-justification and veiled threats from the hunting fraternity which were succinctly summed-up by the *Western Daily Press's* Exmoor correspondent, Chris Rundle. "Be prepared," he wrote,

> "for a deluge of crocodile tears now the Hunting Bill is on its way to the statute book. Prepare to be told that (a) hounds will have to be shot, that; (b) deer will be blasted into oblivion, and; (c) hunt supporters have been the innocent victims of unrestrained police violence while demonstrating in defence of their human rights.
>
> "For those of you who may still be unfamiliar with hunting's black propaganda, let me explain. Firstly, hounds are shot anyway after two or three seasons, when they are no longer able to keep up the pace all day. Secondly, one of the favourite statements of the hunters is: 'We are the best friends the deer have got.' But the sub-text is: 'If we can't hunt them, we'll shoot them.' In other words, if these people can't chase two or three animals a week to exhaustion then they won't be prepared to see them eating their grass and will take them out. All of them. Which is why the Exmoor Society is calling for a post-ban plan to be set up to oversee the management and culling of the national park's 3,000 deer. Sadly, it will require the cooperation of everyone, including those who currently hunt. Even more sadly, the hunters have so far refused to cooperate with the setting up of any such initiative.
>
> "And the poor, blooded hunt followers who limped home from London nursing their wounds? Well, they swaggered into the capital apparently in the belief that they were just as much a law unto themselves as they are on hunting days, when acts of trespass and lunatic driving are not only commonplace but occur while Plod studiously finds some paperwork to do back at the nick. The Metropolitan police had other ideas; the hunt followers got a bloody good hiding. And I have to tell you that, out in the sticks – where they claim to have total support – the cheers have barely died away."

Just to prove the validity of Rundle's argument, on the very day his article appeared the same newspaper carried extensive coverage of a mass stag hunt trespass into Linda's Wood, the eighty-acre sanctuary bought by Sir Paul McCartney in memory of his late wife. Armed hunters threatened LACS warden Paul Tillsley, while over twenty vehicles surrounded the wood as attempts were made to locate the hunted stag. Five weeks later the same wood was invaded, this time by trophy hunters, who killed and decapitated a majestic red stag. The police, of course, had been "talking to the people involved" in the first incident, while DSSH Chairman Tom Yandle stressed that the second was "not something the hunters would get involved in". In fact the only real public protest of any note, which was to prove a publicity disaster for the CA, came on the 28th September when breakaway elements of a mass picket at Labour's annual conference dumped two rotting calves and a dead horse on the streets of Brighton. Referring to the "contorted faces" of the "braying mob" that had carried out this act Deputy Prime Minister John Prescott thundered:

> "How can people who claim to care for the countryside drag dead horses through the streets of this city and call it legitimate protest? Why do they always want to kill animals? I say loud and clear to the fox hunters: you live in a Parliamentary democracy, you lost the argument, now respect what is soon to be the law of the land."

By the time the *Hunting Bill* arrived in the House of Lords, for the Second Reading on 13th October 2004, the issue had gone far beyond a simple matter of animal cruelty, it was now billed as a monumental constitutional clash between Commons and Lords. The Environment Minister Lord Whitty told peers threatening to overturn the ban they were "in the last chance saloon". If they persisted in defying the will of the Commons it could force the government to reform the upper chamber, which could finally spell the end of hereditary peers. To underscore the fact that cruelty had no part in this debate Lords Burns stressed that use of the Parliament Act would be "inconsistent with the procedure" because there was insufficient evidence to endorse a ban. He explained that:

> "Although I fully understand the frustration of those in favour of a ban who feel the issue has been debated long enough, and my own involvement now seems an age ago, I do find it very difficult to accept the use of the Parliament Act in circumstances where there is no clear scientific support for the animal welfare implications of a ban."

Later in the debate, to reinforce their sense of persecution Lord Mancroft, in what had to be one of the most tawdry analogies of the past seven years, claimed that the government was acting like "a fascist dictatorship". This was leading to a situation where "It is OK to abuse hunting people because, like Jews in Nazi Germany, we are undesirables."

Back in the House of Lords on 26th October, for the Committee Stage debates, the peers decided to go for broke. Not only did they reject the Commons Bill by adding an amendment to reinstate a registration system for fox hunting, but turned down a complete ban of stag hunting and hare coursing in favour of licensing. After voting 322 to 72 to send the amended Bill back to the Commons Lord Whitty told the peers, "It is not usually a good move to send back to your negotiating partners a proposal which has already been overwhelmingly rejected, not unless you wish to precipitate a complete breakdown of relations between the two sides." Not only that, but Whitty felt that throwing out a complete ban on deer hunting would be seen as rubbing salt into the wound.

The peers now saw their actions as "calling Tony Blair's bluff" which would demonstrate if he was prepared to use his authority as Prime Minister to secure a compromise, or give in to the anti-hunting majority on his backbenches. The confusion now coming from the government left no doubt that they did not have a clue how to resolve what had become one of the most fiercely fought issues of the Blair years. Downing Street reiterated that the Prime Minister still favoured a compromise based on the original proposals for a ban on stag hunting and hare coursing, but for fox hunting to continue under a system of strict regulation based on the tests of utility and cruelty. But they added the rider that there was little leeway for his intervention as the issue would be taken "on a free vote". Back on the streets another publicity fiasco engulfed the CA when it became known that plans were afoot to "hijack" the 11th November Armistice Day remembrance service at the Cenotaph. Such was the outcry, that come the day, no protest was attempted.

The Bill was again debated in the Lords during its Third Reading on 15th November, amid much talk of "shocking interference with the personal liberties of people who have broken no law..." from Lord Peyton of Yeovil. While Lord Eden of Winton recalled his fox hunting "Uncle Jack" who was killed during the First World War fighting "against tyranny, as were the countless thousands of others whom we have been remembering in this country...over these past few days – against tyranny and for freedom." In closing the debate it became evident that Lord Whitty had had enough, saying he had "sat through many of these debates in which I, the government and those who supported the original Bill have been subject to a lot of abuse, a lot of harassment, and a lot of misleading and occasionally entirely objectionable statements." It was then returned to the House of Commons without a vote.

There had been rumours aplenty in the press that Tony Blair had been working frantically behind the scenes to secure a "middle way" option. Efforts had been made throughout Westminster to "pressure" Labour MPs and "persuade" Liberal Democrats to vote for a compromise, with repeated statements from Downing Street of Mr Blair's continued opposition to a complete ban. By the eve of the final showdown in the Commons there appeared no significant drift of the "payroll" vote of government ministers towards the compromise camp, while Gerald Kaufman was adamant that "we who have been working for a complete ban...are interested only in that". The only good news for the Prime Minister was that MPs appeared willing to agree a stay of execution for fox hunting by supporting a government amendment delaying implementation of a ban for eighteen months. The bad news was that the Lords had now declared their intention to oppose this, going instead for the "kamikaze option" that would force the ban into law by the following February. This way they could ensure that the issue caused maximum discomfort for the government during the general election campaign expected some time early in the New Year by forcing the government to use the Parliament Act.

At 6.30 p.m., on Tuesday, 16th November 2004, a three-hour Third Reading debate began in the House of Commons that would see MPs overturn the "middle way" amendment supported by both the Lords and the Prime Minister. After a lacklustre collection of speeches that ended with a sorrowful Lembit Opik standing "here feeling extremely disappointed" that the House was "on the brink of a vote based on prejudice and not on fact, on victory and not animal welfare – a vote that more than anything is based on the desire to win and pay back the Conservatives for their decisions on the miners and other things that their government did in the 1980s", the votes were taken. In a series of divisions, the most significant two of which, voted by 321 to 204 and 343 to 175 to reject licensed hunting, going instead for a total ban. The Bill was then returned to the Lords, for them to vote on the Commons decision to overturn their amendment to reintroduce regulated hunting.

The following evening, 17th November, defiant peers backed a motion by Baroness Mallalieu by 188 to 79 that reinstated a licensed scheme in the *Hunting Bill.* They again added stag hunting and hare coursing to the list for registration, along with a timetable for implementation now reading 1st December 2007, instead of the three months in the Bill, or eighteen months requested by the government. Much of the two-and-a-half-hour debate was taken up with Baroness Mallalieu moving some fifty odd amendments to the Bill, while Environment Minister Lord Whitty appealed in vain for the peers to back down and not to give the Commons need to invoke the Parliament Act. It was Lord Mancroft, in the last serious speech from the House of Lords during these protracted wrecking tactics, who finally invoked the concept of animal "welfare", albeit as an afterthought, to justify the amendment to extend the delay of a ban until 2007. After citing human rights violation, concerns for hounds and horses and adjustment periods for "all the people involved in hunting", he finally got around to red deer. In a statement that was somewhat selective with its terms of reference he asked for the delayed ban so as to address "the deer management problem" in the West Country. "It is widely accepted," he argued, "that Exmoor is a unique and unusual place, to put it mildly. The herd of red deer on Exmoor is completely unique; there is no other herd like it in the United Kingdom. There are other herds of red deer, but they are nothing like the way they are on Exmoor. It has been said by everyone – the Porchester report, Exmoor National Park, the Burns report, the Phelps report – that it would be deeply irresponsible to change the current system of management of the deer, which is centred around the stag hounds, without putting in place another system."

"It is worth remembering," he continued,

> "that thirty per cent of the deer that the stag hounds take each year are injured or ill deer – they are nothing to do with hunting. Most are either poached and wounded, or involved in car accidents. In the absence of the stag hounds, no one has any ability at all to deal with those injured deer, which is a significant welfare problem. There are a very large number of small landowners down there; they all need to work together. The government, particularly Mr Elliot Morley, have drawn attention to the fact that the local deer management group is the most successful such group in the United Kingdom, and it will take a very considerable time – certainly three years – to put anything else in place. That is why...we need the delayed enactment."

The Bill was then returned to "the other place".

The final act to ban hunting in the House of Commons began at 12.05 p.m., 18th November 2004, on a day that would see high drama and farce. It started with rumours that the government had tabled two amendments to the *Hunting Bill.* One, from Peter Bradley, who was Alun Michael's parliamentary private secretary, to implement a ban in July 2006, with the other in July 2007 from Rural Affairs Minister Alun Michael himself. Confusion reigned, for as MPs had already agreed to accept the original government amendment for a delay until 2006, why was there now a new choice? Many suspected that some kind of "stitch-up" was underway, that would enable the government to avoid using the Parliament Act. The Speaker, Michael Martin, was bombarded with questions from the confused MPs, although he appeared to know as little about the new amendments as anyone else. Demands for the Leader of the House, Peter Hain, to make a statement fell on deaf ears, while many MPs turned on the whips accusing them of "skulduggery". Hilary Armstrong, the Chief Whip, was reported to be having intense discussions in the Members' Tea Room, prompting Gerald Kaufman to raise a point of order complaining that Whips were applying pressure to vote for the 2007 deadline. To defuse the chaos in the chamber the Speaker now suspended the sitting for forty minutes while the situation was clarified. Even a simple vote to set aside one hour's debate on the two options for the delay dates descended into farce. In the division lobbies, an angry mass of anti-hunt MPs became embroiled in a heated argument as to whether the government was pulling a sly trick to make the use of the Parliament Act invalid by changing the format of the Bill.

When Rural Affairs Minister Alun Michael returned he explained that there was nothing sinister in the amendments, but that they were merely to "enable this House not only to be reasonable, but to be seen to be reasonable by going the extra mile..." The vote was 283 to 132 to go for the delayed date of 31st July 2006, while the government's "extra mile" option was rejected by 345 votes to 46. The Bill would now go back to the Lords, where one last chance to salvage an eighteen-month transition period was on offer. If this was voted down then the Bill would revert to its original form of a total ban, coming into effect on 18th February 2005, three months to the day of it becoming an Act.

As the Bill was batted back and forth between the Houses Prime Minister Tony Blair was anything but happy at his failure to broker a compromise. At a Lancaster House press conference, called in honour of a visit from French President Jacques Chirac, he was piqued to find himself bombarded with questions about hunting instead of "important" matters of state. After claiming that "probably the majority of people would have preferred a compromise accepted", he added that the issue was now up to the courts. Later that night he would be angrier still when forced to run the gauntlet of 1,000 jeering CA demonstrators blockading the road to Windsor Castle, where the Queen was holding a state banquet for a by now somewhat bemused President Chirac.

At 6.00 p.m. the Lords, following an impassioned statement from Baroness Mallalieu that "The choice is a simple one: do we throw away our principles or do we vote to support this grubby little banning Bill?", they rejected the Bill by 153 to 114.

At 9.01 p.m. the Speaker, Michael Martin, announced:

> "I have to inform the House that a message has been brought from the Lords as follows: The Lords insist on their amendments to the Hunting Bill, to which the Commons have insisted on their disagreement, for which insistence they assign their reasons. They insist on their amendments to which the Commons have disagreed, for which insistence they assign their reasons, and they disagree to the amendment proposed by the Commons in lieu of the Lords amendments, for which disagreement they assign their reasons."

When MPs asked for an explanation, or possible translation, of that message Michael Martin replied: "I read these messages; I don't understand them." He then continued:

> "As the Minister (Alun Michael) made clear to the House in his remarks earlier today, a rejection on these lines has brought us to the end of the road. I am satisfied that all the provisions of the Parliament Acts have been met. Accordingly, I have to tell the House that I have certified the Hunting Bill under section 2 of the Parliament Act 1911, as amended by the Parliament Act 1949. The Bill endorsed by me will be sent for Royal Assent at the time of prorogation in compliance with the provisions of the Parliament Acts."

The *Hunting Bill* was now sent back to the House of Lords one last time to obtain the Royal Assent. At 9.30 p.m. the Lord Chancellor, Lord Falconer of Thoroton, addressed the assembled peers to inform them that:

> "Her Majesty, not thinking fit personally to be present here at this time, has been pleased to cause a Commission to be issued under the Great Seal, and thereby given Her Royal Assent to divers Acts, the Titles whereof are particularly mentioned, and by the said Commission has commanded us to declare and notify Her Royal Assent to the said several Acts, in the presence of you Lords and Commons assembled..."

Finally, after more than 700 hours of debate, this short ceremony of pomp and pageantry from centuries past turned the Bill into an Act.

At 9.59 p.m. Michael Martin again rose from the Speaker's chair to announce: "I have to acquaint the House that the House has been to the House of Peers, where a Commission under the Great Seal was read, authorising the Royal Assent" to the *Hunting Act 2004.*

It was over. After 103 years of campaigning, stag hunting, along with all other forms of blood sports would be consigned to the history books within three months. Or had they? ***See APPENDIX 15***

Note 1. This new report was commissioned from the consultant company Promar by a partnership comprised of West Somerset District Council, Exmoor National Park Authority, Quantock Hills Area of Outstanding Natural Beauty, Government Office for the South West, North Devon District Council, Devon County Council, Somerset County Council, Mid Devon District Council and the Countryside Agency.

Note 2. In the event, because the *Hunting Act 2004* in no way effected the infrastructure of hunting, not a single hound had to be re-homed or destroyed. Similarly it is unlikely that more than a dozen hunt employees were made redundant.

Note 3. Tony Banks was one of Parliament's staunchest supporters of animal rights, often speaking out against blood sports and vivisection. As vice-president of the LACS he was one of the prime movers behind pushing for a total blood sport ban via the *Hunting Act 2004,* hence the name "Banks Bill".

An example of his pro-animal rights verses human nature views surfaced on 21 May 2004, when he proposed an EDM in response to newspaper reports revealing that MI5 had proposed using pigeons as flying bombs during World War Two. The motion condemned the proposal, describing humans as "*obscene, perverted, cruel, uncivilised and lethal*", and proposed that the House of Commons "*look forward to the day when the inevitable asteroid slams into the Earth and wipes them out thus giving nature the opportunity to start again*".

He was Labour MP for West Ham until standing down prior to the 2005 election, when he became Baron Stratford. He would never take his seat in the Lords as on 5th January 2006 he suffered a serious cerebral haemorrhage while on holiday in Florida, and died in hospital on 8th January, aged sixty-two.

Note 4. The Independent Police Complaints Commission (IPCC) received 425 complaints from demonstrators at this rally – 54 from people claiming to have been injured by heavy-handed police officers. Over two years later (November 2006) the IPCC released a 51-page report published after its investigation into the handling of the riot by the 1,300 police officers involved. There were to be no disciplinary procedures against any office, although the report did reveal serious errors in police procedure. Though a number of protestors received head injuries, no batons were collected for forensic testing. The report also criticised police officers who failed to wear numbered epaulettes on the day.

Chapter Fourteen

"What part of 'no' does the hunting fraternity not understand?"

AT FIRST LIGHT THE FOLLOWING morning, 19th November 2004, CA Chairman John Jackson, in company with two other hunt supporters, marched to the High Count to lodge an appeal for a judicial review of the Parliament Act. His contention being, that as the 1949 Parliament Act had been amended by the use of the 1911 Parliament Act, making its use to force through the Hunting Act unsound. Though he admitted that this challenge had "little to do with hunting" and much to do with "the constitutional arrangements in our country and respect for the law". Obviously desperate for some straw to grasp after what appeared to be the total defeat of the blood sport lobby, this legal case offered a lifeline to the thousands who saw their very reason for existence coming to an end. Certainly the press and television played up the fact that the story was far from over, while giving people like the CA's Simon Hart, appearing on *Question Time* the night of the ban, the chance to remain defiant in the face of defeat. The pending court case also allowed Tony Blair to distance himself from any backlash by acknowledging that the legitimacy of the ban was likely to be resolved in the courts, while government lawyers continued trying to find some way of delaying the ban until after the pending 2005 General Election.

In the immediate aftermath of the ban the more extreme elements of the hunting fraternity promised considerably more than a legal appeal. A breakaway group from the CA, calling itself the Real

Countryside Alliance, led by the former CA chief executive Edward Duke, advocated "aggressive disruption" tactics. Claiming to have studied the actions of animal rights groups for their ideas, the Real CA threatened to contaminate reservoirs with dye, cause damage to major roads and motorways, along with attacks against phone lines and speed cameras. In one interview Duke, trying hard to sound like a hardened ALF activist, warned: "When it comes to it, we will want to set fire to motorways and DEFRA offices. We can do naughty things." Another radical group, the Countryside Action Network, led by former CA press officer Janet George, organised go-slow protests using tractors and farm vehicles to cause chaos on trunk roads and motorways. While a few national monuments such as the White Horse of Kilburn, near Newcastle upon Tyne, were vandalised and an electricity pylon in the Lake District collapsed after being sawn through, the most these "direct action" groups were able to manage was the mass daubing of roads with the slogan "HUNT ON".

The more "responsible" militant campaigners claimed that 50,000 people were ready to disobey the ban with a campaign of civil disobedience. This would be the fulfilment of their Declaration Day promise to carry on hunting after the ban was in force. However, the government appeared more worried by warnings that landowners would also protest by "being obstructive" in withdrawing their traditional "good will" from government agencies such as local authorities and utility service providers. Landowners close to military training areas such as Salisbury Plain threatened to withdraw permission for troops to cross their land on exercise. The CA also announced that other areas where goodwill would be withdrawn included access for flood defence and drainage sites, road improvement schemes, railway maintenance, gas and water pipelines and electricity service provision, plus public access and right of way schemes.

One example of just how spiteful these "acts of revenge" could become was manifest in an action taken by the DSSH in late December. Every February and March one of Exmoor's most beautiful attractions, an area known as Snowdrop Valley, is visited by thousands of people from around the country who come to see the snowdrops in bloom. The Badgworthy Land Company, whose directors include DSSH

Chairman Tom Yandle, joint master Maurice Scott and Somerset CA boss Guy Thomas Everard, decided to close the footpaths to the picturesque beauty spot as a protest against the ban. The damage to tourism and businesses on the moor was regrettable, but as Mr Yandle explained, "The directors feel that they have no choice but to adopt this course of action in order that the effect of this legislation is not allowed to be forgotten and that the consequences are well understood." The ban would be lifted in early January 2005 when it became evident that the only "consequences" to be felt would be from the lost revenue of local businesses, many of whom were pro-hunt.

Though in the main the threatened "rural rebellion" failed to materialise. Farmers throughout the country, shocked to discover that under the *Hunting Act* they could possibly face prosecution for knowingly allowing hunting on their land, began to announce in droves that after 18th February 2005 the hunts would not be welcome. Many die-hard hunters, thinking that a criminal record gained from defying the ban, could result in the revoking of a shotgun licence or failure to obtain a visa to the USA, where many claimed they would go to carry on hunting, suddenly discovered that becoming a "freedom fighter" was not without its drawbacks.

The CA announced on 23rd November that "it would refuse to condone hunts that openly defy the hunting ban", suggesting instead a conversion to drag hunting, or a continuation of hunting in some form which exploited loopholes in the law to "make a mockery of the ban". This dramatic U-turn brought on talk of a split within the CA, prompting the right-wing columnist Anthony Howard to speculate that the pro-hunt movement would go the same way as CND in the early 1960s, and divide between those demanding more militant action and those who wanted to remain within the law. While Professor Roger Scruton, the West Country philosopher who was one of the main architects of the 1st November 2003 Declaration Day pledge to "disobey" any legislation that banned hunting, also had a change of heart. Now it was simply a case that "hunts have to reorganise themselves to obey the law... . Realism has to enter into this, and if hunts can reorganise...to continue without finding their hounds, vehicles and equipment confiscated, then they should."

As for the erstwhile "freedom rider" Noel Edmonds, there was not a peep.

Some sections of the press, desperate to drag the last headline from an apparently lost cause, continued to play up the fight-back. The political commentator Chris Moncrieff was sure that the CA would "relentlessly take this to the bitter end". For the "scale of the street demonstrations in London and elsewhere over the past months and in particular the daring and spectacular invasion of the House of Commons shows clearly that the pro-hunt lobby is in no mood to capitulate whatever the law of the land now is."

The fact that civil war did not explode across the land as a result of the hunting ban came as no surprise to anyone in the anti movement, especially the veteran hunt saboteurs who perhaps knew the character of their enemy better than anyone. The failure of the blood sports lobby to stand and fight reminded some of a final scene from the classic movie *The Wizard Of Oz*, for when Dorothy's little dog pulled aside the curtain to confront the Wizard there was nothing on show but an old man frantically huffing and puffing to maintain the illusion of fear.

The government meanwhile remained mesmerised by the perceived threat of violence and disruption to the pending general election. Apart from the general policy of distancing themselves from the ban, in fact acting as if it was nothing to do with them, every attempt was made to placate the hunters. Within a week of the ban Leader of the Commons Peter Hain was announcing that it was still possible to arrange an eighteen-month delay on implementation, but peers would have to make the first move. It was a simple matter claimed Hain, for, "If the House of Lords changed its mind and came to us and said on reflection we think it's not right to proceed so quickly...then we would have to consider it."

It soon became apparent when the Lords failed to follow up on this olive branch that Downing Street had other straws to clutch in its attempts to delay the ban until after a general election. In a blaze of publicity on 23rd December, Lord Goldsmith, the Attorney-General, announced that he would not oppose any application from the CA for an injunction postponing implementation of the ban before the courts had ruled on its legality. Such an injunction would delay the ban for months, if not years, drawing the political sting from the issue until well after any election. The *Western Daily Press* journalist Chris Rundle was especially outspoken about this piece of soft peddling. "The government's decision not to oppose a legal challenge to the *Hunting Act* must rank as one of its more crass, as well as spineless, decisions," he wrote in late December. In his opinion the hunting set would see "Tony Blair's nervousness as further evidence of him being steamrollered into a piece of bad legislation by backbench class warriors" whereas "a Prime Minister with a little more backbone would have chosen to tough it out and demonstrate from February 18th next year that those who derive pleasure from seeing animals torn to pieces by dogs can't treat legislation like an hors d'oeuvres trolley and agree to abide by only the bits they like."

The threats of civil disobedience continued right up to the Boxing Day meets, with many newspapers running banner headlines to the effect that "EVERY HUNT TO REVOLT ON BAN. Law impossible to enforce – says barrister." Come the day, apart from a number of brutal attacks against isolated groups of hunt saboteurs, it passed without incident. The most radical offering on show was the national distribution of the CA publication *Hunting Handbook 2005* that explained "what you need to know about hunting within the law" and "how hunts and hunting activity *can* continue until the ban is repealed". In the forefront of West Country resistance was the DSSH which drew crowds of upwards of a 1,000 supporters to the village of Exford to hear joint master Diana Scott vow "no way will this be the last Boxing Day meet" for "we shall continue to hunt for the sake of the red deer of Exmoor". Tom Yandle had previously sent a letter to all hunt members outlining the packs' intention once the ban came into force. The letter explained "because of our commitment to the management of deer, we are looking at carrying out some forms of exempt hunting using two hounds only to flush deer for purposes of research and observation, or merely to disperse deer where they may be doing damage."

The LACS, determined not to lose the 18th February deadline for the ban, sought permission to oppose both the legal challenge to the Parliament Act and any possible injunction requested by the CA should they lose the appeal. On 17th January 2005 the High Court granted leave to make both written and oral submissions, whereupon the League immediately retained the London law firm Collyer-Bristow to act on their behalf, who in turn appointed David Pannick QC and Gordon Nardell to take the case.

On 25th January 2005 the first challenge to the validity of the *Hunting Act 2004* began in the Royal Courts of Justice before Lord Justice Maurice Kay and Mr Justice Collins. In what was described as the "most important constitutional case" for a century the two judges would listen to Sydney Kentridge QC, appearing on behalf of the CA, explain the case for the Alliance. The issue had nothing to do with the ethics of blood sports, but was all about the power of the elected House of Commons.

The CA defined Parliament as the House of Commons, the House of Lords and the Sovereign acting together. It was their contention that only if the two houses, Lords and Commons, agree on a Bill and the Sovereign assents should it become an Act of Parliament. Under this definition they maintained that only the *1911 Act* was valid because the then King and both Houses of Parliament agreed to it. Their argument was that the *1949 Act,* which amended the *1911 Act,* was not valid because it was never agreed by the three components of Commons, Lords and Sovereign, but instead passed by virtue of the use of the *1911 Parliament Act* without the Lords' consent. In addition they further argued that the *1949 Act* was not legitimately passed because the *1911 Act* does not make it explicitly clear that it could be used to make further changes to the power of the House of Lords.

Hence the "who rules?" question. If the CA was right the House of Lords, the unelected House, still had the power to delay an Act it did not like for three years, as agreed in the *1911 Act,* not two years as per the *1949 Act.* If the courts were to decide that the *1949 Act* had not been passed correctly, the primacy of the elected House to pass Acts of Parliament would be called into question. No government elected by the people could possibly accept that the unelected House of Lords should have a choke hold on all legislation, for what, in practice, would amount to two-thirds of a five-year Parliament. The government was also faced with the possibility that if the *1949 Act* were found to be invalid they would not only have to reintroduce the *Hunting Act* yet again and use the *1911 Act* terms to force it through, but also the *War Crimes Act*, European Election law and the equalised age of consent law.

Following a spirited defence of the government's use of the Parliament Act (but not opposition to any proposed injunction) by the Attorney General, Lord Goldsmith, the two high court judges ruled on 28th January "that both the *1911* and *1949 Parliament Acts* are valid. The procedures of the *Parliament Act* were, as was certified by the speaker, used correctly. It follows therefore that the *Hunting Act 2004* is valid and was properly passed." Leave to appeal was granted the CA, with 8th February fixed for the next hearing before three of the most senior judges in the land, Lord Woolf QC, The Lord Chief Justice, Lord Phillips, the Master of the Rolls and Lord Justice May.

The Appeal Court hearing would again cover the same ground with arguments from both Sir Sydney Kentridge and Attorney General Lord Goldsmith. The decision of the country's three most senior appeal court judges, when it came on 16th February, was that "the *Parliament Act 1949*, passed without Lords' consent under the *Parliament Act 1911*, could in turn be used to pass the *Hunting Act 2004.*" Lord Woolf added: "The restrictions on the exercise of the powers of the House of Lords that the 1949 Act purported to make have been so widely recognised and relied upon that they are today a political fact." The judges further refused the CA's permission to appeal to the House of Lords, but Sir Sydney Kentridge informed the court that an urgent application for permission would be made direct to the Law Lords.

As it was now no longer possible to apply for an injunction postponing the 18th February ban, as the courts had ruled the *Hunting Act* legal under the 1949 Act, attempts were made to obtain "an injunction staying any prosecutions for defying the ban" until after a decision from the Law Lords. Lord Goldsmith did not object to such an injunction, for with emotions running high in the countryside and the ban less than forty-eight hours away, a stay would have been convenient for the government by postponing the threatened furore until after the general election. But the judges were having none of it and refused the application, while rebuking the Attorney General for trying to "hide behind the courts" on the question of future prosecutions.

When Thursday 17th February 2005 dawned, the last day of legal hunting in Britain, the only comfort for the hunters was the belief that enforcement of the new law would prove difficult, if not impossible, due to the faint-hearted attitude of the government. Offering guidance to police forces across the country Nigel Yeo, the assistant chief constable of Sussex, on behalf of the Association of Chief Police Officers (ACPO), cautioned for a conciliatory approach. After pointing out that offences under the Act carried a fine of up to £5,000 he advised: "It may be felt reasonable and proportionate to warn hunts which we believe to be acting unlawfully, rather than to seek to expend the effort in securing a prosecution." Even if the seriousness of the offence should warrant an arrest and fine, Mr Yeo assured the hunting set that "they (fines levied under the act) are not recordable or notifiable under the national crime recording standards and I am also advised by Home Office lawyers that persons convicted of offences under the *Hunting Act* will not secure a criminal record."

So buoyed in the knowledge that banned by Act of Parliament they may have been, but assured by the Home Office that above the law they remained, the 300 plus hunts throughout England and Wales rode out for one last legal hunt. ***Note 1.*** Their friends in the press did them proud with hundreds of column inches telling that "our birthright has been taken" and of how "tomorrow the fightback begins" accompanied by the standard pictures of sobbing hunt masters, crying children and baleful-looking hounds awaiting the executioner's gun now that their services were no longer required. The *Independent* gave over its front page to a stark black and white photograph of a fox being torn apart by hounds under the by-line "the thrill of the chase is over", then ruined the effect by running an editorial telling its readers a "ban on hunting was not something that this newspaper sought. We regarded hunting as an unedifying practice, but we did not see it as something that required the attention of the law, still less the hours and days of parliamentary and judicial time that was squandered on it." The *Daily Mirror* was the only paper to reflect what many antis actually thought with the headline "NOW JUST...FOX OFF!", while the veteran hunt saboteur Dave Wetton reflected the opinion of the more cultured blood sport opponent. Speaking to the *Daily Telegraph* he mused:

> "Unbelievable isn't it? All of a sudden, it's like we are the sheriff's posse and it's the other side who have become the outlaws. Basically, we've won. After 40 years, that takes some getting used to. From now on, we have to accept that we'll have more of a monitoring role – that we'll be hunt crime watchers. There should be no need for sabbing if the hunters behave themselves."

The stag hunters of Exmoor made the most of their last day within the law, or as their correspondent Pricket put it "our saddest day in a century and a half". After meeting at Hawkridge they chased and killed a stag by 12:45 p.m., after which another was found. This one was "accounted for...in the Barle at 5:15 p.m." after what was described as "one of the great hunts of recent times, including a point of nine miles, and astonishingly appropriate given the circumstances".

There was more of the same on Saturday 19th February, when massed hunters gathered in the first post-ban meets, in what was billed as a Day of Defiance, which would act as the precursor of the "defiant and determined response of hundreds of thousands of people" to start "the process of dismantling the Hunting Act". In reality it was a last chance for the good and the great of the blood sport world to parade upon the public stage before the media lost interest in what was increasingly looking like a "lost cause". A few hundred supporters would gather in the picturesque Quantock village of Bagborough to hear QSH joint master Enid Baker implore "not to forget us – especially financially" before riding off to "exercise" hounds. ***Note 2.*** At Simonsbath the DSSH would meet before "a massive crowd, including nearly 300 mounted and around 1,500 on foot, who came to demonstrate their support and determination to continue and win the fight to preserve our way of life and the wild red deer of Exmoor". After "moving speeches" from stag hunting's elite, including Baroness Mallalieu, the huntsman "took a couple of hounds to the forest to flush deer to guns and a stag in poor condition was accounted for".

A similar spectacle was repeated across the country as every aggrieved blood sportsman, actively encouraged by the media, engaged in an orgy of killing to prove that "Tony Blair's ban" would "not save the life of a single animal". The following day the Sunday papers were plastered with photographs of red-coated gentlemen holding aloft the bloodied bodies of dead foxes "shot by the hunters entirely within the law", while the more intellectually challenged articulated their feelings bedecked with badges bearing the logo "Bollocks To Blair".

By early March a new challenge was underway when the CA was granted leave to take its case against the ban to the European Court of Human Rights. Ten members of the Alliance, including DSSH huntsman Donald Summersgill, planned to argue that the ban contravened the European Convention on Human Rights in that it breached "their human rights to enjoy, work and maintain their own land as they see fit, and also that the government has taken away their livelihoods with no compensation". Even though it was estimated that such a case could take as long as five years to reach a judgement, it would not necessarily mean the ban would be overturned, although it could be seriously compromised. It was evident from this attempt that when the hunting brigade claimed that they were "in the fight to overturn the ban for the long haul" it was no idle threat.

Though the more short-term realities of a pending general election saw the creation of the pro-hunt action group Vote-OK. The operation, run from the loft of a converted barn in the Cotswolds, was set up to direct hunt supporters who wanted to overturn the ban at the ballot box. Vote-OK's intention was to co-ordinate efforts nationwide to get vulnerable Tories re-elected, while trying to depose anti-hunt Labour and Liberal-Democrat MPs. This strategy was seen as the last best hope based on the relative attitudes of the three main parties.

The Labour Party had no wish to mention the hunting issue at all, for this key issue of up until a few weeks ago had been well and truly swept under the political carpet. The Liberal-Democrat rural affairs spokesman Andrew George offered no comfort when he said:

"We do not believe that a ban on hunting, or its repeal, are priorities. I proposed an amendment to the *Hunting Act* to compensate those affected." Whereas the Tories, under the leadership of Michael Howard, promised a Manifesto commitment that read: "We value the diverse nature of our nation and believe in defending traditional liberties. A Conservative government will therefore introduce a Bill, and offer Parliament a free vote, to overturn the government's ban on hunting with dogs."

In the six weeks before the election Vote-OK fielded 20,000 "countryside campaigners" who poured into marginal seats all over Britain to deliver 3.4 million leaflets, address 2.1 million envelopes, and put up 55,000 posters during their 170,000 hours of voluntary service on behalf of blood sports. The only requirement made of them by Conservative Central Office was that during campaigning they did not mention the "H" word, for in some quarters it was considered not the most appropriate subject to help win seats on the doorstep. It all proved fruitless, for when the last vote had been cast on 5th May 2005 Tony Blair remained in power, albeit with a much reduced majority, but large enough to ensure the survival of a Labour government. On the face of it the hunting ban appeared secure for the next five years.

Undaunted by two failed challenges to the validity of the Parliament Act and one lost general election the CA pressed ahead in its attempts to sabotage the *Hunting Act 2004*. On Tuesday, 6th July, the ten hunters who fronted the move to invoke the European Convention on Human Rights appeared before Lord Justice May and Mr Justice Moses at the Royal Courts of Justice in London. This was the first act in the projected two-year, £3 million campaign, which they hoped would ultimately lead to their vindication in the European Court of Human Rights.

The Alliance's barrister, Richard Gordon QC, opened the proceedings by telling the two senior judges that the legislation was "in many ways a sectarian measure". Richard Lissack QC, another Alliance barrister, expanded the argument by emphasising "the deep sense of loss and dismay" felt throughout the countryside. "All feel themselves victims of the ban," he continued, "which by the most bitter irony delivers restriction of human activity without gain in terms of animal welfare. Jobs gone, homes gone, livelihoods destroyed, communities left bereaved – all this will flow if the injustices of the *Hunting Act* are not addressed."

The following day, 8th July, Philip Case, on behalf of the Attorney General, dismissed the human rights challenge as "wholly unprecedented". He argued that although hunt enthusiasts said it was their only pastime, it was only "one of many" pursuits they could enjoy. As far as he was concerned, it could "hardly be said to be integral to their identity or their ability to function socially or as a person".

Mr Case then went on to explain to the court that hunting, despite its historical and cultural links, was no more than a leisure activity and more about pleasure and relaxation than anything else. He dismissed one of the principal complaints of the hunters, that their businesses would suffer and hounds and horses would have to be destroyed. He continued by saying that it was up to the individual hunts whether to kill their animals – the government ban was forcing them to do no such thing. In conclusion, he pointed out that, if businesses were to close, only the most "ambitious" of legal arguments could hope to show that was a violation of the *Human Rights Act*. For "the loss of employment or livelihood is not in itself an interference with the right to respect for private life." The court was then adjourned while Judges May and Moses retired to review the evidence, with their decision expected towards the end of July.

A few days later, 13th July 2005, the CA was back in court again for round three of their challenge to the validity of the *Parliament Act* to pass the *Hunting Act*. This time the battleground was the highest court in the land – the House of Lords, where the importance of the case was indicated by the decision to convene a panel of nine Law Lords rather than the usual five. No one missed the irony of the situation, whereby under the present constitutional arrangements the Law Lords are also entitled to sit in the House of Lords – where their powers can be limited by the Parliament Act.

Sir Sydney Kentridge QC, again representing the CA, opened the proceedings by telling the Law Lords that during the Court of Appeal hearings he had been accused of overstating his case. After requesting

"May I overstate my case again?" he launched into a potted history of the controversy surrounding the *1949 Act*, the gist of which explained that while there had been few instances where the validity of the *Act* had been challenged in the courts "there had been a debate in this country which has defeated constitutional experts for half a century".

He continued by asking the Law Lords to decide whether the Commons had the right to ignore the House of Lords' objections that had been holding up the passage of the Hunting Bill. The same old arguments from the CA (who had already lost in the High Court and Court of Appeal) were trotted out, namely that the *Parliament Act 1949*, which had been used only three times to assert the supremacy of the Commons over the Lords, was unlawful because, unlike the previous *Parliament Act 1911*, only MPs (and not peers) had voted for it. So therefore "the *1949 Act* was beyond the powers of the House of Commons and the *Hunting Act* falls with it" concluded Sir Sydney.

The following day, 14th July, the Attorney General, Lord Goldsmith QC, again representing the government in court, brushed aside the Alliance claim that the use of the *Parliament Act* was invalid. Instead Goldsmith called on the Law Lords to make a ruling over whether the same *1949 Act* could also be used to abolish the very House of Lords where they were now sitting. This was the one concession concerning the limitations of the *Parliament Act 1949* made by the Court of Appeal when it had thrown out the hunters' last attempt to overturn the *Hunting Act* on 16th February 2005. For the appeal judges had ruled that although the *1949 Act* limiting the powers of the House of Lords to hold up Bills was valid, it could not be used to bring about major constitutional changes. Now the hunt supporters listening to the case via a video link from the elegant oak-panelled committee room next door found that their single-issue case had gone to ground as the government went off in pursuit of a much larger quarry – the constitutional challenge to the powers of the House of Commons.

Lord Goldsmith then began his defence by explaining that the reason why there were nine of the existing twelve Law Lords hearing the case – instead of the usual five – was not because of the importance of the challenge to the *Hunting Act*, but because of the "constitutional issues which lie behind this appeal". For "if this appeal were to succeed, it would revive, at least to some extent, the right of the unelected House of Lords to veto legislation, which it has not been able to do for 100 years". He then expressed the government's concern that the Court of Appeal had attempted to place limitations on the use of the *Parliament Act,* concluding that "the House of Commons can insist on *any* public Bill passing". The court then adjourned with a ruling by the Law Lords expected in the autumn.

The dust had hardly settled on this court case when the CA were told their arguments, that the hunting ban breached the European Convention on Human Rights, had been dismissed by the High Court. The two judges who heard the case, Lord Justice May and Mr Justice Moses, dismissed all the challenges comprehensively. Lord Justice May said lawyers for the government had "sufficiently established" the *Hunting Act* had a "legitimate and rational" aim and it was necessary as "part of a democratic society". He added that the Commons would be perfectly entitled to go further than the *Hunting Act* in that there was "sufficient material available for the Houses of Parliament to conclude hunting with dogs was cruel", therefore the legislation was both "proportional" and "justified".

Even so, the judges granted the Alliance leave to appeal, giving its chairman John Jackson the chance to remain upbeat in the press, claiming "the judges have accepted that there is interference with some of the claimant's rights..." ***Note 3.*** For the LACS the outcome of this hearing appeared more black and white. John Cooper, League chairman, was sure that blood sports "in Britain are now dead" and "it is time that its supporters accepted that". As a parting shot he posed the question: "What part of 'no' does the hunting fraternity not understand?"

Actually, to the saboteurs and hunt monitors on the ground, it was becoming abundantly clear that many of the hunters they observed understood very little of the word "no". For by now every perceived loophole in the *Hunting Act* was being pushed to its limit in the sure knowledge that police forces across the country had little, if any, intention of enforcing the law. For instance they began exploiting an exemption in the Act which was included to allow falconers the use of dogs while flushing mammals to their birds when hunting or training. But whereas the *Hunting Act* specifies only two dogs can be used to flush deer or foxes to waiting guns, the law does not put a limit on the number of dogs when they are flushing to a waiting bird of prey.

This anomaly was seized upon by a number of hunts, who learned, following legal advice, that the Act was so vaguely worded that packs of hounds will not even have to employ a bird of prey large enough to capture a fox or deer. For, in theory, hounds could be flushing a piece of ground for any type of wild animal and it would be up to the handler (and the bird itself) whether or not they decided to hunt it. Following discussions with the Association of Chief Police Officers (ACPO) one senior police officer was reported to have described the bird of prey loophole as hunting's "Get Out of Jail Free Card".

On Exmoor and the Quantocks the reluctance of the police to get involved enabled the stag hunts to remain openly "in your face" with their hunting activities. Hunt monitors are in no doubt that the stag hunts have been pushing the boundaries of the law, and sometimes filmed openly flouting them. For whereas any fox hunt "testing" the ban is hard to spot, chasing a large stag across open country is difficult to disguise as something else. Even so, when LACS video footage of such incidents was handed to Avon and Somerset Police showing four hounds from the QSH (not the legal two) in close pursuit of a young stag the police declined to act, with the "official" reason given that "the brief footage did not show enough evidence". Whereas anti-hunt activists thought the real reason was more in line with a comment made by a senior police officer who, when asked during a joint police/hunt monitor liaison meeting, where he thought the *Hunting Act* stood in relation to police priorities replied "roughly on a par with the Litter Law".

Perhaps the most contentious issue with regard to deer hunting has been the creation by the stag hunts of what is known as "relay hunting". Under the *Hunting Act* two hounds are supposed to be used to flush a deer from the woods at which point it must be shot, though in reality a whole collection of "two hounds" are used in succession to harry the animal across country until, exhausted, it stands at bay. Of course, according to DSSH Master Diana Scott, the term "relay hunting was invented by hunt opponents and did not reflect the hunt's practice". Her explanation was that

> "there are times when it would be irresponsible to try to shoot a deer as soon as it was flushed from cover. It may well be moving at speed and it may not be near the guns. We only shoot if it is safe and secure – the welfare of the deer has to come first. We will only go out within the law. But there is nothing in the law to stop you taking out three or four pairs of dogs to flush out different deer. We are just desperately trying to hold together the cohesive force that manages the deer on Exmoor."

A somewhat more honest explanation of the justification for "relay hunting" was contained in an article by Rebecca Austin which appeared in the *Horse & Hound* that informed us: "After 18 February, the Devon and Somerset Staghounds still continues its service to the Red Deer." This is achieved by the use of hounds "as is stipulated in the Hunting Bill, flushing out deer using just two hounds and, as soon as is possible (and safe), shooting the deer. As before, these are deer that need culling: they are inferior in terms of genetic merit."

Though further down the article it becomes apparent that the DSSH are not using just two hounds, but a succession of "two hounds" throughout the hunt. Apparently

> "two hounds do not make the music of a pack. For centuries, these hounds have been bred to hunt as a pack and hence each individual has earned its place out hunting. Some are deep-scenting and help the rest drive on when it gets difficult; others give tongue and so encourage the rest; one might cast particularly well and hit off the scent on a wider cast than usual, and another would be the one to keep a stag at bay, just as a particular foxhound would be the one to come through the pack to kill the fox.
>
> "All that has gone, so a couple of hounds now seem to lose their drive hunting alone a lot quicker than they would under historical

> circumstances. This is where incredible teamwork comes into play and it was not unusual to find a Land Rover waiting at a suitable spot to swap hounds for another couple. Mobile phones are a tremendous aid now to ensure fresh hounds are at the right spot in time and to give an indication of where a stag had crossed the road, in case it is not possible to hear hounds."

So the harrying of a deer from wood to wood, using a succession of "pairs of hounds", is not hunting but "flushing to guns". This was not the interpretation of the law as understood by DEFRA Minister Ben Bradshaw when replying to a request from the LACS to close the loophole that allowed for such practices. According to him the so-called "relay hunting" was already illegal under the law. "To deliberately set dogs on an animal without the intention to shoot is illegal. To use pairs of dogs in relay is illegal. You can use two dogs to flush from cover, but only to waiting guns – not to chase."

Unfortunately for common sense Mr Bradshaw then suggested the classic ministerial Catch 22 solution to deal with the issue. He explained that "ultimately it is for the courts to decide, but the key thing is the intention to shoot as quickly as possible". Which would be fine if the police had not made it virtually impossible for evidence of "relay hunting" to be acceptable, much less passed on to the Criminal Prosecution Service (CPS) for the courts ultimately to make the decision.

The CPS itself, shielded by the police from having to undertake prosecutions that might offend the hunting classes, now added a few refinements of their own. A few days prior to the official November opening meets of fox hunting they "indicated that only masters and whippers-in could *technically* be accused of hunting if they were found to be flouting the law. Followers are classed as observers and would not *technically* be hunting under the Act as it stands." The advice from Robert Rhodes QC was that: "It is essential that those who wish to see the Act repealed should only circumvent the Act by staying firmly on the right side of the law."

The verdict of the Law Lords on the CA challenge to the validity of the *Hunting Act 2004*, and the *Parliament Act 1949* under which it was passed against opposition from the House of Lords, when it was delivered on 13th October, came as a surprise to no one. The highest court in the land, the House of Lords, unanimously decided that the *Hunting Act* was legally valid, although this issue had proved something of a technicality. Hunting itself was hardly mentioned in the eighty-one pages of opinions by the nine Law Lords, with the report's main concern centring around arguments about the powers of Parliament. In essence the Law Lords ruled that the Commons could use the *Parliament Act* as it saw fit, while the Appeal Court's attempt to exclude its use for major constitutional changes had "no support in the language of the Act, in principle or in the historical record". As to any future attempt at abolishing the House of Lords by use of the *Parliament Act* the Law Lords gave the warning that they or a new supreme court "may have to consider whether there is a constitutional fundamental which even a sovereign Parliament acting at the behest of a complaisant House of Commons cannot abolish".

Simon Hart, chief executive of the CA, thought the ruling set a "dangerous, anti-democratic precedent" and vowed to go on fighting "as vigorously as ever" to get the hunting ban repealed. Though by now the twelve-month legal campaign by the CA to overturn the ban had become something of an academic exercise for many rank-and-file hunters. For by now it was becoming evident that many had found a much better way to deal with the Act – they would simply ignore it. Bolstered by the realisation that the police intended to take no action, many hunts just carried on "business as usual". In many instances the opponents of hunting who tried to monitor and film their illegal activities were attacked with ever-increasing severity, with one of the worst cases against IFAW monitor Kevin Hill on 27th October, who was forced to seek hospital treatment after a vicious beating from a supporter of the DSSH. Fortunately the incident was witnessed by a *Daily Mirror* investigation team in attendance at the hunt that day, although it would be another twelve months before the assailant was brought to justice. ***Note 4***

In what would appear the supreme irony, by the time of the "official" start of the 2005/06 hunting season in November, the blame for all this violence had been laid squarely on the shoulders of the opponents of hunting.

Nothing encapsulated the arrogant self-righteousness of the blood sport brigade more than a sanctimonious round-robin sent by Alison Hawes, South West regional director of the CA, to various local newspapers in November 2005. After the usual "hunts have pledged to go out within the law to retain the infrastructure of hunts and hunting", along with "continuing to provide an invaluable pest control service to the farming community" she really excelled. Explaining that "Animal rights extremists have stated their intention of continuing to sabotage hunts," she continued, "They will continue to show no respect for the law, themselves trespassing and harassing those who are going about their legal business, and aggressively filming law abiding families and their children."

The letter continued: "In their desperation to secure a prosecution under the Hunting Act, anti-hunt vigilantes – or hunt monitors as they call themselves – are wasting valuable and already over-stretched police resources by making unfounded allegations against hunts." The solution being of course that: "Anti-hunting organisations and hunt saboteurs should now stop their malicious, prejudiced attacks on the rural community, understand that hunts intend to act within the law until this ridiculous and badly drafted legislation is overturned, and stop causing unnecessary trouble in rural areas." No doubt a few hours of harmless fun was employed in a fruitless endeavour to define "aggressively filming".

No matter how "aggressively the filming" none of it was good enough for the Avon and Somerset Police. The LACS lodged over a dozen complaints during the six months following the ban, the majority concerning the activities of the QSH, but all were dismissed. Even photographs showing four hounds (not the legal two) in pursuit of a young stag, taken within weeks of the ban and witnessed by *Western Daily Press* reporters, were rejected as they did not "identify individuals responsible for the activities shown on the film".

Decisions taken at the League's summer AGM, giving the executive committee power to sell Exmoor deer sanctuaries to raise money for the purchase of shooting land, caused a flurry of speculation in the press. The fact that the LACS was moving into a major campaign against game bird shooting was not the issue, rather how this new venture would be funded. *The Countryman's Weekly* ran major articles maintaining that the issue of selling deer sanctuaries had caused serious divisions within the League, leading to the resignation of West Country spokesman Ivor Annetts, who believed "the League should have an ongoing conservation role". The heat was somewhat taken from the debate when Mike Hobday confirmed "that the League was reviewing the value and intrinsic purpose of its sanctuaries, introduced by the League to provide a safe haven for deer in hunting areas, since the hunting ban introduced in February would render them unnecessary".

He emphasised that no land would be sold until it was clear that the hunting ban would not be reversed, adding:

> "With hunting banned there will come a point at which hunts have packed up or converted to drag hunting. At that point there will no longer be a campaigning purpose to some of the sanctuary land around Exmoor. There is no question of land being sold if there is a danger that hunting might start again. The question is whether we should be involved in conservation or be a campaigning organisation."

The sale of League land following the ban appeared somewhat of an academic issue when the official start of the fox-hunting season in November proved that little, if anything, had changed. The *Independent* editorial for 5th November spoke for many on both sides of the argument when, under the headline "Blair's folly", it pointed out that with all the various exemptions in the Act covering flushing to guns, trail hunting, exercising hounds and the use of birds of prey "it is virtually impossible to distinguish between such activities and illegal hunts". ***Note 5.*** It was certainly true that the number of deer killed on Exmoor had increased since the ban for, according to LACS sanctuary manager Paul Tillsley, whereas the hunt had been satisfied when they killed one deer at a time "now they kill one in the morning and then another in the afternoon".

The first post-ban Boxing Day meet confirmed the unchanged status of hunting with record turnouts across the country. The failure of the Hunting Act to make an appreciable difference was reinforced by a plea for a change in the law from Nigel Yeo, Assistant Chief Constable of Sussex and the public order spokesman for the Association of Chief Police Officers (ACPO), who advised forces on how to police the hunting ban, to Home Secretary Charles Clarke. He requested that police officers be given a right of access on private land to check hunting activity and make arrests, along with making hunting crimes a "recordable" offence, leaving those caught with a criminal record, thus allowing police forces to keep track of persistent offenders.

Even though it had been the Home Office who had requested police chiefs to give their views on enforcement of the Hunting Act, following serious criticism from animal welfare groups that police were taking "a soft approach", it soon became apparent that the government intended to do nothing to give the Act more teeth. A change in the law would require approval of both MPs and peers, and Tony Blair, along with most ministers still badly bruised by the battle to get the existing hunting ban, had no stomach to reopen such a controversial debate in Parliament. *Note 6.*

The year ended in utter confusion for all sides, not a single conviction had been secured, with a private prosecution lodged by the LACS against the Exmoor Foxhounds the only serious attempt to enforce the ban.

Note 1. There were 314 hunts operating as of Boxing Day 2006. 193 packs of foxhounds, 93 packs of harehounds, 3 of staghounds and 25 gun packs.

Note 2. There was a note of no doubt intentional irony in that this meet was held in the grounds of Bagborough House, which had been the former home of Fenwick Bisset – the man who had introduced red deer onto the Quantock Hills in the early 1860s, so as to extend the territory of the DSSH.

Note 3. On 23 June 2006 three judges from the Court of Appeal upheld the High Court ruling that the ban was lawful. Master of the Rolls Sir Anthony Clarke, Lord Justice Brooke and Lord Justice Buxton said imposing the ban was a legitimate and proportionate exercise of government powers.

Note 4. At Exeter Crown Court on 26th September 2006, Christopher Marles (an amateur whipper-in with the East Devon Hunt) was convicted of "causing actual bodily harm". One month later (23rd October 2006) Marles was given "a nine-month sentence suspended for two years". He was also ordered to pay Kevin Hill £2,500 in compensation for the attack.

This was only one of a string of vicious attacks against Kevin Hill over the years. In January 1999, two followers of the Quantock Staghounds were jailed for attacking Kevin Hill as he tried to monitor the hunt at West Quantoxhead. John Bere, of Bishops Nympton, in Devon, was sentenced to four months in prison, while Dean Richards, of Bishmill, Devon, received a six-month sentence for theft (of his camera) and assault.

Journalist Chris Rundle writing of the Marles trial was in no doubt about the levels of violence offered by stag hunt supporters:

> "If ever there was a worthy recipient of a medal for bravery it's Kevin Hill...I have lost count of the number of times he has suffered unauthorised structural alterations to the face as a result of doing nothing more than legitimately recording hunting activities... . He's not the first hunt monitor to be roughed up, of course. Former LACS warden John Hicks was always getting the human punchbag treatment and often turned up at my house still bloodied from his latest encounter."

Note 5. Though the *Independent* had not changed its support for blood sports. The 5th November 2005 editorial ended:

> "This newspaper has long taken the view that pursuing foxes on horseback and then savaging them to death with hounds is an odd, perhaps even cruel, practice. But we have never believed it should be banned. A badly drafted and illiberal law is now resented and ignored in equal measure. The Hunting Act has become a tragic symbol of the follies of the Blair era."

The Times (26th December 2005) editorial stated:

> "This Boxing Day is the first since the pastime was 'banned' in February. Yet exactly the same number of hunts will take to the field this year as were seen 12 months ago. They will have to conduct themselves in a different manner to their traditional techniques to remain within the law, but to the casual observer it will seem to be similar and the Act to be pointless. This is largely because the legislation is not only absurd but virtually designed to be so. Its anomalies make the old Sunday trading regime – which allowed *Playboy* to be bought on the day of rest but not the Bible – appear reasonable."

Note 6. Assistant Chief Constable Nigel Yeo stated:

> "There is no power of entry for police in the Act though there is a power of entry to seize items connected with hunting. There is not a power of entry to see what is going on or even to effect an arrest. Unless we have permission from the landowner we can't go on private land as of right to effect an arrest. We (ACPO) have made the observation to Government that that right is not there and it could be an impediment on occasions. I don't know if this was an oversight or if a view was taken in Government that they did not wish to give us an unfettered right of access. It is a serious step and this country takes privacy very seriously."

Nigel Yeo did feel strongly that hunting offences should be made "recordable" and therefore automatically logged on the police national computer. New offences proposed in the *Animal Welfare Bill* covering cruelty would be recordable and police believe that there should not be this discrimination for hunting law.

Chapter Fifteen

"It is now lame duck legislation..."

THE 17TH FEBRUARY 2006, FIRST anniversary of the hunting ban, was used by the blood sport set to promote the notion that the Act had totally failed to make any serious difference to the practice of hunting in England and Wales. This was a theme taken up by numerous newspapers editorials with comments such as

> "despite all the bitterness, heartache and intransigence on both sides, it seems that in reality very little has changed as a result of the ban. Twelve months on and the financial collapse in the countryside has still not materialised and the hunts are going about their business in much the same way as they always have. *In hindsight, it does make you wonder what all that fuss was really about.*"

Simon Hart, chief executive the CA, fronted the attack against the Hunting Act with a verbal outpouring that concentrated on every issue other than the one that had been the cause of abolition: cruelty. "The issue," Hart claimed,

> "isn't about hunting. It hasn't been for a long time. It is about an unprincipled and prejudiced piece of legislation that is derided, discredited and damaged beyond repair. Hunts have been using the exemptions within the law. They have highlighted the inconsistencies and flaws in the Hunting Act and are determined to keep the infrastructure of their hunts together. In the past

> year, the hunting community has proved itself resilient, adaptable and united and the Hunting Act is being comprehensively dismantled. It is now lame duck legislation, awaiting a sensible administration to put it out of its misery."

Following this statement it was revealed that the ban would be repealed immediately if the Conservative Party won power at a future general election with a simple one-line Bill annulling the Hunting Act to be put through Parliament within a matter of days on a free vote. This surprised no one, as a government Bill to repeal the Hunting Act had been a promise from David Cameron while campaigning to become Tory party leader the previous year.

Regardless of what the press thought, or Simon Hart claimed, the various anti organisations remained upbeat about the situation. Even though the CPS rejected every attempt to force a prosecution, the LACS pressed ahead with its decision to bring a private prosecution against the Exmoor Foxhounds, in the hope that a victory in the courts could create a legal president. ***Note 1.*** Even the HSA was determined to try and enforce the ban, with Press Officer Dawn Preston explaining that

> "the traditional primary tool of a hunt saboteur in the past was always the hunting horn, so we could gain control of the hounds and seek to prevent them successfully hunting the fox, hare, mink or stag. Today our main tool is the video camera, as the very last thing the hunts that are arrogantly breaking the law want is to be caught in the act. The appalling thing is that it is we who are consistently keeping the hunts under surveillance rather than the police."

While the attempts of the CA to both disregard and destroy the Hunting Act came as no surprise, the shock announcement at the end of May that the National Trust was considering a partial lifting of the stag hunting ban brought in after such internal turmoil in 1997, caused great dismay at all levels of animal welfare. So keen were the NT to have the issue resolved in time for the start of the 2006 hunting season that they instigated a working party to study the "possible use of exempt hunting as a means of dealing with sick and injured deer on National Trust land".

The proposals allowed for stag hunts to enter their land "to dispatch sick, weak or injured deer when marksmen are unable to get to them", along with "allowing hunts pursuing sick, weak or injured deer on neighbouring land to follow any deer that cross over". The anti-hunt campaigners naturally saw this move as "allowing cruelty by the back door", while the Masters of Deerhounds Association welcomed it as "common sense". While it would be the LACS sanctuaries manager Paul Tillsley that would sum up the cursory nature of the working parties mandate when he explained "the working group, which contains a member from the pro-hunting Friends of the National Trust (FONT), came to see me and watch a day's hunting. It was misty, they stayed for an hour and then went to the tea rooms in Dulverton, which says it all." ***Note 2***

The first real break-through for the antis came at Barnstaple Magistrates Court on 4th August 2006 when Tony Wright, huntsman with the Exmoor Foxhounds, became the first hunt official to be convicted under the Hunting Act 2004 following a private prosecution by the LACS. ***Note 3***

Following a five-day hearing District Judge Paul Palmer found him in breach of the Act after viewing video footage taken by League monitors Ed Shepherd and Graham Floyd, which showed Wright employing a version of "relay hunting". He was fined £500 and ordered to pay £250 costs for what the judge said was chasing a fox for "a substantial period". Even though Wright was found guilty the LACS was landed with a bill in excess of £65,000, although they considered it a price worth paying for setting a legal precedent that could be used as a benchmark by the police (the Avon and Somerset police had refused to press charges against Wright) and CPS to promote future prosecutions.

The hope of the League was that this landmark verdict could be used as the basis for future prosecutions against the deer hunts, as Wright was convicted for employing a version of "relay hunting" of a type used extensively by deer hunters on Exmoor and the Quantocks since the ban came into force. The type of "relay hunting" practised by the stag hunts, whereby a succession of "two pairs of hounds" are used, despite the insistence of Defra experts that it breached the ban, was now called into question in the courts for the first time. This ruling by District Judge Paul Palmer that the use of two dogs over "a substantial period" was "not exempt hunting" was a clear and obvious interpretation of the Hunting Act that could be used by both police and CPS to seek a prosecution.

Following the Wright conviction a number of allegations of illegal hunting submitted, but previously dismissed by the police and CPS, were revisited with surprising results. One against two members of the QSH, Richard Down and Adrian Pillivant, was again refused, but a reviewing of video evidence by IFAW monitors resulted in charges being brought against leading members of the DSSH. ***Note 4.*** On 17th October both Maurice Scott, master of the DSSH, and Peter Heard, the whipper-in, were arrested and charged by the CPS "with two counts of breaking the hunting ban".

At Taunton Magistrates Court on 19th October the case was adjourned for two weeks for the defence to prepare. For some the setting of Taunton's "unassuming magistrates court (was) an unlikely setting for a piece of British history". The slightly surreal proceedings viewed, not only by a handful of hunt supporters and friends, but "this legal landmark was also witnessed by two dozen children from the local secondary school on an educational visit, who packed the small public gallery". A few days later Donald Summersgill, huntsman with the DSSH, was also charged with two counts of illegal hunting by the CPS, and ordered to appear in the dock alongside Scott and Heard.

The reaction of Exmoor's blood sport supporters was quite extraordinary, with a mixture of righteous indignation and overt self-importance culminating in a demand that representatives of Avon and Somerset police attend a public gathering of hunt members in Exford to explain themselves concerning the arrests of Scott and company. The police were more than happy to acquiesce, with "words of conciliation and respect" in an attempt to smooth over ruffled stag hunt feathers.

More than 350 hunt followers packed into Exford Memorial Hall on Friday, 27th October, to hear CA president and Labour peer Baroness Ann Mallalieu accuse the police of being "unduly influenced" by animal rights groups in their decision to request a prosecution. For his part Superintendent Gary Davies of the Avon and Somerset police, after assuring the gathering that he understood how sensitive and emotive the hunting issue was, promised to "adopt a new sensitive approach" in future dealings with the hunt.

Although it was Baroness Mallalieu who stole the show with her conspiracy theory concerning the RSPCA, police and former Lib-Dem MP Jackie Ballard. After reiterating that the allegations against the DSSH were originally dismissed by Avon and Somerset police, but were reopened in the wake of Tony Wright's conviction, she explained that police officers had told her the case was revisited after pressure from the RSPCA and other animal rights groups. It was certainly "no coincidence that all these three prosecutions for breaching the hunt ban had been against hunts in Ms Ballard's former constituency". *Note 5*

The grapes were extremely sour as Mallalieu continued:

> "Avon and Somerset Police have been unduly influenced by pressure from animal rights campaigners. The normal independent decision-making has succumbed to political pressure. I can think of no other instance where partisan organisations are allowed an involvement in this way. It is no coincidence that all three prosecutions that have been mounted involve video evidence, all three were initially rejected by the police and all three are in Jackie Ballard's former constituency. All three are on hunts which contributed to a task force which lost her her seat."

Tom Yandle, chairman of the MDHA and chairman of the DSSH, was equally indignant that his hunting friends should have experienced something that has been an occupational hazard for the average animal rights campaigner since the 1960s. He was:

> "very upset and absolutely disgusted that a young hunt servant and a senior master of the hunt for 25 years, whose family has farmed the Brendon Hills for generations, should have had the indignity of being locked away in a cell reeking of vomit and urine for two-and-a-half hours while the police discussed their future."

As "a former High Sheriff of Somerset" he was "saddened to say that at the moment I am totally ashamed of my country". ***Note 6***

One week later, on 4th November, the spirits of the stag hunters would be considerably lifted when years of patience and plotting by the Quantock based pro-hunt group Friends of the National Trust (FONT) succeeded in partially reversing the National Trust 1997 no-hunt ban.

Meeting at the Cheltenham Racecourse for its AGM the NT again found itself about to be torn apart internally over the rights and wrongs of allowing the deer hunts access to its properties. LACS director Douglas Batchelor had already courted controversy that morning, causing the NT to request police reinforcements to keep the two sides apart, by suggesting that asking hunters to kill deer humanely was "a concept as ludicrous as asking a known paedophile to supervise a children's playground".

Following the announcement of a reintroduction of hunting five members of the NT, Susannah Steer, Sally Dean, Robert Wilkins, Cerys Roberts and Douglas Batchelor, had put forward a resolution to be debated at the AGM which read in part "that exempt hunting of deer should not be permitted on land controlled by, managed by and owned by the Trust, where it has the power to refuse to allow such activities". ***See APPENDIX 16.***

The NT's opposition to the resolution was argued by Hugh Matheson, a member of the NT Board of Trustees and supported by Peter Nixon, Director of Conservation. They recognised the pivotal role of the staghounds in achieving a swift dispatch of injured deer. An additional counter argument was that if the Trust were to follow the strict wording of the resolution, then professional stalkers would not be able to use their dogs to try and track deer anywhere on Trust property in England and Wales.

The debate was much shorter and much less contentious than the Trust had anticipated. There were well over a dozen members prepared to oppose the resolution and supporters were very thin on the ground. This made for a rather one-sided debate so the chairman limited his call for speakers to those who had specific expertise, who were not members of any staghound pack, and who lived and worked well away from Exmoor. These restrictions left only four main speakers, all of which wished to speak in opposition to the League resolution.

The first was John Young, who was a non-hunting member of the Trust's Working Party, on the potential welfare impact of the Hunting Act 2004. He denounced the LACS for using the Trust AGM as a political platform and urged members to oppose the resolution. Then came Edmund Marriage of British Wildlife Management who spoke persuasively on the value of scenting hounds and their ability to find and follow a line. Mr Marriage urged members not to support a policy that would "promote cruelty and prevent kindness".

Next came Lewis Thomas, a retired veterinary research pathologist, and Secretary of the Veterinary Association for Wildlife Management. He asserted that "injured deer cannot be found without the use of scent hounds and to deny such animals a humane and rapid death because of this resolution is quite frankly a disgrace". Then came Jim Barrington, who again repeated his well-worn mantra that he was "one of four executive directors of the League Against Cruel Sports who have changed their minds about banning hunting with dogs after it became apparent that banning hunting was very different to improving animal welfare". He concluded his argument that "it seems extremely odd that the very people who supported and campaigned for the Hunting Act now argue against it. Banning hunting in every possible way is to them more important than the relief of animal suffering and improving animal welfare."

Following these submissions the NT Chairman, Sir William Proby, could not find any speakers to support the resolution so he called on Peter Nixon and Douglas Batchelor to conclude and then called for a show of hands from the floor. It appeared that about forty to fifty hands were raised in support of the proposal, while some ten times as many were raised against. It was a convincing defeat for the LACS resolution. Although the chairman felt that as the show of hands had not been unanimous, and because stag hunting on Trust land had historically been such a contentious issue, he would now call for the results of a postal ballot from the general membership that had previously been undertaken. The vote from the membership at large would be added to the votes in the hall to give the definitive result required by the NT leadership. The total vote including the postal vote was:

> 12,768 members voted in favour of the resolution that "no exempt hunting of deer should be permitted on NT land"
> 20,182 voted against the resolution
> 1,539 abstained

FONT boss Charles Collins, who had co-ordinated opposition to the motion, was naturally pleased that years of effort had paid off and stag hunting was once again part of the NT agenda. FONT he explained "exists to assist National Trust members through the complexities of the Trust's voting arrangements". All you had to do was send your email address to FONT who would "ensure your vote is an informed one..." ***Note 7***

The year ground on with the usual press support for blood sports on the "official" November opening meets, with the dependable *Independent* stating: "This newspaper has made no secret of its distaste for the business of setting hounds on to a fox to tear the exhausted animal limb from limb." Then explaining:

> "In the past we argued that Parliament had better things to do than legislate on an issue which was totemic for all the wrong reasons, smacking as it did of the facile posturing of an outdated class war. Politicians should not have wasted their time on this. Nor, now, should the police. Animal right activists will be indignant but inaction is, here, the right course of action."

By Boxing Day the newspapers were lauding the actions of redcoats nationwide with headlines such as: "So much for your hunt ban...

we've never been so popular." The *Western Daily Press* editorial for 27th December 2006 could not have been more succinct when it wrote:

> "Thousands of huntsmen and women were out in force across the country yesterday. Indeed, it was almost impossible to tell that a law had been passed in this country banning fox hunting. *It does seem ridiculous that all that time and money was spent by Parliament discussing the issue and yet we appear to have ended up exactly where we started all those years ago."*

The verbal war of attrition continued with the publication of a CA *Hunting Handbook,* which advised hunters on how to make citizens' arrests on monitors and hunt saboteurs, and how to escort them from fields and footpaths physically. The CA's hunting director Phillipa Mayo, no doubt working very hard at keeping a straight face while explaining: "For years and years, the saboteurs have had it their own way. They've been the ones clued up on the law, and have used it to their benefit. This is very much a deliberate policy change now – we don't want to be pushed around by the antis and it's time we stood up for ourselves."

The LACS on its part, faced with police forces treating hunting as a low priority and the difficulties of obtaining conclusive evidence, decided to launch a specialist legal unit to obtain Anti Social Behaviour Orders (ASBOS) against hunters who infringe the law. The unit would advise on the use of the law against hunt members who routinely trespass on private land, who frequently lose control of the hounds resulting in attacks on domestic pets, who block country lanes with four-by-fours, and behave in an aggressive and intimidating manner towards anyone brave enough to complain. League chairman John Cooper was adamant that "ASBOS were not just for hoodies. Taking out ASBOS against hunts is a good way of clipping their wings: after all if they are following a trail there's no need for the hounds to be running through people's gardens or all over a main road."

It was certainly true for many of the older hunt saboteur veterans of countless battles spanning over forty years, with the second anniversary of the hunting ban fast approaching, that the implementation of the ban was now beginning to border on the farcical. Had they really fought so hard, and so long, to see the hunt merely "have their wings clipped" two years after Parliament had allegedly banned blood sports?

The CA's Alison Hawes offered some timely advice to frustrated hunt supporters in early 2007 in a bid to scupper attempts by monitors to gather evidence. In an email, which was leaked to the press, she suggested: "If you have the antis out filming you and they stick a camera in your face the advice is to say something along the lines of, 'Will you stop using threatening language...? Please stop swearing at me... . Now that you have turned the video on, I bet you won't repeat that foul language.' " The advice, which Hawes claimed came from a Police Wildlife Officer, continued with, "I will call the police if you threaten me once more...speak to me like that again and I will call the police...I am about to call the police as you have assaulted me." The reasoning behind these phrases were quite simple she concluded: "By using one of these sentences... or similar, it helps ruin their film as it does not look good if video evidence appears in court or is sent to the police, with a hunt supporter indicating they have been threatened, and the antis absolutely hate it."

The 19th February second anniversary of the hunting ban came and went with the usual mix of claim and counter-claim. A Mori poll, commissioned for IFAW and the LACS, showed that seventy-five per cent of people questioned supported the ban, with twenty-three per cent in favour of repeal, of which only nine per cent "strongly supported the ban being scrapped". The CA hit back with the findings of a survey they had commissioned suggesting that fox and deer numbers had fallen dramatically in the two years since the *Hunting Act's* implementation, while research by the Exmoor and District Deer Management Consensus claimed "a twenty per cent drop in deer numbers in 2006 against a trend of steady rises over a ten-year period".

The government joined in the anniversary celebrations with a ringing defence of the *Act* fronted by Peter Hain, who stated, "I consider this piece of legislation to be one of our proudest achievements since the party came to power in 1997." In a major newspaper article he expanded this view by writing that

> "As the Leader of the House of Commons at the time, I was responsible for taking the Act through Parliament, and saw at close quarters the passion which existed on both sides of the argument. Despite a number of violent protestations in some parts of the country, we stuck to our absolute belief that any policy that outlaws the organised killing of animals for sport and strengthens respect for life is a progressive policy and should be enforced."

A more cynical approach to the *Act* was displayed by a group of protestors who, dressed as policemen and bank robbers, gathered outside Parliament on 19th February under a banner proclaiming "Operation Pick'n'Mix". Their spokesman, John Curtin, voicing the concerns of many explained: "Everyone in the countryside knows that hunting is going on. They are not even pretending to drag hunt any more. There has been a fatal combination of hunts saying they are going to defy the ban and senior police officers saying enforcing it will not be one of their priorities. I'm not aware of a single police investigation to enforce this ban, let alone a prosecution. Is there any other group in Britain who can just ignore the law?"

A few weeks late the redoubtable Tory MP Ann Widdecombe joined the fray with her own attack on the failure of the *Hunting Act.* After hearing pro-hunting MPs openly bragging about deliberately breaking the law in their constituencies she decided to go public. "It was quite wrong," she said,

> "if there is any group of people which believes it is uniquely above the law and furthermore that its breaches of the law may be blatant and rejoiced in. I think there is an absence of understanding throughout the police forces and an absence of willingness among the highest levels of the police forces. It does seem that the message is going out that the law can be broken blatantly and deliberately and nothing will be done."

Despite the assurances of Peter Hain that the *Hunting Act* "should be enforced" the Home Office merely recited the standard cant when responding to Ann Widdecombe. Home Office Minister Joan Ryan dismissed out of hand the attack on police and CPS performance saying, "It's not for the Government to direct chief constables how to deploy their resources to deal with hunting." While Tory leader David Cameron, canvassing during the run-up to the May 2007 local elections, inadvertently confirmed the opinion of Ann Widdecombe. After assuring the party faithful that a future Conservative government would repeal the ban because "I have always believed that country sports are something that have taken place for years and...do not need the approach of the criminal law", he justified that view by stating, "We have passed a law that everyone is openly flouting and it makes the law look stupid."

The long-awaited court appearance of the "Quantock Two", huntsman Richard Down and whipper-in Adrian Pillivant, finally got underway at Taunton Magistrates' Court on 21st May 2007. The LACS presented its video footage taken by monitors Edmund Shepherd and Graham Floyd on 16th February 2006 showing the two involved in chasing eleven deer with two hounds for a considerable distance, prompting Richard Furlong, representing the League, to state,

> "They made no attempt to call the dogs off. The facts of this case are that no reasonable person could have believed this was exempt from the *Hunting Act.* They made no attempt to control the dogs. This is a very simple Act – find, flush and shoot. This case showed no sign of find, flush and shoot, Mr. Down and Mr. Pillivant knew it."

After four days of claim and counter-claim, which CA boss Simon Hart maintained was more about trying to understand the meaning of the *Hunting Act,* with "these two men being dragged through court to try and better define what is, and what is not, exempt hunting", the case was adjourned for a legal ruling.

The verdict came on 7th June at Bristol Magistrates' Court when District Judge David Parsons found both men guilty of illegally hunting deer with hounds, with fines of £500 each, along with £1,000 each as a contribution towards costs. In his summing-up District Judge

Parsons was forthright with his opinion: "The defendants were hunting for sport and recreation to continue their way of life and are disingenuous in attempting to deceive me into believing that they were exempt from hunting." ***Note 8***

Unable to once again face the reality of a court decision in support of the *Hunting Act* Simon Hart resorted to the usual CA mantra that

> "On the day in question they hunted with two hounds, as stipulated by the Act, and ensured there were experienced guns in place to shoot the deer. They shot six deer. If this is not flushing to guns I do not know what is. In the end there is one simple solution to the mess which will end all the confusion and waste of police and court resources. The *Hunting Act* is a bad law and needs to be got rid of."

So once again, this time at a cost of £37,500, a second private prosecution brought by the LACS had been upheld in a court of law, though in the wake of this judgement the stag hunting fraternity exhibited their usual resilience, or denial, depending on your point of view. Tom Yandle, speaking for the MDHA, would explain:

> "We will have to consider this verdict carefully and the wording of the judgement. But it certainly won't set any kind of case law. We have a number of other exemptions to look at and we will have to go over the summer and have another plan in place for when hunting starts again in August. It most certainly is not the end of stag hunting."

For the LACS Mike Hobday was emphatic that stag hunts now had to face up to reality, for "the simple fact is that hunts can no longer do what they used to do" and anything other than a complete conversion to drag hunting "shows that they are in absolute denial" as there "is no way the traditional hunts can still be involved in culling of deer". In reality both sides were steeling themselves for what would be considered the real legal test – the pending prosecution of the DSSH by the CPS later in the year.

Meanwhile it was business as usual on the blood sport war of words front. The CA issued a new document attacking the *Hunting Act* entitled *The Case For Repeal,* which had nothing new to say, being a self-righteous rehash of quotes and opinions from 2001 onwards, though it did come with a facsimile of the much wished for Hunting Act 2004 (Repeal) Act promised by the Tory Party.

This document was complemented by a much weightier offering from the All Party Parliamentary Middle Way Group, in conjunction with the Veterinary Association for Wildlife Management (VAWM), under the title *The Use, Misuse and Abuse of Science in support of the Hunting Act 2004.* The report, launched in the House of Commons on 27th July 2007, was billed as "the first opportunity to scrutinise the reports, submissions and statements made by anti-hunting groups, some scientists and others during the process which led to the passing of the Hunting Act 2004" which "shows that the *'large body of scientific evidence'*, a claim made by the RSPCA, simply does not exist".

Dr Lewis Thomas for VAWM was quoted as saying, "This carefully compiled document comprehensively puts the scientific record straight in respect of the hunting debate and demonstrates that there are not and never were any scientific grounds for banning hunting on the grounds of cruelty." While the Co-chairs of the Middle Way Group, Baroness Golding (Labour), Peter Luff MP (Conservative) and Lembit Opik MP (Lib-Dem) added that "Parliament does not make judgements based purely on science, but science can guide and inform those who create our laws. To invent, deliberately misinterpret or ignore evidence, the results of which are then fed into the legislative process, is a serious charge. This examination of the so-called science put forward to justify the Hunting Act, demonstrates that Parliament, the media and the public were deceived."

A more positive approach to the West Country red deer was offered in September 2007 by both the Exmoor National Park Authority and National Trust when they offered two-day deer safaris to view the forthcoming annual rut. At a cost of £195 per person, the tourist would get two nights B&B, two ranger-led walking tours to view the large stags, followed by an evening meal. The *West Somerset Free Press* later reported (2nd November 2007) that "tourism leaders in Porlock are celebrating the success of the village's first rutting weekend – estimated to have given the local economy a £7,500 boost". The combination of visitors leaving their hotel "under a star laden sky – which many had never experienced before – to journey onto the moor where they saw the sun rise as they watched the wild deer rut" prompted one woman to claim "I've seen whales in the Arctic, orang-utans in Borneo and visited the Galapagos Islands but I've never experienced anything as magical as this." Proof, if such were needed, that the Exmoor economy can benefit immensely from the red deer without the need to kill them in the process.

On 2nd October the 'Quantock Two', Richard Down and Adrian Pillivant, would take centre stage once again with the opening of their appeal hearing against the 7th June conviction for illegally hunting. For three days Mr Justice Wyn Williams, sitting at Taunton Crown Court, would review the evidence and listen to the statements of support for the two hunters. Anthony Trollope-Bellew, who owns 1,000 acres on the Quantock Hills, would tell the court that he gave permission to the hunt because the deer were causing him over £10,000 a year in damage, while QSH chairman Nicholas Gibbons explained that the "only way they could remain in existence was by managing deer within the law" and had taken advice from both the police and CA. The problem, Gibbons continued, was "there was little for followers to see since the Act was introduced and the hunt was now experimenting with trail hunting, which uses a full pack of hounds, because support had dwindled".

A week later, on 19th October 2007, Mr Justice Williams delivered his judgement by ruling that the two men had failed to prove they were not hunting illegally when he stated that, "To conclude, we consider that the appellants have failed to discharge the burden upon them to prove that they were actually engaged in exempt hunting or that they reasonably believed that they were so engaged."

The waters were somewhat muddied when Mr Justice Williams accepted that Down and Pillivant "did not set out to break the law" believing "that they considered they were entitled to enjoy their sport provided they complied with the statutory conditions as they believed them to be", which of course was a direct contradiction of District

Judge David Parsons who had convicted the pair the previous June. In his summing up the pair had been "disingenuous in attempting to deceive me into believing they were exempt hunting", though Mr Justice Williams did stress that the purpose of the hunt's activities on the day in question (16th February 2006) were for "sport, enjoyment and recreation", and did not accept the flush primarily took place to prevent or reduce serious damage to food for livestock and crops. ***Note 9***

In mid-November the Quantock red deer herd again became the centre of attention, this time not from the staghounds, but the Quantock Deer Management and Conservation Group who called for a mass cull of the deer. In a letter sent by the group to landowners in the area it was suggested that an estimated 250 animals should be shot during the early morning and evening of 30th November. Dr Jochen Langbein, deer biologist and secretary of the group, explained that, "We are looking to get the level of deer down to what it was 15 years ago and the group is advising landowners to cull responsibly. The group is organising the cull to bring management of the deer under control but we don't want to eradicate them. One landowner might have a real purge one year and another might not. Doing it that way doesn't work. It needs to be done in a more uniformed way and at the right time. We need to standardise it to ensure damage is limited and deer stocks remain healthy and protected."

While organisations such as the National Trust, Natural England, and the Quantocks Area of Outstanding Natural Beauty Group, supported the cull "because of the risk the creatures pose to ancient woodland and the Quantocks' rural heritage", the outcry from animal welfare groups was predictable. Led initially by a vocal Kevin Hill news of the intended cull soon took on a life of its own, fuelled by such headlines as the *Western Daily Press's* "FURY AT DEER 'KILLING SPREE'", which in turn led to local opposition that would go some way to making sure that the operation remained stillborn. When the dawn arrived on 30th November few local shooters arrived with it, and while some deer were certainly killed, the number was nowhere near the 250 originally suggested. ***Note 10***

In the midst of all this excitement, a situation arose in Portsmouth

Magistrates Court that, while initially going unnoticed by the mainstream media, would ultimately prove to be the possible death knell of the Hunting Act 2004. On Thursday, 22nd November 2007 the Act was thrown into further confusion on the first day of what was scheduled to be a seven-day trial of the Isle of Wight Foxhounds following a prosecution brought by the LACS when the court was unable to determine where the burden of evidence of proving exempt hunting lay.

After submissions based on Section 101 of *The Magistrates Court Act,* which mired the Portsmouth Court, four barristers, two solicitors, four defendants and the District Judge took part in futile legal wrangling on points of law. This was followed by frantic phone calls to the District Judge in Bristol, who was scheduled to hear the case against the DSSH the following week and who was also unable to clarify the situation. It was therefore decided to adjourn the Isle of Wight case, provisionally, to at least the beginning of May 2008. ***Note 11***

The net result of all this was that all legal teams in cases concerning future prosecutions for "exempt hunting" suspended future action until a legal definition of Section 101 was forthcoming, not from a Magistrates Court, but following an appeal to the High Court. The much awaited CPS test case against the DSSH was of course included, with the provisional date for a possible trial now put somewhere around the middle of 2008.

The following week (28th November) the House of Lords predictably, but rather academically, ruled against the CA's appeal, which had been brought by ten individuals including the DSSH Donald Summersgill, that the Hunting Act "infringed their human rights".

A panel of Law Lords voted unanimously that the Hunting Act should remain law, adding that campaigners should not be allowed to overturn democratic decisions made in Parliament by using the law. Lord Bingham said the Hunting Act 2004 must "be taken to reflect the conscience of the majority of the nation", while Lord Hope commented that: "The history of legislation in the United Kingdom for the prevention of cruelty to animals leaves no room for doubt that in this country the subject is deeply rooted in public policy." Following this judgement the CA began packing their bags ready for the trip to the European Court of Human Rights in Strasbourg.

Then, on Friday, 30th November 2007, came what many on both sides of the blood sport debate saw as the *coup de grace* for the Hunting Act, when Judge Graham Cottle, sitting with two magistrates at Exeter Crown Court, acquitted convicted huntsman Tony Wright on appeal. After a four-day trial that began on 5th November, followed by three weeks of deliberation, Judge Cottle upheld Wright's appeal by saying "the law was so uncertain that it was open to different interpretations" and because he believed the huntsman thought he was working within the law.

The words of Judge Graham Cottle in that Exeter court threw into doubt the future of the entire Hunting Act. In a scathing indictment of the Act's failings he said: "It seems to us that any given set of facts may be susceptible to differing interpretations. The result is an unhappy state of affairs which leaves all those involved in a position of uncertainty. We do not consider that the hunt was simply paying lip service to the obligation to comply with the law. We are satisfied the appellant has proved that he reasonably believed, perhaps optimistically, that he had put the safeguards in place that he thought would ensure compliance with the requirements of the Act."

So while the verdict was celebrated long and hard across Exmoor, at the HQs of the main protagonists the point scoring began all over again. The CA carping that "the Hunting Act is not only a pointless and prejudicial piece of legislation, it is a very bad law. If the courts cannot be sure what is hunting and what is not, how on earth can anyone else"

For the LACS the

> "judgement in the Tony Wright case has in many ways opened up a legal can of worms. In the cases so far, the courts seem to have been quite clear about what is and isn't legal and convictions have resulted. In the Tony Wright case, first time round the Judge seemed quite clear as to what did and did not constitute hunting. This time the Judge in the crown courts was not so sure. If

> nothing else, the fact that the Judge has said the law is open to interpretation means that it is very likely that the Crown Prosecution Service will appeal this case to the High Court for a ruling on what does and does not constitute hunting. While the hunters may claim the law is unclear, it is also the case that by appealing the Tony Wright case in the Crown Court they have also opened the doors to the High Court to make a definitive judgement in the case that they will long live to regret."

For Douglas Batchelor the future path that the League must travel left no room for doubt. For him

> "the whole saga has taught us that we need to fight the battles in court case by case, that we have to get the incontrovertible evidence of what we believe to be wrong doing and that in court we have to win the legal arguments. It has taught us that it isn't enough to be experts in hunting, we have to be experts in the law and experts in the advocacy of the law. The lessons are clear: more professional monitoring of hunts, better case preparation and first class advocacy in court. All this is costly, in court and in the field, and it teaches us that belief in our case is not a legally persuasive argument in court. A ruling on Section 101 will help, a High Court ruling on what does and does not constitute hunting will help, but the key to all this is making absolutely sure that the facts of the case brought to court are beyond legal dispute. This is a legal battle, not a campaign."

The key was in the last sentence, and to prepare for the legal struggles ahead the League began "planning to reorganise its resources to meet these challenges", while at the same time "making sure that they had the financial resources to take the fights to the courts of appeal that would set the precedents in law that were so clearly needed."

So while the LACS prepared to mount a titanic legal battle to test the ultimate worth of the Hunting Act 2004, many former animal rights activists had already concluded that the Act was now beyond salvation, having long taken on the mantle of a farce worthy of the Monty Python team. It all seemed a long way away from the heady days of 1963 when a seventeen-year-old youth joined a group of aspiring hunt saboteurs in the mistaken belief that he was about to smoke-bomb blood sports into the dustbin of history within a few years. None of us realised that it would take another forty years for an Act of Parliament to ban hunting, or that such a ban would be so loosely worded and cluttered with exemptions, that the courts of law are unable to obtain any meaningful convictions.

Of one thing though we can be certain: the saga of West Country stag hunting verses the Hunting Act 2004 as it stands will, like the best soap operas, continue to run and run. ***Note 12***

Note 1. The CPS would not confirm any reason for refusing to prosecute the various hunts brought to their attention, though the antis were given to understand that problems with proving the intent of the huntsmen were crucial to the decision. For the law states prosecutors must prove huntsmen intended their hounds to pursue the fox, hare, mink, or deer. There were also issues with identification of those in control of the hounds, and whether the dogs were under control at all.
Note 2. Brendan McCarthy, Director of Wessex National Trust, wrote the following letter to the *Western Daily Press* on 6th June 2006:

> "In contrast to the impression given by your article on hunting and the National Trust, 'A staggering U-turn on hunting', I would like to make clear that the National Trust will NOT be allowing exempt hunting of deer on its land. Your headline suggests that we have reversed a decision made by the trust in 1997 when stag hunting was banned on trust land. We have not.
>
> "At the forefront of our policies regarding the deer populations on the trust's Holnicote Estate is deer welfare. The trustees of the National Trust have considered whether exempt hunting within the law would be compatible with deer welfare, and have concluded that it is not. They have, however, looked at the issues of sick and injured deer coming onto trust land. In these rare and exceptional cases, they have determined that, in the best interest of deer welfare and to avoid unnecessary suffering of the animal,

> the trust would allow the minimum number of hunt staff necessary to kill the deer humanely to come onto trust land and shoot the deer.
>
> "This is in line with our own practice to shoot sick or injured deer to reduce their suffering, and is subject to the requirement that the hunt informs the trust's local staff in advance. It will be monitored closely by trust staff."

Ironically, the first instance of deer hunting on NT land since the announcement to reverse the 1997 ban came in a video taken by LACS monitors on 14th August 2006. The incident showed the deer being chased for over two hours by hounds and rider, who is seen cracking his whip at the animal which is clearly frightened and exhausted. The incident was given prominent coverage in the *Independent on Sunday* of 27th August 2006.

Note 3. The first conviction in England under the Hunting Act was against a Merseyside man who had been hunting rabbits with dogs, but Wright's was the first for any "official" blood sport since the ban came into force.

Note 4. Following the Wright conviction the LACS would bring another private prosecution against the Quantock Staghounds following film taken by its monitors in February 2006, which the CPS had refused to act upon. The QSH huntsman Richard Down and whipper-in Adrian Pillivant were both named to appear at Taunton magistrates on 21st September to answer charges of illegal (relay) hunting. The police and CPS again looked at the evidence following the Wright case and again decided not to pursue a prosecution. It was this refusal, plus the approaching six-month deadline to mount a prosecution, that prompted League lawyers to pursue the case privately.

Note 5. The ex-Liberal Democrat MP made a name for herself as an out-spoken anti-hunt campaigner. She was defeated in the 2001 General Election after a major mobilisation of stag hunt supporters targeted her seat – and the loss of her seat was widely acknowledged as having been due to the hunting issue.

Within months, Jackie Ballard became chief executive of the RSPCA, and she was thought to have moved the society closer towards an anti-blood sport agenda. The RSPCA helped form the Campaign for the Hunted Animal along with the LACS and IFAW, a pact that helped bring about the hunt ban.

Note 6. The same type of arrogance exhibited by stag hunters when they are caught breaking the law, such as demanding that the police appear at public meetings to explain their action, also transfers to the hunting field as this story from August 2006 illustrates.

Magistrate Catherine Hodgson used her body as a human shield, in August, against two staghounds as they ripped apart her pet dog in a horrific attack. Mrs Hodgson of East Worlington, near Tiverton, threw herself on top of the family terrier as the hounds attacked just yards from her front doorstep. By the time the hunt intervened, Pippa, a fourteen year-old border cross Jack Russell, was fatally wounded and had to be put down by a vet.

The Hodgsons' condemned the actions of the Tiverton Staghounds, which offered compensation for "shock and trauma" – on the condition they kept the incident quiet. The hunt later withdrew the confidentiality demand when she pointed out her duty to inform the police. Mrs Hodgson, who was chairperson of the North Devon magistrate's bench, said:

> "Pippa was old and slow and they caught her barely a stride away from me. One had its jaws into her back and the other had her throat. They literally peeled her apart. I could see flesh opening up and she was desperately wounded. When we got the hunt's letter offering hush money it made me so angry..."

In a letter of apology to Mrs Hodgson, the hunt's solicitor, Hole and Pugsley of Tiverton, offered £1,000 compensation and promised to pay vet bills plus the cost of a new dog. Mrs Hodgson later accepted the compensation package, while Tiverton Staghounds joint master John Lucas, said both hounds involved were immediately destroyed.

Reported by *Western Daily Press* on 24th August 2006 & *HOWL 86*, Winter 2006.

When this case was brought before Exeter Crown Court, on 13th/14th August 2007 under the *1991 Dangerous Dogs Act*, Judge Jeremy Griggs ordered the jury to find huntsman John Norrish "not guilty because the hounds had effectively been allowed on to the private garden...where the attack took place." As Mrs Hodgson had allowed the hounds to range through her garden on a regular basis without complaint Judge Griggs concluded that "what happened was an exceptional event" caused by the fact that "dogs will be dogs".

A somewhat different slant on the story was given in an article by Clive Bainbridge, the solicitor who defended the TSH, which appeared in the *Horse & Hound* of 4th October 2007. He wrote that:

> "The well-reported demise of Mrs Hodgson's terrier was only part of the story that unfolded in court number three. When the huntsman and the then master John Lucas tried to resolve matters, Mrs Hodgson lambasted them with: 'Do you know who I am? I'm the chairman of the North Devon Bench. I sat in on the Tony Wright case.' (Tony Wright was the first huntsman to be privately prosecuted under the Hunting Act) In open court she conceded that such 'pulling rank' was a misuse of her office.

"Within five days of the incident the magistrate wrote accepting the hunt's offer of £450 for a replacement terrier, payment of vet bills and £1,000 payment for her distress. She admitted that the hunt had acted honourably throughout and that £1,000 was very generous compared with the £50 to £100 that would be awarded in her court for such minor injury.

"On the same day as writing to accept the hunt's money she made a formal complaint to the police. From that moment, the matter was 'sub judice'. That notwithstanding, the magistrate and her husband procured extensive media coverage that could only be prejudicial to the huntsman and the Tiverton Staghounds, with copy appearing in both local and national press. During the trial the jury enquired of the judge as to whether this was a private prosecution. Indeed they might. The Crown Prosecution Service chose not to heed defence representations made in February as to the futility of the case. Mrs Hodgson may have publicly thanked the police and CPS for bringing the case, yet others have grave concerns as to why it was ever brought in the first place and how a magistrate can, under oath, admit to misusing her office and still sit in judgement upon the people of North Devon."

The conflicting elements of this case are recorded here merely to show how complex an apparently simple and straightforward-looking hunting incident can become when played out in a court of law. It must be for the reader to draw their own conclusions.

Note 7. Much of the information contained in this section on FONT and the NT resolution was obtained from the CA web site for 6th November 2006.

A later press statement from FONT stated: "Just one per cent of the charity's members – 33,000 – had bothered to vote on the resolution. In the past deer hunting was a subject that had attracted upwards of 100,000 on both sides of the argument. This shows that the public are bored by the subject."

Note 8. The various options following the judgement in this case were succinctly explained as part of an article by Tristan Cork entitled "What now for stag hunting in the wake of court blow?" that appeared in the *Western Daily Press* on 9th June 2007.

The stag hunts

This judgement shatters the main exemption all three have depended on since the ban came into force in February 2005. The hunts have used "relay hunting" – using two dogs at a time to flush deer to guns, instead of whole packs. The judge said that was illegal as there was still a chase of sorts. Their only other options now are converting fully to drag hunting, or employing a mix of hounds exercising with deer management marksmen.

The fox hunts

Foxhunts are worried by the judgement because it appears to say you can't mix pest control with the set-up, paraphernalia and colour of hunts. The law is the same for both, but foxhunts have more obvious exemptions open to them.

The police and CPS

They will now be under even more pressure to take anti-hunt monitors' evidence more seriously and to mount prosecutions. The police said they had "learned the lessons" of the Tony Wright case – the first private prosecution – but still turned down the evidence against the Quantocks. A lot rests on the prosecution of the Devon and Somerset Staghounds.

The antis

Jubilant and victorious, they have two cases to justify the setting up of their special legal team. They will put more pressure on the police, but are likely to face more hostility out in the field.

The law

Both huntsmen Tony Wright and the Quantock Two relied on an exemption in the hunt ban which allows two dogs to be used to flush animals to waiting guns. In both cases, the judge ruled that the time between the flushing and the shooting constituted a chase. In the latest case, the judge said because the hunt was an arranged and seemingly traditional hunt meet, they couldn't argue the delay was unintended. Antis say the law has been cemented, pro-hunt groups that it is even more confused.

Note 9. While the appeal hearing did not overturn the original conviction of the "Quantock Two" much of the final judgement did allow the blood sport lobby to claim that it gave some clarity in attempting to work within the Hunting Act. Tim Hayden, solicitor for the QSH, gave the following assessment in the *Horse & Hound* on 25th October 2007:

"Although Mr Justice Wyn Williams dismissed Richard Down and Adrian Pillivant's appeal against their conviction for offences under the Hunting Act, there were significant implications in his judgement for the two men involved, the Quantock Staghounds and anyone involved in deer hunting.

"Crucially for those seeking to engage in lawful exempt hunting, the judge did not find that deer hunting could never fall within an exemption. The judge accepted that deer cause significant damage to crops, one of the statutory purposes of exempt hunting. He accepted that, if it could be established that one of the statutory purposes was the 'primary purpose' of a particular hunt, then the fact that those engaged in hunting enjoyed their sport would not, in itself, make their activities unlawful. He accepted that the primary purpose of the first flush the QSH engaged in on the day was to prevent damage to crops, but found that later flushes were not made for this purpose. He noted that the meet on the day had been organised well in advance of a request by the landowner to hunt deer that were causing damage to his grass.

"He held that reasonable steps must be taken to shoot dead all deer flushed if the flushing and stalking were to be relied upon.

"In this regard he took the view that the three guns in the Quantock case were not a sufficient number to have killed the 10 or more deer that were likely to have been flushed. He also found that the pursuit of deer over several hundred yards following a flush at Longstone Hill meant that the deer had not been shot 'as soon as reasonably practicable'. The result of this judgement is that it should enable the QSH to continue to hunt within the scope of an exemption if the following steps are taken:

"When relying on the 'flushing' exemption, guns must be placed close to the flushing point with no extended pursuit outside cover.

"Reasonable steps must be taken to shoot dead all deer flushed. This does not mean that all deer flushed must be killed, but that there are sufficient marksmen in place to kill all deer flushed.

"Hunting must only be undertaken if its 'primary purpose' is one defined by an exemption. It would be unwise to continue to organise meets in the traditional manner well in advance and respond to requests from landowners on the day, as it is likely that hunting and enjoyment will be found to be the 'primary purpose' of the meet."

Note 10. The following letter from Dr Jochen Langbein that appeared in the 23rd November 2007 edition of the *West Somerset Free Press,* giving as it does a fascinating insight into the deer management issues relating to the Quantock Hills, is reproduced here in full.

> "In reporting on the call by the Quantock Deer Management and Conservation Group for more female deer to be culled in and around the Quantock Hills this winter, several papers have widely used emotive terms such as mass slaughter and bloodbath.
>
> "I was pleased to see the more balanced reporting by the Free Press last Friday but would nevertheless like to clarify some points and ask readers to do some of the necessary elementary maths for themselves, and to consider the wider reasons that have led the very broad array of individuals and conservation organisations which make up the QDM&CG to ask local landowners to move towards culling – yes, more deer, but do so also in a more collaborative, selective and sustainable manner.
>
> "A visual spring (pre-calving) count of red deer on the Quantocks has been organised annually with the help of 50 volunteers for the past 17 years.
>
> "Deer are difficult to count accurately, not least when within concealing cover, but this standardised count enables at least minimum numbers to be confirmed and trends to be monitored.
>
> "The average of counts obtained during the five years from 1993-1997 was 555, rose to 745 from 1998-2002 and taken across the last five counts has averaged 830 red deer.
>
> "Aside from the rise in overall numbers, the population of adult males in the population has fallen, thus raising also the rate of population growth.
>
> "The spring count records merely the annual minima before at least 350 or more calves will have been born last summer, taking the total by autumn to somewhere near 1100 red deer.

"Culling of deer on the Quantocks is nothing new – in the absence of any significant natural mortality, around 200 to 250 or more red deer will have been culled in most recent years.

"The exact number and breakdown of the cull is not known, as rightly or wrongly (the latter in my view) game laws in England remain so lax that there is no legal obligation on landowners to report to anyone how many deer (or indeed foxes or crows etc) they cull nor limit the totals culled in any way.

"While only a minority of landholders report their culls to the group at present, culls taken over recent years have clearly been inadequate to prevent the observed increasing trend in deer numbers and distribution; in part because the total cull has been too low, but mostly because the proportion of adult females included in the culls needs to be greater if the trend is to be reversed.

"The Quantocks are far from being alone in all this. A report by the British Association for Shooting and Conservation in 2006 estimated that the annual cull of deer taken by its members in the UK approached 250,000 head including over 155,000 culled within England. In addition near 60,000 deer are killed as a result of collisions with vehicles every year.

"That carnage of deer and other wildlife arising from our ever-increasing levels of road traffic might indeed justify terms like indiscriminate and mass slaughter, but even when added to the quarter of a million deer that are culled legally with rifles each year, the national deer cull has to date been insufficient to prevent increases seen in the numbers and distribution of roe, red, fallow, sika and muntjac deer in numerous parts of the country.

"For appropriately qualified and experienced stalkers, red deer are not an especially difficult species to cull. The more complicated task lies in getting the many owners whose land the red deer herds roam over to agree and jointly work towards maintaining a healthy and sustainable herd, to be conserved as a highly valued part of our wildlife and asset to local tourism, but which remains in balance with the environment without unacceptable levels of damage to farm and timber crops or detrimental impact on semi-natural habitats.

"The QDM&CG is fully committed to the long-term conservation of a substantial population of red deer on the Quantocks. However, its members (which include individual Quantock landholders, as well as Natural England, Friends of Quantocks, Forestry Commission, National Trust, DEFRA, British Deer Society, The Quantock Staghounds, The Deer Initiative, BASC, and the Quantock AONB Service) have jointly reached the conclusion that concerns about damage to farmland, forestry, and woodland bio-diversity make the current size of deer populations unsustainable in the longer term.

"The need to reduce winter grazing levels of both deer and sheep is particularly pertinent for conservation of the ancient semi-natural oak woods within the Quantock Hills, which are designated as a SAC (Special Area of Conservation) of international importance, but are considered by Natural England to be in unfavourable condition at least partly due to overgrazing.

"The group has therefore asked local landholders to liaise in attempts at a gradual reduction of the population over the coming five years, and then retain a population nearer 500 head. To accomplish this, annual culls will need to be around 25 per cent higher than they have been in recent years.

"In other words, while recent culls estimated at around 250 head have helped to hold spring counts at around 800 head, an extra 50 to 100 mature females will need to be culled annually to initiate a more significant reduction also in the breeding herd.

"The purpose of the collaborative cull proposed for the end of November is not as reported in the press an attempt to achieve the whole annual cull in a single day. Rather, the aims are firstly to provide a day when, by virtue of most local deer managers being available in their own usual management areas, their combined culling is likely to be more efficient overall, because if a deer does not provide a safe shot on one holding, it may nevertheless well do so if it moves onto a neighbour's land. And secondly to enable provision of practical assistance for landholders if required through loan of equipment such as mobile high seats and/or with the sale and collection of venison.

"The focus for the collaborative day is purely on achieving a higher cull of hinds not of stags, and is planned to be an addition, not a replacement, of other culling activity throughout the season.

"This approach has been applied successfully with the backing of the Deer Initiative in other parts of England, and only if feedback from local landowners suggests it has also been helpful here will consideration be given to organising further similar days in the future.

"Whilst the optimum deer population level for the Quantocks remains debatable and will always require compromises between landholders and other interest groups, in the absence of any natural predators of deer, direct management intervention does become inevitable at some point.

"When deer become so abundant that the majority rather than minority of landowners regard them as excessive, standards of control also tend to decline, including resort by some to night shooting and other illegal practices.

"Therefore as a biologist and wildlife enthusiast with a lifelong passion for deer, but no interest at all in hunting or shooting game, I nevertheless have no problem in accepting the need for culling as one part of deer management. I also have no reservation in recommending that more people should eat venison, which is a high quality meat usually reared far more humanely than the 20 million or more poultry that will be slaughtered en masse next month in the name of Christmas.

"The more important issue is that deer culls should be undertaken in a humane, professional and highly selective manner and that a significant and healthy population is retained which remains valued as an asset rather than perceived as a pest by the majority of landholders."

Note 11. The following LACS 3rd December 2007 Information Mailing from Douglas Batchelor explains the implications of Section 101 of the *Magistrates Court Act,* along with other issues pertinent to the various late 2007 court cases.

"Basically, what Section 101 says is that if you, the accused, are going to rely on an exemption or an excuse in law as a defence for your actions that would otherwise have been illegal, it is up to you, the accused, to prove that you were acting within the law. This is unusual because in most cases it is for the prosecution to prove that you, the accused, broke the law. Section 101 puts the burden of proof on the accused, if he or she relies on an excuse or an exemption in law.

"In the Quantock Staghounds related case it was accepted that Section 101 did apply. In the Tony Wright case first time round it wasn't raised as an issue and in both the Isle of Wight case and the Devon and Somerset Staghounds case it is accepted that it may well be an issue. In the Tony Wright appeal, the Judge said he thought it didn't apply but he gave no grounds for that decision whatsoever.

"All that leads to a legal situation where everyone wants to know whether or not Section 101 does apply and for that reason alone the CPS will almost certainly have to appeal the Tony Wright case to the High Court for a ruling on the Section 101 issue.

"But life is never simple in law. There are also other issues in relation to the Tony Wright case, whatever the High Court ruling with regard to the burden of proof. Chief amongst those issues are first, does hunting include or exclude searching for with a view to pursue, and secondly whether knowingly following the scent of a quarry animal constitutes hunting. In most of the cases so far the Judges have been clear in that pursuit of a scent is hunting and that searching for, is hunting. The only exemption to that has been flushing to guns or a falcon where the objective is not a pursuit, but a flush so that the quarry can be shot at the earliest opportunity with the dogs having been called off.

"At the time that the Hunting Act was going through Parliament, Alun Michael the Minister responsible, was very clear that hunting included searching. To quote the *Oxford English Dictionary*: "1. to pursue and kill (a wild animal) for sport or food. 2. search diligently for. Hunting, noun: an act or the process of hunting, an association of people who meet regularly to hunt, especially with hounds", and so on. The reason that hunting was not defined in the Act was because it was felt in Parliament that it was already sufficiently well described in the *Oxford English Dictionary.*

"The effect of the Tony Wright judgement is that the hunters, the CPS and the League all need clarification as to the applicability of Section 101 of the Magistrates Court Act and with regard to the definition of hunting. Common sense would suggest that pursuit of a wild mammal by a dog was hunting, but the law is about people not dogs, so there is a need for the High Court to judge this issue and that is I suspect exactly what will happen.

> "The parliamentary precedents on all of the legal issues are pretty clear. The Minister's intent in the Hunting Act is clear in Hansard; the precedents in relation to the Magistrates Court Act are also clear in law. But when all is said and done, one of the key issues will be the intent (the mens rea) of the hunter. If their intent was to provide sport and entertainment then it cannot in my view have been at the same time to hunt in an exempt manner. The core question in all this was, was this sport or was it something else? The first court said it was not exempt hunting, the second said it appeared to them to be arguably within the rules of exempt hunting as they saw them and the third, the High Court have yet to opine."

NB. There is another theory regarding the *Hunting Act 2004* that has taken root amongst the more conspiracy-minded element of animals rights which holds that the passing of this Act was nothing more than a confidence trick perpetrated by the Blair government on a gullible public. Desperate to placate a vociferous back bench who were intent on forcing the government to honour its Manifesto commitment to abolish blood sports, but unwilling to anger the countryside/ruling elite, an ingenious plot was hatched. The Act would be passed but in such a way that it would be legally ambiguous, loosely worded and open to so many legal interpretations that it would be unenforceable. This would give the appearance of honouring the Manifesto promise, remove the threat of anti-hunt protest and legitimacy of such groups as the hunt saboteurs, turning the whole issue into a protracted legal battle that would consume the financial resources of such groups as the LACS and IFAW for the foreseeable future. When the next Tory government repealed the Act, then the opposition would be so weakened, having exhausted its resources with endless court actions, while the saboteurs would be virtually non-existent as a result of their years of inactivity, that there would be little, if any, effective opposition to the return of full hunting in all its glory.

But then, it is only a theory.

Note 12. Of all the exemptions within the *Hunting Act 2004*, the most worrying to hunt monitors and the one that could be used as a catch-all to justify all other exemptions, comes in Schedule 1, Section 2 (9)(2) under the heading "*Research and observation*". This states that the hunting of a wild mammal is exempt if "the hunting is undertaken for the purpose of or in connection with the observation or study of the wild mammal", while further on it states that "each dog used in the hunt is kept under sufficiently close control to ensure that it does not injure the wild mammal". The inference that it is perfectly legally acceptable to chase a wild animal all over the countryside so long as it was done in the name of "*research and observation*" is abundantly obvious. The stag hunters could and no doubt will use this clause in much the same way as the Japanese use similar "exemptions" within the International Whaling Commission's (IWC) commercial whaling ban to justify their slaughter of minke whales, fin whales, sei whales, Bryde's whales, sperm whales and humpback whales in the name of *"scientific research"*.

It was not only in the West of England that a Pythonesque farce was underway, for the Republic of Ireland was running a very close second. Following intense public pressure and hard campaigning from ICABS the Dublin Government had at last been forced to act against the Ward Union carted deer hunt.

On 19th December 2007, John Gormley, Minister for the Environment, Heritage and Local Government, notified the Ward Union Staghounds of his decision to grant the hunt a licence under the *Wildlife Act 1976*. However the licence was strictly conditioned so that the actual pursuit of a stag by hounds was not permitted.

According to the government press statement:

> "Section 26 of the *Wildlife Act 1976* provides that the Minister may issue a licence for the hunting of stags with a pack of stag hounds. Minister Gormley has examined the Ward Union's licence application for the 2007/2008 season. The Minister raised a number of serious concerns...including in relation to animal welfare, conservation and protection of stags generally and compliance with previous licence conditions. These concerns have arisen particularly since the incident last January (2007) when a stag ran into a school playground in Kildalkey, Co. Meath, while parents waited to pick up their children from the school.
>
> "The Minister said, 'The licence with the conditions I have granted to the Ward Union Staghounds will allow for the hunting of stags in a manner which will provide for the protection of the stag and the general public. *In effect it permits the Ward Union Staghounds to release a deer to lay a scent trail along the course of the hunt, but I am insisting that the deer must be recaptured before the hounds are released and the full hunt gets underway* (author's italics). I believe that the conditions to the licence address my concerns from a wider public policy perspective about the public safety issues surrounding the hunting of a large animal by a large group on horseback and a pack of hounds through an increasingly urbanised countryside.' "

In early February 2008 the Ward Union were granted an injunction against the hunting licence by the Dublin High Court pending a judicial review of the issue, which allowed them to revert back to the 2006 licence and chase the tame deer as before.

Conclusion

BEFORE ATTEMPTING TO ADDRESS the two prime questions that are often asked – was the hunting ban justified, and will it work? – it must be stated that much of this book was written during the 2002-2004 push for abolition and therefore without the benefit of hindsight. The initial heady euphoria, experienced by many in the animal rights movement, has since given way to a cynical acceptance that, in reality, the *Hunting Act 2004* has had little overall effect on blood sports, give or take the odd inconvenience.

To the first question, as to whether an attempt to ban blood sports was justified, the answer must be an unequivocal YES. For it cannot be right, or realistic, to claim that in the first decade of the twenty-first century the only satisfactory method of controlling red deer, fox, hare and mink is the continuation of a practice that predates the Norman Conquest of 1066.

The hunting of wild red deer in the West Country is primarily a "sport", with the concept that it serves to both protect and control an invention of the late nineteenth/early twentieth centuries, when the opposition to blood sports began to gain ground in the public consciousness. It was, and remains, primarily, a social activity that is pursued by a small number of individuals for the gratification of personal pleasure. If there is any genuine intention to operate an expensive form of pest control service then this aspect takes second place in the minds of hunt officials whose primary concern is offering "good sport" to the subscribers, who in some instances have travelled long distances to participate in the chase. Chapter One explains the concept of what constitutes a good hunt, with the "glorious gallop" high on the list. Such a hunt would be recorded in the annuls of hunting mythology in flowery terms of countryside traversed, or miles covered, in some cases twenty or twenty-five miles; the reality was a stag or hind pursued relentlessly by a pack of baying dogs while running for its life from human pursuers.

Another falsehood perpetrated by the hunting set is that one of the prime functions of stag hunting is to maintain a healthy herd. This they claim is undertaken by *only* hunting the old, sick, weak and injured, and, in the case of red deer stags, leaving the prime specimens (often identified by exceptional antler spread) to ensure prime breeding stock. In reality this is often far from the truth, for not only do poor stags offer second-rate trophies (antlers to hang on the wall), while the weakest animals certainly do not offer the best runs. Today it is fashionable to play down the "long run" as a product of days gone by with a point of nine miles considered "one of the great hunts of recent times", as per the last legal hunt of 2005. For anyone wishing to delve deeper into the mythology of this aspect of deer hunting I recommend Paddy King-Fretts' book, *Staghunter: The Remarkable Story Of Ernest Bawden.* Not only does it conjure up a fascinating picture of this famous DSSH huntsman against the back-drop of early twentieth century Exmoor, but includes detailed descriptions of ten "classic runs" (with maps) between 1924-1935 that covered distances, in some instances, of thirty-five miles. There is little doubt from reading these types of reports that within the mindset of stag hunters the animal on the receiving end of their "sporting interests" are given about the same consideration as the ball in a game of rugby. ***Note 1***

Another reason why blood sports should be removed from the equation is the disproportionate influence they command in relation to their importance, coupled with the damage caused to animal welfare issues generally. Every attempt to legislate on behalf of animal welfare (wild mammals) in Britain has been hampered, weakened, or blocked by blood sport supporters determined that no Act of Parliament, no matter what the issue, or how abstract the threat, should in any way impinge on their sporting interests. Name any piece of proposed legislation (*Conservation of Seals Bill, Protection of Badgers Bill, Wildlife and Countryside Bill,* the various *Deer Bills, Wild Mammals [Protection] Bill)* and somewhere behind the scenes will be found the hand of blood sport interests, fronted by the BFSS/CA, attempting to water down or neutralise its effectiveness.

These same people, who constantly try to convince us that they, and they alone, are the only ones who not only care about animals, but understand the issues, are also curiously absent on any animal or environmental issue that does not directly, or indirectly, relate in some way to blood sports. In over forty years of involvement with animals rights, encompassing opposition to such issues as the Canadian seal culls, international whaling, live exports, fur trade, cosmetic testing on animals, etc., I cannot remember a single instance of encountering any prominent hunting figure, nor saw any active opposition to the general issue of animal abuse.

Equally, having worked over twenty-five years in mental health social work, I was amused to see a nurse paraded by the CA on one of their "fight prejudice" posters. Quick though they were to forge a connection with the caring professions as typical of blood sport adherents, I fail to remember a single instance of ever meeting one during all my years of service, whereas the number of animal activists in people-related employment are legion. So much for the taunt that people who show concern for animal suffering are indifferent to human misery.

As to the second question – will the *Hunting Act* work? – the answer must be, not in its present form. What appeared truly amazing to some sceptics was that the *Hunting Act* ever reached the statute book at all. The obstructions that were overcome from many of the most prominent figures in British public life, entrenched opposition from large sections of both Houses of Parliament, and most of the media who are in favour of blood sports, it was incredible that abolition was finally achieved through a right-wing Labour government controlled by ministers who made every attempt to placate the hunters. And it was only being brought to fruition after relentless pressure from backbench MPs with the use of the Parliament Act to force it through, with this followed by twelve months of legal challenges by the CA to the validity of the Parliament Act, going all the way to the highest court in the land – the House of Lords. After such a monumental struggle no one who worked so hard over all the years to make it happen now wants to admit it was all for nothing.

On the other hand, for those of a cynical disposition with eyes to see, the future course of New Labour's plan to deal with hunting appeared in the 17th January 2000 *Guardian* article by David Henckle. The strategy was simple he explained:

> "The Tories will...start a guerrilla campaign to make the government's Hunting Bill as flawed and as sloppy as possible with the aim of ensuring a fox hunting ban is unenforceable when the new law is implemented.... The Shadow Cabinet is expecting the government to get a big majority...*but has given the nod to a detailed parliamentary strategy to hide faults in the legislation with the aim of making the ban impossible to police.*" (author's italics)

That statement, four years before the implementation of a ban, leaves little to the imagination regarding the strategy, so that same imagination does not need to make any great leap to conclude that either through the expediency of hiding behind Tory duplicity, or with actual complicity, New Labour had a preconceived "get-out clause" concerning the implementation of their promise to end blood sports. It is therefore not surprising that the more "conspiracy-minded" smelt slightly more than the proverbial rat.

Thus was born a train of thought which concluded that to pass a law abolishing blood sports, but allowing "exempt hunting" to continue via an entire collection of loopholes (trail hunting, flushing to guns with two dogs, the use of a bird of prey with unlimited numbers of dogs, exercising the pack, etc.), while the infrastructure of the hunt remained intact, could in fact be seen by the more astute observer as a means of legitimising, or legalising, blood sports.

The conclusions are not hard to fathom. New Labour, the leadership of which had no wish to abolish hunting, though finding itself hounded by back benchers and public alike to honour its Manifesto pledge, hit upon the idea of the *Hunting Act 2004*, which actually abolishes nothing. It merely offers the illusion of ending the cruelty of blood sports, while leaving the structure of hunting in place until the return of the Tories and their "one line bill to repeal the Act".

Hunting will weather the minor inconveniences of the *2004 Act*, while wearing their opposition to "prejudice" as a badge of honour, until their ultimate vindication at the inevitable repeal. What has actually happened of course is that with the act of abolition, without the realisation of dismemberment of hunting's infrastructure, the future of blood sports has been secured in perpetuity. For once the *Hunting Act 2004* is repealed who else in the future would ever dare to try for abolition again?

One question that can't be avoided at this point, and must be taken into account when considering the options of the government, is just how feasible was it to abolish well in excess of 300 various hunts? One argument must be that any government with the desire to impose its will, especially one with majorities the size commanded by Blair, would have had little problem if they had been willing to weather the inevitable, albeit short-term, CA-orchestrated storm. Had the government ordered the disbanding of the hunts, the destruction of the hound packs, and the dismantling of the infrastructure, along with redeployment of hunt servants, it could have been achieved, though the constant television and press coverage of hounds facing execution, with accompanying photographs of heartbroken hunt masters burying the dead dogs, would have been very difficult for cabinet ministers to stomach, the more so with an election in the offing.

Maybe the sheer size of the fox-hunting industry makes any attempt to dismantle it next to impossible. Not to mention the composition of hunt enthusiasts that include half the Tory top brass, most of the British aristocracy, including a fair smattering of royalty, along with many of the masters of industry, before you even arrive at the thousands of assorted peasantry that make up the rank and file. For a weak-willed government, regardless of massive public support on the issue, along with the largest election majority in living memory, maybe it was just too tall an order.

What *could* have been achieved was the end of the two most hated blood sports: stag hunting and hare coursing. Had the Blair administration had the courage of its convictions then the three remaining deer hunt packs could have been disbanded, the hounds rehomed, or the pack converted to fox or drag hunt. The arrangements for any real, or imagined, contribution to deer control they made could have been taken over by such agencies as the Exmoor Society, National Trust, British Deer Society, or private deer stalking operations that operate in the area. The slightest of initiatives on Defra's part, which were sadly lacking on all fronts, could have solved the problem of the West Country deer control issue once and for all.

Regardless of the "what might have been" there were always going to be a number of blood sport fanatics who would attempt to ignore the law and push the legal definition of hunting, within the Act, to breaking point. The refusal of the Blair government to insist upon judicial redress for their actions would only later be seen as a bonus by these burgeoning rural freedom fighters. The eventual aim of the CA always was to see the Act repealed at the earliest opportunity following the future re-election of a Conservative government. David Cameron, during his campaign to become party leader, had promised "the hunting ban would be repealed immediately by the Conservatives if the party won power at the next general election". He stated the favoured option was a one-line Bill annulling the *Hunting Act* to be put through Parliament within a matter of days on a free vote. ***Note 2***

Kate Hoey, the pro-hunt Labour MP, spelled out not only the intention, but the strategy as well, on taking over as the CA's chairwoman in October 2005. "We will get it lifted. It may take a few years, but ultimately it will only take a very small one-clause Bill to go back to where we were before." This will be achieved by the hunts employing a mixture of drag and trail hunting, increasing intimidation of hunt monitors, and blatant disregard of the law to maintain the survival of hunting's infrastructure for the next few years.

The authorities have no intention of upholding the law, given that the police and courts, actively encouraged by an unwilling government, will vacillate at every occasion. The fact that the first two years of the Act has seen only two successful private prosecutions, regardless of many instances of serious violation, gives many on the anti side serious cause for concern. What will happen when the monitors from the LACS, HSA, IFAW, POWA and the various other groups that were formed to police the hunts, come to realise that, however much evidence they amass, the authorities will by and large fail to prosecute is open to question. The only certainty is that the hunt saboteurs will revert to their traditional role.

The abolitionists will also have to deal with a mainly hostile press that appears to offer ever more support for blood sports as time passes. While their tacit support is no doubt born of a desire to "bang the drum of political correctness", fearing to be accused of attacking minority issues, the mainly one-sided reporting in many papers tends to constantly cloud the issue, maintaining the spurious concept that the *Hunting Act* was about class warfare and not cruelty. In fact, the killing of animals by people who regard such activities as good fun is seen by many newspapers as perfectly acceptable. One of the better examples appeared in *The Times* on 29th October 2005 when it reported that a group of four- to fourteen-year-olds formed their own rabbit hunt following the ban, with twelve-year-old Tom Small quoted as saying: "We came up with this idea as a bit of fun. It's a way of enjoying ourselves now we can't hunt foxes anymore."

Though the implications of press bias can prove more serious, such as when Delly Everard, Wessex representative for the CA, was given free rein in the regional media in August 2005 to claim that "the contrast between the healthy deer maintained by deer hunting and the diseased and dying animals found on the League Against Cruel Sports so-called 'sanctuaries' could not be greater". This accusation was based on spurious statements from a disgruntled former LACS employee to the *Sunday Telegraph* in 2002 concerning the condition of deer on the Baronsdown sanctuary. Not only did the newspaper allow Everard to present these allegations as true, but also to intimate that the deer chased by the hunt were somehow different from the ones living within the boundaries of the sanctuary. The truth was that the claims of "diseased and dying animals" were disproved a considerable time prior to her outburst, while of course the deer that are hunted are the same animals that frequent the League sanctuaries.

It is of course an entirely different matter when the "boot is on the other foot", as the *Western Daily Press* found in August 2004 following the publication of a letter from M J Haines asking: "Why is it perfectly all right for hunts to chase to exhaustion, drag down and maul pregnant deer to death?" The CA Head of Media, Tim

Bonner, then wrote a letter threatening to take the paper to the Press Complaints Council (PCC) if it continued allowing readers to describe people who hunt as "barbaric and cruel", or "morons" inflicting "agony and terror" on wild animals. Tim Bonner's letter was followed by a faxed message from Simon Hart, Chief Executive of the CA, which also threatened to involve the PCC unless a "correction" and apology for having published the Haines letter was printed.

When the *Western Daily Press* refused to bow to what it described as "bully-boy tactics" Bonner went to the PCC accusing the editor, Terry Manners, of breaching the code of conduct by which all editors are bound by allowing "gross inaccuracies" to appear in the letters page. A full meeting of the PCC was held on 27th October 2004 during which the paper was fully exonerated, although Bonner did not agree with the adjudication. This led to another meeting of the PCC to review his further complaints, which were also rejected. Having considered the issue one of press freedom the newspaper felt more than justified in its full report published on 26th November to state "Mr. Bonner cannot complain that he has not had a fair hearing, but we fully expect him to disagree with the findings because we have come to expect him to insist that there is no truth but his truth..."

The experience of the *Western Daily Press* could go some way in explaining the marked decrease of informed opinions on the letters page of many smaller regional papers, who may well have found themselves under similar pressures. Most newspapers rigidly maintain the "we will continue to report the hunting issue even-handedly, without fear or favour from either side" approach, but the absence of hunting issues now appear markedly missing in many. The prize must go to the *Independent* (5th November 2005) who admitted: "This newspaper has long taken the view that pursuing foxes on horseback and then savaging them to death with hounds is an odd, perhaps even cruel, practice. But we have never believed it should be banned." So apparently on the grounds that this "badly drafted and illiberal law is now resented and ignored in equal measure" the killing of deer, hare, fox and mink for pleasure should be allowed to continue. Quite on what grounds apart from the apparently inalienable right to kill for fun, the *Independent* fails to tell us.

The almost total blackout of serious in-depth press coverage on the issues of hunting, coupled with fatuous reporting of ageing rock stars fronting pop concerts for the CA, laced with spurious statements from the likes of Delly Everard that their motives are based on "the principle of how a minority has been treated and that the government has introduced law on the basis of no evidence but through prejudice", only add to a sense of foreboding. The news that the National Trust has now instigated "a partial lifting" of the 1997 ban so as to allow huntsmen on to their land "to deal swiftly with sick and injured deer" appears to be the thin end of the wedge.

Unless some drastic reappraisal of the Act is undertaken by the government, which would seem most unlikely, then the *Observer's* Nick Cohen will be about right when he says the "ban will join Margaret Thatcher's prohibition of the promotion of homosexuality and Jack Straw's curfews for children in the list of fatuous legislation that was designed to make vocal minorities feel good and succeeded only in bringing the law into disrepute". But then again, there are those who think that may have been Tony Blair's plan all along?

Note 1. A good idea of how living creatures are perceived by the blood sport brigade can be perceived from a statement that appeared in the *Daily Telegraph* of 11th August 2007. In an article extolling the 12th August annual grouse slaughter (better known as the Glorious Twelfth) Jonathan Young wrote concerning "those born to the purple moors, men such as the van Cutsems, Sir Edward Dashwood and the Dukes of Norfolk and Northumberland. Their thoroughbred performance, expending just one and a half cartridges for every grouse killed, makes most of us look like donkeys. *But while they are essential for successfully harvesting the grouse crop, they rely on their grouse keepers to grow it."* (my italics)
Note 2. David Cameron's views on the *Hunting Act* were spelled out into a question and answer interview published in the 21st August 2007 *Western Daily Press.*

> Question: In view of your so-called modernisation of the Tory Party, why have you pledged to repeal the Hunting Act and restore the barbaric practice of torturing and killing our wildlife in a most inhumane fashion in the name of "sport"? Does this abhorrent pastime not belong in the Middle Ages?

Answer (Cameron): I am not a big fan of government banning things and I don't think that the current law is working or even credible. That is why I have said that a future Conservative government would make time available for a vote whether to repeal the hunting ban, but it would be a free vote for Conservative MPs.

I understand the strong feelings there are on both sides of the issue. But actually, trusting people to take more decisions themselves is one of the principles which I think modern political parties should hold dear. So I don't think allowing people a choice on whether they want to participate in hunting is incompatible with that modern approach at all.

Appendices

Appendix 1

To understand fully how deer and fox hunting are conducted it is necessary to describe the role of the persons involved in a day's "sport". The following descriptions are taken from the *HSA 1980 Tactics Booklet.*

THE HOUNDS. The hounds are not bred for speed but for stamina and scenting ability; so although the deer runs much faster than the hounds the hound's superior stamina will eventually enable it to kill the quarry. Different hounds in a pack may have different scenting abilities – some better on grass, others on the road, etc. Usually no feed is given to hounds the day before the hunt in order to increase their sensibilities. Most hounds only have a hunting life of six to seven years, after which they are either killed off or kept for breeding purposes.

THE MASTER. He is the one that has to dig into his pocket at the end of the year and pay the outstanding hunt debts. Hunting is so costly that some hunts have joint masterships, where up to four people may share the title and the overheads. The Master is responsible for controlling the kennels, the season's programme and for showing good sport. The Master in his turn is directly answerable to the hunt committee.

THE HUNT COMMITTEE. This is elected by the hunt subscribers, and will appoint the Master. They are responsible for the "hunt country" and overall policy. They are also responsible for raising the money to run the hunt, which includes the Master's pay and expenses, wages for hunt servants, food for hounds, maintenance of hunt premises and equipment, damage to non-hunt property, etc. The money raised will come from subscriptions, caps, Hunt Supporters' Club events, point-to-points, sales items and hunt races, etc.

THE HUNTSMAN. He "hunts" the hounds and is responsible for their welfare and for the cleanliness of the kennels. He is usually a professional (i.e. paid wages) but sometimes the Master will "hunt" the hounds, in which case the professional in charge is known as the Kennel Huntsman who will usually act as first Whipper-in.

THE WHIPPER-IN. This one acts as the right-hand man to the Huntsman. Some hunts have more than one; he may be a professional or an amateur (i.e. not paid wages). His job is to aid the huntsman, while hunting hounds, by keeping the pack together, collecting stray and struggling hounds, helping to sight the deer and keeping followers away from the hounds.

THE MOUNTED FIELD. These are the hunt followers who pay their annual subscriptions or "cap" (money paid on the day), which varies from hunt to hunt, in order to have a good ride across the countryside. They rarely see a kill or the hounds "working" as they are kept in strict control, either by the Master or a person known as the Field Master, who may be a Joint Master or an elected member of the Committee. About ninety per cent of the field are there for the social side of hunting and are more interested in whether Rodney knows that Cynthia is having an affair with Guy, than whether hounds have killed. The majority seem to care little for the technicalities of hunting and are the most likely to come out with clichéd defences of hunting, which they have learnt parrot-fashion.

The field are kept well in the background while hounds are "drawing" the animal to be hunted and it is not until the hounds are well on the scent that they are permitted to follow on. If it is a slow day – scent wise – the huntsman may come in for a great deal of criticism for "not hunting his hounds properly".

THE HUNT SUPPORTER (OR FOLLOWER). Each hunt has its own idiosyncratic followers, but generally this breed comes in three varieties:

MR THERMOS FLASK. He is out for a picnic with a difference. He can be seen leaning on his car, a thermos lid in one hand, a pair of binoculars in the other. His wife is usually passing sandwiches out of the window with a bored expression on her face and a travelling rug over her knees. He prefers to travel in convoy, following "holloas" rather than hounds. He thinks that he knows all about hunting but is quite often looking in the wrong direction.

MR BORED. He can be seen aimlessly driving about the lanes looking for the hunt (or possibly the infamous Guy), but not putting a lot of effort into it. He is always mildly surprised when he finds them. Don't be deceived by his posh accent, as he swears like a trooper.

MR HEAVY. He likes to travel in a gang, usually in a Land Rover. He is very boisterous, likes to force a confrontation, and will punch a suspected hunt monitor or saboteur at the drop of a hat. A few of Mr Heavy will always be present when the deer is killed and can always be relied upon to undertake any dirty work required.

HUNT SUPPORTERS' CLUB. Most hunts have their own club, membership of which is made up of car followers of the hunt. They will organise fund raising events throughout the year and supervise the point-to-point, etc.

FIXTURE LIST. The fixture list is drawn up before the season starts and is distributed to all members of the Supporters Club. The hunts follow a similar agenda each season, but much relies on crop rotation and deer distribution. It is possible to work out approximate dates and venues from old fixture lists, along with the projected route a hunted deer will take. Until the so-called hunting ban, the stag hunts would publish detailed accounts of the day's chase, from these could be worked out (with something like a seventy/thirty per cent success rate) the general area of where the deer would finish its run, quite often enabling the hunt saboteurs to keep ahead of the pack.

POINT-TO-POINT. A greater part of the hunt revenue comes from these events. The programme is organised and run by the hunt, in conjunction with the Jockey Club, and entries come from riders both inside and outside the hunt. It is a one-day event, usually in early summer.

HUNT BALL. An end-of-season jamboree, where the hunt master may rub shoulders with the hunt heavy and an odd magistrate or chief inspector of police can be spotted. It is at this event where Guy will most likely have his first serious encounter with Cynthia!

HOUND PARADES. These take place at local country shows and

serve to show the general public what fine fellows stag hunters really are.

PONY CLUBS. These are registered with the British Horse Society. Hunts will arrange a special meet during the season for children belonging to these clubs, which is a great way to foster indoctrination. It must be stressed that there are a number of pony clubs throughout Britain that *do not* have any affiliation to blood sports.

HUNT TERMINOLOGY.

ACCOUNTED FOR. The deer is never "killed" at the end of a hunt, always "accounted for".

ALL ON. When every hound in the pack is present, the whipper-in reports to the huntsman "All on".

ANTLERS. Red deer have antlers, never horns. The spread of a deer's antlers, or head, are comprised of "rights" and "points on top". The "rights" are called, from base of skull upwards, Brow, Bay & Trey, followed by the "points a'top". The main stem of an antler is the Beam. The most sought after hunting trophy would be a "twelve pointer", meaning the Brow, Bay, Trey, with three points on top on both antlers. For an example of what is considered a classic trophy head see the photograph of the Haddon Stag, killed in 1926, in E R Lloyd's *The Wild Red Deer of Exmoor.*

BAY. The cry of a hound, as in "the baying of the hounds'.

BAY, at. Stag nearing the end of a hunt, stands **at bay** to face the hounds

BEAT-UP. Hunted deer walking, trotting or swimming up-stream.

BELLING. The roaring made by a stag during the October/ November breeding season, or rut.

BREAK OUT. A hunted deer, when leaving a covert, is said to break out.

CAP. A donation on the day of the meet towards the upkeep of the hounds, or may be a special collection for broken fences, hunt servants, Countryside Alliance fighting funds, etc.

CAST. The action taken by the huntsman in directing his hounds to regain the scent, which has been temporarily lost.

CAST OFF. Releasing hounds at the start of a hunt.

CHALLENGE. When hounds, being cast off, find the scent and begin to cry, they are said to challenge.

CHANGE. When hounds quit a scent for a new one.

CHECK. Hounds are said to check when a scent is temporarily lost.

COUPLE. Correct hunting term for two or more (even numbered) hounds i.e.: ten couple indicating twenty hounds.

COUPLE AND HALF. Correct tern for three or more (uneven numbered) hounds, i.e. ten and half couple indicating twenty-one hounds.

COVERT. Pronounced "cover" and generally used to describe a wood, but also encompasses any type of habitation, where the hunted animal may lay for shelter.

CHECK. When hounds momentarily stop and sniff about for the scent.

DRAWING. The act of encouraging the hounds through the wood to search for the quarry.

FEATHER. A hound's feathers when he waves his stern before being certain of the scent.

FIELD. Collective name for the mounted followers of a pack of hounds.

FOUND. When hounds rouse the stag he has been found.

GIVEN BEST. To let the hunted animal escape, possibly to be hunted another day.

GIVES TONGUE. A hound gives tongue on picking up the scent during a day's hunting.

HARBOUR. Stag retiring to rest is said "to harbour".

HARBOURER. The member of the hunt whose job it is to find a suitable (warrantable) stag for hunting.

HEEL. Hounds are said to run "heel" when they go in the reverse direction taken by the hunted quarry.

HOLLOA. Pronounced "holler" and is a loud high-pitched screaming shout, often accompanied by a cap-holding arm, to point out the direction taken by the quarry.

MEET. Correct term for the meeting of hounds and riders prior to a day's hunting.

LINE. Route taken by the hunted animal.

NOTT STAG. West Country term for a male red deer that never produces antlers (in Scotland the term is"“hummel”).

PRICKET. Two year old male deer. The word “brocket” is also used to describe a two-year-old male red deer.

REWARD. The term used when giving hounds the deer’s entrails after a kill, i.e. to reward the hounds.

RIOT. Hounds are said to riot when they chase after animals other than the hunted ones, such as birds, cats, sheep, etc.

RUN TO HERD. Hunted deer joining up, or attempting to hide, in a herd of deer.

SCENT. The smell (or odour) made by the hunted animal and followed by hounds.

SCRATCH PACK. Pack of hounds made up of differing breeds, mainly used in deer hunting by the unregulated packs that hunt roe deer.

SPEAK. The sound made by a hound when hunting.

STERN. The tail of a hound.

TUFTERS. Name of hounds used to rouse the harboured stag.

TUFTING. Describes the method of rousing the stag by means of three or four couple of steady hounds known as tufters.

Appendix 2

Early Day Motions

An Early Day Motion, or EDM, is in practice a petition from MPs to the government. In theory, it is a motion for discussion in Parliament at an early day – or in plain language, when there is time for it to be heard.

The Parliamentary timetable is always crammed with business, so there is not normally the opportunity to debate Early Day Motions. However, it is a way in which MPs are able to express and gauge the popularity of an issue by the number of signatures which the motion attracts. For organisations like the LACS it is a way of demonstrating support in Parliament and an opportunity to present their case to MPs.

10 Minute Rule Bills

Under this procedure a Member of Parliament may move a motion at the start of the day's business on a Tuesday or Wednesday. The MP is allowed to make a short speech in favour of his or her Bill – a "ten minute" speech. Following this, another MP may rise to make an equally short speech against the Bill. The Speaker then puts the question that the MP be given leave to introduce the Bill. If this is successful, the Bill is presented for its First Reading, is printed, and joins the queue of Private Members Bills waiting for a second reading.

However, unless the government provides time for the Bill to be debated, it is unlikely that it will get any further. The Parliamentary timetable is always crowded and unless the government provides time for the Bill to be properly debated, any such Bill can be defeated by the objection of just one MP

In practice, the real importance of 10 Minute Rule Bills is that the House "divides" (votes) at a time when most MPs are present, thus giving an indication of support within the House of Commons. As the issue is debated early on a Tuesday or Wednesday afternoon, most MPs are able to be in the House. The Whips are not involved, so MPs have a free vote.

PRIVATE MEMBERS' BILLS

"Private Members" are MPs who are not Ministers or Shadow Ministers. Ten Fridays are set aside each session for Private Members' Bills and ten Fridays and four other days for Private Members' motions. The precedence for a Private Members' Bill is decided through a Ballot which is held in the first few weeks of the parliamentary session. Twenty names are drawn from the ballot and the successful Members of Parliament are invited to introduce their Bills within a few weeks of this. Once the names are known, the MPs are often subject to intense lobbying from a wide range of interest groups.

MPs will be aware that controversial Private Members' Bills very rarely become law. Exceptions to this are Bills with government support (one of the best examples of this being David Steel's *Abortion Law (Amendment) Act of 1967)*, but in reality this is very rare. A handful of determined MPs can give long speeches so that no vote is taken by the end of business for that day. The second reading debate has still to be concluded. Given the very limited amount of time available, it stands next to no chance of getting into its Committee Stage.

MPs who are selected in the ballot have to judge how best to use their place. They can use a high place to introduce non-controversial Bills and will stand a good chance of success, they can also introduce Bills which will have government backing (often in response to topical public concerns) but they can also use their place in the ballot to introduce Bills which they know will not proceed beyond Second Reading or Committee. They will not secure new legislation, but they will be able to use the time put aside for Private Members' Business to ensure a debate on the area of their choice.

HOW A BILL BECOMES LAW

First Reading: The Bill is introduced to the relevant House.

Second Reading: A debate on the general principles of the Bill.

Committee: The Bill is considered in detail, clause by clause, and amendments are made. In the Commons the Committee is made up of a group of MPs representative of their party's seats. In the Lords the whole House sits as a Committee.

Report: Amendments to meet points raised in Committee can be made. MPs who are not on the Committee also have the opportunity to propose amendments.

Third Reading: Where MPs or peers can express dissatisfaction or satisfaction with the Bill as amended.

Bills can be introduced through either House of Parliament, but must follow the same stages through both Houses. The Bill then passes through the same stages in the other House.

If the Bill is amended in the passage through the second House it must be returned to the House from which it originated for their consideration of the amendments which have been made. In theory both Houses need to agree to the Bill, including all amendments. In practice, the Lords will usually accept the Commons' decisions.

Once the Bill has received Royal Assent, it becomes an Act and comes into effect at a time specified in the Act.

Appendix 3

HUNT SABOTEUR TACTICS *(DETAILS FROM THE HSA TACTICS BOOKLET 1980)*

The best method of sabotage for a stag hunt (in fact the only one of merit) is to flush the woods in the area of the hunt on the night before. This should be done between midnight and seven in the morning. If the harboured deer has been scared off and all the other deer in the area are "jumpy", then it will take the hunt quite a time to find a deer that is worth hunting and by the time they do quite often it is late in the day. This method makes the harbourer's job very difficult and denies the hunt an easy find. When eventually a deer is found, the time can be fairly late in the day (one-two p.m.) and the hunted animal has a good chance of outrunning the hounds.

The night before a hunt the woods within a two-to-three-mile radius of the meet can be systematically cleared of all deer by stringing rook scarers at regular intervals and using whatever other means of noise making are at hand, such as bangers, exploding rockets, etc. To obtain the best results, four teams of two saboteurs, are required to work from the centre of the woods outwards. This method though simple, proved surprisingly effective on most occasions it was used. A variation was used with regard to hind hunting (as these are not harboured) that worked in much the same way. The night before a hind hunt the area of the meet is "soaked" with rook scarers, exploding rockets, etc. thus driving many of the hinds some distance away, causing long delays in the morning.

The problem with these tactics is trying to co-ordinate eight saboteurs blundering around in the dark woods (Exmoor and the Quantocks can be *very dark),* although it is possible for just two or three sabs who know what they are doing (and the area well) to prove quite disruptive. The cost can prove very expensive, considering the numbers of rook scarers and other explosives needed, while the noise is apt to awaken the local population and police.

During the actual hunt itself, calling the hounds with a horn, or voice, and shouting holloas can of course add to hunting time lost, but because of the nature of the terrain and the large number of supporters, it can prove much more difficult to sabotage a stag hunt in this way.

The normal tactics for disrupting the average mounted hunt (fox or deer) are as follows:

Keep one step ahead of the hunt. Spray (Antimate /sab special, etc) in the woods before the hunt arrives.

Confuse and distract the hounds by using whistles and calling the hounds by name (mimic the huntsman).

Pretend that you have seen the hunted animal and "holloa" (a sort of loud, high-pitched "woooo" yell). This will often bring the hunt and/or the hounds over. Then you have to either "disappear", or misdirect the hunt.

Use a hunting horn to bring some or all of the hounds over to you and away from the huntsman. Used in conjunction with hunting calls this is often very effective, it can be used to split the pack or to draw hounds off a scent. If the pack is split it may take the hunt a long time to reassemble the hounds. It is essential to learn the various horn calls, so as to use the correct call, when it will be most effective etc. If you can't blow a horn, try calling the hounds to you with a sharp "Yut", "Yut", "Yut" or "C'mon", "C'mon". There will be many local variations, so best to listen to the master's calls.

Hunts often lose hounds. If you see a stray one, take it to the local police station. It is worth detaching a sab from "active duty" for an hour or two for both the police and hunt staff love this "game".

In the exceptional circumstances, were the hounds get close to their quarry, and the sabs can intervene, use the tactics detailed below, but smoke bombs can also be used between the quarry and the hounds. This should not be done unless absolutely necessary.

If the hunted animal passes, it is important to remember that the scent will drift, therefore don't spray only just behind the animal, try to cover about ten yards either side and also downwind.

Keep spraying. Even if the hounds are not in sight they will often come up very suddenly. Try to call them off the scent, or use a hunting horn. Avoid driving them past the area you have sprayed or they will locate the scent of the hunted animal.

Remember, scent is wind-borne, so spray the air (fox height if a fox, deer height if a deer) as well as the ground. If in doubt, spray downwind from the actual path of the hunted animal.

If a hunted animal crosses a field it is better, if possible, to spray in the middle of the field as there is more likelihood of the hounds checking or splitting than at the edges where hedgerows and lack of wind will not dissipate scent. Ideally spray the middle of the field first and then the edge.

Spray the far side of the hedge rather than the nearside if the deer goes through a gap. (In this way if the hounds check, the huntsman is more likely to try casting on the nearside to relocate the scent).

If the hounds check and you are certain that the huntsman is trying to push them back, then call the hounds forward and vice versa.

If the hunt is drawing a wood with a road, railway, river or other obstacle at one end, they will enter the hounds at this end and flush away from the obstacle. Position yourself accordingly at the far end (do not block the hunted animals' escape route). If the animal breaks cover try to intercede between it and the hounds. Use sprays, horn and whistles. Try to call the hounds up.

Don't let the hunt get away while you argue with the supporters.

When following a hunt, always try and stick with the hounds and not the field (mounted followers).

Keep your OS maps with you at all times – they can be invaluable if you get lost and can give an indication of where the hunt is likely to go. They also show public footpaths, which is very useful when you fall foul of "Mr Get Orf My Land". It is also worth marking the projected run of a hunted stag (this is not so difficult if you study the detailed reports in the press) on your map, as quite often by this method it is possible to be in the right place at the crucial moment. (NB: Since the 2005 ban the stag hunt reports no longer appear in the local press.)

Ideally it is best to have sabs in the field, plus sabs in cars so that the hit can proceed on various fronts. Also the mobile sabs will sometimes be in a position to move everyone on to a better position – or arrive in the nick of time, like the 7th Cavalry, when the hunt heavies move in for the kill (of your mates).

The following article from the 20th October 1975 *Daily Mirror* by Donald Gomery entitled "THE STAG THAT GOT AWAY: How a night on the moors prevented death in the afternoon" will give an indication of not only the successful nature of stag hunt saboteur tactics, but a taste of the good fun we had at playing that "giant game of chess":

IAN PEDLER arrives on Exmoor shortly after midnight. "A good night for sabotage," he says, "No moon." By one o'clock, now wearing heavy clothes, he is stalking through the woods with three companions, two of them girls. They carry rook scarers – small "bangers" strung together to explode at half-hour intervals. And they have an oscillator which gives out a high-pitched note beyond the range of human hearing. But the oscillator – and the bangers – will be audible to deer in the woods. The noise should frighten them into moving away – out of danger.

For the Devon and Somerset Staghounds are meeting in the morning to hunt down the big red stags that roam Exmoor. Tonight the hunt saboteurs are doing their best to spoil their fun.

Already the hunt's "harbourer" has selected a strong animal capable of being chased for up to six hours. Tonight the saboteurs, travelling from wood to wood by car, are pitting their wits against the harbourer and the hunters. "It is like a giant game of chess," says Pedler, who has driven from Bristol to try to prevent a "kill".

Pedler, twenty-eight, an industrial consultant and former chairman of the Hunt Saboteurs Association, is founder of the Save Our Stags campaign, now in its first full season. He once had five front teeth knocked out with a riding crop. But that was at a foxhunt. "Stag hunting is much more dangerous," he says. "Passions run high on Exmoor." But he is against "violent" sabotage.

Farm men, supporters of the hunt, are also patrolling tonight, on the watch for saboteurs. There is always the risk of confrontation. Police cars are on the move. "That's the fourth we've seen," says Pedler edgily as he approaches Exford. "People must know we're coming." But he adds: "Don't think I treat this as an adventure. I can think of better ways of spending a night than creeping through the woods. Disruption of hunts is only twenty per cent of our work. The rest is mostly propaganda and bringing pressure on Parliament to outlaw hunting."

Pedler thinks the Devon and Somerset will hunt around the village of Dulverton. Lights in Dulverton homes flash on as exploding rook scarers waken villagers. "Sometimes," says Pedler, "we hang the 'rookies' outside the kennels. That keeps the hounds awake and tires them for the hunt." By five a.m. the night saboteurs' work is over. Pedler snatches a couple of hours sleep in his car, then confers with the main body of saboteurs who have now arrived, with fifteen saboteurs involved in this "strike".

Today ninety riders, including children, of the Devon and Somerset meet at eleven a.m. on Mounsey Hill, 1300 feet up on Exmoor, with about 300 followers in cars. Sir Bernard Waley-Cohen, a former Lord Mayor of London, and chairman of the hunt, is riding today. So too is Bob Nancekivell, the grand old man of West Country hunting, now in his seventies. *Nancekivell, always ready to argue the merits of hunting, talks affably with Pedler, whom he has known for years.* Pedler says, "He's the best advert blood sports ever had. An all-round gentleman."

The day is sunny as the hunt moves off. An hour passes, two hours. The hunt seems to be having difficulty "drawing" a stag. Then, on a distant hillside, a stag is said to have been sighted. "Beautiful he is, beautiful," says a local woman. A mass of cars makes for the scene. In front of me a saboteur's car sprays Jeyes Fluid to put the hounds off the scent. A saboteur is leaning out of the window, blasting on a hunting horn, hoping to draw riders and hounds away.

But down the Bridgetown-Exbridge road, the hunters sense their prey is near. They turn off, through the shallow River Exe, into a dense wood. Pedler stops his car. What sounds like a shot echoes from the wood. Unseen from the road, pandemonium breaks loose. The hounds are baying, whips are cracking and, above all, rises the savage "hallooing" of the hunters.

One of the girl saboteurs, twenty-seven-year-old Maralynn Jones, begins to weep. "They've killed him," she sobs. "The swine, the murdering swine." Pedler tries to comfort her. He too is upset and angry, believing there has been a kill.

From the road they can see nothing, though they know the scene well: *The stag turns at bay, it is shot by a humane killer, its throat is cut (to preserve the meat), then the body is gutted and the entrails thrown to the hounds.*

But they are wrong. Later they learn that one of the saboteurs has exploded rook scarers in the path of the hounds. The stag has escaped. The hunt goes on. But, by 4.30, rain begins to lash the moor. Despondent riders begin to make their way back to their horse boxes, back to their homes.

The Master of the hunt, Mrs Nora Harding, tells me later that she knows nothing of the incident in the woods. Saboteurs, she says, are "just a nuisance, not so much to the hunt, but to other people on the roads". She admits, "It was a very poor day," and blamed the stag. "He was an unenterprising stag, he wouldn't run straight. A twisty gentleman."

But the saboteurs record it as a victory. Another stag has been saved.

★

The same incident as told by Marley Jones (minus the "sobbing", which with the passing of over thirty years, I still recall as *Daily Mirror* "poetic licence" – for it was just not her style) to American journalist Odean Cusack:

We had been after them all day, and they had no luck at all. Then, about 3:30 p.m., we heard a shot coming from the woods where we knew the stag to be. I jumped from the car, which at the time was in the midst of many hunt supporters, and started to run down the road towards the wood. I was calling the hunters just about everything possible, while at the same time, Ian was holding me back, as he feared the redcoats would hurt me.

I remember thinking, "After all our efforts the bastards have still killed." It later turned out that some other saboteurs had been in the woods, seen the deer followed by hounds, and exploded some rockets to drive the stag away."

Appendix 4

The following report from the LACS *Exmoor Deer Hunting: Past and Present* pamphlet gives a clear indication as to the strategic importance of Alfoxton Wood as a deer sanctuary, while giving a good idea of the type of abuse suffered by Gladys and Lionel Mantle during their years as residents in Holford. It is worth pointing out that Alfoxton Wood surrounded the Mantles' house on three sides, with the front of the house facing Holford village green.

"Crowcombe Meet, Quantock Staghounds. 3rd October 1957. Extracts from Investigator's Report:

At 11 a.m. I went to Crowcombe. About 20 to 30 cars and Land Rovers already assembling and many mounted…The horses and hounds moved off…*On taking the Stowey Road I saw the stag cross over into the hills.* I followed the horses and hounds over the track…I waited on the hill and *they turned the stag, it having jumped over a fence and catching itself on the wire netting fence gate.* Mr Mantle saw the incident and warned the hunters to get off his ground. Mr Mantle walked across the small roadway by a parked Wolseley car. The driver, a hunt follower, started immediately throwing verbal insults at Mr Mantle accusing him of raising a hunting whip. Some 20-30 hunt followers also shouted filthy and dirty remarks at Mr Mantle.

After some ten minutes they moved off as the stag moved on. I made my way to the main road…I observed over 20 cars parked in a very dangerous bend along the road…a police car stopped in the bend…and warned all drivers to move on as they were causing an obstruction… I saw the hunt below Savages Farm 30 yards away. *The stag came out of Alfoxton Woods to the stream. It was turned by the hounds.*

Several hounds were close to it and one ran by its side snarling at the stag. The stag turned and ripped the side of the hound with its horns. The hounds were called away and the wounded hound put into a Land Rover. *The stag ran on to Alfoxton Wood again in the direction of Mr Mantle's ground. I saw it running below me along the stream. The hounds were close to it.* Time about 2.30 p.m. *The stag came up by the wall and the two cottages adjoining Mr Mantle's ground. It looked over the wall but was unable to jump due to 30 or 40 people gathered there... The stag stood at bay by a ledge below the wall.* A shot gun was produced but they afterwards decided not to shoot it.

It stood up and was sweating...and appeared very exhausted. Whilst the Hunt Master and followers decided on a course of action a number of people threw stones near the stag in hopes it would run off again. I heard a boy about seven say, "Oh Mummy, have they killed the stag? I want to see it." A number of other children were present. Whilst conversing the stag moved off again down into the wood. A man then shouted that Mr Mantle had impounded two of the hunt hounds on his premises. The hunt master, hounds and horsemen and some 50 followers all moved round the road facing Mr Mantle's ground. Mr Mantle was standing by his gateway in company with his wife and another grey-haired lady and another man. The crowd shouted at Mr Mantle and several swore at him and threw insults. One man laughed and another remarked that he had earlier told Mr Mantle to "Take two pills and go to bed." Another man said he "would like to drop a bomb on his house and his neighbours". They all held conversations about him.

The Hunt Master then conversed with Mr Mantle and accompanied him into the house. Some 15 minutes later they emerged from within with two hounds...I noted that Mr Mantle was very polite to the Hunt Master. The Hunt moved off with the Master. The followers still stood in small groups insulting Mr Mantle, who approached them in a very curt manner alone, expressing his views about the situation. He then wished them a good day and returned to his house."

Appendix 5

The cross-examination of Richard Prior during the 1985 High Court action between the League Against Cruel Sports and the Devon and Somerset Staghounds. This report from LACS *Cruel Sports* (Summer 1985), which in turn was based on the sixty-page court report and further fifty-seven pages of judgement:

The Hunt called a Mr Richard Prior as their own deer "expert". He has written books about deer and purports to be the greatest living expert on deer and their conservation and control.

What an unbelievably pompous and oily character he was. He dismissed Mr Yeo's evidence (the previous witness) as "rubbish" and went on. "Only the Devon and Somerset Staghounds ensure the survival of the deer on Exmoor, there is no other way of controlling them except by hunting." His superior air and dismissive pomposity would have irritated a saint and it clearly irritated Mr Blom-Cooper. The cross-examination was pure magic and, because it is on record, sworn under oath, has forever demolished any claim that Prior may make for being an "expert".

Mr Blom-Cooper asked: "Would you not agree that there are two perfectly reasonable schools of thought, one being that hunting is the best way to manage the (deer) herd, and the other being shooting?"

"No," replied Mr Prior. "The shooting argument is not reasonable."

Mr Blom-Cooper was off: "Surely red deer are controlled in Scotland, Norway, and Germany by shooting – is that not reasonable?"

"No," replied Mr Prior, "hunting is the best way to do it."

Mr Blom-Cooper – "These other people do not agree with you – they are reasonable people – can't you admit that although it is diametrically opposed to your view, nevertheless they are reasonable people?"

Mr Prior became flustered and appealed to the Judge for help. The

Judge said, "Simply answer the questions put to you and don't become flustered by Mr Blom-Cooper."

Blom-Cooper: "Have you ever hunted?"

Prior: "No"

Blom-Cooper: "Do you know anything about hunting?"

Prior: "No."

Blom-Cooper: "How can anybody who, on his own admission knows nothing about hunting presume to be an expert on the subject?"

No answer from Prior.

Blom-Cooper: "How many red deer are there on Exmoor?"

Prior: "I do not know."

Blom-Cooper: "You have stated to my learned friend (Mr Cazalet) that the herd was 1,200 strong, now you say you don't know. How do you explain the contradiction?"

Prior: "I was told it by the Devon & Somerset Staghounds, but I do not know myself."

Blom-Cooper: "Ah! You were told but you do not know. Very well, if the herd is 1,200 strong, as you have been told, what percentage of the herd would have to be taken out (culled) each year to maintain the herd at that size?"

Prior: "About thirty per cent."

Blom-Cooper: "In fact, about 350?"

Prior: "Yes."

Blom-Cooper: "Do you know how many deer the hunting people take out each year?"

Prior: "No"

Blom-Cooper: "If I told you that in 1983 they killed forty deer and that in 1984 they had an exceptionally high kill of eighty what would you say to that?"

Prior: "Nothing."

Blom-Cooper: "About 300 deer have to be killed by shooting because the hunt kill only about 50. Do you still maintain that hunting is the best method?"

Prior: "I have already given my answer to that question."

Bloom-Cooper: "Do you shoot deer?"

Prior: "Yes."

Blom-Cooper: "Do you enjoy killing deer?"

Prior: "I am not so bloodthirsty as I used to be so I don't shoot so much."

Blom-Cooper: "I asked if you enjoyed killing deer?"

Prior: "No, not anymore."

Blom-Cooper: "No more questions."

Appendix 6

The following article from the Winter 1988 (Issue No.9) *Wildlife Guardian*, by one-time LACS Administrative Officer Jessica Drewery, gives a good indication of John Hicks' life at this time:

"No matter how many stag hunts I patrol, I always feel a sickening knot in my stomach as I go to them," said John, "but as soon as I arrive, I'm all right – rather like actors feel before going on stage, I imagine."

John Hick, Sanctuaries Manager for the League Against Cruel Sports, was taking me to a stag hunt as I was curious to see what attraction it might have for its *aficionados.*

As we approached the meet, John observed that it was comparatively small – three Joint Masters of the Devon and Somerset Staghounds, about forty riders, one hundred hunt followers in cars and twenty-five to thirty on motor-bikes, all wearing outdoor gear – Barbours, wellies and woollies – which made me think that they were anticipating a day of strenuous exercise, an impression which was compounded by the fact that many of the cars had dogs in them and sported National Trust stickers.

John and I parked in the League sanctuary, Lowtrow Cross, which was diagonally opposite the meet. As we strolled over to watch the hunt taking the stirrup cup, John pointed to an ugly wire fence which added some three feet to the high bank adjacent to the sanctuary. The hunt had erected it to prevent their quarry from leaping to safety.

Our arrival caused a ripple of interest. John was obviously well-known, but no one greeted him. For his part, he nodded cheerily to one or two stony faces and then busied himself videoing the hunt setting off. This was to record the day and the time in case there was an incident later on (trespass for example). Soon after, the dogs were put away and the "tufters" (experienced hounds) sorted out. "Now comes a boring bit," said John. "There'll be a wait of about three-quarters of an hour while they select their quarry, so I'll drive you around the sanctuary and some of the locality." Meanwhile, hunt followers were getting into their vehicles and heading for likely vantage points. All day, as we drove around, we passed parked car lining the lanes, their occupants standing peering over a hedge, or out in a field, binoculars raised, scanning the countryside. We were more active, our purpose being to establish the most likely route of the quarry and if it was anywhere near a sanctuary or land banned to the hunt, to patrol that area to ensure that if the stag went onto it, the hunt did not follow. As the day progressed, I was impressed by John's intuitive knowledge of the quarry's movements. The hunt followers would have done better to follow him than jeer and gesticulate as he drove past since, today at least, he went unerringly to the very place where minutes later the hunt appeared.

By 11.30 a stag had been selected and the hunt was on. We drove up to a vantage point and stood on a bank overlooking a field which adjoined a coniferous wood. A few hunt followers arrived and stood nearby. We all stared at the empty field, listening. Suddenly a stag burst out of the woods and ran towards us, but on seeing a row of people, swerved away and disappeared. One of the followers leapt onto his motorbike and raced off to report that the stag had been sighted, another got out his CB radio and broadcast the information. Not long after, the dogs appeared and were set on the trail. John motioned to me and we drove off in the direction he expected the stag to take. Once more, we stopped and waited. Sure enough, riders soon came galloping down the road. John videoed them and as the third rider thundered past, I noticed her arm jerk as if it had caught on something – as indeed it had. An instant replay of the video revealed that she had deliberately struck John on the face with her riding crop. He was unperturbed by the incident, just disappointed that her face was indistinct on the video recording.

We drove on again – the traffic in those narrow country lanes at times rivalled the M25 – and got "stuck" behind a rider who, glancing back and recognising the League sticker mockingly prominent on John's vehicle, slowed her mount to a sedate walk in the middle of the lane.

John bore this with an air of resignation, but after a few minutes tooted gently at her, provoking a dismissive wave of the arm. He waited, then tooted again more loudly, whereupon the rider kicked her horse into a trot, jerked it over to the side and began shrieking louder than any car hooter at John for "frightening" her horse. The same rider later galloped past our parked vehicle and once again screamed angrily at John for his "bad manners". By now, we had driven around the same area four or five times and I was beginning to recognise some of the hunt followers, some of whom stayed put most of the day, while others moved around like us. The hunt seemed to spend as much time galloping down the roads as the cross-country bikes did charging across the fields.

Once more, we were in a traffic jam, third in line, behind a land rover full of children making faces at us. An elderly countryman came up to John and jabbed him angrily on the shoulder, "Next time you tell me to get out of a field, I'm going to hit you," he promised. "Why not do it now?" suggested John. "That'll get the court case over sooner and you might be out for Christmas." Somewhat put out by John's helpfulness, the old man tried again, "You've no right to stop me having a piss."

"Of course not, but if you're trespassing on my land, I have every right to ask you to leave immediately," smiled John. This response infuriated the old man and after a couple of uncomplimentary sentences he departed, cursing. We were still in the traffic jam, so John decided to take action. The leading car had stopped in the middle of the lane, but when John walked up to it, the driver got out and began an elaborate charade of examining a rear tyre, letting out some air and getting out a tool box. Several hunt followers were highly entertained by this and encouraged him to continue. Calmly, John videoed the performance, informing the joker that he would be reported to the police for deliberately causing an obstruction on the highway and then returned to his car. "Well," he said, "it's their day out he's spoiling. I'm quite happy to sit here all day – it saves petrol at least." I was less enthusiastic as it seemed we might be doomed to do just that – the people ahead clearly enjoying the fun – but other hunt followers were becoming impatient. Believing John to be the cause of the hold-up (as he was, indirectly) one treated him to a volley of abuse. "If I didn't already have a conviction" he added, "I'd land one on you."

"I'm sorry, but as you can see, I'm not responsible for the delay," said John. "Your friend up there is pretending to have a puncture." Still cursing us, the hunt follower persuaded his colleague to move on, for which assistance John thanked him warmly.

Once again we drove, stopped, looked and listened. I had been warned not to enter any fields which were not League land or banned to the hunt. Passing a banned field, John told some supporters standing in it that they were trespassing. This provoked a diatribe about the value of hunting and vileness of hunt saboteurs. John's attempts to point out that the League and the hunt saboteurs were separate organisations were ignored as the speaker became more and more heated and his colleagues chipped in. The video whirred into action as they refused to move off the land. "The bastard – we ought to do him over," muttered one. "We did him over a couple of years ago, and it's time we did it again."

More time passed with us driving around, inspecting fresh hoof prints on banned hand and checking the whereabouts of the hunt, until about 4.30 when John said he was sure the hunt was over. He spotted a couple of regulars leaving and so we went back to the meet and he asked a ticket collector (*author: I presume she means the person who collects the daily cap)* what had happened. As John had guessed, the stag had entered land banned to the hunt, and the hunt had failed to drive it out. So we too went home, with a last glance back at some hunt followers still standing on the bank gazing into the distance.

"Well, did you enjoy it?" asked John. I said I thought it was interesting for me, but I couldn't imagine that it was anything but monumentally boring for most of the hunt followers, many of whom cannot have seen anything much all day. It seemed as if the stag had been hunted by CB radio and motorbike. I could understand that the riders might enjoy a "mystery" gallop, but then the entire day seemed to be a mystery to many of them who galloped up and down tarmac lanes looking for the others. As for the "upper class" image of the hunt, that myth was well and truly scotched for me, listening to the coarse language of the thugs who threatened John. I wondered how John coped with the overt aggression unremittingly directed at him, but he just shrugged it off. Apparently, he had been dragged from his car and severely beaten (just as I had overheard), but he expressed admiration for the courage of those landowners who banned the hunt. He said they were put under tremendous social and economic pressure as a result. He at least was only doing his job and he felt that it was important that the stag had one person on its side!

Appendix 7

In 1982 the National Trust issued a statement regarding its policy on blood sports; this recorded a long-standing practice and was further expanded in November 1988 in the Council statement in response to the resolution proposed at the 1988 AGM which sought to prohibit all fox, deer, hare and mink hunting with hounds on National Trust land. In the Spring 1989 issue of the Trust's magazine, the policy was again stated as follows:

> "Since its foundation in 1895 the Trust, very dependent on the goodwill of country people, whether as donors, neighbours, tenants or staff, has adopted the following practice on field sports. Where hunting is rooted in local tradition, does not contravene the wishes of former owners of land and is not harmful to nature conservation, public recreation or its tenant's rights or interests, the Trust has allowed it to continue. In some instances, where land was let on a full agricultural tenancy prior to Trust ownership, the contract precludes the Trust from having any say in the matter.
>
> "Because the disturbance caused by field sports can be incompatible with the protection of rare animals and birds and fragile habitats, there are a number of places where the Trust forbids them permanently or at sensitive times of the year.
>
> "For some properties donors have recorded their wish that hunting should not be permitted. This is the case on the Arlington Court Estate in North Devon. Conversely, there are properties where donors have expressed the wish that hunting should continue; on the Holnicote Estate, for example, on Exmoor."

Appendix 8

The 1990 National Trust resolution proposed by Doreen Cronin and Diana Wilson was passed in the following terms:

> "This meeting recommends to the Council of the National Trust that wherever the Trust has the right to decide whether or not hunting should be permitted on land it owns, the hunting of deer with hounds should be prohibited from 1st August 1991; and, notwithstanding any expressed wishes of a donor for hunting to continue, where any donated land has subsequently been designated as a Site of Special Scientific Interest that the hunting of deer with hounds should be prohibited."

Appendix 9

Recommendations of the Bateson Report. Chapter VI:

This chapter draws together conclusions, in relation to the terms of reference about suffering as a welfare factor in red deer culled by different methods. My first point is that , although it would have been possible to have done a great deal more work, the study has generated a clear-cut coherent body of data.

It is clear that lengthy chases in the course of hunting with hounds impose on red deer stresses that are likely to cause great suffering. These hunts cause red deer to experience conditions that lie far outside those conditions that would normally be experienced by the species living in a natural environment. Therefore, hunting with hounds raises very serious issues about the welfare of the deer.

The stresses on the deer are at least at the same level as those of the injured deer in our study, which were put down because of their injuries. The duration of these stresses, and associated injuries, is in no sense fleeting, the minimum period being usually measured in hours in deer killed by the hunt and probably much longer in those that escape after being hunted.

We were not able to judge the extent to which there is, in the long-term, recovery from the stresses of hunting by those deer that escape from the hunt. Even so, possible ultimate recovery, in whole or in part, for most or some of these deer, is not a reason for ignoring the effect of the chase. If a man beats his dog causing it injury, the fact that the dog may recover does not justify the beating or the injuries.

I acknowledge that the degree of suffering, which I regard as unacceptable, may not occur in every deer that is hunted. Even so, it is not possible to say in advance of a hunt whether an unacceptable level of stress is likely to occur. It is therefore necessary to act on the basis that the potential for an unacceptable level of suffering arises in any hunt.

If deer are to be culled, the only realistic alternative to hunting red deer with hounds is to shoot them. As explained in Chapter Two, most of the culling of red deer which occurs on Exmoor and the Quantocks is already carried out through shooting, whether by professional stalkers or others. I am clear, from the evidence discussed in the two preceding chapters, that the level of individual suffering from this form of culling is, on average, much less than with hunting.

Of the 130 or so red deer killed annually by the hunts, I believe that all experience an unacceptable level of suffering because of the stresses and strains put on them. At least a further 100 that escape would present a serious welfare problem because of the distance travelled before they escaped. This makes a conservative total of 230 deer a year presenting a serious welfare problem. If the 130 or so animals killed by the hunts were culled by stalkers instead, then on the basis of the five per cent wounding estimate we obtained, less than seven deer would present serious welfare problems because of their injuries. These are broad calculations but the greater than thirty-fold reduction in numbers of suffering animals ought not to be ignored.

I therefore conclude that the level of total suffering should be markedly reduced if hunting with hounds was ended. Hunting with hounds can no longer be justified on welfare grounds given the standards applied in other fields discussed in Chapter Three, such as the transit and slaughter of farm animals, the use of animals in research and so forth. This is the key conclusion of my report to the Council of the National Trust. I accept that the National Trust will want to weigh this conclusion against other issues, including their wider responsibilities, considerations about the social and economic benefits of hunting and the problems of conservation. On the final point, I believe, it is proper for me to relate our concern about welfare to some wider issues of deer management.

Deer management was considered in depth in the 1993 Savage Report on Deer Management. I recognise that even if a ban on stag-hunting were to be imposed on National Trust land alone, the result might nevertheless bring an end to all hunting of red deer, at least on the Quantocks. It has been put to me that the lack of hunting would disorganise the management of red deer, since much of the management is co-ordinated by, or depends on the co-operation of, the Hunts; the result could be an increase in indiscriminate and inexpert shooting which might increase the proportion of deer injured from shooting and also reduce the overall red deer population on the Quantocks. Further, the Hunts would no longer be available to help find and put down injured deer.

I recognise the risks of a sudden implementation of a ban on stag-hunting on National Trust land and fully endorse the need set out in the Savage Report for an effective system of deer management to control numbers and to supervise organised culling programmes. An efficient wardening system to deal with injured deer would need to be part of this scheme. It may be argued that any ban on hunting over National Trust land should await such a new management programme. I note that this could be a recipe for unacceptable delay in reducing a serious welfare problem and add the comment that it may be necessary to consider facing the risk of a temporary decline in the deer population, especially on the Quantocks, on the basis that this would provide a stimulus for the creation of effective local deer management programmes.

I believe that the problems of inexpert and unorganised shooting could be greatly reduced if, as already under discussion in Scotland, stalkers were obliged to put identifiable tags on each carcass shot so that each carcass could be traced through game dealers. A ban on night shooting would also further reduce the incidence of wounding.

Because the evidence points so strongly to the fact that all hunting with hounds has the potential to cause an unacceptable level of suffering in red deer, I have not felt it necessary to advise the Trust on how hunts might be limited to particular sexes or age classes of deer or particular times of year.

My remit was confined to red deer on "National Trust properties on Exmoor and the Quantocks". However, scientific evidence may have general validity. If the findings of this study are accepted, the implication is that hunting with hounds can push red deer beyond acceptable physiological and behavioural limits and in so doing is likely to cause considerable suffering. Before the study was carried out, it was possible to argue that views about suffering in hunted deer were subjective and open to debate. This position is, I believe, no longer tenable. Both those who hunt red deer and those who are concerned more widely with the welfare of these animals will need to take the new evidence into account. That having been said, I repeat that extending the results of this study to the hunting of other species with hounds would need careful evaluation of the various differences between red deer and other species.

Appendix 10

FONT members standing for 1998 NT election:

Robert Waley-Cohen. Mentioned in his NT biography that he "enjoys holidays in Exmoor", but failed to reveal that he was a board member of the Countryside Alliance and hunts with the DSSH. His proposer was Nicholas Serota, Director of the Tate.

Lucinda Green. Mentioned that she is an Olympic Gold medal winner, but not that she hunted with the DSSH. She was proposed by Lord Mancroft, board member of the Countryside Alliance, and was seconded by Sir Robin Dunn of the DSSH.

Hugh Van Cutsem. Mentioned that he was a farmer, but failed to reveal that he was a founder and council member of the CA.

John Jolliffe. Wrote for *The Spectator.* Described his special interests as "gardening and trees". His sister hunted with the DSSH.

The Hon George Lopes. Deer stalker. His wife hunted with the DSSH. He was proposed by former Foreign Secretary Lord Carrington and seconded by actor Jeromy Irons.

Peter Walwyn. Famous racehorse trainer. Hunted with the Vale of White Horse fox hunt and enjoyed stag hunting.

Henry Keswick. Former proprietor of *The Spectator* and Director of the *Telegraph* group. His wife hunted. He was seconded by Jeremy Brown, paid up member of the DSSH.

Timothy Myers. He was seconded by Catherine Nicholls, a paid up member of the DSSH and Master of the Dulverton West Foxhounds.

Appendix 11

Estimates of deer numbers on Exmoor and the Quantocks.
Conservation and Management of Deer on Exmoor and the Quantocks:
The Southampton Report: Jochen Langbein & Rory J Putman. 1992:

"Previous objective study into the ecology and management of deer populations in the West Country has been minimal, with just a single one-year scientific study into density and habitat use of red deer in a small part of the Exmoor area (Malcolm et al.,1984), and one recent, yet unpublished study on the Quantocks (Winder and Chanin). Given this scarcity of previous objective data, we concentrated in our work on obtaining our own assessment of current deer numbers, distribution, and population structure against which we might assess such other objective, subjective or anecdotal data as we could obtain from published and unpublished sources."

Results: "Visual census methods enabled us to establish a *minimum* estimate of current end of winter population numbers at 2100 red deer based on the Exmoor National Park and 650 within the Quantocks AONB. Visual censuses unless undertaken in entirely open country are notorious for producing significant underestimates of the true population number. Our second, indirect approach based on assessment of deer faecal accumulation suggest that true winter population numbers are likely to be as high as 4750 red deer within the Exmoor National Park, with probably a further 1,000 living within 10 km of its southern and eastern boundaries. Recent estimates, again based on study of dung accumulation, carried out by Exeter University, suggest that current populations within the Quantocks AONB number at least 800-900."

The Red Deer of Exmoor: Conservation of a Population (Peter Donnelly, *Exmoor Review,* 2004):

"Over the past decade the deer population on Exmoor has been counted annually by teams of local deer-orientated people. The 1997 census recorded a population of 2,800 Red deer. (The 2003 census recorded 3,000: this suggests that the population *could* be up to 4,000!) It has been demonstrated time and again that visual censuses will always be an underestimate. Counting deer is notoriously difficult, especially in a mixed landscape with woodland, farmland and open moorland as on Exmoor. Here scientific surveys have indicated that these visual counts account for, on average, some 75% of the resident deer population. It is also worth noting that deer numbers on Exmoor have been rising annually for the past ten years, despite a cull estimated to be between one thousand and twelve hundred deer each year."

Annual deer count results 1991-2005 undertaken by the Quantock Deer Management & Conservation Group (Secretary: Dr Jochen Langbein)

1991 (753), 1992 (655), 1993 (610), 1994 (676), 1995 (535), 1996 (381), 1997 (482), 1998 (534), 1999 (802), 2000 (745), 2001 (no count), 2002 (893), 2003 (819), 2004 (881), 2005 (958)

Quantock Wildlife: Its Ecology and Conservation. Pat Wolseley and Ernest Neal, Somerset Trust for Nature Conservation, 1980:

"With the extermination of the wolf, man has largely determined deer numbers. The deer are hunted regularly by the Quantock Staghounds, many of the followers being farmers who tolerate the winter damage to crops while enjoying their hunting. The population is maintained at around 250-300 deer."

E R Lloyd *(The Wild Red Deer of Exmoor,* 1975):

"The question of the number of deer on Exmoor at any given moment is a fruitful subject for discussion and some very varied estimates are given. As mentioned above, the deer is a woodland animal, so with the best of intentions no figure can be more than an informed guess, but it is generally considered that the total in 1975 lay somewhere between six and eight hundred."

Waddy Wadsworth and Dick Lloyd (*Vive La Chasse,* 1989):

"The total number of deer killed by the three hunts does vary depending on the severity of the winter, but the usual number is somewhere between 150 and 200. In addition there must be allowed a margin of a very small number legally shot of which there is no record and an infinitely variable number removed by poaching. I suggest that neither of these activities remove a significant total and the estimates, particularly of poaching depredation, are frequently wildly exaggerated. A recent survey in the Devon and Somerset country suggests that the total number of deer is about 1,000 and that there are another 500 in other parts of the West Country."

Noel Allen (*Exmoor's Wild Red Deer,* 1990):

"The greatest density (of red deer) is in South West England with about 500 on the Quantocks , 1,500 within the Exmoor National Park, and some 400 immediately south of the border towards South Molton and Tiverton. The problem today and perhaps casting a shadow over the future is the indiscriminate shooting of deer for venison."

Appendix 12

The following article (8th February 2005) by Martin Cassidy, BBC Northern Ireland rural affairs correspondent, explains the workings of the modern County Down Staghounds.

"It is a peaceful scene with the rolling farmland of County Down bathed in a weak winter sun. The hedgerows are frost burnt and bare. This is the hunting season. Far below, the horses and hounds are moving off. The bright red jackets are clearly visible as a group of 20 or more mounted figures take to the fields. The hounds fan out and in just a few minutes they are on to something. From a wooded field boundary their quarry breaks cover – it is a stag.

"Hearing the baying pack and the thunder of hooves, the deer flees. It is heading for higher ground and the safety of the distant Dromara hills. If it escapes the hounds, it must use this early speed to give the dogs the slip. And indeed its early speed is too much for the pack. Head raised like a steeplechaser, it clears a tall hedge cleanly. The deer gallops across a grass field, opening up a gap with the chasing pack. But the advantage proves short lived. Ten minutes later and the stag is already flagging.

"The pack is running it down and once again the deer tries to out-jump the dogs, clearing a fence into a garden. But the pack pours over and through the wire as it continues its pursuit. Now there is the bizarre sight of stag and following pack running across a lawn, within just a few yards of someone's front door. Back into open fields now and the stag's early speed has gone. The hounds are relentless. Instinctively, the deer knows its best chance of escape now is through a field boundary – but the thorn hedge represents a formidable barrier to a tiring stag. The hounds are all around it but are still wary about moving in on an animal of this size. Exhaustion of the quarry is their primary hunting strategy. Surrounded, the deer forces itself through a narrow gap in the thorns.

"The spectacle draws crowds of onlookers – the narrow roads are jammed as people vie for the best view. But we too have been spotted and the hunt seems to be uncomfortable being watched by the media. There is something of a stand-off now, some 40 minutes into the hunt. Hunt organisers say they are going to call off proceedings if we don't withdraw. We have asked for an interview with the master of the hunt. We wanted them to explain exactly what was happening. But they declined. Instead they referred us to the umbrella group for field sports – the Countryside Alliance.

"Ronan Gorman of the Alliance tells me stag hunting is a 'non-lethal way of dealing with the problem of a rapidly increasing deer population. There are problems with forestry, damage to crops, road accidents and deer need to be moved on from problem locations and stag hunting does that very well.'

"But while the Countryside Alliance is keen to emphasise that at the end of the hunt, the stag is free to go, animal welfare campaigners are not impressed with the argument. Stephen Philpott of the Ulster Society for the Prevention of Cruelty to Animals says the hunt needs to be viewed from the stag's point of view. 'That animal is pursued over a great distance by one of its most feared predators, a pack of hounds,' he says. The USPCA maintains that the deer is stressed and says that stag hunting is unacceptable. Stephen Philpott adds that 'by the very definition of the Welfare of Animals Act it is causing unnecessary suffering, therefore it is cruel'.

"Back in Dromara, the County Down Staghounds are packing up for the day. The hounds have been called off and many of the riders have dismounted and are unsaddling. It has been a frustrating day for them due to unwanted media attention. Today there is an early escape for the stag. But the County Down Staghounds will be back to pursue a sport which it has been pursuing for more than 150 years."

The Southern Ireland Ward Union Staghounds carry on much as before. A fact sheet issued by the Irish Council Against Blood Sports in 2006 gives an up-to-date picture.

"Carted deer hunting is a cruel 'sport' which causes horrific suffering to defenceless red deer. It subjects the deer – captive bred specifically for the abuse – to a distressing ordeal, leaving them exhausted, injured and severely at risk of dying from heart failure.

"The red deer used are taken from a herd which is privately owned by the Ward Union hunt. This hunt is based in Dunshaughlin, County Meath.

"Every Tuesday and Friday between November and mid-March, two deer (stags and hinds) are taken out in a cart to a hunt location. They have their antlers sawn off to prevent injuries being caused to the dogs and the manhandlers who wrestle them to the ground at the end of each hunt.

"One deer is turned out of the trailer, and forced to run. The other is kept as a spare in case the first deer is caught too soon. During the hunt, the deer is at risk of sustaining injuries as it frantically tries to outrun the horseback riders and the pack of dogs. Being in unfamiliar terrain, the deer has an extremely hazardous route ahead. Crashing through hedges, over walls, across busy public roads and even into lakes and rivers, the terrified creature does everything it can to stay ahead.

"A Department of Agriculture Veterinary Inspector who monitored a Ward Union hunt wrote: 'One stag was seen attempting to jump a very high fence and getting his front legs caught on a top strand of barbed wire and hanging thus suspended for some seconds before his struggles and/or weight tore him free.' He also outlined how a stag 'having run at least 8 miles in 90 minutes showed extreme physical distress, panting through its mouth and with a lather of white foam around its muzzle.'

"Reported fatalities highlighted how one deer died of an aneurysm while another was 'accidentally' choked to death during capture. In a suppressed 1997 document (only obtained by ICABS in Autumn 2003), another Department of Agriculture Veterinary Inspector concluded that the deer hunt was 'inhumane'.

"Yet, no action was taken to stop the hunt which, we contend, is in breach of the 1911 *Protection of Animals Act*. We have appealed to the Minister for Agriculture, who is well aware of the cruelty involved, to follow the example of her counterparts in Northern Ireland who outlawed a similar hunt, The County Down Staghounds, in 1997. It was ruled that the deer used by that carted deer hunt were domestic animals and thus covered by animal welfare legislation."

Appendix 13

Letter sent to regional newspapers on 10th May 2001 by Graham Sirl.

"Having recently left the League Against Cruel Sports after nine years as head of West Country operations, I now feel I should put forward my own views on deer hunting with hounds.

"I have not changed my view that hunting with hounds is unnecessary and involves cruelty to the individual deer being hunted. However, I do now believe that hunting with hounds does play an integral part in the management system for deer on Exmoor and the Quantocks. In some instances, hunting in general is a constitutive part of West Country rural community life. Those who do not acknowledge this to be true, or similarly choose to ignore same, are turning their backs on an argument they know is difficult to win.

"Before going to the West Country, I had followed deer hunting in the New Forest. There this form of hunting was truly carried out for recreational purposes. Management was carried out by Forestry Commission keepers and the use of the rifle. Following the Commission's ban on deer hunting on its land, the forestry authorities increased cull figures. This was not surprising as they do regard deer as pests. In the West Country, more deer are shot than killed by hounds. Take away hunting and the management system will break down.

"Over the years, and many meetings with landowners and others, I have come to the conclusion that, in the event of a total hunt ban, the deer population will be decimated. This view is shared by many, including some who remain independent on the hunting issue.

"As well as the 50-plus registered stalkers already operating on Exmoor, a ban will attract an influx of inexperienced guns from outside the area. The end result will be a significant drop in deer numbers, together with an increase in injured and wounded animals. Because of landowners such as the National Park and the National Trust, the deer will survive, but it will take many years before the population recovers to today's figures.

"Sadly, a ban on hunting will not save one animal's life. The current Bill before Parliament will do little for animal welfare. It seeks the abolition of one method of killing, hunting. Unfortunately, it still leaves many more, which will continue to be used for so long as they are legal. Greater protection is needed for the quarry species, therefore prior to, or following a ban, amendments must be made to the Wild Mammals Protection Act 1996. Failure to bring such protection will inevitably lead to an increase in activities such as fox, deer, and hare drives. This will be nothing short of unmanaged, indiscriminate slaughter.

"Deer must become an asset to the local community via tourism, not to be hunted, but to be viewed and photographed by visitors and residents alike. Finally, I would urge all those currently involved in deer management, on both sides of the argument, to sit down and plan for the future. Hunting as we know it could be finished. It is up to you to seek and find the humane alternative before it is too late."

In fairness to Graham Sirl it must be pointed out that the author of this book also sent a "round robin" of a similar vein to the regional press back in April 1983:

"Now that the Labour Party has finally announced its intention to abolish all blood sports following a possible victory at the next General Election, I wonder what alternative form of deer control will be forthcoming for the West Country. For while it is perfectly true to say that an end to fox and hare hunting will make little overall difference to the number of these animals killed annually, the same cannot be said with regard to deer hunting.

"To anyone who has been involved with deer control in this area it is an unmistakable fact that a blanket abolition of deer hunting with hounds, backed up without a serious alternative, will be disastrous. Quite simply the people who live in stag hunting country will no longer have a reason to tolerate the deer, or the damage they cause, and will decimate this unique collection of animals, leaving nothing but a few scattered individuals.

"Therefore, a workable compromise has to be found that will safeguard the interests of both farmers and deer. There are numerous ways. The government could pay the farmers for not killing deer, in much the same way as they are now paid for not ploughing the open moorland. A government financed Deer Control Team could be appointed with a mandate to maintain the herds at the acceptable level of around 1,000 deer. Financial inducement could be offered to the British Deer Society to appoint and operate a deer control team in the area. Funding could be made available to the Exmoor National Park Authority and Somerset Trust for Nature Conservation to undertake such a control programme.

"All these ideas, feasible though they seem, are fraught with many difficulties and would encounter considerable opposition, simply because little or no deer damage compensation would be forthcoming. Consequently, it would appear that any type of control venture would have to prove self-financing and that the funding would have to come from within the area of control itself.

"Regrettably there would seem to be only one suitable solution to this problem and that is the possibility of a limited stalking operation. A number of professional stalkers would have to be appointed (all proficient in the use of fire-arms and deer management) who would supervise all shooting. The stalkers would pay a fee for the 'privilege' of hunting an Exmoor deer (in much the same way as happens in Scotland) and from this fee, coupled with the sale of the venison, would come the salaries of the professional stalkers and compensation payments for the farmers.

"Landowners could be encouraged to harbour a limited number of stags on their land and to inform the stalking centre as to their numbers and size, in much the same way as they now do for the stag hunt."

While it is true that the passage of over twenty years had modified my views on the practically, or morality, of a deer stalking programme it remains my belief that it is essential for a structured deer management scheme to be formulated, and implemented, without delay. The way forward, in lieu of stalking, would be to capitalise on the present Exmoor safaris, encouraging the photographing, rather than the killing, of deer. I also believe that the failure of the Blair government to offer post-ban protection to the red deer could still prove disastrous, and that this serious defect in the *Hunting Act 2004* must be addressed as soon as possible.

This same argument was reinforced by Peter Donnelly writing in the 2004 *Exmoor Review:*

"In his Annual Report to the Exmoor Society in 2002 the Chairman, Michael Hawkins, stated: 'The Society has responded to the Government's invitation during the (hunting with dogs) consultation process. At the heart of our response is the conviction that to remove the present system of control without putting in place an equally effective form of management would be irresponsible and would put the Red deer herd at risk...any such management would be worthless if not backed up by enforceable legislation monitored and administered by a publicly accountable body.'

"Simply put, if hunting Red deer with hounds is banned in the future, many farmers and landowners will be unable or unwilling to afford to play host to considerable numbers of deer feeding on their crops without any form of *quid pro quo.* (One Red deer eats as much as at least two sheep.) Therefore if the presence of deer at their current numbers cannot be sustained the deer population on Exmoor will be reduced drastically, by fair means or foul!

"Irrespective of whether hunting deer with hounds becomes outlawed, for its future well being the deer herd needs to be cared for in a carefully planned and co-ordinated manner under a Management Plan. This can only be achieved with the full co-operation of all those on and over whose land the deer live and travel.

"If the hunting bill goes through, banning deer hunting, there will be those who, for whatever reason, will attempt to kill all the Red deer on Exmoor. They will not succeed. Yes, in the short term the population will be savagely reduced and thrown into even greater imbalance, but those who actually care for the deer, as well as those who provide 'sanctuaries' will ensure that Red deer remain on Exmoor for the foreseeable future.

"The wisdom of Solomon and the patience of Job are the pre-requisites for the person who will someday draw up a management plan which will achieve the long-term well-being of the Red deer of Exmoor, whatever the outcome of the deliberations of the Palace of Westminster."

Much the same argument, coupled with a somewhat "Utopian" vision of the future, was expounded by the hunt supporter turned anti Graham Floyd in his book *All His Rights.*

"Conservationists are often reminded by the blood sports lobby of what happened to the red deer during the mid 18th century when stag hunting on Exmoor failed and with it deer numbers sunk to low levels. The Exmoor of today is a very different place, a 'National Park' and despite most of the land remaining in private ownership, there is good reason today to be very optimistic over the chances of a number of red deer being around for a very long time. The National Park Authority itself owns around 6.8% of the land, a further 10% is under the control of the National Trust another large landowner is the League Against Cruel Sports. None of these landowners would ever adopt a policy of complete eradication of deer.

"76.8% of Exmoor remains in private ownership, of which there are likely to be many who would be sympathetic to the deer, even without hunting. Another significant sanctuary will be Exmoor's wonderful wild and inaccessible coastline. The most likely outcome of a deer hunting ban in Parliament, without legislation passed to assist in management and preservation of this wild animal, is a few fragmented pockets of wild red deer with a low number of stags. They may well survive well into the next century and beyond thanks to a few friends, but mainly due to inaccessible habitat coupled with the deer's cunning powers of survival against all the odds and under intense pressure.

"In an ideal world it would be nice to read a naturalist's report on the wild red deer of Exmoor in, say 2050. I hope it might read something like this:

" 'Despite the abolition of hunting deer with hounds, a sound working system of deer management and conservation was put in place to protect the wild red deer of the West Country. The deer on Exmoor are today highly regarded as an asset to the Park and have been given lawful wildlife status. Long gone are the days when they could be treated as a pest. Immediately after the abolition of deer hunting the government set up a "Red Deer Commission", with its base on Exmoor and working with the National Park Authority. To qualify for conservation grants, farmers and landowners have to co-operate and adhere to the Commission. Generous extra grants are paid out to compensate for deer damage.

" 'All culling, when necessary, is carried out by "only" Commission appointed stalkers, who each have their own areas to control. Each stalker is highly trained and uses a trained dog to, on the rare occasion, follow up a wounded deer. Licences for possession of rifles are not issued to any individual or landowner, who must as part of the scheme, only allow Commission appointed stalkers on their land. Shotgun licences are granted for pest control and game shooting, but it is a serious offence to use a shotgun on deer. A new set aside grant for woodlands was implemented on Exmoor to preserve undisturbed woodland covers for deer and wildlife and curtail the massive increase in commercial pheasant shooting.

" 'The commission is still partly funded from government grants, but is striving to be self-sufficient through the "Red Deer Fund". Money is raised in various ways including tourism, stalking, venison sales, lottery grants and much fund raising by the local community, proud of their wildlife. The Commission have their own sanctuary area in the Exe Valley, which is also a Visitor Centre and Deer Interpretation Centre. Safaris around the sanctuary, as well as around Exmoor, led by National Park rangers, benefit the Red Deer Fund. Some of the culling is let to the paying gun who has to pass a regular, rigorous stalking proficiency test and must be led by a Commission appointed stalker. All revenue from stalking benefits the deer through the Red Deer Fund.

" 'The Commission appointed stalkers know their areas intimately and the deer situation. Each regularly reports to the Commission on numbers and the cull is set by the Commission with the issue of official tags for hinds and for stags. The number one aim is to maintain a high quality herd and an even balance of the sexes. As well as setting the cull, the Commission also manages the granting of compensatory payments to farmers for deer damage to crops and hedges. All culled deer from Exmoor have to be sent with their official cull tag to the Red Deer Commission's central hanging and dressing point at Exford. Some carcasses are sold on to game dealers, some venison can be distributed to farmers and landowners as part of their compensation and there is also a good local market for Exmoor venison. Today one can eat venison from Exmoor in the knowledge that it is the harvest from a sound working management and conversation system for the wild red deer and that all profits from venison benefit the species.

" 'Such is the merest sketch of a system that has saved this animal when a few years ago the future was in doubt. It is a cold January day in 2050 and I am standing on the heather clad slopes of Mill Hill on Exmoor, watching a wintering bunch of Exmoor stags. There are forty or more of them and I can only marvel at their array of antlers, a moving forest, as they make their way towards a feeding point run by the Red Deer Commission. The roots they are given only in winter help them through this leanest of times.'

"I sincerely hope that such a system is put in place. It could be put in place now and stag hunting for as long as it remains a legal method of killing an animal, could be incorporated into the scheme, and bring hunting and shooting back in harmony again.

"Surely then the future for the wild red deer of Exmoor would be assured and there would not only be plenty of fine old Exmoor stags with Brow, Bay and Trey, carrying all the rights on their heads, and so, not before time, being given all the rights to a secure future, for they were here first."

Appendix 14

Press release issued by the LACS: Friday 5th September 2003:

A poll being widely publicised by the pro-hunt Countryside Alliance during its "weekend of action" has been heavily criticised by independent marketing experts. They have condemned it for having "flawed logic, ambiguity and potentially biased wording" and recommend that its results should be "discounted as measures of public opinion".

The Countryside Alliance claims that the results of its poll prove that "59 per cent want to keep hunting". However the question used to arrive at this figure was ambiguous.

Q1: "Looking at the hunting debate over recent years do you believe that...

Hunting should be allowed to continue because it is essentially a matter of civil liberties.

Hunting should not be allowed to continue at all as cruelty is more important to me than liberty.

Allowing hunting to continue under regulation would strike a balance between civil liberties and animal welfare.

The experts said that, in option 3, the term "under regulation" which was selected by 41 per cent of those interviewed: *"could be interpreted by some as a near complete ban (maybe most fox hunting, maybe all deer hunting and hare coursing) – or, on the other hand, as no ban at all. Given this potential confusion, responses to this question should neither be counted as supporting hunting nor being against it. The Countryside Alliance however seems to count the 41% in this ambitious category as supporting hunting and adds it to the 18% who certainly do (explaining the Countryside Alliance's total of 59%.) Added to this ambiguity are a number of potential biases in wording which seem further to invalidate the question."*

Three references to civil liberty in the same question were also criticised. The experts concluded that the wording of the three options is odd, saying: " '*Cruelty is more important to me than liberty*' *almost suggests a liking for cruelty.*"

The findings of the Countryside Alliance poll were analysed by Martin Evans, Senior Teaching Tutor, University of Cardiff and author of Applied Marketing Research; Dr John Pallister, Head of Strategy and Marketing Section, University of Cardiff and specialist in opinion surveys; Dr Alan Tapp, Senior Lecturer, Bristol Business School, University of West England and specialist in research methodology.

Appendix 15

Hunting Act 2004

Contents

PART 1 OFFENCES
1 Hunting wild mammals with dogs
2 Exempt hunting
3 Hunting: assistance
4 Hunting: defence
5 Hare coursing
PART 2 ENFORCEMENT
6 Penalty
7 Arrest
8 Search and seizure
9 Forfeiture
10 Offence by body corporate
PART 3 GENERAL
11 Interpretation
12 Crown application
13 Amendments and repeals
14 Subordinate legislation
15 Commencement
16 Short title
17 Extent

Schedule 1 — Exempt Hunting
Schedule 2 — Consequential Amendments
Schedule 3 — Repeals

ELIZABETH II c. 37
Hunting Act 2004
2004 CHAPTER 37

An Act to make provision about hunting wild mammals with dogs; to prohibit hare coursing; and for connected purposes. [18th November 2004]

BE IT ENACTED by The Queen's most Excellent Majesty, by and with the advice and consent of the Commons in this present Parliament assembled, in accordance with the provisions of the Parliament Acts 1911 and 1949, and by the authority of the same, as follows:—

PART 1 OFFENCES

1 Hunting wild mammals with dogs

A person commits an offence if he hunts a wild mammal with a dog, unless his hunting is exempt.

2 Exempt hunting

(1) Hunting is exempt if it is within a class specified in Schedule 1.

(2) The Secretary of State may by order amend Schedule 1 so as to vary a class of exempt hunting.

3 Hunting: assistance

(1) A person commits an offence if he knowingly permits land which belongs to him to be entered or used in the course of the commission of an offence under section 1.

(2) A person commits an offence if he knowingly permits a dog which belongs to him to be used in the course of the commission of an offence under section 1.

4 Hunting: defence

It is a defence for a person charged with an offence under section 1 in respect of hunting to show that he reasonably believed that the hunting was exempt.

5 Hare coursing

(1) A person commits an offence if he—

(a) participates in a hare coursing event,

(b) attends a hare coursing event,
(c) knowingly facilitates a hare coursing event, or
(d) permits land which belongs to him to be used for the purposes of a hare coursing event.

(2) Each of the following persons commits an offence if a dog participates in a hare coursing event—
(a) any person who enters the dog for the event,
(b) any person who permits the dog to be entered, and
(c) any person who controls or handles the dog in the course of or for the purposes of the event.

(3) A "hare coursing event" is a competition in which dogs are, by the use of live hares, assessed as to skill in hunting hares.

PART 2 ENFORCEMENT

6 Penalty

A person guilty of an offence under this Act shall be liable on summary conviction to a fine not exceeding level 5 on the standard scale.

7 Arrest

A constable without a warrant may arrest a person whom he reasonably suspects—
(a) to have committed an offence under section 1 or 5(1)(a), (b) or (2),
(b) to be committing an offence under any of those provisions, or
(c) to be about to commit an offence under any of those provisions.

8 Search and seizure

(1) This section applies where a constable reasonably suspects that a person ("the suspect") is committing or has committed an offence under Part 1 of this Act.

(2) If the constable reasonably believes that evidence of the offence is likely to be found on the suspect, the constable may stop the suspect and search him.

(3) If the constable reasonably believes that evidence of the offence is likely to be found on or in a vehicle, animal or other thing of

which the suspect appears to be in possession or control, the constable may stop and search the vehicle, animal or other thing.
(4) A constable may seize and detain a vehicle, animal or other thing if he reasonably believes that—

(a) it may be used as evidence in criminal proceedings for an offence under Part 1 of this Act, or

(b) it may be made the subject of an order under section 9.

(5) For the purposes of exercising a power under this section a constable may enter—

(a) land;

(b) premises other than a dwelling;

(c) a vehicle.

(6) The exercise of a power under this section does not require a warrant.

9 Forfeiture

(1) A court which convicts a person of an offence under Part 1 of this Act may order the forfeiture of any dog or hunting article which—

(a) was used in the commission of the offence, or

(b) was in the possession of the person convicted at the time of his arrest.

(2) A court which convicts a person of an offence under Part 1 of this Act may order the forfeiture of any vehicle which was used in the commission of the offence.

(3) In subsection (1) "hunting article" means anything designed or adapted for use in connection with—

(a) hunting a wild mammal, or

(b) hare coursing.

(4) A forfeiture order—

(a) may include such provision about the treatment of the dog, vehicle or article forfeited as the court thinks appropriate, and

(b) subject to provision made under paragraph (a), shall be treated as requiring any person who is in possession of the dog, vehicle or article to surrender it to a constable as soon as is reasonably practicable.

(5) Where a forfeited dog, vehicle or article is retained by or

surrendered to a constable, the police force of which the constable is a member shall ensure that such arrangements are made for its destruction or disposal—

(a) as are specified in the forfeiture order, or

(b) where no arrangements are specified in the order, as seem to the police force to be appropriate.

(6) The court which makes a forfeiture order may order the return of the forfeited dog, vehicle or article on an application made—

(a) by a person who claims to have an interest in the dog, vehicle or article (other than the person on whose conviction the order was made), and

(b) before the dog, vehicle or article has been destroyed or finally disposed of under subsection (5).

(7) A person commits an offence if he fails to—

(a) comply with a forfeiture order, or

(b) co-operate with a step taken for the purpose of giving effect to a forfeiture order.

10 Offence by body corporate

(1) This section applies where an offence under this Act is committed by a body corporate with the consent or connivance of an officer of the body.

(2) The officer, as well as the body, shall be guilty of the offence.

(3) In subsection (1) a reference to an officer of a body corporate includes a reference to—

(a) a director, manager or secretary,

(b) a person purporting to act as a director, manager or secretary, and

(c) if the affairs of the body are managed by its members, a member.

PART 3 GENERAL

11 Interpretation

(1) In this Act "wild mammal" includes, in particular—

(a) a wild mammal which has been bred or tamed for any purpose,

(b) a wild mammal which is in captivity or confinement,

(c) a wild mammal which has escaped or been released from captivity or confinement, and

(d) any mammal which is living wild.

(2) For the purposes of this Act a reference to a person hunting a wild mammal with a dog includes, in particular, any case where—

(a) a person engages or participates in the pursuit of a wild mammal, and

(b) one or more dogs are employed in that pursuit (whether or not by him and whether or not under his control or direction).

(3) For the purposes of this Act land belongs to a person if he—

(a) owns an interest in it,

(b) manages or controls it, or

(c) occupies it.

(4) For the purposes of this Act a dog belongs to a person if he—

(a) owns it,

(b) is in charge of it, or

(c) has control of it.

12 Crown application

This Act—

(a) binds the Crown, and

(b) applies to anything done on or in respect of land irrespective of whether it belongs to or is used for the purposes of the Crown or a Duchy.

13 Amendments and repeals

(1) Schedule 2 (consequential amendments) shall have effect.

(2) The enactments listed in Schedule 3 are hereby repealed to the extent specified.

14 Subordinate legislation

An order of the Secretary of State under this Act—

(a) shall be made by statutory instrument,

(b) may not be made unless a draft has been laid before and approved by resolution of each House of Parliament,

(c) may make provision which applies generally or only in specified circumstances or for specified purposes,

(d) may make different provision for different circumstances or purposes, and

(e) may make transitional, consequential and incidental provision.

15 Commencement

This Act shall come into force at the end of the period of three months beginning with the date on which it is passed.

16 Short title

This Act may be cited as the Hunting Act 2004.

17 Extent

This Act shall extend only to England and Wales.

SCHEDULES

SCHEDULE 1 Section 2
EXEMPT HUNTING

Stalking and flushing out

1 (1) Stalking a wild mammal, or flushing it out of cover, is exempt hunting if the conditions in this paragraph are satisfied.

(2) The first condition is that the stalking or flushing out is undertaken for the purpose of—

(a) preventing or reducing serious damage which the wild mammal would otherwise cause—

(i) to livestock,

(ii) to game birds or wild birds (within the meaning of section 27 of the Wildlife and Countryside Act 1981 (c. 69)),

(iii) to food for livestock,

(iv) to crops (including vegetables and fruit),

(v) to growing timber,

(vi) to fisheries,

(vii) to other property, or

(viii) to the biological diversity of an area (within the meaning of the United Nations Environmental Programme Convention on Biological Diversity of 1992),

(b) obtaining meat to be used for human or animal consumption, or

(c) participation in a field trial.

(3) In subparagraph (2)(c) "field trial" means a competition (other than a hare coursing event within the meaning of section 5) in which dogs—

(a) flush animals out of cover or retrieve animals that have been shot (or both), and

(b) are assessed as to their likely usefulness in connection with shooting.

(4) The second condition is that the stalking or flushing out takes place on land—

(a) which belongs to the person doing the stalking or flushing out, or

(b) which he has been given permission to use for the purpose by the occupier or, in the case of unoccupied land, by a person to whom it belongs.

(5) The third condition is that the stalking or flushing out does not involve the use of more than two dogs.

(6) The fourth condition is that the stalking or flushing out does not involve the use of a dog below ground otherwise than in accordance with paragraph 2 below.

(7) The fifth condition is that—

(a) reasonable steps are taken for the purpose of ensuring that as soon as possible after being found or flushed out the wild mammal is shot dead by a competent person, and

(b) in particular, each dog used in the stalking or flushing out is kept under sufficiently close control to ensure that it does not prevent or obstruct achievement of the objective in paragraph (a).

Use of dogs below ground to protect birds for shooting

2 (1) The use of a dog below ground in the course of stalking or flushing out is in accordance with this paragraph if the conditions in this paragraph are satisfied.

(2) The first condition is that the stalking or flushing out is undertaken for the purpose of preventing or reducing serious damage to game birds or wild birds (within the meaning of section 27 of the Wildlife and Countryside Act 1981 (c. 69)) which a person is keeping or preserving for the purpose of their being shot.

(3) The second condition is that the person doing the stalking or flushing out—

(a) has with him written evidence—

(i) that the land on which the stalking or flushing out takes place belongs to him, or

(ii) that he has been given permission to use that land for the purpose by the occupier or, in the case of unoccupied land, by a person to whom it belongs, and

(b) makes the evidence immediately available for inspection by a constable who asks to see it.

(4) The third condition is that the stalking or flushing out does not involve the use of more than one dog below ground at any one time.

(5) In so far as stalking or flushing out is undertaken with the use of a dog below ground in accordance with this paragraph, paragraph 1 shall have effect as if for the condition in paragraph 1(7) there were substituted the condition that—

(a) reasonable steps are taken for the purpose of ensuring that as soon as possible after being found the wild mammal is flushed out from below ground,

(b) reasonable steps are taken for the purpose of ensuring that as soon as possible after being flushed out from below ground the wild mammal is shot dead by a competent person,

(c) in particular, the dog is brought under sufficiently close control to ensure that it does not prevent or obstruct achievement of the objective in paragraph (b),

(d) reasonable steps are taken for the purpose of preventing injury to the dog, and

(e) the manner in which the dog is used complies with any code of practice which is issued or approved for the purpose of this paragraph by the Secretary of State.

Rats

3 The hunting of rats is exempt if it takes place on land—

(a) which belongs to the hunter, or

(b) which he has been given permission to use for the purpose by the occupier or, in the case of unoccupied land, by a person to whom it belongs.

Rabbits

4 The hunting of rabbits is exempt if it takes place on land—

(a) which belongs to the hunter, or

(b) which he has been given permission to use for the purpose by the occupier or, in the case of unoccupied land, by a person to whom it belongs.

Retrieval of hares

5 The hunting of a hare which has been shot is exempt if it takes place on land—

(a) which belongs to the hunter, or

(b) which he has been given permission to use for the purpose of hunting hares by the occupier or, in the case of unoccupied land, by a person to whom it belongs.

Falconry

6 Flushing a wild mammal from cover is exempt hunting if undertaken—

(a) for the purpose of enabling a bird of prey to hunt the wild mammal, and

(b) on land which belongs to the hunter or which he has been given permission to use for the purpose by the occupier or, in the case of unoccupied land, by a person to whom it belongs.

Recapture of wild mammal

7 (1) The hunting of a wild mammal which has escaped or been released from captivity or confinement is exempt if the conditions in this paragraph are satisfied.

(2) The first condition is that the hunting takes place—

(a) on land which belongs to the hunter,

(b) on land which he has been given permission to use for the purpose by the occupier or, in the case of unoccupied land, by a person to whom it belongs, or

(c) with the authority of a constable.
(3) The second condition is that—
(a) reasonable steps are taken for the purpose of ensuring that as soon as possible after being found the wild mammal is recaptured or shot dead by a competent person, and
(b) in particular, each dog used in the hunt is kept under sufficiently close control to ensure that it does not prevent or obstruct achievement of the objective in paragraph (a).
(4) The third condition is that the wild mammal—
(a) was not released for the purpose of being hunted, and
(b) was not, for that purpose, permitted to escape.

Rescue of wild mammal

8 (1) The hunting of a wild mammal is exempt if the conditions in this paragraph are satisfied.
(2) The first condition is that the hunter reasonably believes that the wild mammal is or may be injured.
(3) The second condition is that the hunting is undertaken for the purpose of relieving the wild mammal's suffering.
(4) The third condition is that the hunting does not involve the use of more than two dogs.
(5) The fourth condition is that the hunting does not involve the use of a dog below ground.
(6) The fifth condition is that the hunting takes place—
(a) on land which belongs to the hunter,
(b) on land which he has been given permission to use for the purpose by the occupier or, in the case of unoccupied land, by a person to whom it belongs, or
(c) with the authority of a constable.
(7) The sixth condition is that—
(a) reasonable steps are taken for the purpose of ensuring that as soon as possible after the wild mammal is found appropriate action (if any) is taken to relieve its suffering, and
(b) in particular, each dog used in the hunt is kept under sufficiently close control to ensure that it does not prevent or obstruct achievement of the objective in paragraph (a).

(8) The seventh condition is that the wild mammal was not harmed for the purpose of enabling it to be hunted in reliance upon this paragraph.

Research and observation

9 (1) The hunting of a wild mammal is exempt if the conditions in this paragraph are satisfied.
(2) The first condition is that the hunting is undertaken for the purpose of or in connection with the observation or study of the wild mammal.
(3) The second condition is that the hunting does not involve the use of more than two dogs.
(4) The third condition is that the hunting does not involve the use of a dog below ground.
(5) The fourth condition is that the hunting takes place on land—
(a) which belongs to the hunter, or
(b) which he has been given permission to use for the purpose by the occupier or, in the case of unoccupied land, by a person to whom it belongs.
(6) The fifth condition is that each dog used in the hunt is kept under sufficiently close control to ensure that it does not injure the wild mammal.

SCHEDULE 2 Section 13
CONSEQUENTIAL AMENDMENTS

Game Act 1831 (c. 32)

1 In section 35 of the Game Act 1831 (provision about trespassers: exceptions) the following words shall cease to have effect: “to any person hunting or coursing upon any lands with hounds or greyhounds, and being in fresh pursuit of any deer, hare or fox already started upon any other land, nor”. Game Licences Act 1860 (c. 90)

2 In section 5 of the Game Licences Act 1860 (exceptions) exceptions 3 and 4 (hares and deer) shall cease to have effect.

Protection of Animals Act 1911 (c. 27)

3 In section 1(3)(b) of the Protection of Animals Act 1911 (offence of cruelty:

exceptions) a reference to coursing or hunting shall not include a reference to—

(a) participation in a hare coursing event (within the meaning of section 5 of this Act), or

(b) the coursing or hunting of a wild mammal with a dog (within the meaning of this Act).

Protection of Badgers Act 1992 (c. 51)

4 Section 8(4) to (9) of the Protection of Badgers Act 1992 (exception for hunting) shall cease to have effect.

Wild Mammals (Protection) Act 1996 (c. 3)

5 For the purposes of section 2 of the Wild Mammals (Protection) Act 1996 (offences: exceptions) the hunting of a wild mammal with a dog (within the meaning of this Act) shall be treated as lawful if and only if it is exempt hunting within the meaning of this Act.

SCHEDULE 3 Section 13

REPEALS

Short title and chapter	*Extent of repeal*
The Game Act 1831 (c. 32)	In section 35, the words "to any person hunting or coursing upon any lands with hounds or greyhounds, and being in fresh pursuit of any deer, hare or fox already started upon any other land, nor".
The Game Licences Act 1860 (c. 90)	In section 5, exceptions 3 and 4.
The Protection of Badgers Act 1992 (c. 51)	Section 8(4) to (9).

Appendix 16

Statement by the proposers of the LACS exempt hunting of deer (NT AGM 4th November 2006) resolution:

The Hunting Act 2004 makes the hunting of deer with dogs illegal, leaving exemption for stalking or flushing of deer to guns. The conditions are that such activities must not involve the use of more than two dogs, and that reasonable steps must be taken to ensure that the deer is shot dead by a competent person as soon as possible.

While there is a specific exemption in the Hunting Act for the hunting of deer undertaken to relieve suffering, we do not believe that this hunting is appropriate in the case of sick or injured deer. The chasing of sick or injured deer amounts to the infliction of cruelty on an animal which is already suffering. Professional stalkers experienced in the dispatch of injured deer know that great care should be taken not to make disturbance which could cause the deer to bolt during stalking. The use of hunting hounds is intended to cause the deer to run, making a humane kill next to impossible. This is futile cruelty.

In May 2006, the National Trust made the important decision that "exempt hunting of deer as generally practised by the local hunt should not be licensed on Trust property because of the uncertainties over the nature of the activity". Evidence collected by hunt monitors does indeed show the stag hunts systematically using pairs of hounds in relay to chase deer to exhaustion.

However, the Board of Trustees has resolved that, where hunts chasing "clearly sick and injured deer" cross into National Trust land, members of the hunt staff should be allowed to follow and kill the deer. This gives licence for the hunts to flush and chase sick and injured deer from the outset, increasing their suffering in a way which traditional stalking does not do.

The National Trust's current position does not require hunts to prove that their target deer are sick or injured, nor does it make clear that deer exhausted from long chases inflicted by the hunts do not qualify as such. It does not prohibit the use of hounds on the land, and therefore cannot stop prolonged chasing and the use of relay hunting continuing on to Trust land. It does not require that hunts report incursions in pursuit of deer, or set out how frequently they expect the "exceptional cases" where the hunt will have to undertake this to occur.

We call on National Trust members to support this resolution and prevent the hunts from using hounds on Trust land to pursue deer. By only using traditional stalking to target sick and injured deer, the Trust can ensure the good welfare of deer on their land.

Statement by the Board of Trustees in response to the resolution:

Animal welfare is a prime concern of the Trust in the management of deer. The Board of Trustees understands the concerns expressed in this resolution, but recommends members to vote against it because "exempt hunting" under the Hunting Act 2004 includes activities which would not generally be thought of as hunting and which we believe are essential to the management and welfare of the increasing population of deer on our land.

For instance, if the Trust were to follow the strict wording of the resolution our professional stalkers would not be able to use trained dogs to track a deer if it is stalked and wounded but not killed outright. This would prolong the injured deer's suffering. Nor would the use of up to two dogs be possible for research or observation purposes, for example flushing deer from thick cover to enable them to be counted.

Contrary to some press reports the Trust is not permitting exempt hunting as generally practised on some adjacent property. However, on rare occasions, the welfare of a sick or injured deer may best be served by allowing members of the hunt to locate and dispatch the animal. This is in those circumstances where the use by the hunt of up to two hounds to locate an already wounded or sick deer enables it to be dispatched more quickly and humanely than would be possible using only our own staff. We will allow this. That will be the full extent of the hunt's involvement. We are confident that the concerns expressed in the supporting statement to this resolution can be satisfactorily addressed in the detail of the arrangement determined by our staff at local level. We will review this arrangement after a year.

The Board of Trustees therefore recommends that you vote against the resolution.

Bibliography

IN A BOOK OF THIS type, where one attempts to tell a story not only covering over one hundred years, but where the subject matter tends to be of a highly controversial and contentious nature, the recourse to published material is extensive. While some is readily accessible through previously published books, much tends to be found in obscure pamphlets and bulletins issued by the various interested bodies, plus long-forgotten newspaper and magazine articles. To attempt a bibliography listing every source would prove not only tedious to the general reader, but would require many extra pages of print. Therefore I have taken the liberty of only including the most significant sources, divided into books, pamphlets, and articles of primary interest from the press. If the reader would like more information on any specific issue in this book then the author would be pleased to supply a copy of any reference point, all of which will be on record in his personal archive.

Books & General Publications:

Aldin, Cecil: *Exmoor, The Riding Playground of England* (H F &.G Witherby, London, 1935)

Allen, Noel: *Exmoor's Wild Red Deer* (Exmoor Press, Dulverton, Somerset, 1990)

Baily's Hunting Directory (J Allen, London, annually)

Bateson, Professor Patrick: *The Behavioural and Physiological Effects of Culling Red Deer* (National Trust, 1997)

Bryant, John: *Fettered Kingdoms: an examination of a changing ethic* (privately printed c.1979)

Burton, S H: *Exmoor* (Westway, London, 1952 & Hodder & Stoughton, London, 1969)

Centre for Rural Studies: *Economic and Social Aspects of Deer Hunting on Exmoor and the Quantocks* Royal Agricultural College, Cirencester, 1993)

Chapman, Norma: *Deer* (British Natural History Series, Whittet Books Ltd, London, 1991)

Clayton, Michael: *Endangered Species: Foxhunting – the history, the passion and the fight for survival* (Swan Hill Press, 2004)

Collyns, Charles Palk: *Notes On The Chase Of The Wild Red Deer* (Alston Rivers Ltd, London, 1907)

Cresswell, Beatrix F: *The Quantock Hills* (The Homeland Association, London, 1922)

Cronin, Doreen: *A View from the Wild Side (*DSRADP, June 1993)

Delderfield, Eric R: *Exmoor Wanderings* (The Raleigh Press, Exmouth, 1956)

Evered, Philip: *Stag-hunting with the Devon and Somerset 1887-1901: An Account of the Chase of the Wild Red Deer on Exmoor* (Chatto & Windus, London, 1902)

Floyd, G C: *All His Rights: A study of the Wild Red Deer of Exmoor* (Published by the author) Printed by West Somerset Free Press, Williton, Somerset. 1998

Fortescue, Hon John: *Records of Staghunting on Exmoor* (Chapman & Hall Ltd, London, 1887)

Fortescue, Hon John: *The Story of a Red Deer* (Macmillan & Co, London, 1938)

Goss, Fred: *Memories of a Stag Harbourer* (H F & G Witherby, London, 1931. Facsimile edition Halsgrove 2001)

Griffin, Emma: *Blood Sport: Hunting in Britain since 1066* (Yale University Press, New Haven & London, 2007)

Hamilton, Archibald: *The Red Deer of Exmoor* (Horace Cox, London, 1907)

Hendy, E W: *Wild Exmoor Through The Year* (Eyre & Spottiswoode, London, 1946)

Hendrick, George & Willene (Ed): *The Savour Of Salt: A Henry Salt Anthology* (Centaur Press, Sussex, 1989)

HMSO: *House of Commons Official Report: Parliamentary Debates (Hansard) (*London, 1809-2004)

HMSO: *Exmoor National Park Guide No.8* (London, 1970)

HMSO: *Report of the Committee on Cruelty to Wild Animals* (London, June 1951, 1964)

Hewett, H P: *The Fairest Hunting: Hunting and Watching Exmoor Deer* (J A Allen, London, 1963)

Huskisson, Mike: *Outfoxed* (Michael Huskisson Associates/League Against Cruel Sports, London, 1983)

Hutchings, M M & Caver, M: *Man's Dominion: our Violation of the Animal World* (Hart-Davis, London, 1970)

Jackson, John: *Deer in the New Forest* (Moonraker Press, Bradford-on-Avon, 1977)

James, David & Stephens, Wilson (Eds): *In Praise Of Hunting* (Hollis & Carter, London, 1960)

Jefferies, Richard: *Red Deer* (Longmans, Green & Co.1884 & 1892. Facsimile edition Halsgrove 2001)

Kean, Hilda: *Animal Rights: Political and Social Change in Britain since 1800* (Reaktion Books, London, 1998)

King-Fretts, Paddy: *Staghunter: The Remarkable Story Of Ernest Bawden* (Halsgrove, Tiverton, Devon, 2005)

Langbein J & Putman R J: *Conservation And Management Of Deer On Exmoor And The Quantocks* (National Trust, 1992)

Lethbridge, Richard: The *Tiverton Staghounds* (Privately printed, 2001)

Lloyd E R: *The Wild Red Deer of Exmoor* (Exmoor Press, Dulverton, Somerset, 1975)

Macdermot, E T: *The Devon and Somerset Staghounds 1907-1936* (Collins, London, 1936)

Mann, Keith: *From Dusk 'til Dawn: An insider's view of the growth of the Animal Liberation Movement* (Puppy Pincher Press, London, 2007)

Marshall, H J: *Exmoor: Sporting & Otherwise* (Eyre & Spottiswoode, London, 1948)

Martin, E W: *The Case Against Hunting* (Dennis Dobson, London, 1959)

Moore, Patrick (Ed): *Against Hunting: A Symposium* (Victor Gollancz Ltd, London, 1965)

Moss, A W: *Valiant Crusade: the History of the RSPCA* (Cassell, London, 1961)

National Trust: *The Conservation & Management of Red Deer in the West Country* (Report to the council of the National Trust by the Deer Hunting Working Party) (National Trust 1993)

North, Richard D: *The Hunt At Bay* (Wildlife Network, 1999)

Page, F J Taylor: *Field Guide To British Deer* (The British Deer Society, Blackwell Scientific Publications, Oxford & Edinburgh, 1957 & 1971)

Page, Robin: *The Hunter And The Hunted* (Davis-Poynter Ltd, London, 1977)

Peel, J H B: *Portrait of Exmoor* (Robert Hale, London, 1970)

Pine, Leslie: *After Their Blood* (W Kimber, 1966)

Pine, Leslie: *The History of Hunting* (LACS, London, 1973)

Prior, Richard: *Living With Deer* (White Lion Publishers Ltd, London, 1976)

Roberts, J J: *Against All Odds: Animal Liberation 1972-1986* (Ark Print, London, 1986)

Shackle, Major E W: *Hunting the Carted Deer.* Contribution to *Deer, Hare & Otter Hunting* (Lonsdale Library, Vol. XXII) (Seeley, Service & Co Ltd, London, 1936)

Sheppard, Vera: *My Head against the Wall: A Decade in the Fight against Blood Sports* (Moonraker Press, Bradford-on-Avon, Wiltshire, 1979)

Smith E H: *Quantock Life & Rambles* (The Wessex Press, 1945)

Soulsby, Lord: *Review of the Report on The Behaviour and Physiology of Hunted Deer (Bateson Report)* (August 1997)

Thomas, Richard H: *The Politics of Hunting* (Gower Publishing Co Ltd, Aldershot, 1983)

Turner E S: *All Heaven In A Rage* (Michael Joseph, London, 1964)

Vowles, Alfred: *Stag-hunting on Exmoor* (Barnicott and Pearce, The Wessex Press, Taunton, 1920)

Vowles, Alfred: *Wild Deer Of Exmoor* (Cox & Sons, Minehead & Williton, 1936)

Wadsworth, Waddy (Ed): *Vive La Chasse: A Celebration of British Field Sports Past and Present* (Dickson Price, Kent, 1989)

Waite, Vincent: *Portrait Of The Quantocks* (Robert Hale, London, 1972)

Watson, Paul: *Ocean Warrior: My Battle to End the Illegal Slaughter on the High Seas* (Vision Paperbacks, London, 2003)

Whitehead, Kenneth: *Hunting and Stalking Deer in Britain through the Ages* (B T Batsford Ltd, London, 1980)
Wiggin, Col W W: *Stag Hunting on Exmoor.* Contribution to *Deer, Hare & Otter Hunting* (Lonsdale Library, Vol.XXII). Seeley, Service & Co Ltd, London, 1936)
Williamson, Henry: *The Wild Red Deer Of Exmoor: A Digression on the Logic and Ethics and Economies of Staghunting in England To-day* (Faber & Faber, London, 1931)
Williamson, Henry: *The Old Stag and other hunting stories* (G P Putnams & Sons, London, 1942)
Windeatt, Philip: *The Hunt and the Anti-Hunt* (Pluto Press, London, 1982)
Wolseley, Pat & Neal, Ernest: *Quantock Wildlife: Its Ecology & Conservation* (Somerset Trust for Nature Conservation, Broomfield, Bridgwater, 1980)

Pamphlets

The Beginning. Booklet dealing with birth of the BFSS by Suzanne Beadle. (BFSS, c.1971)
Control or Carnage? A countryman's views on hunting by Lt Col A Milner Brown, TDMA.) (BFSS, c.1970s)
Field Sports: The Truth (BFSS, June, 1957)
Exmoor Deer Hunting (National Committee for the Abolition of Deer Hunting, c.1958)
Map Of The Devon and Somerset Staghounds Country. (Reid-Hamilton Publication, c.1950s)
NO HUNTING-NO DEER (BFSS, c.1987/88)
Sport and Wild Animals (NSACS, c. 1960)
Staghunting: A Barbarian Brutality (NSACS, Third Edition, 1959)
Stag-Hunting (NSACS, c. 1969)
The Staghunting Controversy: Some provocative Questions…with straight Answers (Masters of Deerhounds Association, c. 1990 & reprint Endangered Exmoor 2002)

The "Tradition" of Staghunting on Exmoor and the Quantocks (Devon & Somerset Residents Association for Deer Protection, 1988)
What do you know about Staghunting: some questions answered. Pamphlet No. 7 in the Young Sportsman Series, written by H P Hewett. (BFSS, c. 1970)

Articles

Adams, Tim: *Fantastic Mr Fox: the unspeakable, the uneatable, the unconsolable (GRANTA 90,* Summer 2005)
ANON: *Stag Hunters At Bay (Daily Mail,* 19th February 1965)
Ashe, Larry: *The next victims? (TV Times,* c.1982)
Austin, Rebecca: *Casualties of this War (Horse & Hound,* 31st March 2005)
Boffey, Daniel: *Baying For Blood (Daily Mirror,* 29th October 2005)
Burnand, Tony: *A Death or a Good Day's Sport (Animal Life,* c.1968)
Cook, Ralph: *A Quarter Century Of Sabbing (HOWL,* Spring 1989)
Cookson, Rich: *Hunting the hunters (Independent Review,* 21st August, 2003)
Cusack, Odean: *Direct Action For Animals: Interview with England's Marley Jones (AGENDA,* May/June 1983)
Donnelly, Peter: *The Red Deer of Exmoor: Conservation of a Population (Exmoor Review,* Vol. 45, 2004)
Edmonds, Noel: *"Individuals CAN make a difference" to ban (Horse & Hound,* 13th December 2003)
Fazey, Ian Hamilton: *The deer hunters (Financial Times,* 16th November 1985)
Francis, Pam: *Death at the end of a "perfect day" (Reveille,* 28th April 1978)
Gibson, Rob: (pictures Douglas Doig): *BARBARIC: A cruel end for the stag at bay (Daily Star,* 9th October 1979)
Gomery, Donald: *Death in the afternoon-English style (Daily Mirror,* 16th September 1970)
Gomery, Donald: *The Stag That Got Away (Daily Mirror,* 20th October 1975)

Grant, Ned: (pictures Reg Lewis): *"A Copybook Finish" To A Staghunt* (*Daily Mirror,* 20th March 1957)

Harrison, Fred: *BARBARIC! They poach deer without mercy (Sunday People,* 4th June 1976)

Hill, Kevin: *There's no rebellion over the hunts in the Shires (Western Daily Press,* 23rd August 2002)

Hill, Kevin: *Consider all the options before cull (Western Daily Press,* 27th January 2004)

Hughes, Darren: *Sinister side of hunt saboteurs (Western Daily Press,* 22nd September 2004)

Hughes, Robert: *Even The Vicar Hunts (Daily Telegraph,* 25th October 1968)

Kendall, Ena: *Wearied In The Chase (*the *Observer,* 24th January 1982)

Kingdom, Johnny: *I don't want the deer wiped out (Western Daily Press,* 24th September 2004)

Lawless, Maureen: *Hounded To Death (News of the World,* 6th March 1983)

Leyhart, Edward: *Brow, Bay and Trey* (*Riding,* November 1970)

Lucas, Pat: *He's given his best to Sport in the West (Horse & Hound,* 12th April 1974)

Lucas, Pat: *At Home On Exmoor: with Sidney Bazeley...the harbourer (Horse & Hound,* 9th April 1976)

MacEwen, Malcolm: *Stag at Bay: being cruel to be kind (The Times,* 21st April 1973)

Monteith, Malcolm: *The Hunter and the Hunted (Lilliput,* November 1958)

Moorhouse, Geoffrey: *The Hunt At Bay (*the *Guardian,* 30th December 1964)

Pedler, Ian: *Red Deer and the Trust (HOWL,* Spring 1991)

Pedler, Ian: *Carnage or Control: What Price Deer Hunt Abolition (HOWL,* Winter 1992)

Pedler, Ian: *A Roe for the Killing (HOWL,* No.53, Autumn/Winter 1993/94)

Pedler, Ian: *SAVE OUR STAGS: saboteurs at the deer hunt (HOWL,* Summer 2004)

Poole, Steve: *1963: From Protest to Resistance (HOWL,* Spring 1989)
Ridout, Alan: *Blood Lust Of The Deer Hunters (Sunday People,* 11th December 1983)
Rodgers, Lucy: *We've got the huntsmen on the run (Western Daily Press,* 5th July 2003)
Rowe, Mark: *On Porlock Hill they are baying for blood (Independent on Sunday,* 8th December 2002
Rundle, Chris: *Go for the swift kill (Western Daily Press,* 5th December 2002)
Rundle, Chris: *Hunters threaten our red deer herd (Western Daily Press,* 1st February 2003)
Stoneley, Jack: *Torture In The Forest (Sunday Mirror,* 23rd June 1974)
Tierney-Jones, Adrian: *A Way of Life? (Exmoor Country Magazine,* No 20 Autumn 2002)
Treharne, Mal: *Why country folk oppose hunt ban (Western Daily Press,* 6th December 2002)
Wainwright, Peter: *Enemy of conservation? (Shooting Times,* 13-19th July 1978)
Waley-Cohen, Sir Bernard: *The Case For Stag Hunting (Animal Life,* c.1968)
Wetton, Dave: *21 Years Of Sabbing: a personal recollection (HOWL,* Spring 1985)
Wetton, Dave: *The Open Door breakthrough (HOWL,* Summer 2004)
Windeatt, Phil & Marten, Michael: *Hunt Is A Four Letter Word (The Beast,* No.3, Oct-Nov 1979)

DVD

The Animals Film (Beyond The Frame, 27 Old Gloucester Street, London, WC1N 3XX)

Bulletins

DSRADP: *Newsletter April/May 1988-Autumn 1999*

HSA:
Newsletter 1964
Newsletter 1971-1973

HOWL 1973-2005

LACS:
Cruel Sports 1927-1940
League Doings 1940-1958
Cruel Sports 1958-1986
Wildlife Guardian 1986-2005

SWDP:
Deer Diary (Winter/Spring 2000-Spring/Summer 2003)

Index

Amos, Henry 42, 52, 83
Animal Liberation Front (ALF) 103, 136, 143, 267
Animals Film, The 32, 142, 143, 402
Annetts, Ivor 285
Ashby, Eric 162, 167, 214
Association of Chief Police Officers (ACPO) 280
August, Bob 148

Badgworthy Land Company 18, 66, 267
Baillie, Peter 124
Baker, Enid (Hunt Master) 274
Ballard, Jackie 202, 217, 293, 309
Banks, Tony, MP 237, 239, 244, 245, 246, 248, 253, 254, 255, 264
Barrington, Jim (James) 180, 193, 195, 211, 217, 220, 233, 247, 295
Barter, Gwen 63, 73, 74, 75, 76, 81, 83, 216
Batchelor, Douglas 238, 241, 294, 295, 307, 317
Bateson, Patrick 181, 182, 183, 184, 185, 187, 189, 190, 191, 192, 216, 230, 233, 359, 395
Bawden, Ernest (Huntsman) 26, 322
Beadle, Fred 44, 45, 46, 47, 59
Beaufort, Duke of 47, 93, 94
Behavioural and Physiological Effects of Culling Red Deer (Bateson Report) 182, 395
Bell, Ernest 33, 42, 52
Berkshire and Buckinghamshire Farmers' Harriers 37
BFSS (see British Field Sports Society)
Bisset, Fenwick M 17, 19, 286
Blair, Tony, Prime Minister 219, 224, 229, 236, 239, 241, 251, 255, 258, 259, 262, 266, 270, 275, 276, 285, 286, 287, 325, 326, 329
Blom-Cooper, Louis, QC 3, 159, 160, 203, 348, 349, 350
Boles, Col Denis, 24
Boles, Sir Jeremy 69
Bonner, Tim 328
Bonsor, Sir Nicholas, MP 171
Bradshaw, Ben, MP 282
Brimble, Steve 147
British Deer Society (BDS) 32, 124, 125, 151, 153, 204, 326, 372
British Field Sports Society (BFSS) (now CA) 2, 4, 6, 16, 30, 47, 53, 57, 59, 61, 70, 76, 78, 79, 81, 83, 96, 101, 106, 107, 108, 110, 116, 122, 125, 161, 171, 173, 174, 175, 180, 185, 186, 188, 190, 196, 200, 204, 205, 208, 209, 212, 220, 230, 322, 399
Brook-Popham, Lady 101
Bryant, John 101, 110, 133, 152, 169, 175, 176, 238, 242, 395
Burns Report: Report of the Committee of Inquiry into Hunting with Dogs in England and Wales 231, 232, 233, 234, 240
Butler, Sam 229

Callender, Dave 147
Cameron, David, MP 290, 300, 326, 329, 330
Campaign for Nuclear Disarmament (CND) 103, 268
Campaign for the Protection of Hunted Animals (CPHA) 212, 220, 233, 238
Campaign for the Relief of Wildlife (CROW) 106
Cann, Edward du, MP 67
Case For Repeal 302
Cavanagh, Bill 166, 172
Cheldon Buckhounds 15, 198, 199, 201
Chorley, Lord 175, 176, 177, 180, 181
Churchill, Lord Randolph 34, 39
Churchward, Robert 88
Cinema Advertising Association 215
Cirencester College Report: Economic and Social Aspects of Deer Hunting on Exmoor and the Quantocks 170, 178, 230, 249, 396
Clutton-Brock, T H 118, 192
Cocks, F Seymour, MP 56, 57, 58, 59, 70, 84
Collins, Charles & Jo 156, 188, 271, 296
Collyns, Charles Polk 5, 6, 10, 11, 17, 25, 26, 32, 396

Conservation and Management of Deer on Exmoor and the Quantocks (Southampton University Report) 178, 363
Conservation of Seals Bill 108, 322
Conservation of Wild Creatures and Wild Plants Act (1975)121
Cook, Ralph 147
Cook, Robin, MP 238, 239, 240
Cooper, John 231, 279, 297
Corbyn, Jeremy, MP 171
Countryside Alliance (CA) (formerly BFSS) 2, 4, 30, 47, 152, 169, 188, 189, 190, 212, 217, 229, 233, 234-239, 241, 243, 247, 248, 249, 250, 252, 257, 259, 263, 264, 266, 267, 268, 269, 270, 271, 272, 275, 276, 277, 278, 279, 282, 283, 284, 289, 290, 293, 297, 298, 300, 301, 302, 303, 305, 306, 311, 322, 323, 325, 326, 327, 328, 329, 334, 363, 368, 377, 378
Countryweek Hunting 199
County Down Staghounds 15, 193, 210, 226, 242, 366, 367, 368, 369
Course, Richard 101, 133, 134, 137, 138, 142, 143, 145, 147, 154, 155, 167, 173, 212
Cox, Nora (DSSH Master) (later Harding) 66, 68, 82
Criminal Prosecution Service (CPS) 282, 290, 291, 292, 300, 301, 308, 309, 312
Cronin, Doreen 166, 172, 174, 176, 181, 184, 191, 357
Cruelty to Animals Act (1876) 38, 39
Cruelty to Wild Animals in Captivity Bill 39
Culmstock Otterhounds 92

Daily Chronicle 43
Daily Express 50, 92, 120
Daily Graphic 63
Daily Herald 43, 74, 75
Daily Mail 253, 255, 400
Daily Mirror 46, 72, 82, 87, 93, 95, 108, 114, 123, 188, 274, 283, 343, 345, 400, 401
Daily Sketch 42
Daily Telegraph 68, 81, 162, 188, 192, 220, 244, 274, 329, 401
Davies, Mark 211
Dawes, Mandy 144
Day of Defiance 274
Deacon, Bob 148
Deadline 2000 233, 234
Declaration Day 2003 248, 267, 268

Deer Act (1963) 79, 80, 127
Deer Act (1980) 130
Deer Act (1991) 131, 211
Deer Hunting and Hare Coursing (Abolition) Bill (1969) 107, 130
DEFRA: Department for Environment, Food and Rural Affairs 32, 238, 240, 243, 244, 267, 282
Denby, Maeve 137, 138
Devon and Somerset Staghounds (DSSH) 3, 8, 12, 16, 18, 19, 24, 38, 44, 46, 47, 50, 51, 54, 64, 65, 66, 68, 72, 73, 80, 82, 91, 95, 97, 99, 100, 103, 105, 106, 107, 109, 117, 142, 151, 152, 154, 157, 158, 159, 160, 161, 162, 164, 171, 182, 187, 197, 198, 204, 226, 227, 233, 242, 245, 257, 267, 270, 274, 275, 280, 281, 283, 286, 292, 293, 301, 322, 362
Disney, Florence 66, 67
Doig, Douglas 114, 400
Donoughue, Lord 237, 251
Down, Richard (QSH huntsman) 292, 300, 303, 309, 313
DSRADP: Devon and Somerset Residents Association for Deer Protection 176, 177, 186, 191, 396, 402

East Anglian Daily Times 74
Edmonds, Noel 247, 269
Edwards, Jimmy 69
European Convention on Human Rights 275, 276, 279
European Court of Human Rights 275, 276
Evening Standard 11, 255
Everard, Delly 327, 329
Everard, Guy Thomas 268
Everard, Philip 44
Exeter Express 64
Exmoor Foxhounds 245, 286, 290, 291
Exmoor Red Deer Survey 1981-82 152
Exmoor Society 129, 171, 256, 326, 373

Farr, John, MP 125, 130
Ferry, Otis 254
Fewings, Bill (QSH Master) 156, 165, 195, 226
Floyd, Graham 8, 9, 28, 291, 300, 374, 396
Foot, Isaac, MP 42, 43
Foot, Michael, MP 155, 163
Forestry Commission 3, 31, 32, 126, 151, 153, 157, 167, 187, 213, 215, 233, 370
Fortescue, John 11
Foster, Michael, MP 220, 221, 223, 224, 225
Fraser, Lovat, MP 43, 44, 45, 52
Friends of the National Trust (FONT) 187, 188, 189, 191, 291, 294, 296, 311, 362

Garfield, Rorke 111, 147
GECCAP: General Election Co-ordinating Committee for Animal Protection 133, 155
George, Janet 185, 212, 267
Gibbons, Nicholas (QSH chairman) 303
Gibbs, Jeromy 198, 217
Goldsmith, Lord 269, 272, 278
Goss, Fred (DSSH harbourer) 22, 396
Gooch, Colonel Brian (Norwich Staghounds Master) 75
Gray, Charles, MP 246, 247, 248
Greenwood, Anthony, MP 56, 58, 79
Greenwood, Sir George,MP 36, 40
Greig, Morland (DSSH Master) 24, 25
Groves, Paddy (QSH Master) 228

Hague, William (MP) 220
Hain, Peter, MP 248, 250, 251, 252, 262, 269, 298, 299
Hale, John 147

Hall, Daisy 166, 191
Hall, Richard 63, 108
Hansen, Neil 220, 243
Harding, Nora (DSSH Master) (formerely Cox) 82, 159, 160, 161, 162, 345
Harding, William (DSSH harbourer) 68
Hardy, Peter, MP 124, 130
Harris, Brigadier H R (Norwich Staghounds Chairman 76
Harris, Dr Roger 189, 190
Hart, Simon 266, 283, 289, 290, 300, 301, 328
Hashman, Joe 215
Hawes, Alison 284, 298
Heard, Peter (DSSH servant) 292
Heffer, Eric, MP 97
Hemingway, Edward 49, 50, 51, 64, 65, 66, 67, 68, 69, 72, 73, 77, 78, 81, 83, 85, 86
Hicks, John 147, 154, 159, 160, 164, 170, 171, 176, 193, 195, 196, 287, 351, 352
Hill, Kevin 14, 191, 197, 198, 199, 200, 202, 204, 205, 227, 242, 247, 283, 287, 304
Hirst, Patrick 121
Hobday, Mike 285, 301
Hobhouse, John 106, 110
Hoey, Kate, MP 326
Hollis, Miriam 147
Horse & Hound 16, 175, 242, 247, 281, 400
Hough, Sue 111, 148
Houghton, Lord 116, 117, 130, 133, 134, 137, 167
Hounds off the New Forest 167
Hounds off Our Wildlife (HOWL) 113
Human Rights Act 250, 277
Humanitarian League 33, 36, 37, 40, 42
Hunt Saboteurs Association (HSA) 82, 87, 88, 89, 93, 96, 97, 98, 99, 100, 101, 103, 104, 106, 110, 111, 112, 113, 115, 134, 135, 137, 138, 139, 141, 147, 148, 155, 231, 290, 326, 331, 340, 403
Hunting Act 2004 264, 271, 272, 276, 282, 291, 295, 321, 324, 325, 379-391, 374, 393, 394
Huskisson, Mike 14, 143, 144, 397

Independent, the 188, 247, 273, 285, 287, 309, 328
International Animal Rescue (IAR) 177, 196
International Fund for Animal Welfare (IFAW) 14, 177, 191, 204, 208, 212, 219, 226, 242, 249, 283, 292, 298, 309, 326
Irish Council Against Blood Sports (ICABS) 193, 368
Isle of Wight Foxhounds 305
Isle Valley Buckhounds 16, 198

Jackson, John 266, 279
James, Ken 216, 227
Jefferies, Richard 5, 6, 9, 13
Jenkins, Dame Jennifer 174
Jenkins, Roy, (Home Sec) 111, 124, 174
Johnson, Howard, MP 81
Joint Universities Study on Deer Hunting (JUS) 189
Jones, Jeanette 147
Jones, Marley 121, 141, 144, 146, 344, 345

Kaufman, Sir Gerald, MP 237, 245, 251, 259, 262
Kimball, Marcus, MP 79, 101, 108, 121, 125

Langbein, Dr Jochen 304, 314, 363, 364
League Against Cruel Sports (LACS) 8, 14, 26, 31, 42, 43, 47, 51, 52, 53, 55, 56, 60, 63, 64, 69,

72, 76, 78, 81, 83, 86, 87, 92, 96, 97, 100, 101, 104, 106, 108, 110, 112, 115, 116, 119, 130, 133, 134, 135, 137, 142, 143, 145, 147, 148, 151, 152, 155, 156, 157, 158, 159, 161, 163, 164, 167, 168, 170, 173, 175, 179, 180, 182, 184, 188, 195, 198, 202, 203, 204, 205, 208, 209, 211, 212, 213, 214, 216, 219, 220, 226, 231, 233, 238, 241, 242, 247, 249, 257, 264, 270, 279, 280, 282, 284, 285, 286, 287, 290, 291, 294, 295, 297, 298, 300, 301, 309, 326, 327, 337, 347, 349, 352, 371, 375, 377, 392, 398, 399, 403
League for the Prohibition of Cruel Sports (later League Against Cruel Sports 42, 48, 55
Lewis, Leo 90, 92
Liberty and Livelihood Rally 243
Linzey, Professor Andrew 243
Lipton, Marcus, MP 79, 95, 99, 100, 105
Lloyd, Dick 2, 3, 15, 199, 366

Magistrates Court Act 305, 317, 318, 319
Mallalieu, Baroness Anne 30, 188, 212, 220, 236, 237, 240, 248, 260, 263, 274, 293
Manchester Guardian 43, 51
Mancroft, Lord 30, 205, 208, 249, 258, 260, 363
Mantle, Gladys 63, 64
Mantle, Lionel 100, 346, 347
Marles, Christopher 286, 287
Martin, Michael, MP 252, 262, 263, 264
Martin, Richard (MP & founder RSPCA) 38
Masters of Deerhounds Association (MDHA) 14, 16, 62, 198, 291, 399
Maxwell-Hyslop, Robin, MP 130
McCartney, Paul 195, 198, 257
McFall, John, MP 207, 208, 209
McNamara, Kevin, MP 162, 196, 207
McNay, Iain 111
Messer, Sir Frederick, MP 66, 67, 82, 83, 84
Michael, Alun, MP 240, 245, 246, 253, 261, 262, 263
Mid Kent Staghounds 41
Middle Way Group 233, 234, 249
Mikardo, Ian, MP 108, 129
Monica Coleman 167
More, Jasper, MP 79, 108, 125
Mr Lawrence Clark's Buckhounds 198
Murphy, Col Louis (DSSH Master) 68, 69, 71, 77, 78, 82

Nancekivell, R H, (Bob) (DSSH Master) 8, 38, 91, 92, 95, 99, 100, 102, 103, 105, 344
National Animal Rescue Association (NARA) 147
National Anti-Hunt Campaign 220
National Committee for the Abolition of Deer Hunting (NCADH) 12, 66, 84, 400
National Farmers Union (NFU) 125
National Society for the Abolition of Cruel Sports (NSACS) 52, 53, 56, 60
National Trust (NT) 1, 3, 18, 31, 32, 61, 100, 128, 168, 171, 177, 181, 187, 188, 190, 191, 290, 291, 294, 296, 308, 326, 329, 356, 357, 358, 360, 361, 362, 371, 374, 392, 393, 397, 399
New Forest Animal Protection Group (NFAPG) 167, 213
New Forest Buckhounds (NFB) 15, 95, 109, 156, 193, 196, 213, 214, 215, 216
New Forest Deer Protection Council 162, 167
New Forest Deerhunt Abolition Alliance (NFDAA) 156, 161, 213

News Chronicle 64
Norman, Mrs Cicely 66, 67, 70, 82
North Devon Staghounds 17
Northfield, Lord 124, 125, 129
Norwich Staghounds 15, 74, 75, 76, 83
Nunnely, Charles 189
Nunnerley, Ian 148

Opik, Lembit, MP 212, 222, 250, 260

Pamment, Flod 147
Parliament Act (1911) 263, 272, 278
Parliament Act (1949) 263, 272, 278, 282
Pedler, Jane (now Heath) 94
Peel, J H B 14, 15
Pilger, John 93
Pillivant, Adrian (QSH whipper-in) 292, 300, 303, 309, 313
Pine, Leslie 120
Portcullis Inquiry 241, 243
POWA (Protect Our Wild Animals) 226, 242, 326
Prescott, John, MP 219, 239, 251, 257
Prestidge, John 86, 87, 88, 90, 92, 93, 96, 102
Preston, Dawn 290
Prior, Richard 2, 3, 160, 348, 349, 350
Prohibition of Foxhunting Bill (1949) 56, 61
Protection of Animals (Hunting and Coursing Prohibition) Bill (1949) 56, 57
Protection of Animals (No 2) Bill (1930) 43
Protection of Animals (Prevention of Deer Hunting) Bill (1939) 53
Protection of Animals Act 1911 40, 41, 42, 60, 77, 84, 162, 166, 207, 211, 368, 391
Protection of Animals Bill (1924-1931) (1937-1939) 42, 53
Protection of Animals Bill (1969) 105
Protection of Badgers Act (1992) 391
Protection of Badgers Bill 322
Protection of Deer (Hunting Abolition) Bill (1958-1960) (1965) 66, 82, 95
Pyke, Jean 63, 81

Quantock Deer Forum 152
Quantock Deer Management and Conservation Group (QDMCG) 32, 314, 316
Quantock Staghounds (QSH) 19, 32, 64, 95, 101, 105, 139, 141, 177, 185, 287, 309, 347, 365
19, 32, 51, 64, 69, 95, 98, 100, 101, 105, 113, 127, 131, 132, 135, 136, 138, 139, 141, 146, 148, 150, 151, 153, 154, 156, 157, 165, 170, 175, 176, 177, 185, 187, 188, 195, 196, 197, 202, 203, 206, 226, 228, 241, 245, 274, 280, 284, 287, 292, 309, 346, 364
Queen Victoria 34, 37
Quicke, Sir John 169
Quicke Working Party 169, 178

Redman, Norman 89, 96
Rennison, Jan 115, 116
Report of the Committee on Cruelty to Wild Animals 59, 397
Richardson, Jo, MP 129
Roach, Brian 121
Robins, Walner (QSH Master) 135, 139, 141, 151, 156
Roffe-Silvester, Godfrey Peter (QSH Master) 100
Rowley, Raymond 73, 74, 75, 78, 81, 87, 88, 92, 96, 97, 98, 99, 100, 101, 106, 107, 112, 115, 116, 134
Royal Buckhounds 33, 36, 37, 41, 54, 62
Royal Society for the Prevention of Cruelty to Animals (RSPCA) 1, 35, 37, 38, 40, 41, 42, 43, 45, 46,

52, 59, 65, 70, 73, 75, 78, 101, 106, 110, 115, 124, 133, 151, 161, 207, 208, 209, 212, 217, 233, 242, 249, 293, 309, 397
Rundle, Chris 256, 257, 270, 287, 402
Ryder, Richard 101, 176

Salt, Henry 33, 34, 37, 42, 397
Savage Working Party Report 176, 177
Save Our Seals Campaign 111
Save Our Stags Campaign (SOS) 113, 114, 115, 116, 117, 135, 136, 138, 139, 140, 141, 142, 143, 144, 146, 150, 153, 156, 157, 158, 214
Savernake Staghounds 64, 95
Schonfeld, Victor 142, 143
Scott, Arminel 228
Scott, Diana (DSSH Master) 233, 270, 280
Scott Henderson Report (1951) (see also Report of the Committee on Cruelty to Wild Animals 61, 95, 108, 230
Scott, Maurice (DSSH Master) 159, 268, 292
Scruton, Roger 249, 268
Sea Shepherd 144, 145, 146, 148, 149
Section 101 305, 307, 317, 318
Sharp, Joseph 53, 66, 68, 78, 83
Shaw, Arnold, MP 107, 108, 130, 137
Shaw, George Bernard 37, 42
Shepherd, Ed 291
Sheppard, Vera 63, 81, 110
Shooting Times 118, 119, 120, 122, 124, 126, 131, 175, 402
Sir John Amory's Staghounds 18
Sirl, Graham 162, 196, 220, 239, 242, 370, 371
Sizer, Ann 102, 105
Skeffington, Arthur, MP 67
Smith, Angela 208, 220
Smith, Sue 113, 121, 140, 143
Somerset County Council 18, 152, 202, 264
Somerset Trust for Nature Conservation 152, 175, 196, 365, 372, 399
Soper, Lord 116, 167, 179, 180
Soulsby, Lord 185, 230
South Devon Foxhounds 87, 102
South West Deer Protection (SWDP) 12, 191
Sporting League, The 35
Stag Hunting with Hounds (Abolition) Bill (1968) 101
Stratton, Rev J 33, 34, 35, 36, 37, 41
Straw, Jack, MP 219, 224, 229, 230, 231, 233, 234, 235, 329
Stride, John (NFB Huntsman) 214, 215
Summersgill, Donald (DSSH huntsman) 275, 292, 305
Sunday Mirror 96, 97, 114, 402
Sunday Telegraph 93, 143, 327
Sunflower 158

Tebbit, Norman, MP 163
Thomas, Aubrey 148
Thorpe, Jeremy, MP 95
Thrower, Ruth (QSH Master) 105
Tillsley, Paul 285, 291
Times, The 46, 107, 147, 191, 205, 225, 255, 287, 327, 401
Tiverton Staghounds (TSH) 11, 18, 196, 198, 310, 397
Trollope-Bellew, Anthony 170, 175, 303
Trollope-Bellew, Major T F 126, 128, 152

Use, Misuse and Abuse of Science in support of the Hunting Act 2004 302

Veterinary Association for Wildlife Management (VAWM) 302
Vote-OK 275, 276
Vowles, Alfred 5, 15, 23, 27, 70, 83, 398

Waley-Cohen, Sir Bernard 65, 97, 107, 109, 344
Ward Union Staghounds 193, 320, 368
Watson, Paul 145, 148, 149, 398
Waugh, Auberon, 220
Welfare of Animals Act (Northern Ireland)(1972) 211, 225
West Somerset Free Press 16, 43, 44, 48, 57, 67, 69, 70, 82, 91
Western Daily Press 100, 105, 256, 270, 284, 297, 308, 310, 311, 327, 328, 329, 401, 402
Wetton, Dave 98, 99, 104, 106, 110, 111, 274, 402
Whitaker, Ben, MP 105
White, Peter 215, 227, 242
Whitehead, Kenneth 3, 7, 15, 23, 126, 127, 399
Whitty, Lord 248, 257, 258, 259, 260
Widdecombe, Ann, MP 221, 239, 299, 300
Wild Animals in Captivity Protection Act (1906) 40
Wild Mammals (Hunting with Dogs) Bill (1997) 220, 221, 222, 224, 229
Wild Mammals (Protection) (Amendment) Bill 237
Wild Mammals (Protection) Act (1996) 210, 211, 212, 237, 391
Wild Mammals (Protection) Bill 196, 207, 208, 209, 251, 322
Wildlife and Countryside Act (1981) 121, 169, 385, 386
Wildlife Guardian 152, 167, 188, 220, 238, 352, 403
Wildlife Network 1, 211, 217, 218 233, 398
Williamson, Chris 137, 148
Williamson, Henry 24, 50, 55, 120, 399
Wilson, Mrs Diana 166, 172, 176, 191, 357
Wilson, Harold, Prime Minister 94, 108, 109
Wright, Tony (Exmoor Foxhounds huntsman) 291, 293, 312, 318

Yandle, Tom 152, 257, 268, 270, 293, 301
Yeo, Nigel 273, 286, 288